HELLENIC STUDIES SERIES 85

DEMETRIOS OF SCEPSIS
AND HIS *TROIKOS DIAKOSMOS*

T0334680

Recent Titles in the Hellenic Studies Series

http://chs.harvard.edu/chs/publications

DEMETRIOS OF SCEPSIS
AND HIS *TROIKOS DIAKOSMOS*

ANCIENT AND MODERN READINGS
OF A LOST CONTRIBUTION TO
ANCIENT SCHOLARSHIP

Alexandra Trachsel

Center for Hellenic Studies
Trustees for Harvard University
Washington, D.C.
Distributed by Harvard University Press
Cambridge, Massachusetts, and London, England
2021

Demetrios of Scepsis and His Troikos Diakosmos
By Alexandra Trachsel
Copyright © 2021 Center for Hellenic Studies, Trustees for Harvard University
All Rights Reserved.
Published by Center for Hellenic Studies, Trustees for Harvard University,
Washington, D.C.
Distributed by Harvard University Press, Cambridge, Massachusetts and
London, England
Printed by Total Printing Systems, Newton, IL
Cover Design: Joni Godlove
Production: Jen Jackowitz

Library of Congress Cataloging-in-Publication Data

Names: Trachsel, Alexandra, author.
Title: Demetrios of Scepsis and his Troikos diakosmos : ancient and modern
readings of a lost contribution to ancient scholarship / Alexandra
Trachsel.
Other titles: Hellenic studies ; 85.
Description: Washington : Center for Hellenic Studies, Trustees for Harvard
University, 2020. | Series: Hellenic studies ; 85 | Includes
bibliographical references and index.
Identifiers: LCCN 2019021519 | ISBN 9780674237933
Subjects: LCSH: Demetrios, of Scepsis, active 2nd century B.C. Troikos
diakosmos. | Homer--Criticism and interpretation.
Classification: LCC PA3948.D55 T73 2019 | DDC 883/.01--dc23
LC record available at https://lccn.loc.gov/2019021519

Contents

Acknowledgments

The story began in 2007 with a Junior Fellowship at the *Center for Hellenic Studies* in Washington, DC. It is therefore with much satisfaction and deep recognition that I would like to thank this institution for having accepted to publish the present study. Moreover, this institution should also come first, as I could count, throughout the years, on the interest and support from Prof. Gregory Nagy, its director. Other members from the *Center for Hellenic Studies* were also very supportive, and I would like to mention in particular the members of the *Homer Multitext Project*. As they work on a digital edition of the Homeric scholia, they were very interested in a research on the Homeric scholarship carried out by Demetrios of Scepsis.

As the present work is a slightly reworked version of part of my habilitation-thesis, which I submitted at the University of Hamburg in 2014, I would also like to mention here the Department of Greek and Latin Philology of this university. The research could not have taken the form it has, without the academic position I held at the University of Hamburg. In particular I would like to thank Prof. Christian Brockmann for the six years during which I could work at this department and for his support and supervision during this time. However, other members of the staff should also be remembered here for their encouragements in the course of the long journey the writing of the present study represented for me. I would like to thank in particular Prof. Claudia Schindler and Prof. Klaus Lennartz, who knew, from their own experiences, the challenges one may face while writing a habilitation-thesis and could give me the support that was most needed in each phase of the undertaking. This does not mean, however, that the other members of the department should be forgotten. I benefitted from a large number of very positive colleagues, who were always helpful, friendly, and encouraging.

However, most of the research was written in London during the Marie Curie Intra-European Fellowship that I was awarded for the academic year 2012–2013 at King's College, London. Therefore, I am very grateful to Prof. Charlotte Roueché (Department of Digital Humanities) and to Prof. Giambattista D'Alessio (Department of Classics) for their support during the application process and during the time I spent in London. I was especially touched by the great interest for my project and the very kind welcome I received at the Department of Digital Humanities, and I would like to mention in particular Dr. Gabriel Bodard, who also was an important figure during the application process, and Dr. Simona Stoyanova, who worked with me on the more editorial aspects of the research. The discussions with them, and with all the other members of the Department of Digital Humanities, were very inspiring.

Finally, for the several levels of proofreading I would like to thank Dr. Christiane Krause and Cosima Schwarke, M.A. (both from the University of Hamburg) and Dr. Charlotte Tupman and Dr. Rebecca Kahn (both from King's College London).

Introduction

Studying an author like Demetrios of Scepsis implies that we are dealing, as is often true in the field of Classics, with a topic to which we have only a very limited access. In the case of Demetrios, this limit comes from the fact that the work he wrote has not been transmitted in its entirety, but was preserved only indirectly through quotations in other ancient authors' works. Therefore, we have to deal with fragments, which means here textual sequences that have been separated, in several steps and in various ways, from the original work. These pieces of evidence have now to be reassembled so that an image as accurate as possible of the research Demetrios undertook can be established. However, the task seems particularly challenging with Demetrios of Scepsis, as only very few fragments have been preserved from a work that must initially have been particularly voluminous, so that we must assume that only the smallest portion of his work can now be assessed. Therefore, it becomes crucial to pay particular attention to the scholar who undertook the research and to the period in which he lived. This will be the aim of the first chapter of our investigations. It will provide, in three steps, a thorough analysis of the historical and literary context in which Demetrios carried out his research. We shall first provide a close reading of the passages considered as testimonia and highlight the evidence that can be gained from these texts. In a second step, we shall attempt to locate Demetrios within the literary background of ancient scholarship to which the evidence points. Finally, we shall expand our investigations to the time in which Demetrios lived and define some aspects that may have been particularly influential on the scholar in order to help us understand his undertaking. From a methodological point of view, this means that, because we are dealing primarily with the testimonia about Demetrios, this chapter will be dedicated to the scholar rather than to the fragments of his work. In this respect, Chapter 1 is an attempt to understand Demetrios as a historical figure by focusing on the place, the time, and the scholarly tradition to which he belonged.

It is therefore only from Chapter 2 onwards that we shall focus more specifically on the remaining fragments. In this, we will be guided by the new approach that scholars developed in recent years for the study of fragmentarily preserved writings from Antiquity.[1] Our research on Demetrios shares many of the concerns raised by this new approach, and the output of these discussions substantially contributed to shape the form of the present book.[2]

First of all, the indirectness of the access to Demetrios' work made it necessary to concentrate our efforts on the transmission of the fragments, before any new edition of these textual remains could be considered. This is the reason why the present work is neither an edition nor a collection of the remaining fragments of Demetrios' work. It should rather be seen as a preliminary step towards such an edition, which still remains a desideratum.

Second, as just said, Demetrios' work is preserved primarily through quotations, and this means that we have to focus, in our investigations, on two stages of the transmission of his text: the ancient readings of Demetrios' work and the modern interpretations of the remaining fragments. To both aspects one chapter of the present study is dedicated. In Chapter 2, we shall not only investigate how Demetrios' work was read and studied in Antiquity, but also examine how it was incorporated into new works by the scholars who had access to his study and found parts of it interesting for their own research. Finally, these analyses should also help us to define how this process of reuse may affect our modern understanding of Demetrios' contribution. The ancient reception of Demetrios' work can be observed roughly between the Hellenistic period and the twelfth century CE, when we have the last allusions in Tzetzes and Eustathius, before we are left alone with the meager evidence preserved in the different corpora of scholia.

In Chapter 3, we shall focus on modern scholars and see how they deal with the fragments and according to what criteria they judged Demetrios' scholarly achievement. Indeed, as our understanding of Demetrios' work, and especially the collecting of the remaining fragments, also depends on the readings that modern scholars made of the ancient texts in which Demetrios is quoted, this step is a necessary complement to Chapter 2. As we shall see, their interpretations varied, often considerably, which led to completely different pictures of Demetrios' work. These variations are often explained by the context in which these scholars lived and the value they gave to the authors in whose texts the witnesses from Demetrios' work were preserved. This chapter aims therefore to highlight the multiple factors that influenced the way modern scholars dealt with Demetrios, so that this bias can be taken into consideration when

---

[1]   Derda/Hilder/Kwapisz 2017 bear witness to the current scholarly interest in fragments. Earlier examples are Most 1997, Darbo-Peschanski 2004, and Lenfant 2007a. See also, for instance, Schepens 2002, Berti 2013, and Lenfant 2013.

[2]   For instance, Trachsel 2012 and Trachsel 2017b.

evaluating their works on Demetrios, and more importantly when using their editions of the remaining fragments for further studies on Demetrios.

The goal of the research should therefore be seen as an attempt to assemble, in three steps, each of which is represented by one chapter, all that what we still can know about Demetrios, so that we may draw a clear outline of the scholar's work. This may help us to assess correctly his contribution to ancient scholarship and to give him the place that he deserves in the history of this field. It should, however, also provide some ideas about his methodological choices in interpreting the Homeric text and about the literary tools he used to compose his commentary. Third, the study is certainly also undertaken to spark interest in this scholar and to pave the way for a reevaluation of the remaining fragments that may ultimately lead to a new edition of their corpus.

Finally, in order to help our own reader, we should give some preliminary indications about more practical issues of our work. First, because the texts of the fragments are not to be found in our study, we shall direct our reader either to Gaede's edition from 1880 or to Biraschi's more recent contribution for the wording of the passages involved. Therefore, our references to the fragments are always composed of the numbers of both editions. Our discussions should, however, allow our reader to appreciate their contributions in an appropriate way and to understand when we depart from their conclusions. Moreover, since Chapter 2 in particular should demonstrate the difficulty we have in finding a way back to Demetrios' work through the quotations that were preserved, we also give for each fragment the precise reference to the ancient work in which the wording of the fragment can be found. In this way, the reader may also consider the source texts and take account of the context in which the piece of evidence has been transmitted. Likewise, for the fragments quoted in the present study that do not come from the work of Demetrios, the reader will find the reference to the editions used in the List of Abbreviations, if not specified otherwise. In this way, she or he may easily find the source texts from which they come. There are, nonetheless, a few quotations from ancient works that figure in our study, and in these cases the translations are our own.

Second, as far as the transliteration of Greek names is concerned, we have taken an intermediary stance. We have tried to stay as close as possible to the original spelling of the Greek, especially when the meaning of the Greek word under discussion is important. We have kept, however, to a more Latinized version with well-known proper names. Finally, in Chapter 3, the reader will sometimes find references to more than one edition of a given work, especially for those written in the nineteenth century, for which it was important in connection with our discussion to know when the different versions appeared.

List of Abbreviations

DK   Diels, H., and W. Kranz, eds. 1956. *Die Fragmente der Vorso
                      kratiker.* Vols. 1–3. 8th ed. Berlin.

Eudocia   Flach, I. 1880. *Eudociae Augustae Violarium.* Leipzig.

Festus [Müller]   Müller, K. O., ed. 1839. *Sexti Pompei Festi de verborum significa-
                      tione quae supersunt cum Pauli epitome.* Leipzig.

Festus [Lindsay]   Lindsay, W. M., ed. 1913. *Sexti Pompei Festi De verborum signifi-
                      catu quae supersunt cum Pauli epitome.* Leipzig.

Grammatici graeci   Hilgard, A., et al., eds. 1867–1910. *Grammatici graeci.* Leipzig.

Kassel-Austin   Kassel, R., and C. Austin, eds. 1983–2001. *Poetae Comici Graeci.*
                      Berlin.

Körte   Körte, A., ed. 1957–1959. *Menandri quae supersunt.* 2nd ed.
                      Leipzig.

P. Aphrod. Lit. II   Fournet, J.-L. 1999. *Hellénisme dans l'Egypte du VIe siècle. La
                      bibliothèque et l'oeuvre de Dioscore d'Aphrodité*, 87–173. Cairo.

P. Oxy.   Grenfell, B. P., A. S. Hunt, et al., eds. 1898–. *The Oxyrhynchus
                      Papyri.* London.

P. Köln 1   Kramer, B., and B. Hübner. 1976. *Kölner Papyri. Band 1.* Opladen.

SoudaOnline   Whitehead, D., ed. n.d. *Suda On Line: Byzantine Lexicography.*
                      http://www.stoa.org/sol/.

1

The Life of Demetrios
Testimonia, Literary and Historical Background

The aims of the first chapter of our study will be threefold. First, we shall discuss, in Section 1, the remaining testimonia and define what they may tell us about the author who is the subject of our study. This task is now much easier as we have had, since 2011, a new collection of the fragments of Demetrios of Scepsis, the contribution made by A. M. Biraschi in the continuation of Felix Jacoby's *Fragmente der griechischen Historiker*.[1] The Italian scholar has assembled the testimonia for the first time,[2] thus providing a new tool, which will help us to reevaluate the texts much more precisely. In the two subsequent sections, we shall broaden our approach to locate the contribution of Demetrios, following the information gained from the close reading outlined in the first section, in its wider literary and historical context. We shall therefore focus in Section 2 on the tradition of Homeric scholarship and discuss Demetrios' work within this tradition, and then in Section 3 go on to describe more fully the period in which the scholar lived and the changes it brought for the inhabitants of the Troad. This division and the focus on the testimonia is necessary because we are dealing with an author of whom very little remains,[3] whose fragments have very disparate contents, and who has been, as we shall see, the object of much specu-lation over the last two centuries. We aim, therefore, by working at the begin-ning only with the texts considered as testimonia, to separate the content of these texts from the opinions their ancient authors had of Demetrios of Scepsis. This separation will then help us to define, here in Chapter 1, the chronological framework and historical background in which Demetrios lived, whereas the

---

[1] Biraschi 2011.
[2] Some of them were discussed by Stiehle 1850:528–529 and by Gaede 1880:1. But neither of the two German scholars has dedicated a specific section to them.
[3] There are 75 fragments in Gaede's and 76 in Biraschi's edition. However, we shall see that the Italian scholar adds, besides the mentioned fr. 76, six further passages to complete some of Gaede's fragments. She does it without changing Gaede's numbering. These additional frag-ments are fr. 17a, fr. 18a and b, fr. 55a, fr. 67a, and fr. 70a [Biraschi].

opinions, which we may encounter during the analysis of the passages involved, will lead us to Chapters 2 and 3. Indeed, we shall have to compare the image that we define ourselves through our analysis of the remaining evidence not only with ancient opinions about Demetrios, but also with that of modern scholars, which was made from the same starting point. Therefore, Chapter 2 will be dedicated to the ancient appreciation of Demetrios of Scepsis, whereas Chapter 3 to modern opinions of him. Nevertheless, the discussion in Chapter 1 is not only a preparation for the two subsequent chapters, but will also raise a whole range of questions about Demetrios and his work, which will open new ways for the study of the remaining fragments.

1.1 Evidence From the Testimonia

There are ten, or, according to Biraschi, even eleven, remaining testimonia on Demetrios.[4] These are unfortunately very few, but the content of these passages can nonetheless help us to draw an initial picture of the context in which the author lived and composed his work. In order to do so, we shall offer a close reading of the texts collected as testimonia by Biraschi and shall reevaluate the texts and the statements about Demetrios they contain. Such a reexamination is necessary, because, as we shall see, in the last two centuries many different and often contradictory conclusions about Demetrios and his scholarly activity have been drawn. These statements were often based on the same texts, but until now it was difficult to follow or evaluate these statements, because scholars quoted different versions of the passages under discussion or considered different parts of the source texts as testimonia about Demetrios.[5] This sharpened their disagreements, and in order not only to better understand their lines of argument but also to highlight the actual content of the passages, we shall have to go back to the texts themselves and discuss their contents so that we can single out what they tell us about the time and place in which Demetrios lived.

The testimonia, though small in number, still contain a lot of information about Demetrios, his work, and what ancient authors knew and thought about the scholar. We shall therefore divide our section into three parts and begin the discussion with the dating of the author and his work before dealing with the other elements. This order of priority is justified, in our opinion, by the fact that establishing the chronological framework is not only crucial to enabling us to

---

[4]   T1–11 [Biraschi]. T11 [Biraschi] is dubious and this explains the hesitation.

[5]   This is especially true with the text of Strabo, and the scholars themselves were aware of this difficulty, not only with regard to the passages that were considered as testimonia, but also with those classified as fragments. See for instance Brentano 1877:37 and Brentano 1881:31–35. We shall return to this several times throughout Chapter 3.

place the work of Demetrios in context, but is also the least controversial information about Demetrios preserved in the testimonia. We shall then shift our focus, in the second part of the section, to elements characterizing Demetrios, first as a man and then as a scholar. Finally, in the third part, we shall list the characteristics that have been attributed to Demetrios' work, discuss the title in more detail, and give a first description of what the testimonia reveal about its contents. This should not only prepare us to distinguish the opinions of ancient and modern scholars on Demetrios from the content of these passages, but should also provide the necessary elements to appraise in a more appropriate way the remaining fragments of Demetrios.

1.1.1 Dating

The clearest evidence for chronology comes from a passage of Strabo, in which the geographer describes the visit of Demetrios to Troy when the scholar was a young man (μειράκιον):

> καὶ τὸ Ἴλιον δ’ ὃ νῦν ἐστι κωμόπολίς τις ἦν ὅτε πρῶτον Ῥωμαῖοι τῆς τ’ Ἀσίας ἐπέβησαν καὶ ἐξέβαλον Ἀντίοχον τὸν μέγαν ἐκ τῆς ἐντὸς τοῦ Ταύρου. φησὶ γοῦν Δημήτριος ὁ Σκήψιος μειράκιον ἐπιδημήσας εἰς τὴν πόλιν κατ’ ἐκείνους τοὺς καιροὺς οὕτως ὠλιγωρημένην ἰδεῖν τὴν κατοικίαν ὥστε μηδὲ κεραμωτὰς ἔχειν τὰς στέγας, [...]

> The present Ilion was a village-town, when the Romans came to Asia for the first time and expelled Antiochos the Great from the territory on the inner side of Mount Tauros. For Demetrios of Scepsis says that, after having visited the place in those days, still in his youth, he saw the settlement being so neglected that the roofs did not even have tiles [...]

> Strabo 13.1.27 [C594][6]

In this passage the date of the visit is well-defined, as Demetrios places it during the time when the Romans first entered Asia Minor, which must mean between 190 and 188 BCE.[7] This suggests that the time of his activity must have been in the first part of the second century BCE, as one can consider that a μειράκιον was a man in his 20s.[8] Further information is given by another passage of Strabo:

---

[6]   = T3 [Biraschi] (= fr. 21 [Gaede/Biraschi]).

[7]   We shall discuss this in more detail later in Section 1.3.

[8]   In Menander (fr. 494 [Kassel-Austin] = fr. 724 [Körte]) for instance, the word is mentioned between ἔφηβος and ἀνήρ. See Chantraine 1968:678. In Lucian's *Dialogue of the Deaths*, a μειράκιον is given the age of about twenty (See *Dialogi Mortuorum* (Lib. 77) 19 (9), 4 = 362 (dialogue between

ἐκ δὲ τῆς Σκήψεως καὶ ὁ Δημήτριός ἐστιν, οὗ μεμνήμεθα πολλάκις, ὁ
τὸν Τρωϊκὸν διάκοσμον ἐξηγησάμενος γραμματικός, κατὰ τὸν αὐτὸν
χρόνον γεγονὼς Κράτητι καὶ Ἀριστάρχῳ, καὶ μετὰ τοῦτον Μητρόδωρος,
ἀνὴρ ἐκ τοῦ φιλοσόφου μεταβεβληκὼς ἐπὶ τὸν πολιτικὸν βίον καὶ
ῥητορεύων τὸ πλέον ἐν τοῖς συγγράμμασιν.

And also from Scepsis comes Demetrios, whom we mention often, the
scholar who explained the Trojan Catalogue and who was born at about
the same time as Crates and Aristarchos, and after him Metrodoros, a
man who moved from philosophy to a political life and mostly practised oratory in his writings.

Strabo 13.1.55 [C609][9]

The geographer tells us that Demetrios was a contemporary of the two Homeric
scholars Aristarchos of Samothrace and Crates of Mallos. We shall see more
precisely in Section 2, on the literary background, what this means for the
literary context of Demetrios' work.[10] Here we may note that, as Aristarchos
lived from about 216 to 144 BCE[11] and Crates visited Rome around 168 BCE,[12] we
have confirmation of the indications from the first testimonium, which means
that Demetrios probably lived and worked during the first part of the second
century BCE.[13]

The rest of Strabo's paragraph 13.1.55 [C609–610] is also interesting for
us and gives further information about the wider context in which we should
situate Demetrios. This part of Strabo's text has not, however, been included
either in Biraschi's new edition or in the collection assembled by Pagani.[14] This
is mainly due to the fact that the paragraph is about Metrodoros of Scepsis, who
lived shortly after Demetrios (καὶ μετὰ τοῦτον). However, this second scholar
from Scepsis also appears, along with Demetrios, in a passage from Diogenes
Laertios:

Simylos and Polystratos). Leaf 1923:xxviii (and Leaf 1917–1918:23) gives Demetrios, therefore, an
approximate age between fourteen and twenty.

[9] = T1 [Biraschi].

[10] See below Section 1.2.

[11] Cohn 1896:862–873 and Montanari 1996c:1090–1094. Further, see Pfeiffer 1968:210–233,
Marastoni 2007:28n9, and for a recent bibliography on Aristarchos, see Razzetti 2010.

[12] Kroll 1922a:1634–1641 and Broggiato 1999:812–814. Further, see Pfeiffer 1968:238–243, Marastoni
2007:28n8, and for a more detailed discussion on the testimonia, now Broggiato 2001:131–140.

[13] For further elements for a relative dating, see Ragone 2009:652.

[14] For Pagani, see Pagani 2006. As she does not distinguish the testimonia from the fragments in
her collection, Strabo 13.1.55 [C609] appears at position 49 in her list. It is the same with Strabo
13.1.27 [C594] quoted above as T3 [Biraschi]. It is also considered as a fragment of Demetrios (=
fr. 21 [Gaede/Biraschi]). Therefore, the passage appears at position 41 in Pagani's collection.

ἑνδέκατος Σκήψιος, πλούσιος καὶ εὐγενὴς ἄνθρωπος καὶ φιλόλογος
ἄκρως· οὗτος καὶ Μητρόδωρον προεβίβασε τὸν πολίτην.

The eleventh [Demetrios] is the one from Scepsis, a rich and noble man, and a skilful scholar. He also fostered Metrodoros, his fellow citizen.

Diogenes Laertios 5.84[15]

Therefore, we should perhaps give more weight to the Straboian passage and to what it tells us about Metrodoros of Scepsis, since it will also give us, as we shall see, some information about Demetrios. In fact, Strabo gives us a reasonably detailed portrait of Metrodoros.[16] First, we learn that he was a philosopher who later made a political career (ἐκ τοῦ φιλοσόφου μεταβεβληκὼς ἐπὶ τὸν πολιτικὶν βίον "who moved from philosophy to a political life"), leaving mainly rhetorical works (καὶ ῥητορεύων τὸ πλέον ἐν τοῖς συγγράμμασιν "and mostly practised oratory in his writings").[17] Strabo then gives us some details about the date and the circumstances of Metrodoros' death, which occurred in 72/71 BCE, during the third Mithridatic war, when, sent on an embassy to Tigranes by Mithridates VI Eupator, Methrodoros allegedly betrayed the king.[18] Strabo does, however, leave open the question of the circumstances of Metrodoros' death, suggesting that he was either killed by order of King Mithridates VI Eupator or died of illness.[19] This dating is confirmed by evidence from Cicero, who quotes Metrodoros in his *De oratore*. The historical background for this dialogue is the year 91 BCE and there Metrodoros is mentioned as an older contemporary.[20] We are, therefore, rather well-informed about the second part of Metrodoros' life, which occurred in the first quarter of the first century BCE. His hatred of the Romans,[21] for which he was famous, also fits into this period. We shall see later in Section 3, about the historical background, that during the time of

---

[15] = part of T2 [Biraschi] (= A1 [Marastoni]).

[16] See Marastoni 2007 for a modern appreciation of the scholar and a recent collection of his fragments. Otherwise the fragments are found in *Die Fragmente der griechischen Historiker* 184 and now in *Brill's New Jacoby* 184.

[17] Strabo 13.1.55 [C609–610] = A2 [Marastoni].

[18] King Mithridates VI Eupator's reign goes from 120 to 63 BCE, during which three wars against Rome took place. See Marastoni 2007:6 and e.g. Sartre 1995:122–133 or Mayor 2010:296–297.

[19] The death of Metrodoros is also told by Plutarch *Lucullus* 22 (= A3 [Marastoni]), but in a rather different way. This is, however, an element that is less important for the appreciation of Demetrios, and we shall not develop this further here. See e.g. Marastoni 2007:30–31 and 59 with a recent bibliography on this topic.

[20] Cicero *De oratore* 2.88 = 2.360 (= A5 [Marastoni]), Cicero *De oratore* 2.90 = 2.365 (= A4a [Marastoni]) and Cicero *De oratore* 3.20 = 3.75 (= A4b [Marastoni]).

[21] Pliny *Natural History* 34.16.34 (= A10 [Marastoni]) and Ovid *Ex Ponto* 4.14.37–40 (= A11 [Marastoni]). See also Marastoni 2007:56–59.

Metrodoros, the discontent against the Romans and their exploitation of the wealth of Asia Minor was increasing.[22]

From these elements about Metrodoros we may now draw two conclusions about Demetrios of Scepsis. First, it is certainly interesting to know, because of his rather uncommon origin of Scepsis, that another scholar from the same place had some success in the fields of philosophy and rhetoric. This background, given that both were well-educated scholars, must have allowed them to receive some kind of education in their hometown, or at least the prosperity of this city must have been such in those days that it enabled two of its citizens to amass enough resources to ensure a good education. Second, if Metrodoros, living roughly between 133 and 71 BCE, witnessed on the one hand the breakdown of the stability in Asia Minor following the end of the kingdom of the Attalids,[23] and on the other the extension of Roman influence in Asia Minor, then Demetrios, who preceded Metrodoros in the first part of the second century BCE, was able to work in a calmer period, in which it was possible to deal with the Roman presence in Asia Minor in a way that was not yet so polarized as it became later that century, particularly during the Mithridatic wars.

There remains, however, a difficulty with regard to the link between Demetrios and Metrodoros. In the passage from Strabo alluded to above, the geographer uses, as we have seen, the expression "καὶ μετὰ τοῦτον" to indicate that he continues in his narration and passes from one native of Scepsis (Demetrios) to another (Metrodoros). This formulation would allow for a certain timespan between the two scholars. Diogenes Laertios, on the other hand, defines the link between the two scholars by the verb προεβίβασε and indicates that Demetrios must have had some influence on the future career of the young Metrodoros and that the lives of the two men must have overlapped for some time. This is, however, difficult to believe, especially when we consider the elements discussed above concerning Metrodoros' death. The timespan between Demetrios having been in his youth in 190/188 BCE, and Metrodoros having died in 72/71 BCE is almost impossible for only two men.[24] Some modern scholars have therefore put forward the hypothesis of two men named Metrodoros, a father and his son,[25] but the issue is still controversial.[26] The difficulty and its possible answer does not, however, affect the two conclusions we have drawn

---

[22] See e.g. Sartre 1995:148. As mentioned, we shall come back to this more fully in Section 1.3.

[23] Bresson 2001:14-15. Further details will be discussed in Section 1.3.

[24] Leaf 1923:xxviii estimates the timespan to be 135 years. See Marastoni 2007:53-55 for a recent summary of the question.

[25] Jacoby 1930:608-612 (= commentary to *Die Fragmente der griechischen Historiker* 184) and Pédech 1991:66-71.

[26] Alonso Núñez 1984:253-258, Ferrary 1988:229 (in particular note 18) and Briquel 1997:124n23.

from the connection between Demetrios and Metrodoros, and we may add them to the picture of the scholar that we are trying to create.

1.1.2 Characteristics of the Scholar

Having ascertained that Demetrios must have lived in Scepsis during the first part of the second century BCE, when it was a rather prosperous town, even if its citizens were observing the arrival of the Romans in Asia Minor, we can now focus on the elements in the testimonia that define Demetrios as a scholar and look for indications that may help us to analyze the content of his work, his methods, and his aims. It seems, indeed, important, with regard to the way Demetrios' work has been transmitted, to mention this here independently for the passages considered as fragments, so that we may draw a distinction between the elements we may gain from the testimonia and those contained in the fragments. In the testimonia, the information is given by scholars who may be influenced by their opinions about Demetrios while composing their comments, and it may be very different from the evidence that we can gather ourselves by reading the remaining fragments. Therefore, we seem justified in separating the different layers of information about Demetrios and his work, and in focusing first on what has been transmitted in the testimonia, postponing the discussion on the fragments for future studies.

As first element we may mention the fact that Demetrios was said to have been wealthy (πλούσιος) and of good birth (εὐγενής).[27] These characteristics are not helpful with regard to the content of his work, but are still relevant for our appreciation of Demetrios for two reasons. First, they were very important in Antiquity as they enabled Demetrios to benefit from a good education, which was obviously the necessary basis for any scholarly activity. Second, they should also remind us of the fact that with the work of Demetrios, as with many other works from Antiquity, we have the point of view of someone belonging to the privileged social classes. This is perhaps even more important when we consider, as we shall see in greater detail later, that some of his statements were linked to political issues of the time and had direct influence on the status of his hometown Scepsis, such as for instance the town's alleged foundation by the son of Aeneas,[28] or the localization of the cult of the goddess Rhea in the Troad.[29] Both subjects not only illustrate the wide and thorough scholarly

---

[27] Diogenes Laertios 5.84 = part of T2 [Biraschi]. For the text see above p. 5.

[28] Strabo 13.1.53 [C607] = fr. 35 [Gaede/Biraschi] and Stephanus Byzantius s.v. Ἀρίσβη (Stephanus Byzantius 119, 3 [Meineke] = Stephanus Byzantius α 426 [Billerbeck]) = fr. 20 [Gaede/Biraschi].

[29] Strabo 10.3.19–20 [C472] = fr. 61 [Gaede/Biraschi], Stephanus Byzantius s.v. Ἀλύβη (Stephanus Byzantius 79, 6 [Meineke] = Stephanus Byzantius α 233 [Billerbeck]) = fr. 60 [Gaede/ Biraschi] and

education of Demetrios, which we shall discuss shortly, but more importantly they contain issues that influenced the status of his hometown. Thus, we may imply from these two characteristics that Demetrios was not only working as a skilled scholar hunting down the less well-known versions of a myth, as some other testimonia suggest, but was also acting as a citizen of his hometown who had the social position to take part in debates about the political situation of Scepsis.[30]

This tie to his hometown is another characteristic mentioned in the testimonia that we may highlight. Demetrios is indeed often considered as someone well-acquainted with his country (ἔμπειρος; ἐντόπιος; ἐπιχώριος).[31] This information has two implications for us. First, even without giving direct indications about the content of the work of Demetrios, this characteristic can, nonetheless, tell us something about its scope and subject areas. If it was known that he was well-acquainted with the landscape of his hometown, and this fact was judged important enough to be noted by ancient scholars—at least by Strabo, from whose text the two testimonia come—we may understand that his research must somehow have involved the landscape of his hometown and its surrounding region. Second, if we focus on one of the testimonia that mentions his acquaintance with the topography of his hometown, we could perhaps make some further suppositions about the aims that he pursued in his work, or at least about the way in which they were perceived in Antiquity. Strabo describes in the passage under discussion the peculiar position that Demetrios defended in one of the many controversial issues about the localization of Homeric toponyms in the Trojan landscape. By the way the geographer phrases his text, he seems to suggest that the Hellenistic scholar may have worked in the interests of his own hometown:

ἀλλ᾽ οὐδ᾽ οἷς συνηγορεῖ τούτοις ὁμολογεῖ. τὰ γὰρ περὶ τὴν Σκῆψιν τοποθετῶν, τὴν ἑαυτοῦ πατρίδα, πλησίον τῆς Σκήψεως καὶ τοῦ Αἰσήπου Αἰνέαν κώμην καὶ Ἀργυρίαν λέγει καὶ Ἀλαζόνιον.

Stephanus Byzantius s.v. Σκῆψις (= Stephanus Byzantius 574, 8 [Meineke] = Stephanus Byzantius σ 202 [Billerbeck]) = fr. 34 [Gaede] or fr. 34b [Biraschi]. For another modern hypothesis where the erudition of a Hellensistic scholar may have been used in a political context, see Ridgway 2000:33—Crates of Mallos could have provided the scholarly input to the representation of the Gigantomachy from the Pergamon Altar.

[30] See Dreyer 2009:33–46 for a few elements, gathered, however, independently from any considerations concerning Demetrios, about what we can know about the local elites of those days.

[31] Strabo 13.1.45 [C603] = T4 [Biraschi] and Strabo 13.1.43 [C602] = T5 [Biraschi]. For the use of the adjective ἐπιχώριος as applied to a specific genre of local historiography, see Ambaglio 2001:7–21.

> But, he [Demetrios] does not even agree with those whose opinion he is defending. For, while localising the places around Scepsis, his own hometown, he mentions near Scepsis and the Aisepos, the villages Ainea, Argyria and Alazonion.
>
> Strabo 12.3.23 [C552][32]

In this example, Strabo suggests that, when touching on a topic involving places near his hometown, Demetrios departs from the opinions of other scholars and defends his own, which were, however, so far-fetched that even Strabo could not follow them.[33] We may infer from this that Strabo sees a difference between the way in which Demetrios handles topics involving his hometown and the approach he takes when dealing with other issues in which his hometown is less involved, and he states this in a rather allusive way. If our interpretation of this passage is correct, it could explain why the characteristic of being a native of Scepsis, and therefore well-acquainted with the landscape of his hometown, is so crucial for the appraisal of Demetrios and his contribution, making it so peculiar among ancient scholarship. This characteristic has been judged so important that some modern scholars, especially Walter Leaf, claimed that Demetrios had founded a new branch of scholarship by this peculiar approach,[34] but we shall have to discuss the appraisal of modern scholars later. For the time being, we may keep to the idea that Demetrios was considered a scholar who was not only well-documented, but was also personally acquainted with the place that formed to a large extent the subjects of his work.

Another slightly more controversial characteristic emerging from the testimonia concerns the way in which Demetrios is defined with regard to his scholarly activity. In three of the remaining testimonia,[35] Demetrios is described as having acquired a deep knowledge, and is called either a γραμματικός, a φιλόλογος, or perhaps also a ἱστορικός, if we take into account the dubious T11 [Biraschi].[36] We shall discuss this in more depth in the section on the literary background, but, for the time being, we would like to highlight the fact that there is no evidence in any of the testimonia that would suggest where Demetrios received his education and/or undertook his research. The absence of this information is surprising, as all three adjectives, even without taking into

---

[32] = T8 [Biraschi] = part of fr. 45 [Gaede/Biraschi].

[33] See Leaf 1917–1918:28–31.

[34] Leaf 1917–1918:23–24 repeated by Leaf 1923:xxviii.

[35] Strabo 13.1.55 [C609] (= T1 [Biraschi]); Diogenes Laertios 5.84 (= part of T2 [Biraschi]); Eudocia 128, as found in Flach 1880:221 (= T11 [Biraschi]).

[36] The addition of this fragment is controversial. There only a Demetrios of Ilion is mentioned. See Biraschi 2011, commentary ad T1–11, for her reasons for including it in her collection.

consideration their specific meanings, point to an activity for which one has to have at one's disposal a considerable amount of sources on which to build one's research.[37] But nothing on this is found in the remaining testimonia, and we have to rely here on two modern hypotheses about the place where Demetrios could have acquired this knowledge. These two possibilities are Scepsis or Pergamon: either he was working in his hometown of Scepsis or he went to Pergamon, the famous center of scholarship, to carry out his research. For the first hypothesis, Schwartz suggested, by emphasizing either a Platonic or an Aristotelean tradition, that Demetrios could have acquired his knowledge in his hometown,[38] perhaps even by using the library of Aristotle, which had been brought to Scepsis after the death of the philosopher.[39] However, the fate of this library is controversial and it is difficult to prove the scholarship of Demetrios on the basis of the presence of Aristotle's library in Scepsis;[40] but certainly his acquaintance with the landscape of his homeland and its presence in his work may speak in favor of this hypothesis. On the other hand, since it is clear that for his work and research he must have used an extensive library,[41] another hypothesis is that he had access to the library of Pergamon.[42] Elements in favor of this suggestion can be found in fr. 68 [Gaede/Biraschi],[43] in which Strabo emphasizes a scholarly disagreement between Demetrios and Crates of Mallos, and suggests, by doing so, a close link between the two scholars. However, the wording of the Straboian passage unfortunately does not allow us to go beyond this link and to define, for instance, whether Demetrios read the work of Crates or had access to his statements through other means, or, finally, whether Strabo juxtaposed the opinions of the two scholars who may have stated them independently of one another. We shall come back to this later, but we may keep in mind here that none of these three options can really resolve the question of where Demetrios carried out his scholarly activity. If he read Crates, he may have done so either

---

[37] The presence of a library for the scholarly activity has also been highlighted by Montana 2015:82–90.

[38] Schwartz 1901:2808.

[39] This is a hypothesis recently defended by Ragone 2009:669–674.

[40] For the fate of the library, see e.g. Gottschalk 1972:335–342, Lindsay 1997:290–298, Nagy 1998:200–206, Schubert 2002:225–237, Primavesi 2007:51–77 and finally also Irigoin 1994:50–53 and Richardson 1994:8–12, both with further bibliography. For the most recent bibliographical references, see also Radt 2008:504–505, Berti/Costa 2010:49–55, and now Montana 2015:78, 167–170.

[41] This is not only inferred from the relevant adjectives, but can also be suggested by the number of authors that Demetrios quotes himself (see below pp. 21–22).

[42] See, for instance, Montanari 1993b:651, who considers, however, the links between Demetrios and Pergamon to be not very tight. Pfeiffer 1968:249–251 also discussed Demetrios' achievement in the chapter on Pergamene scholarship emphasizing, however, the scholar's independence. So does Sandys 1903:153–154 and most recently Montana 2015:147.

[43] Strabo 9.5.18 [C438–439].

in Pergamon or in Scepsis. Likewise, when considering the second option, which suggests that Demetrios was only aware of the discussions carried out in the surroundings of the library of Pergamon without having access to physical writings through which he learned of Crates' position in the debate, we may postulate that he may have known them either because of the circulation of ideas that was certainly already happening in those days, or because he himself was present in Pergamon, either visiting or as a more permanent resident. Finally, in the hypothesis suggesting that the link is provided by Strabo, the piece of evidence would only allow us to say that Strabo used the books from both scholars together as sources for his own work, giving no indication about the two scholars involved. We see, therefore, how difficult it is, because of the nature of the evidence, to determine facts about Demetrios and the place where he carried out his activity. We may thus summarize our reading of the passages attributing to Demetrios the adjectives γραμματικός, φιλόλογος, or ἱστορικός by stating that, strictly speaking, they only define Demetrios as one among the ancient scholars—after all, he is alluded to with the same adjectives as the other Pergamene or Alexandrian scholars—but without linking him to a special center of scholarship. This uncertainty about the place where he carried out his activity may, however, not only be seen as a lacuna in our understanding of Demetrios' historical background: it could also be connected with the characteristic of focusing on his hometown. As Demetrios' acquaintance with Scepsis and the topography of its surroundings was so important for the content of his work, an author quoting from it or speaking about Demetrios' achievements may have left out or dismissed the information about the place where Demetrios actually undertook his research in order to highlight the scholar's acquaintance with the landscape of his hometown.

1.1.3 Characteristics of His Work

Having defined the scholar in the previous section, we shall now move on to his work and focus on the way it was characterized, judged, and appreciated in the testimonia, keeping in mind that the two aspects—the image a reader has of a given author and the perception he has of his work—are closely linked. Nevertheless, it may be interesting to separate them, particularly in the case of an author like Demetrios about whom almost nothing is known apart from the elements that remain of his work.

First, we should discuss here the title of the work, or more precisely, the way the work was alluded to or quoted in Antiquity. For this, we are in a rather good position as the title of Demetrios' work is well attested as ὁ Τρωϊκὸς διάκοσμος, at least in the fragments from Athenaeus.[44] In Strabo, however, who is quoting Demetrios most of the time only by his name, no title is given. Nevertheless, at least two paraphrases of the title are preserved in his work that are reasonably close to Athenaeus' formula: ὁ τὸν Τρωϊκὸν διάκοσμον ἐξηγησάμενος γραμματικός "the scholar who explained the Trojan Catalogue"[45] and ὥστε τριάκοντα βίβλους συγγράψαι στίχων ἐξήγησιν μικρῷ πλειόνων ἑξήκοντα, τοῦ Καταλόγου τῶν Τρώων "that he has written thirty books about the little more than sixty lines of the Trojan Catalogue."[46] Furthermore, the same words are again used to refer to Demetrios' work in Strabo's fragmentarily preserved book 7, in which we find the formula ἐν τοῖς Περὶ τοῦ Τρωϊκοῦ διακόσμου.[47] Here, however, it is not so much the words themselves that are striking, but the presence of the preposition περί in its wording. Indeed, because of the presence of this preposition, the expression from Strabo's book 7 is actually a formula, which would point to a well-attested type of scholarly writing, the so-called περί-*literature*,[48] and we shall have to take account of this in our discussion. Finally, since in the dubious T11, which Biraschi added to her collection, the work is called a Τρωϊκά,[49] we may have to consider this variation as well, and examine what this may tell us about the ways in which Demetrios' work has been understood.

Beginning with the formula of Athenaeus, ὁ Τρωϊκὸς διάκοσμος, we must first draw attention to an ambiguity it contains, but which will also be of some importance for our understanding of Demetrios' work. Indeed, it seems that the formula can be used either to designate the work of Demetrios, as in Athenaeus, or to refer to the Trojan Catalogue, the part of the Homeric text on which Demetrios commented, as for instance in the two aforementioned paraphrases from Strabo. This second meaning of the formula is also found in

---

[44] Fr. 1 [Gaede/Biraschi] (= Athenaeus 4.141e–f); fr. 3 [Gaede/Biraschi] (= Athenaeus 14.658b); fr. 5–11 [Gaede/Biraschi] (= Athenaeus 8.346c; 15.697c; 4.155b; 14.644a; 3.80d; 4.173f–174a and 7.300d); fr. 15 [Gaede/Biraschi] (= Athenaeus 3.91c) and fr. 16 [Gaede/Biraschi] (= Athenaeus 10.425c). Fr. 12 [Gaede/Biraschi], giving also the title, is from Stephanus of Byzantium (Stephanus Byzantius s.v. Σιλίνδιον (= Stephanus Byzantius 569, 6 [Meineke] = Stephanus Byzantius σ 159 [Billerbeck])). As fr. 13 [Gaede/Biraschi] (= Athenaeus 15.697d) is following immediately fr. 6 and fr. 14 [Gaede/Biraschi] (= Athenaeus 4.174a) fr. 10, they do not have the full title. Finally in fr. 4 [Gaede/Biraschi], from Harpocration (s.v. Θυργωνίδαι), the title is abbreviated to ἐν β´ Διακόσμου.

[45] Strabo 13.1.55 [C609] = T1 [Biraschi].

[46] Strabo 13.1.45 [C603] = T4 [Biraschi].

[47] Strabo 7, fr. 22a [Radt] = fr. 47 [Gaede/Biraschi]. We shall discuss this in more details below.

[48] Schröder 1999:11–12 suggests that for prose texts the expected title would include περί. But Dubischar 2015:565–568 rightly points out that there may not have been such a strict rule about the choice of the title for a scholarly work.

[49] Eudocia 128 (= Flach 1880:221) = T11 [Biraschi].

two further passages from Strabo's *Geography*,[50] and, for at least one of them, modern scholars suggested that the issue discussed there was linked to the work of Demetrios.[51] The passage concerns two plus-verses about the Caucones that were added by Callisthenes to the Trojan Catalogue:

> Καλλισθένης δὲ καὶ ἔγραφε τὰ ἔπη ταῦτα εἰς τὸν διάκοσμον, μετὰ τὸ "Κρῶμνάν τ' Αἰγιαλόν τε καὶ ὑψηλοὺς Ἐρυθίνους" τιθεὶς "Καύκωνας δ' αὖτ' ἦγε Πολυκλέος υἱὸς ἀμύμων, / οἳ περὶ Παρθένιον ποταμὸν κλυτὰ δώματ' ἔναιον·" [...]

> Callisthenes actually inserted, after the line "Cromna, Aegialos and the heights of Erythinoi," these plus-verses to the Catalogue: [52] "The noble son of Polycles led the Caucones, / who dwelt in their splendid houses around the Parthenios River." [...]

Strabo 12.3.5 [C542]

It is, however, not only in the context of Demetrios' work that the word διάκοσμος was used for κατάλογος when the formula designates the Trojan Catalogue in the Homeric text. We find other examples, which are completely unrelated to Demetrios. The clearest comes from a papyrus dated to the second century CE in which a line from the Trojan Catalogue (*Iliad* 2.848) is quoted as ἐν διακόσμῳ.[53] We know that this refers to the Homeric passage considered as the Trojan Catalogue, because, in the scholia transmitted by the manuscripts tradition, the same line is quoted as belonging to the κατάλογος.[54] Both words seem therefore to be used for this part of the Homeric text, almost like a title.[55] This can also be seen in several other references in the scholia to the *Iliad*,[56] and in

---

[50] Strabo 12.3.5 [C542] and Strabo 12.3.10 [C544] where a part of the Trojan Catalogue is called ὁ παφλαγονικὸς διάκοσμος.

[51] Radt 2008:350–351 quoting Gaede 1880:10. Also in other places Radt suggests that Strabo's vocabulary might have been influenced by Demetrios' work. See Radt 2008:479 where the remark concerns the verb μεταλαμβάνεσθαι, which occurs in Strabo 13.1.34 [C597] and in Strabo 13.1.35 [C598].

[52] In his 1928 edition Jones translated this formula as "in the treatise of Callisthenes" (his translation being: "Callisthenes in his treatise on *The Marshalling of the Ships* was for inserting [...]"). In this case, Callisthenes' work would have had the same title as the work of Demetrios, ὁ Διάκοσμος. See further Radt 2008:351, who keeps to a more circumspect translation, and Nicolai 2005–2006:62 who understand the formula as meaning the Homeric passage defined as the Trojan Catalogue.

[53] P. Oxy. 2.221 (column 6, lines 18 and 23–24) = Erbse 1977:89–90.

[54] Σ bT *Iliad* 21.140 [Erbse].

[55] See for instance Schröder 1999:36 and also Lohan 1890:5–9.

[56] Σ AT *Iliad* 11.422b [Erbse]; Σ T *Iliad* 14.511 [Erbse]; Σ A *Iliad* 17.73 [Erbse]; Σ A *Iliad* 17.218b1 [Erbse].

addition the verb διακοσμεῖν is used to describe the ordering of the troops a few lines before the Catalogue of the Ships.[57]

From all this, we may draw two consequences for our appreciation of Demetrios' work. First, we will have to take account of the fact that Demetrios seems to have had the choice between κατάλογος and διάκοσμος, but opted for διάκοσμος. Therefore, we may have to investigate further what his choice for this word may tell us about the scholar and his work. Second, and more importantly, the evidence also suggests that this closeness between the formula chosen for his title and the designation of the part of the Homeric text on which Demetrios was commenting may not have been coincidental. It was probably meant to emphasize the constitutive link between Demetrios' work and the part of the Homeric text with which it dealt. Such a choice may then be interpreted as an effort to tighten, in commentaries or commentary-like works, the link between the explicandum (the Homeric text here) and the explanation as suggested by Dubischar.[58] Indeed, the German scholar points out that, by emancipating the commentary from the text it was meant to explain, by giving the comments the forms of *hypomnemata*, the scholars had to redefine how the now self-standing text of their commentary could be linked back to the primary text they were explaining. Moreover, such an interpretation could also explain why the formulation of the title lacks, at least in Athenaeus' text, the introductive περί that would perhaps be expected for a title of a scholarly work written in prose.[59] As we have seen, such a formula has been transmitted in the version preserved in fr. 47 [Gaede/Biraschi] of Strabo's book 7 (ἐν τοῖς Περὶ τοῦ Τρωϊκοῦ διακόσμου).[60] However, the passage involved comes from the *Vatican Epitome* of Strabo's book 7 and should therefore be used with cautions as evidence for the title of Demetrios' work.[61] Still, as it contains a formulation of the title that associates Demetrios' work with one category of scholarly works, the so-called περί-literature, the passage and its formula raise a further question about the form that Demetrios' work may have taken. Therefore, we should perhaps mention this debate here before proceeding further. It is also noteworthy in this context to mention that Baladié suggests, in his translation of the Straboian passage involved, that the formula should be completed with the word ὑπομνήμασι.[62] In doing so, he blurs the distinction that is commonly made between two forms of scholarly writing, the *hypomnemata* and the *sungrammata*. With regard to

[57] *Iliad* 2.476.
[58] Dubischar 2015:554–556.
[59] Schröder 1999:11–12. See above p. 12.
[60] Strabo 7, fr. 22a [Radt].
[61] For the value of the text from the *Epitome*, see for instance Radt 2007:331–332.
[62] Baladié 1989:179.

Demetrios of Scepsis, this question has been discussed most prominently by Rudolf Pfeiffer, who suggests in his *History of Classical Scholarship* that Demetrios' work must have taken the form of a *hypomnema*.[63] He takes, however, another starting point for his argumentation and begins by comparing Demetrios' work, commonly known as ὁ Τρωϊκὸς διάκοσμος, with the work of Apollodoros of Athens, which is quoted as Περὶ τοῦ τῶν νεῶν καταλόγου.[64] He then goes on to claim that Demetrios' work seems never to have been quoted with a formula containing περί, somehow ignoring the evidence from Strabo's book 7, and concludes from the difference between the two formulas used for these titles that the two works may have belonged to different categories of scholarly writings. He suggests that the work of Demetrios was a *hypomnema* (ὑπόμνημα) whereas that of Apollodoros took the form of a *sungramma* (σύγγραμμα), and justifies his assumption by the fact that the title of the *sungrammata* tends to be given with the preposition περί when the topic is thematic, or with πρός when the work is directed against another scholar.[65] However, Felix Jacoby had already remarked, in his commentary on Apollodoros, that one has to be more cautious when trying to give a general definition of the content or structure of the so-called περί-*literature*.[66] Furthermore, it has been shown more recently on the basis of papyrological findings how difficult it is to distinguish remaining fragments of scholarly works and to attribute them to one of the two categories.[67] This is not only due to the poor state of preservation of the fragments, but also because the ancient scholars could combine several categories and compose rather heterogeneous works.[68] This distinction between the different works must have been less sharp and the title may thus have been attributed less systematically than is assumed by Pfeiffer. Here we may once again refer to the recent study by Dubischar and to the systematization he proposed there.[69] He divides both categories of scholarly writings (the *hypomnemata* and the *sungrammata*) into several subgroups, demonstrating, for instance, that the presence of the preposition περί is not always the best criterion to distinguish different types of *sungrammata*. Nonetheless, he maintains a clear distinction

---

[63] Pfeiffer 1968:249–251. He has recently been followed by Ragone 2009:663, who emphasized, however, a second characteristic of Demetrios' work, the exegesis, to which we shall return later.

[64] The formula is, however, not uniformly transmitted. Schwartz 1894:2863–2864 mentions the variants ὁ Νεῶν κατάλογος, ὁ Κατάλογος, ὁ περὶ νεῶν κατάλογος, ὁ Περί νεῶν, ὁ Περὶ νεῶν κατάλογος. Jacoby 1930 (*Die Fragmente der griechischen Historiker* 244) reconstructs Περὶ τοῦ Νεῶν καταλόγος; whereas Pfeiffer 1968:257 suggests Περὶ τοῦ τῶν νεῶν καταλόγου.

[65] Pfeiffer 1968:213.

[66] Jacoby 1930:760 (= commentary to *Die Fragmente der griechischen Historiker* 244 F88–153).

[67] Montanari 1993a:243, Dorandi 2000:15–27, Hardings 2006:13–20, Lundon 2011:163.

[68] Montanari 1993a:243.

[69] Dubischar 2015:554–570.

between *hypomnemata* and *sungrammata*, in so far that the latter show an even great autonomy from the primary text, which was at the center of the discussions, than the former. All these remarks may then strengthen our first hypothesis, which suggests that the absence of the περί in the title of Demetrios' work should be explained, first and foremost, by the closeness that Demetrios wanted to establish between the content of his work and the part of the Homeric text on which he made his comments, the Trojan Catalogue. We may therefore have to focus in what follows in more detail on Demetrios' choice for the words in the title rather than on the formula transmitted to get further details about the scope of his work.

In order to do so, we may begin by investigating if the word διάκοσμος occurs in the title of other works and how it was used there. By comparing the evidence, we may then be able to deepen our understanding of Demetrios' work. Our first example is provided by a text, which not only has the word διάκοσμος in its title, but was probably also composed in a context similar to that in which Demetrios worked. This is the work of the rather unknown Mnesimachos of Phaselis,[70] who has been dated to the early Hellenistic period.[71] In one of his preserved fragments, the word διάκοσμοι, in its plural form and in a formula without the expected περί, has been used—or has at least been transmitted—as the title of one of his works.[72] As far as the content of the work is concerned, in this fragment, as well as in a second,[73] Mnesimachos is quoted as having attempted to classify the different categories of Nymphes, and as far as we can tell from these very few pieces of evidence, it seems that it was a very learned work where the author tried to classify parts of traditional mythological elements. Unfortunately we kept only the two fragments on Nymphes, and cannot tell what would have been other topics he discussed. However, with regard to Demetrios of Scepsis, the evidence suggests that Mnesimachos' work was composed independently of any previously existing text, and with the aim of collecting, systematizing, and explaining disparate mythological elements found in several texts.[74] This fact would then point to a work being a monograph

---

[70] Bux 1932:2279 and for the text of the three preserved fragments *Die Fragmente der griechischen Historiker* 841 F1–3 and now also *Brill's New Jacoby* 841 F1–3 with further comments. They all come from the scholia to Apollonios Rhodios.

[71] Because of the scarcity of the evidence, modern scholars hesitate, however, and suggest that any time between Charon of Lampsacos (dated to the fifth century BCE) and Eirenaios (dated to the first century CE) would be possible. See Baumbach 2000:307 and Bux 1932:2279.

[72] *Die Fragmente der griechischen Historiker* 841 F2 = *Brill's New Jacoby* 841 F2 =Σ Apollonios Rhodios 4.1412 [Wendel].

[73] *Die Fragmente der griechischen Historiker* 841 F3 = *Brill's New Jacoby* 841 F3 = Σ Apollonios Rhodios 2.477 [Wendel].

[74] As far as the scope of this systematization is concerned, it is extremely difficult, because of the scarcity of the evidence, to give an accurate picture of the work. Modern scholars hesitate, for

rather than an interpretation of any preexisting selected text or work, as has been supposed for Demetrios, and we see once again how difficult it is to apply the distinction suggested by Pfeiffer to authors like Demetrios or Mnesimachos of whose work very little remains.

However, by expanding our discussion to other works that were titled with a formula containing the word διάκοσμος, we may gain further information about Demetrios' work. A good example of this is actually the oldest preserved attestation of the word διάκοσμος as a title. It comes from the context of Presocratic philosophy: the title Διάκοσμος, completed with either μικρός or μέγας, is attested for works of either Democritos or Leucippos.[75] In these works, the idea of ordering was emphasized, in particular the ordering of the whole earth or cosmos, and their contents are probably very different from that of Demetrios' work. Still, this evidence allows us to identify a further feature of Demetrios' work. First, we may briefly note that this example shows once again, in connection with the discussion above, that the word διάκοσμος could be used as a title even without the more common περί-formula, although this choice may be explained here by the content of the work rather than by a special tradition with regard to the formulation of a title.[76] Focusing now on the Presocratic environment in which the title appears, it is possible to see another aspect of Demetrios' work, which would, moreover, attribute it to a special field of Homeric scholarship. The link is established through the fragments of another scholar, Metrodoros of Lampsacos, a pupil of Anaxagoras.[77] In one of his few fragments, he uses the word διακόσμησις in its plural form, διακοσμήσεις, in the context of an allegorical interpretation of the Homeric poems, even if not for the title of his study.[78] The word is used to designate the elements for which the gods stand in the poems, and seems therefore embedded in allegorical interpretation.[79] There is, however, a link to be drawn between this early allegorical interpretation and Demetrios of Scepsis. First, we may mention that in another of Metrodoros' fragments he is qualified as one of the first Homeric scholars to deal with the so-called physical elements in the Homeric poems

---

instance, about the rendering of the title: either *"Descriptions des Mondes"* (Lachenaud 2010:510) or *"Gruppierungen"* (Baumbach 2000:307). See also *Brill's New Jacoby* 841 F2 for further thoughts on this.

[75] Ὁ μικρὸς Διάκοσμος or ὁ μέγας Διάκοσμος. See e.g. Bodnár 1997:455. For Leucippos 67 B1 [DK] and B1a [DK], for Democritos 68 A33 [DK] and B5 [DK]. The expression τὸν Ἀναξαγόρειον διάκοσμον (Anaxagoras 59 A20c [DK]) would link the word to Anaxagoras, but in this context the expression does not seem to be a title.

[76] They wanted to create an order, not to write about it. It was probably also the reason why Lachenaud 2010:510 translates the title of Mnesimachos' work as *"Descriptions des Mondes."*

[77] Pontani 2005:27–28, Nestle 1932:1476–1477, and most recently Novokhatko 2015:37–38.

[78] Metrodoros 61 F3 [DK] (= Tatian *Oratio ad Graecos* 21, pp. 24.5–14 [Schwartz]).

[79] See Janko 1997:76–79 and Hammerstaedt 1998:28–32.

(ὃν καὶ πρῶτον σπουδάσαι τοῦ ποιητοῦ περὶ τὴν φυσικὴν πραγματείαν "who was the first to focus on the physical elements used by the poet").[80] Therefore, already in the time of Metrodoros, a scholar who was aiming at an interpretation and/or an explanation of the Homeric poems, moreover in the context of an allegorical approach, could be interested in the physical elements belonging to the setting in which the story was believed to have taken place.[81] Second, this tradition seems to have been known by Demetrios. This is proved indirectly through one of his fragments. Indeed, in fr. 61 [Gaede/Biraschi],[82] Demetrios is quoting Stesimbrotos of Thasos,[83] another of the early interpreters of Homer, as an authority on the mysteries of Samothrace. This Stesimbrotos is quoted in a passage of Plato's *Ion*, together with Metrodoros of Lampsacos, and is considered, along with Metrodoros, as one of the best commentators on Homer.[84] Thus, Demetrios must have known this early tradition, as he used one of its two representatives as his authority. It could therefore be plausible that the presence of the word διάκοσμος instead of κατάλογος in the title of Demetrios' work may somehow indicate this affinity. Such a connection between Metrodoros and Demetrios through the similarities of these words (διάκοσμος and διακοσμήσεις) has already been suggested by Porter.[85] He mentions the fragment of Metrodoros containing the word διακόσμησις in connection with Crates of Mallos while discussing his allegorical interpretation of the arrangement of the Achaean ships on the Trojan coast (*Iliad* 14.31–36), a topic very relevant to ours. The modern scholar does not, however, justify his statement, and we shall have to return to the link between Demetrios and Crates in our section on the literary background. However, the discussion of the more philosophical use of the word διάκοσμος provides us with some hints as to the literary tradition to which Demetrios' work may have belonged.

However, we should not go too far with such speculation, and must remember that there were other formulations that alluded to Demetrios' work. For instance, as mentioned above, Demetrios' work could also be called a Τρωϊκά.[86] The closest example is certainly the Τρωϊκά of Hegesianax of Alexandria Troas, Demetrios' contemporary, who is quoted several times by the Hellenistic scholar.[87] But this

---

80   Metrodoros 61 F2 [DK] = Diogenes Laertios 2.11.

81   Janko 1997:77.

82   Strabo 10.3.19–21 [C472–473].

83   Pontani 2005:27, Nestle 1932:1476–1477, and most recently Novokhatko 2015:38.

84   Plato *Ion* 530c = Metrodoros 61 F1 [DK].

85   Porter 1992:110.

86   As mentioned above, the evidence comes from T11 [Biraschi] (= Eudocia 128 as in Flach 1880:221) about a Demetrios of Ilion whom Biraschi identifies with our Demetrios.

87   Fr. 7 [Gaede/Biraschi] = Athenaeus 4.155b and fr. 9 [Gaede/Biraschi] = Athenaeus 3.80d. See also fr. 20 [Gaede/Biraschi] = Stephanus Byzantius s.v. Ἀρίσβη (Stephanus Byzantius 119, 3 [Meineke]

category of work must have been quite heterogeneous,[88] as we see, for instance, when we cite the example of Timolaos of Macedonia, who composed under the title of Τρωϊκόν, a recomposition of the *Iliad* with a new line inserted after each Homeric line.[89] Moreover, the formula Τρωϊκὸς διάκοσμος could also be used for other works. It is, for instance, attributed by the *Souda* to Dictys of Crete.[90] However, Dictys' work definitely does not belong to the same category of work as that of Demetrios: Dictys composed a narrative fiction whereas Demetrios' work, with all the lacunae we have about its exact form, is still clearly designated in the testimonia as an exegetical work (a text on a text), as shown for instance in the two passages from Strabo alluding to Demetrios' work by paraphrasing its title.[91] We should therefore add to the considerations about the title other elements that we find in the testimonia to progress in our task here. We may, however, take from the discussion about the title that not only the absence of the expected περί in the formula of the title but also the presence of the word διάκοσμος instead of κατάλογος were significant. It should particularly be highlighted that because of both of these singularities the title was identical to the formula used in Antiquity to designate the part of the Homeric text on which Demetrios commented.

For the discussion of a further characteristic attributed to Demetrios' work we should go back to the passages of Strabo we just mentioned above containing the two paraphrases of the title.[92] In both of these, Demetrios' work was defined as an ἐξήγησις and this characteristic has recently been highlighted by Ragone.[93] But with the concept of ἐξήγησις we face another difficulty. This word, and its meaning, have often been treated by modern scholars independently of the debate about the opposition between *hypomnemata* and *sungrammata*, in which Demetrios' work was involved, and we shall therefore have to deal with a third category of ancient scholarly works and try not only to understand what kind of works this category represented, but also to discover how it was related to the two other forms of writings. Indeed, the word ἐξήγησις itself seems older than

---

= Stephanus Byzantius α 426 [Billerbeck]) and fr. 21 [Gaede/Biraschi] = Strabo 13.1.27 [C594].

[88] See Jacoby 1957b:521 (= commentary to *Die Fragmente der griechischen Historiker* 43–51), Merkle 1989:45–46 and Fry 1998:75–76.

[89] See Souda s.v. Τιμόλαος (τ 626 [Adler]) and Pontani 2005:47.

[90] Souda s.v. Δίκτυς (δ 1117 [Adler]).

[91] Strabo 13.1.55 [C609] = T1 [Biraschi]: ὁ τὸν Τρωϊκὸν διάκοσμον ἐξηγησάμενος γραμματικός "the scholar who explained the Trojan Catalogue" and Strabo 13.1.45 [C603] = T4 [Biraschi]: ὥστε τριάκοντα βίβλους συγγράψαι στίχων ἐξήγησιν μικρῷ πλειόνων ἑκήκοντα, τοῦ Καταλόγου τῶν Τρώων "that he has written thirty books about the little more than sixty lines of the Trojan Catalogue." See above p. 12

[92] Strabo 13.1.55 [C609] = T1 [Biraschi] and Strabo 13.1.45 [C603] = T4 [Biraschi].

[93] Ragone 2009:663 and previously Pfeiffer 1968:249–251. See further Pontani 2005:23–103 for a very detailed account of the activities placed in Antiquity under the category of ἐξήγησις.

the other two, as it was used for the explanation of literary texts from at least Plato[94] down to Dionysios Thrax,[95] and it can be applied to a very large category of works that includes all kind of interpretations and extends to domains others than philology, such as philosophy, especially at its beginning.[96] The only common feature in all these works seems to be, according to Dettori for instance, the fact that the works deal with previous literary traditions and aim to interpret them.[97] When considering Demetrios' work as an ἐξήγησις, we are therefore in a completely different field that does not take account of the distinction between *hypomnemata* and *sungrammata* alluded to above. This distinction is mostly used in the context of the scholarly productions of the Alexandrian critics. Their works have been classified into four groups: editions (ἐκδόσεις), commentaries (ὑπομνήματα), monographs (συγγράμματα), and finally lexica (λέξεις).[98] But we have already seen how limited this approach may be in the discussion about the title of Demetrios' work. We reach a similar conclusion when focusing on the concept of ἐξήγησις, as, for instance, the presentation of ancient exegetical works given by Pontani shows how diversified this field was.[99] This is even more visible when taking into consideration philosophical commentaries, as, for example, Baltussen does.[100] It may still be a good idea, because Demetrios' work is defined as an ἐξήγησις and, despite that fact, we are going beyond the distinction between *hypomnemata* and *sungrammata* to include in our discussion elements taken from Baltussen's considerations about philosophical commentaries. For instance, a very interesting element of Baltussens' discussion is the fact that the Australian scholar makes a distinction between an exegesis and a commentary. He defines the exegesis as a more general act of interpretation of a work (written or oral), whereas a commentary is a written explanation intended to clarify another text.[101] Moreover, for Baltussen the two forms of interpretative activities are not simultaneous: as the form of the commentary presupposes a fixed text that was the object of the commentary, it comes later than the exegesis, which can exist, according to Baltussen, even without a written form of the work. Furthermore, in order to create a more accurate picture

---

[94] Especially in Plato's *Ion*, for which see now also Hunter 2011:27–40. Another example is Plato *Cratylus* 407b.

[95] Dionysios Thrax *Techne* § 1 (= Grammatici graeci I.1, 5–6).

[96] Baltussen 2004:24–25, Richardson 1975:71–77, and Pontani 2005:27–33.

[97] Dettori 2000:187. He mainly contrasts it with the activity of a poet who privileges the words themselves.

[98] Turner 1968:112 and more recently West 2001:50–85. This division is maintained by Dubischar 2015:546–549 and 586–587, although he refines it.

[99] Pontani 2005:23–103. He, however, only focuses on works dealing with the *Odyssey*.

[100] Baltussen 2004:21–35.

[101] Baltussen 2004:23.

of the emergence of the philosophical commentary, the Australian scholar divides the tradition of interpretative activities into three stages, now, however, without making a distinction between ἐξήγησις and commentary.[102] He calls the first stage "emergence of exegesis," where the exegesis is clearly defined as a precursor of the commentary, and dates it between the sixth and fourth century BCE.[103] He paraphrases a second phase as "formalisation and *Gelehrsamkeit*" and makes it extend over a long period from the fourth century BCE to the second century CE. It is then followed, in the philosophical perspective Baltussen takes, by a final stage from the second century CE to the sixth century CE, during which the exegesis evolves into a certain "professionalism and maturity." This distinction can roughly be found for the philological commentaries too, as for instance Pontani mentions a turning point in the second century CE.[104] However, for the philological tradition, this turning point is in fact the beginning of a decline, whereas, for the philosophical commentary, the huge works of Porphyry and Proclos, for instance, were still to come.[105] For our study, it is Baltussen's second phase that is the most relevant, not only from the chronological point of view, as Demetrios' work belongs, as shown above, to the second century BCE, but also for the two characteristics Baltussen mentions for this phase. First, we have the emergence of a typical form for such works, which is accompanied by a reflection on this process. It is therefore here where the debate, linked to Demetrios' work, about the difference between the *hypomnemata* and *sungrammata*, two rather well-defined forms of scholarly writings, could be placed. Second, there is the scholarly polymathy that the authors displayed in their works, and it is this second characteristic mentioned by Baltussen, the polymathy, that seems to be a further feature of Demetrios' work, and may lead us to a third characteristics of Demetrios' work that we would like to discuss.

It has often been noted by modern scholars that Demetrios himself quotes a lot of other works.[106] This characteristic has also been used, for instance in the context of glossographical works, to distinguish a more poetically creative approach from a more exegetical one.[107] Therefore, an abundance of authors

---

[102] Baltussen 2004:26–27.

[103] For this beginning phase, see also Richardson 1975:25–37, Ford 2002:80–85, and the more comprehensive study by Novokhatko 2015:3–59.

[104] Pontani 2005:84.

[105] It is noteworthy to mention that Porphyry and Proclos are also mentioned in Pontani 2005:84–87 as taking part in the exegetical tradition on Homer. See also Dubischar 2015:595 who dates the beginning of the decline of the philological tradition a little earlier (shortly after Didymus).

[106] Stiehle 1850:543–544 gives a list of twelve authors found already in the rather incomplete collection he presented. Ragone 2009:667 has extended the list up to thirty-one authors quoted or alluded to in the context of the fragments of Demetrios.

[107] Dettori 2000:186–187, mainly about Philetas of Cos.

quoted as authorities or as targets to whom to direct one's criticism, as found in Demetrios' fragments, could be another indication (independent of the title and its classification as ἐξήγησις), which could help to qualify it as a scholarly work. However, in the case of Demetrios, it is not only the abundance of quotations that allows us to draw such a conclusion, but also the nature of these quotations. They often come either from poets, often archaic poets, like Mimnermos[108] and Callinos,[109] or from rather unknown scholars, such as, for instance: Democles, quoted in fr. 48 [Gaede/Biraschi]; Hestiaia of Alexandria Troas, quoted in fr. 26 [Gaede/Biraschi];[110] Stesimbrotos of Thasos, in fr. 61 [Gaede/Biraschi];[111] or finally Callisthenes, who is better known to us, in fr. 44 [Gaede/Biraschi].[112] This is already an impressive selection, even if there are many other authors who appear by name in or around the passages that have been taken as fragments of Demetrios' work; and Ragone counted up to thirty-one names. However, the Italian scholar's list has to be taken with caution, as it is not always possible to define, from the preserved wording, whether the authors Ragone mentions are quoted by Demetrios or whether they were simply used together with Demetrios by the source text, for instance, by Strabo. Therefore, it seems safer to break down his list and to start, as we did, with those among the authors whose names appear in the fragments of Demetrios' work, for whom verbs are used that we would most likely translate as "quoting," like τίθεσθαι and παρατίθεσθαι, παραλαμβάνειν μάρτυρα or μιμνήσκεσθαι, and where there is, therefore, no ambiguity. We may, however, add in a second step those authors whom Demetrios contradicts. These are Timaeus, Ephoros, Neanthes of Cyzicos, and Euripides.[113] Finally, we may make a further exception for Hegesianax and Palaephatos, even if they are among the authors for whom it is unclear how Demetrios used their works. They are of particular interest here and deserve a longer development. This is due to the fact that they have a rather prominent position in the fragments from Demetrios' work. Moreover, as we shall see,

---

[108] Fr. 50 [Gaede/Biraschi] = Strabo 1.2.38–40 [C45–47].

[109] Fr. 41 [Gaede/Biraschi] = Strabo 13.4.8 [C627].

[110] See T7 [Biraschi] (Strabo 13.1.36 [C599]) and Funaioli 1913:1313–1314. Besides the above-mentioned occurrence in Strabo, her name is mentioned in Σ D *Iliad* 3.64 [van Thiel] and appears twice in Eustathius, however, in the form Ἱστιαία (Eustathius *Commentarii ad Iliadem* 2.537 (= 280, 15–20 or van der Valk I:430–431) and Eustathius *Commentarii ad Iliadem* 3.64 (= 384, 20 or van der Valk I:606–607).

[111] Strabo 10.3.19–20 [C472–473]. He is one of the early interpreters of Homer mentioned above in the discussion of the title of Demetrios' work. See Pontani 2005:27 and Nestle 1932:1476–1477 and above pp. 17–19.

[112] Strabo 14.5.26 [C680].

[113] Fr. 27 [Gaede/Biraschi] Timaeus (ψεύσασθαί φησιν); fr 45 [Gaede/Biraschi] Ephoros (οὔτε τὴν τούτου δόξαν ἀποδεξάμενος); fr. 50 [Gaede/Biraschi] Neanthes (ἀντιλέγων); fr. 61 [Gaede/Biraschi] Euripides (ὑπεναντιούμενος).

when discussing these authors in more detail, we obtain some further information about Demetrios himself.

As far as the weight Demetrios attributes to these authors, we may mention first that Hegesianax is mentioned twice by Demetrios for episodes of his life.[114] Palaephatos, on the other hand, is praised (ἐπαινεῖ), together with Hecataeus and Menecrates, in fr. 45 [Gaede/Biraschi].[115] This suggests that they were certainly among the sources he used as documentation for his work. Moreover, the fact that the same title, Τρωϊκά, is attested for all three scholars may even suggest that a certain proximity may have been felt by some readers to exist between the content of Demetrios' work and that of the two other scholars. However, strictly speaking, the wording of the Straboian passages under discussion here tells us only that Demetrios knew the scholars and their opinions. And, while this may certainly imply that Demetrios dealt with their statements and may have used them, it is more difficult to take this evidence as proof that Demetrios actually quoted from their works.

When turning to the additional information that we may gain about Demetrios from the presence of Hegesianax and Palaephatos in his work, we see that two elements can be added to the picture of Demetrios that we are trying to establish. First, we may reevaluate the negative opinions of some modern scholars about Demetrios of Scepsis. They often based their appreciation of the scholar on the fact that Demetrios approved of or used some of the statements from authors like Hegesianax and Palaephatos. However, as very few fragments of such works have been preserved, it is not always possible to appreciate their works accurately today. Therefore, Demetrios' approval of these authors can be seen in either a positive or a negative light, and he may be considered either as a well-documented scholar or as too credulous a man, willing to accept, without discrimination, any comment on his topic.[116] From this we see that it is more the opinions of modern scholars about Hegesianax and Palaephatos that further influenced them in their appraisal of Demetrios' contribution, rather than the scholar's work itself and his working method. We may therefore have here at least one example in which the separation of the discussion about the content of the testimonia from the opinions of modern scholars about these statements brought us a step further. We see now that, on the one hand, the fact that Demetrios used several sources to compose his work should be seen

---

[114] Fr. 7 [Gaede/Biraschi] = Athenaeus 4.155b and fr. 9 [Gaede/Biraschi] = Athenaeus 3.80d. See also fr. 20 [Gaede/Biraschi] = Stephanus Byzantius s.v. Ἀρίσβη (Stephanus Byzantius 119, 3 [Meineke] = Stephanus Byzantius α 426 [Billerbeck]) and fr. 21 [Gaede/Biraschi] = Strabo 13.1.27 [C594] for Hegesianax.

[115] Strabo 12.3.20–23 [C549–552].

[116] See Cameron 2004:124–125 for a statement about Demetrios based on such assumptions. Further such statements shall be discussed in Chapter 3.

as something positive, whereas, on the other hand, we have to acknowledge that his choice for these two sources can be interpreted in a more negative way, depending on how modern scholars appreciate these sources. We shall come back to this subject in Chapter 3.

Second, the link between the three authors through the common title, Τρωϊκά, which was given by some readers to their works, may provide the context for a final testimonium on Demetrios. This is T10 [Biraschi] taken from Photius' summary of Ptolemaios Chennos' *New History*, which mentions the largely unknown Tellis:

ὅτι τελευτήσαντος Δημητρίου τοῦ Σκηψίου τὸ βιβλίον Τέλλιδος πρὸς τῇ κεφαλῇ αὐτοῦ εὑρέθη.

That, when Demetrios of Scepsis had past away, the book from Tellis was found close to his head.

Photius Bibliotheca 190, 151a 6–8[117]

In order to make sense of this text, modern scholars tried to connect this Tellis to another author with the same name who is known for having written about the death of Penthesilea.[118] No title for the work has been transmitted from Antiquity, but it has been suggested by Richard Stiehle that the work should be considered as a Τρωϊκά.[119] However, even as it stands, and without taking into account the hypothesis of modern scholars, the passage can give us some information about how Demetrios' work was perceived by ancient scholars. Indeed, when taking into account the context in which the testimonium has been transmitted, we see that it is the first of several entries on a list of more or less well-known people who were found at their death with a text by their side that had been important to them during their lives. This list, even if the episodes themselves may have been invented,[120] may still bear witness to the fact that, at some point in the transmission of Demetrios' text, he was perceived as someone for whom it was important, and perhaps even too important, to have rather unknown books at his side, whether or not they were valuable from

---

[117] = T10 [Biraschi].

[118] *Die Fragmente der griechischen Historiker* 61 T1 and F1a. Indeed, Jacoby assembles the two relevant passages (Photius *Bibliotheca* 190, 151a 6–8 and Eustathius *Commentarii ad Odysseam* 11.538 (= 1696, 51 [Stallbaum]) and identifies, by doing so, the Tellis mentioned in the passage about Demetrios with the one quoted by Eustathius as one author. See also Biraschi 2011, commentary ad T10, Ragone 2009:673–674, and most recently *Brill's New Jacoby* 61, with up-to-date comments on the Greek passages.

[119] Stiehle 1854:509. We shall discuss the contribution of this German scholar about the fragments of Demetrios in Section 2.2.1.1.

[120] Ragone 2009:673–674.

a scholarly point of view. This kind of emphasis, or overemphasis, on his scholarly activity that we interpreted in this testimonium can also be found in the Straboian passage counted as T4 by Biraschi:

> ταῦτα μὲν οὖν ἔνστασιν ἔχει τοιαύτην, τἆλλα δὲ ὑπολαμβάνομεν, ἢ τά γε πλεῖστα, δεῖν προσέχειν ὡς ἀνδρὶ ἐμπείρῳ καὶ ἐντοπίῳ φροντίσαντί τε τοσοῦτον περὶ τούτων ὥστε τριάκοντα βίβλους συγγράψαι στίχων ἐξήγησιν μικρῷ πλειόνων ἑξήκοντα, τοῦ Καταλόγου τῶν Τρώων.

These elements face then such objections, for the rest, however, or at least for most of it, we assume that we have to follow him as a man who is acquainted with and native of the place and who has thought so much about this, that he has written thirty books about the little more than sixty lines of the Trojan Catalogue.

Strabo 13.1.45 [C603]

Indeed, when contrasting the rather small number of Homeric lines that form the Trojan Catalogue with the huge number of thirty books that Demetrios wrote about those lines, Strabo may also have suggested that Demetrios may have been unexpectedly or excessively long in his analysis. However, this is a rather subjective interpretation of Strabo's statement, as the appreciation of the length of ancient works could vary in Antiquity. For Athenaeus, for instance, only a number of 144 books in one work elicits the qualification of πολύβυβλος,[121] and it may therefore be more promising to proceed to the final characteristic ancient scholars mention about Demetrios' work.

If we continue to focus on the ways in which ancient scholars appreciated Demetrios' work, we see that, despite this slight form of a critique that may have underlain some of the testimonia we have alluded to, it is well-attested in others that Demetrios' work was considered in Antiquity as a well-documented and serious work that brought a certain fame to its author. Besides the list of authors in whose work the fragments have been preserved and that we shall analyze in Chapter 2, we have evidence, again from Strabo, who acknowledges explicitly at least twice how much he owes to Demetrios whom he used abundantly.[122] He can, however, still be fairly independent from Demetrios, as is shown, for instance, in T9 [Biraschi], given in the discussion about the itinerary of Jason in Strabo's book 1[123] or in T8 [Biraschi], occurring in Strabo's exposition of the

---

[121] See Athenaeus 6.249a–b and Jacob 2000:95.
[122] Strabo 13.1.55 [C609] = T1 [Biraschi] and Strabo 13.1.45 [C603] = T4 [Biraschi].
[123] Strabo 1.2.38 [C45]. This is actually part of fr. 50 [Gaede/Biraschi] = Strabo 1.2.38–40 [C45–47].

controversy about the Halizones in books 12 and 13.[124] This second passage is of particular interest here, as Strabo takes a rather complex stance. He states that he will put forward his own opinion against that of Demetrios and those of others, showing, therefore, a certain independence, but he also acknowledges in the same discussion that he has to follow Demetrios for the most part, as the Hellenistic scholar is an expert in that topic. Therefore, Strabo's allusions to Demetrios' achievements could not only be seen as a form of critique, but could also be interpreted as a kind of justification or an indirect attempt to increase Demetrios' fame or scholarly value: indeed by stating that even with his mistakes Demetrios is still the authority on the subject, Strabo emphasizes the uniqueness of Demetrios' work.[125] A similar ambiguity can be found in a passage in which Strabo discusses the debt Apollodoros of Athens has to pay to Demetrios of Scepsis.[126] Strabo says that in his discussion of Ephyra, Apollodoros mostly used elements from Demetrios, but that he could also show his independence from Demetrios, where necessary. So, even if the testimonium about Apollodoros is on one level again a kind of critique of Demetrios' achievements (as Apollodoros had opposing opinions about the issue under discussion), it also bears witness to the fame Demetrios must have had, as he was the author to whose work Apollodoros felt the need to respond. Apollodoros was a pupil of Aristarchos and clearly belonged to the scholarly tradition of Alexandria, even if he also worked later under the Attalids in Pergamon. Therefore, the fact that a scholar of such stature took the time to write a book against or in response to Demetrios shows that the latter's work was considered worthy, at least to the extent that a response was thought to be necessary. This response could of course be a polemic and contain many critical elements, but even so, Demetrios' work seems to have been considered worthwhile of scholarly activity.

To summarize what we have discovered about Demetrios' work, we see that its characteristics are complementary to what we have seen of the scholar himself. We know that Demetrios was called either γραμματικός, φιλόλογος, or even ἱστορικός. This is in alignment with the fact that his work was alluded to as an ἐξήγησις and contained a great number of quotations. But we have also seen that he was not only acquainted with the texts (shown by the many authorities he quotes and alludes to), but also with the territory of the Troad (ἔμπειρος; ἐντόπιος; ἐπιχώριος). Furthermore, and perhaps precisely because of

---

[124] Strabo 12.3.23 [C 552]. Here too the testimonium is actually part of a passage that reappears as a fragment. This is fr. 45 [Gaede/Biraschi] = Strabo 12.3.20–23 [C549–552]. We could also add here once again T4 [Biraschi] = Strabo 13.1.45 [C603] (a part of fr. 31a [Biraschi] = Strabo 13.1.44–45 [C602–603]), which alludes to the same discussion about the Halizones.

[125] Leaf 1923:xxxiii and Nicolai 2005–2006:62 for a discussion of Strabo's opinion.

[126] Strabo 8.3.6 [C339] = T6 [Biraschi]. See also T9 [Biraschi] = Strabo 1.2.38 [C45], where Strabo even goes so far as to make Demetrios responsible for some of the mistakes ascribed to Apollodoros.

this characteristic, he is himself used as authority by Strabo and by Apollodoros, despite the fact that both must have occasionally argued against him in order to defend their own opinions, and Strabo perhaps even alludes ironically to the length of Demetrios' work. Finally, the discussion of the title suggests that Demetrios' work, was, despite its length, limited to a special and rather small part of the Homeric text: the lines of the Trojan Catalogue. It was not meant to be extended to a whole book of the poem, as has sometimes been done.[127] This restriction is at least true for its framework, even if the actual content of Demetrios' comments could imply, as the preserved fragments still show, either a much wider topographical area or could allude to any relevant part of the Homeric poems.

1.2 Literary Background

In this part of Chapter 1 we shall focus on two elements highlighted in the previous section on the testimonia. First, as told above, Demetrios is considered by ancient authors as a contemporary of Aristarchos and Crates of Mallos.[128] This allusion to the two famous Homeric scholars is certainly more than just a chronological indication. By mentioning them in connection with Demetrios, Strabo may also have wanted to characterize the work of Demetrios and to locate it within the tradition of Homeric scholarship.[129] This field of research was, however, only one part of a much larger scholarly activity that could focus on any text, not only on the Homeric poems, and that had started before the Hellenistic period in the form of the ἐξήγησις, as discussed.[130] We shall therefore not only locate Demetrios within the tradition of Homeric scholarship, but also define this field of research within its wider literary context. Second, as we have seen in the previous section, the discussion on the testimonia made us enumerate many ancient scholars who were linked either to Demetrios or to his work. This will also be the case in our present discussion as some of them are the main representatives of the scholarly activity we shall describe in the first part of our discussion. Therefore, we shall dedicate the second part of the section to these scholars and define more closely the different types of links that connected them to Demetrios.

---

[127] For instance, in the work preserved in P. Aphrod. Lit. II = Fournet 1999:87–173.

[128] Strabo 13.1.55 [C609] = T1 [Biraschi].

[129] For recent summaries of the different stages and developments of Homeric scholarship, see Pontani 2005:47–48, Dickey 2007:5–6, Costa/Berti 2010:156, and Montana 2015:93–94. The standard works are still Pfeiffer 1968 and Frazer 1972.

[130] See above Section 1.1.3 (pp. 19–21), as well as Pontani 2005:23–103 and Baltussen 2004:21–35.

1.2.1 Ancient Scholarly Activity and Its Subjects

Turning to the first task of this section, the positioning of Demetrios' work in its wider context, we must address a first difficulty. There seems to be no overall or unproblematic name for the scholarly activity in Antiquity of which Demetrios' research, and, more generally speaking, Homeric scholarship, was a part. Even if this activity may have developed its methodological principles by working on the Homeric texts,[131] it was not limited to these, as recent studies have shown.[132] Therefore, we have to go beyond this field and look for a broader concept. The notion of ἐξήγησις, mentioned above and appearing in the testimonia of Demetrios, unfortunately does not really fit, as it is either too wide or too narrow. It is too wide, if we take it as being applied to all interpretations or explanations of any preexisting work. Indeed, such a definition would then also include the philosophical tradition of interpretation, which seems, however, to have been distinguished at some point from a more literary one.[133] Furthermore, such an understanding of the word would then also be applicable to the interpretation of oral works, as we saw in Section 1 when discussing the approach of Baltussen, who tried to introduce a distinction between the exegesis, as a more encompassing term, and the commentary, which would be linked to the written form.[134] The term ἐξήγησις can, however, also be seen as too narrow, even if it has been used to describe Demetrios' work,[135] especially if we consider the use that ancient scholars made of this term. In Dionysios Thrax, for instance, as we shall see, the term ἐξήγησις is applied only to one part of the scholarly activity, which was then called either γραμματική or κριτική.[136] These two terms are again problematic, even if the first brings us back to Demetrios.[137] They seem not to have been used in a coherent way in Antiquity, and modern scholars struggle to define them, especially when it comes to the distinction between

---

[131] Nesselrath 1997:90 highlights that the well-known principle of Homeric scholarship (Ὅμηρος ἐξ Ὁμήρου σαφηνίζειν "to clarify Homer through Homer") was used later, for instance by Galenos, for any author (ἕκαστον τῶν ἀνδρῶν ἐξ ἑαυτοῦ σαφηνίζεσθαι "to clarify for me each author through his own writings"). See *De pulsuum dignotione* 8, 958 [Kühn].

[132] Dettori 2000:183–207, Schenkeveld 2006:189–202, Gutzwiller 2010:365–337, and Nünlist 2011:105–117. For the evidence from the scholia, see Nünlist 2009 and, more specifically, for *hypomnemata*, see Turner 1968:100–124, and more recently now Lundon 2011:159–179.

[133] For the link between philosophy and philology and an attempt to present it as having its roots in philosophy, see Diehle 1998:86–93. For the early phase of such a scholarly activity, see Novokhatko 2015:30–32.

[134] Baltussen 2004:23.

[135] T1 [Biraschi] = Strabo 13.1.55 [C609] and T4 [Biraschi] = Strabo 13.1.45 [C603].

[136] For the link between κριτική and γραμματική, see for instance Schenkeveld 1994:263–301, and for the field of γραμματική in particular, see Ax 1991:276–301 and now Wouters/Swiggers 2015.

[137] Indeed the first one, γραμματική, recalls the adjective γραμματικός, which is applied in some of the testimonia to Demetrios. See again T1 [Biraschi] = Strabo 13.1.55 [C609].

the activity carried out by a φιλόλογος and that undertaken by a κριτικός.[138] Therefore, not even the modern term of philology, built on the adjective φιλόλογος, may be convenient,[139] so we may have to start our discussion from a completely different angle. In order to do so, we shall try to switch to the point of view of ancient scholars and analyze their own considerations about this field of research. This means that we shall focus on the various aspects of ancient scholarly activity without defining it as a whole, as this is the way in which ancient scholars spoke of it. Indeed, we shall see that the definitions they provided, or at least those that are preserved, consisted mainly of a list of tasks and skills that ancient scholars had either to perform or to possess when they took part in this activity. Such an approach has, however, the advantage not only to describe in more detail the literary tradition to which Demetrios belonged, but also to provide a better tool to understand the content of Demetrios' work and the methodological devices he used for his interpretations.

The interpretative activity in which we are interested was very diversified,[140] which is perhaps one of the reasons why it is so difficult to find a single term to describe it. Moreover, it was divided, as far as we know, into several domains, among which textual criticism is the part best documented.[141] In this part of the scholarly activity, the interpretations and the comments on the content were subordinated to the finding of the best and most authentic text of the literary work under discussion. However, other domains were included in the interests of ancient scholars.[142] When taking into consideration the testimonia from the scholia, as does Nünlist, we see that throughout Antiquity scholarly activity encompassed, besides the above-mentioned textual criticism, literary criticism, semantic and linguistic questions, and finally a whole range of explanation

---

[138] For the opposition between φιλόλογος (title taken by Eratosthenes) and κριτικός (title taken by Crates of Mallos), see Pfeiffer 1968:89, 156–159, and 238, and now Dihle 1998:88–89 and Gutzwiller 2010:338–339. For evidence from Antiquity, we may allude to the title Galenos gave to one of his treatises: εἰ δύναταί τις εἶναι κριτικὸς καὶ γραμματικὸς ἕν "whether it is possible for one person to be a 'kritikos' and a 'grammatikos' in one"). See *De libris propriis liber* 19, 48 [Kühn].

[139] A good description of this issue is given by Bravo 1971:325–335. For him the ancient concept of philology was the largest, which could contain, alongside so-called antiquarian research and the domains of the γραμματική, research on mathematics or other natural sciences. Furthermore, the field called γραμματική, as one part of philology, shares one of its domains with antiquarian research. However, antiquarian research was not limited to those dealt with in this common field, but could take the form of other investigations, such as chronological studies or periegetical works. See also Bravo 2002:248–249 or Bravo 2007:521–523. Finally, for a more comprehensive overview of the occurrences of φιλόλογος/*philologus* in Antiquity, see Nuchelmans 1950 and Kuch 1965.

[140] Turner 1968:118–121.

[141] Nünlist 2009:16.

[142] Turner 1968:112–113.

of background information.[143] These subcategories are rooted in Antiquity, as they already appear in the ancient descriptions of such scholarly activity. Three are preserved: one by Tauriscos, a second from Dionysios Thrax, and a third by Asclepiades of Myrlea.[144] Each divides this activity into different fields and lists the subjects that each of these parts deals with. Moreover, with regard to our own research topic, these pieces of evidence are extremely relevant as they are close in time to Demetrios of Scepsis. Indeed, all three scholars are either contemporaneous with Demetrios or lived a little later than his time: Tauriscos was a pupil of Crates of Mallos; Dionysios lived at the end of the second century BCE; and Asclepiades was dated by modern authors between the second and the first century BCE.[145] Their considerations about the field and its methodological tools may therefore turn out to be the most useful to help us to understand the scope of Demetrios' work and to locate it within this tradition, even if the three testimonia we shall discuss are very controversial today and two of them are preserved only indirectly in the work of Sextus Empiricus.[146] We shall therefore spend some time trying to find out what they tell us about the activity to which Demetrios contributed.

The most relevant definition for our study is given by Dionysios Thrax, as the notion of ἐξήγησις appears there. He divides the scholarly activity (here called, as we have seen above, γραμματική) into six parts: skills in reading (ἀνάγνωσις); interpretation (ἐξήγησις); explanation of obscure words and historical facts (γλωσσῶν τε καὶ ἱστοριῶν ἀπόδοσις); discovery of the origin of words (ἐτυμολογίας εὕρεσις); account of analogy (ἀναλογίας ἐκλογισμός); and critical judgment of poems (κρίσις ποιημάτων).[147] This is already extremely interesting, as we have evidence in the remaining fragments of Demetrios' work that the Hellenistic scholar carried out some of the other tasks besides that of ἐξήγησις, by which his work was defined. For instance, fr. 29 [Gaede/

---

[143] Nünlist 2009:14–16. The Euphonist critics mentioned by Gutzwiller 2010:346–354 should also be added here.

[144] All three are called grammarians by modern categories, but as Lallot 1998:28 suggests, the definition of the activity they call grammar is actually overlapping with that of their predecessors in Alexandria. (See also Schenkeveld 1994:265) Lallot 1998:74–75 defines the work that Dionysios carried out as a subsequent interpretation, once the text is corrected. So it could be considered as a second type of studies on the text (commenting and explaining) that come after the more fundamental one (correction = διόρθωσις).

[145] For Tauriscos, see Wendel 1934:15, Baumbach 2002:54, Broggiato 2014:145–153, and Montana 2015:149–150. For Dionysos Thrax, see Pfeiffer 1968:266–272, Montanari 1997c:632–635, Lallot 1998:19–20, and Wouters/Swiggers 2015:522–528. Finally, for Asclepiades, see Pagani 2007:11–46, Montanari 1997a:92, Trachsel 2008, and Wouters/Swiggers 2015:536–539.

[146] Sextus Empiricus *Adversus Mathematicos* I.

[147] Dionysios Thrax *Techne* § 1 (*Grammatici graeci* I.1, 5–6). See Wouters/Swiggers 2015:526–528 for further explanations about the six parts and Montana 2015:159–161 for a summary on the question of authenticity concerning this passage.

Biraschi][148] and fr. 74 [Gaede/Biraschi][149] are concerned with the explanation of special Homeric words, others deal with dialectal forms,[150] and still others with etymologies.[151] But the two other definitions are also very helpful and may provide further details about how ancient scholars like Demetrios were supposed to deal with the texts on which they wanted to comment. Tauriscos, for instance, who is from the entourage of Crates, divides the domain he calls κριτική into three parts:[152] a "rational part" (λογικόν) in which grammatical and phraseological issues were discussed; an "empirical part" (τριβικόν)[153] in which dialects and style were dealt with; and a "historical part" (ἱστορικόν). In this last part, the focus was on considerations about rather heterogeneous material defined as the preexisting subject-matters, which could not be discussed using one special method[154] and which is sometimes qualified as commentary.[155] Asclepiades finally, also following a tripartition, names a technical (τεχνικόν), a historical (ἱστορικόν), and a philological (γραμματικόν) part.[156] The content of these three parts is given in another passage in which Sextus speaks in his own words, even if he follows the point of view of Asclepiades:[157]

ἀπαρκέσει λέγειν ἀσυκοφαντητότερον ὡς ἄρα τῆς γραμματικῆς τὸ μέν ἐστιν ἱστορικὸν τὸ δὲ τεχνικὸν τὸ δὲ ἰδιαίτερον, δι᾽ οὗ τὰ κατὰ τοὺς ποιητὰς καὶ συγγραφεῖς μεθοδεύεται. ὧν τεχνικὸν μέν ἐστιν ἐν

---

[148] Strabo 13.1.43–44 [C602], about the adjective πολυπῖαξ.

[149] Athenaeus 6.236c, about the noun εἰλαπιναστής.

[150] Fr. 16 [Gaede/Biraschi] = Athenaeus 10.425c, fr. 41 [Gaede/Biraschi] = Strabo 13.4.8 [C627], and fr. 70 [Gaede] (fr. 70a [Biraschi] = Σ Apollonios Rhodios 1.1123 [Wendel] and fr. 70b [Biraschi] = *Etymologicum Magnum* s.v. χεράδες). For further details, see below.

[151] Fr. 2 [Gaede/Biraschi] = Σ Theocritos 5.83a [Wendel], fr. 18 [Gaede] (fr. 18a [Biraschi] = Harpocration s.v. Ἀδράστειαν and fr. 18b [Biraschi] = Souda s.v. Ἀδράστεια (α 524 [Adler]), fr. 23a [Gaede/Biraschi] = Σ bT Iliad 20.53c [Erbse], fr. 23b [Gaede/Biraschi] = Σ A Iliad 20.3 [Erbse] (or Σ D Iliad 20.3 [van Thiel]); fr. 32 [Gaede/Biraschi] = Σ A Iliad 6.35 [Erbse] (or Σ D Iliad 6.35 [van Thiel] completed by Σ bT and b Iliad 6.35 [Erbse], fr. 34 [Gaede] (fr. 34b [Biraschi] = Stephanus Byzantius s.v. Σκῆψις (= Stephanus Byzantius 574, 8 [Meineke] = Stephanus Byzantius σ 202 [Billerbeck]) and fr. 34a [Biraschi] = Strabo 13.1.52 [C607]) and fr. 52 [Gaede/Biraschi] = Σ Apollonios Rhodios 1.238 [Wendel].

[152] Sextus Empiricus *Adversus Mathematicos* I, 248–249. See Broggiato 2014:145–153 for a thorough commentary on this passage.

[153] Dickey 2007:218 for the translation of τριβή (use, practice). For an Italian rendering of the three domains, see Bravo 2002:250.

[154] See Pagani 2007:32n84 and the translation from Blank 1998:49. Another translation (*la materia inaccessibile a quasiasi metodo*) is given by Bravo 2002:250 in which he also discussed several modern interpretations of the term ἀμέθοδος ὕλη.

[155] Baumbach 2002:54.

[156] Sextus Empiricus *Adversus Mathematicos* I, 252–253. We are following for this third part the translation given by Pagani 2007:33. In Wouters/Swiggers 2015:538, the translation is expert part (τεχνικόν), historical part (ἱστορικόν), and grammatical part (γραμματικόν).

[157] Bravo 2002:252.

ᾧ περὶ τῶν στοιχείων καὶ τῶν τοῦ λόγου μερῶν ὀρθογραφίας τε καὶ ἑλληνισμοῦ καὶ τῶν ἀκολούθων διατάττονται, ἱστορικὸν δὲ ὅπου περὶ προσώπων οἱονεὶ θείων τε καὶ ἀνθρωπίνων καὶ ἡρωικῶν διδάσκουσιν, ἢ περὶ τόπων διηγοῦνται καθάπερ ὁρῶν ἢ ποταμῶν, ἢ περὶ πλασμάτων καὶ μύθων παραδιδόασιν ἢ εἴ τι τῆς αὐτῆς ἰδέας ἐστίν. ἰδιαίτερον[158] δὲ τὸ κατὰ τοὺς ποιητὰς καὶ συγγραφεῖς ἐπισκοποῦσι,[159] καθ᾽ ὃ τὰ ἀσαφῶς λεγόμενα ἐξηγοῦνται, τά τε ὑγιῆ καὶ τὰ μὴ τοιαῦτα κρίνουσι, τά τε γνήσια ἀπὸ τῶν νόθων διορίζουσιν.

It will be enough to say without more sophistry that one part of grammar is historical, one technical and one specific, in which the production of poets and writers are dealt with. Of these the technical part is that in which one makes arrangements concerning the elements, the parts of speech, orthography, Hellenism, and what follows from these. The historical part is where one teaches about persons, for example divine, human, and heroic ones, or describes places such as mountains or rivers, or transmits traditions about fictions and myths or anything else of this kind. One considers as the specific part the one that concerns poets and writers, where one explains what is said unclearly, judges what is sound and what is not sound, and sorts the genuine from the spurious.

Sextus Empiricus *Adversus Mathematicos* I, 91–93.

For Demetrios of Scepsis, these divisions are again revealing as further fragments can be associated with the tasks mentioned in these texts. There are, for instance, the fragments quoted above on dialectal variants (fr. 16 [Gaede/Biraschi],[160] fr. 70 [Gaede],[161] and up to a point also fr. 41 [Gaede/Biraschi][162]), which would then belong either to the empirical part, if we follow the division of Tauriscos, or to the technical part of Asclepiades (in the form presented by Sextus). Other more famous fragments of Demetrios can be linked to the historical part in which the scholars were supposed to focus on the realia and their

---

[158] Note that Sextus has another name for this third part here instead of Asclepiades' γραμματικόν.

[159] The text is difficult here and several alternative readings have been suggested, as for instance by Blank 1998:20 or by Bury 1949:55. We keep, however, to the version given by the manuscripts (and found in Mau 1954) and try to make sense of it.

[160] Athenaeus 10.425c. This is about an alternative name of wine-pourer (ἐπεγχύτης) used by the Hellespontians.

[161] Fr. 70a [Biraschi] = Σ Apollonios Rhodios 1.1123 [Wendel] and fr. 70b [Biraschi] = *Etymologicum Magnum* s.v. χεράδες. This word was used, according to Demetrios, by the inhabitants of Apollonios Pontica.

[162] Strabo 13.4.8 [C627]. The name Esiones, used by Callinos, is explained as an Ionian form for Asiones, who Demetrios believes to be the inhabitants of Asia.

localization or on their history. The most prominent among them are certainly those linked to the discussion about Troy and the description of the Trojan plain: fr. 21 [Gaede/Biraschi],[163] fr. 22 [Gaede/Biraschi],[164] fr. 23 [Gaede],[165] fr. 24 [Gaede],[166] fr. 25 [Gaede],[167] fr. 26 [Gaede/Biraschi],[168] fr. 27 [Gaede/Biraschi],[169] and fr. 28 [Gaede].[170] But actually almost all of the fragments from Demetrios' work touch on an issue dealing with some kind of realia, either linked to the Homeric text and the Trojan story or completely detached from them.[171] Therefore, we may understand that this part on the realia or on the so-called preexisting subject-matters must have been the most extended in Demetrios' work. However, we may add here that his distribution of topics among the fragments is certainly also due to the part of the Homeric text Demetrios chose as his field of investigation. In the Trojan Catalogue, topographical issues linked to place names mentioned there are obviously very important, even if it does not prevent Demetrios from developing other topics. There are also fragments that illustrate textual criticism, the clearest examples being fr. 17 [Gaede],[172] fr. 39 [Gaede/Biraschi][173] together with fr. 40 [Gaede/Biraschi],[174] fr. 45 [Gaede/Biraschi],[175] and fr. 75 [Gaede/Biraschi];[176] and this should remind us that Demetrios also touched on the third part (the more specific part called either τὸ

---

[163] Strabo 13.1.27 [C594].

[164] Strabo 13.1.33–34 [C596–597].

[165] Fr. 23a [Gaede/Biraschi] = Σ bT *Iliad* 20.53c [Erbse]; fr. 23b [Gaede/Biraschi] =Σ A *Iliad* 20.3 [Erbse] (or Σ D *Iliad* 20.3 [van Thiel]), and finally fr. 23c [Biraschi] = Strabo 13.1.35 [C597].

[166] Fr. 24a [Biraschi] = Strabo 13.1.35 [C598] and fr. 24b [Biraschi] = Hesychios s.v. Θύμβρα.

[167] Fr. 25a [Biraschi] = Strabo 13.1.35 [C598] and fr. 25b [Biraschi] = Σ A *Iliad* 11.166–168 [Erbse].

[168] Strabo 13.1.36 [C599].

[169] Strabo 13.1.39 [C600].

[170] Fr. 28a [Biraschi] = Strabo 13.1.41 [C601] and fr. 28b [Biraschi] = Σ B *Iliad* 6.92 [Bekker] = Porphyry *Quaestiones ad Iliadem* (*Iliad* 6.273).

[171] We may give here as example fr. 3 [Gaede/Biraschi] (= Athenaeus 14.658b) and fr. 4 [Gaede/Biraschi] (= Harpocration s.v. Θυργωνίδαι) where Demetrios speaks about Achaian cheese and about the toponym Thyrgonidai. Here may certainly also figure all the fragments in which Demetrios gives precise indications about the distance between two places, as in fr. 8 [Gaede/Biraschi] (= Athenaeus 14.644a) (distance *Plakous* to Thebes) or in fr. 47 [Gaede/Biraschi] (= Strabo 7, fr. 22a [Radt]) (distance Perinthos to Byzance). Also the very precise description of Mount Athos in fr. 46a [Gaede/Biraschi] = Strabo 7, fr. 15a [Radt] and fr. 46b [Gaede/Biraschi] (= part of Σ bT *Iliad* 14.229 [Erbse]) belongs here.

[172] Fr. 17a [Biraschi] (= Strabo 10.5.19 [C489]) and fr. 17b [Biraschi] (= Stephanus Byzantius s.v. Κάλυμνα (= Stephanus Byzantius 350, 12 [Meineke] = Stephanus Byzantius κ 39 [Billerbeck]). Demetrios changes the wording of *Iliad* 2.676–677.

[173] Strabo 13.4.6 [C626]. The discussion concerns a plus-line after *Iliad* 2.866.

[174] Eustathius *Commentarii ad Iliadem* 2.865–866 (= 366, 14–15 or van der Valk I, 577).

[175] Strabo 12.3.20–23 [C550–552], which deal with the many variants for the Halizones and the toponym Alybe occurring in *Iliad* 2.856–857.

[176] Tzetzes Σ *ad Lycophronem* v. 530. Here Demetrios discusses an alternative reading of *Iliad* 2.701. See Trachsel 2011:153–167.

γραμματικόν or τὸ ἰδιαίτερον) if the text, or the passage he wanted to explain, required this. Therefore, we see that Demetrios of Scepsis belongs fully to the scholarly tradition described by the three ancient scholars. However, this list may also suggest that he gave different weight to each of these parts, driven by the overall aims that he pursued in his research or by the topics in which he was most interested.

We may then conclude that it was probably the text a commentator chose as his topic and its difficulties that defined the tools he used. Indeed, it seems likely that the actual wording of a text and its content may have called for several levels of interpretation depending on the difficulty of the text, its history or state of preservation, and finally also on the commentator's skills and resources and on the audience he had in mind when composing his work. It may also have been difficult for a scholar, starting from a given text and applying different interpretative tools to it, to keep separated the different categories of approaches, which were, using a more abstract approach and thinking about the activity itself, as did Tauriscos, Dionysios Thrax, and Asclepiades of Myrlea, quite distinct. A good example of this, which constitutes, moreover, a rather close parallel to Demetrios of Scepsis, comes from the fragments of Parmeniscos, a pupil of Aristarchos.[177] Very few fragments from him remain, and among them just one title, *Against Crates*. Now, as far as the texts in which Parmeniscos was interested are concerned, some of the fragments seem to have focused on the Homeric texts as they have been preserved in the scholia to either the *Iliad* or the *Odyssey* and in Stephanus of Byzantium.[178] Others must have dealt with some of the plays of Euripides, as here again fragments have been preserved in the scholia to *Medea*, to the *Troades*, and to the *Rhesus*.[179] The last four have been attributed by Breithaupt to two independent works, one dealing with astronomy and the other with the grammatical concept of analogy.[180] When, on the other hand, we consider the problems Parmeniscos seems to have explained, we see that some of them concern textual criticism, whereas others are dealing with topographical issues, such as for instance the localization of the toponym of

---

[177] See Wendel 1949:1570–1572, Ax 2000:343. For the collection of his fragments, see Breithaupt 1915 and now also Ippolito 2005.

[178] Fr. 1–11 [Breithaupt]. For the precise indication of their provenance, see the list given by Breithaupt 1915:60.

[179] Fr. 12–17 [Breihaupt].

[180] Fr. 18–20 [Breithaupt] on astronomy and fr. 21 [Breithaupt] on analogy. The 22nd fragment is a dubious one that Breithaupt does not attribute to any work, but it seems to be dealing with the orthography of a toponym (the Gargaphian spring near Plataea: Herodotus 9.25.3, 9.49.2, and 9.51.1, and Pausanias 9.4.3).

Ephyra, a problem we also find in Demetrios' fr. 55 [Gaede] and fr. 56 [Gaede].[181] Therefore, as in the case of Demetrios of Scepsis, Parmeniscos seems not to have privileged any of the methodological tools for his research.

Further evidence of the fact that ancient scholars often mixed in their works, or in their research interests, several of the domains of scholarly activity can be found in what we know about the two great Homeric scholars, Aristarchos and Crates. They are generally considered as the most important representatives of textual criticism with regard to the Homeric poems. However, Aristarchos himself wrote a work on the disposition of the ships (Περὶ τοῦ ναυστάθμου) in which his focus seems to have been on the topographical setting of the Homeric narrative rather than on the wording of the Homeric text.[182] Crates of Mallos also took an interest in these issues and responded to the Aristarchean Περὶ τοῦ ναυστάθμου by commenting on *Iliad* 14.31–36, the very passage in which the disposition of the ships was given.[183]

However, even if such considerations seem very fitting when discussing works that appear to have been composed in close relation to a given text they were supposed to explain, there are also some difficulties linked to this approach. Indeed, already with Aristarchos' Περὶ τοῦ ναυστάθμου we feel its limits, especially if we follow the hypothesis that it was a work written independently from the Homeric text, and this is even more so when we consider scholars such as Polemon of Ilion. This is actually the reason why modern scholars, for instance Benedetto Bravo, suggested that the works of authors like Polemon of Ilion or Apollodoros of Athens do not fit into the three ancient definitions of the scholarly activity discussed above and should therefore be classified within another domain of literary activities, that of antiquarianism.[184] Indeed, Polemon's Περιήγησις Ἰλίου, for instance, seems to have been composed independently from the Homeric text, in the sense that its outline seems not to have been shaped, as far as we can see from the three remaining fragments, to follow another preexisting text to which the author added comments when

---

[181] Fr. 2, fr. 3, fr. 5, fr. 6 [Breithaupt] about textual criticism in the Homeric texts. As far as topographical issues are concerned, these are fr. 9, fr. 10, fr. 11 [Breithaupt] for the Homeric texts, and fr. 14 and fr. 15 [Breithaupt] for Euripides' *Troades*. For Demetrios, we have fr. 55 [Gaede] (= fr. 55a [Biraschi] = Strabo 8.3.6 [C339] and fr. 55b [Biraschi] = Strabo 7.7.10 [C328]) and fr. 56 [Gaede] (= fr. 56a [Biraschi] = Strabo 8.3.5 [C338] and fr. 56b [Biraschi] = Σ T *Iliad* 15.531 c and d [Erbse] + Σ D *Iliad* 15.531 [van Thiel]).

[182] See Dubischar 2015:566 for the place of this work in the tradition of scholarly writings.

[183] Fr. 19 [Broggiato] and Porter 1992:109. We have already alluded to this previously in Section 1.1.3 (pp. 17–19) when we considered the title of Demetrios' work and its link to the word διακόσμησις), but for a more detailed description of the difference between the approaches the two scholars took, see Porter 1992:110–111 and Pontani 2005:53.

[184] Bravo 2002:250–251, and for the link between antiquarianism and philology in particular, see Bravo 2007:520–523. See now also Montana 2015:147.

necessary. This difference brings us back to the distinction between commentaries (*hypomnemata*) and more independently composed treatises (*sungrammata*) discussed previously in connection with the title of Demetrios' work and the example of Mnesimachos of Phaselis.[185] We have seen that, because of its title, Mnesimachos' work may have been very close to that of Demetrios, but we have had to conclude that there must have been a great difference between the two works, as Mnesimachos seems not to have followed a preexisting text. However, if we return to Polemon and Apollodoros, the distinction Bravo made between these two scholars may have been too sharp. First, he himself concedes that both Polemon and Apollodoros were during Antiquity already called γραμματικοί, ἱστορικοί, or φιλόλογοι, as was Demetrios in some of the testimonia.[186] Second, in the three ancient definitions, one part of the scholarly activity should deal with historical facts, either about persons or about places. This would indeed have included some of the research qualified by modern authors as antiquarianism, even if we would then have to acknowledge that in some of them the weight would have been given exclusively to this part, so that it could be detached from any preexisting text and be carried out for its own sake and become an independent category of scholarly work.[187] For Apollodoros of Athens this could fit very well, as we know that he composed an answer to Demetrios' work that focused on the Catalogue of the Ships. This part of the Homeric text could then have functioned as the preexisting text that had to be explained. We know, however, that he had written a treatise on the gods (Περὶ θεῶν) in which he focused on religious or cultural elements without following any preexisting texts, even if he may have quoted from them to illustrate or to prove his case.

Therefore, even without claiming that our approach resolves all the difficulties trying to describe the scholarly tradition to which Demetrios' work belonged, and while remaining well aware that ancient definitions were certainly not meant as a tool to classify scholarly works,[188] but should rather be seen as a reaction to the many scholarly works that were written in those days,[189] our approach may still have shown some interesting aspects of this activity. It has shown, for instance, regarding the works Aristachos and Crates dedicated to the realia,[190] that this field of research and in particular the topographical background of the Homeric text was a topic *en vogue* and that Demetrios of Scepsis

---

[185] See above Section 1.1.3 (pp. 16–17).

[186] Bravo 2002:252–253.

[187] This would then still be compatible with the way Bravo describes the different parts of scholarly activity. See Bravo 2002:248–253.

[188] Wouters/Swiggers 2015:544 define the different ancient definitions as an effort to assess the epistemological status of grammar.

[189] Gutzwiller 2010:337 speaks of three centuries of intense activity.

[190] See for this also Broggiato 2001:xx–xxi.

did not create his work in a vacuum, but composed it as his own response to a developing domain.[191] This impression may be strengthened when we add works like that of the largely unknown Hestiaia of Alexandria Troas (συγγράψασα περὶ τῆς Ὁμήρου Ἰλιάδος "she who has written about Homer's *Iliad*") quoted by Demetrios himself,[192] that of Apollodoros of Athens about the Catalogue of the Ships, and finally an even less well-known work on the Catalogue of the Ships written by an otherwise unknown Menogenes, quoted by Eustathius alongside that of Apollodoros of Athens.[193]

Our discussion has also highlighted some details of Demetrios' approach. First, he seems to have expanded the idea of Aristarchos and Crates of working on the world or geographical conception behind the Homeric text. The two Homeric scholars were dealing with a rather short passage of five lines (*Iliad* 14.31–36), whereas Demetrios dedicated his research to a much larger part of about sixty lines (*Iliad* 2.816–877), even if the Trojan Catalogue is not yet a whole book of the *Iliad* nor the work of Demetrios a treatise about the entire geographical background involved in the Trojan narrative of the *Iliad*. Still, by focusing on the Trojan Catalogue, he chose a part of the Homeric text in which the topography played a particularly important role and that takes into consideration a much wider portion of the landscape than the passage commented on by Aristarchos and Crates. This part only involved the topography of the Achaean camps and the disposition of the ships within this camp, which was thought to have been established on the shore of the Hellespontos near the mouth of the Scamandros. The discussion therefore involved only a very small space. The Catalogue of the Trojans on the contrary involves the whole of the Troad and the regions from which the Trojans' allies came. This could become a rather large geographical area, depending on which localization theories the scholars were defending. Second, the length of Demetrios' work was also exceptional. With his thirty books about a subject only sixty lines long, he must have exceeded the others, even if we do not have preserved, for instance, information about the length of the work of Aristarchos. It can still be hypothesized that the length of Demetrios' work was exceptional when comparing it to the others for which we possess such information. The work of Apollodoros had only twelve books and was, moreover, about a much longer part of the Homeric text, the Catalogue of the Ships comprising 265 lines. Furthermore, the work of the unknown Menogenes on the same subject was only twenty-three books long, which is still much longer than that of Apollodoros, but is not yet comparable

---

[191] Pontani 2005:52–54.

[192] Strabo 13.1.36 [C599] (= T7 [Biraschi]). See above Section 1.1.3 (p. 22) and below Section 1.2.2 (p. 42).

[193] Eustathius *Commentarii ad Iliadem* 2.494 (= 263, 36–37 or van der Valk I, 401).

in length to that of Demetrios. Finally, we may add the example, mentioned by Pontani,[194] of Heracleon of Tilotis, who wrote a commentary on Homer in forty-eight books. But here the comparison is perhaps less immediate since the work by Heracleon seems to have been on Homer in general, and not on a part of one of his poems. However, the comparison with the length of Demetrios' work still shows how much longer his treatise must have been than was customary.

We may then conclude this part of our discussion by summarizing what we have discovered. This review of scholarly activity has revealed a very complex situation. Many different types of work existed. Their form and content depended on the skills, means, interests, and entourage of the scholars. For many of them, not only for Demetrios' work, it is difficult nowadays, because of the scarcity of the remaining elements, to attribute them definitely to one category or another. As far as Demetrios' contribution is concerned, it can, however, roughly be defined as an interpretative work, focusing on a specific part of a previously existing text, in our case obviously the Trojan Catalogue in book 2 of the *Iliad*. Because of the content of this passage, and also because of the interests and experiences of the scholar, the work focused on the realia appearing in the Homeric text, and among the realia particular interest was given to the landscape. This special focus did not, however, mean that Demetrios excluded other topics from his work. Furthermore, we could also see that, from the methodological point of view as well, Demetrios used several approaches in his argumentation. Finally, we have also seen that he was not the only scholar who dealt with this subject. In his time there were several examples of other scholars composing similar works, and this last remark allows us to turn precisely to these scholars and to define more closely their links with Demetrios.

1.2.2 The Scholars

We shall not mention here all the authors whose names occur in the remaining fragments of Demetrios' work, as they have been alluded to in the previous section.[195] Here we would just like briefly to come back to the scholars mentioned in the discussion outlined above who were contemporaneous with Demetrios and for whom some information is preserved about their interaction with him. This will not only help us to define the links between Demetrios and these scholars, but should also provide us with further information about the context in which Demetrios worked, by throwing light upon it from a different angle.

We shall begin with Aristarchos and Crates of Mallos, for whom we have already seen how they contributed to the field in which Demetrios was

---

[194] Pontani 2005:64.
[195] See above Section 1.1.3 (pp. 21–23).

interested. They both focused in some of their research on the realia mentioned in the Homeric text and in particular on the landscape. They both worked, as we have seen, on the disposition of the Achaean ships, aiming to give an interpretation of the Homeric passage from book 14, which contains allusions to the disposition of the ships. Unfortunately, the link between Aristarchos and Demetrios cannot be clarified from the evidence that remains. Therefore, we must rely on what we know about the interaction between Demetrios and Crates of Mallos. For this we have to focus on fr. 68 [Gaede/Biraschi][196] from which we learn that Demetrios must have defended a position that was opposed to a statement of Crates, and that he contradicted the Pergamene scholar.[197] The discussion concerns Phoenix's birthplace.[198] Demetrios claims a Thessalian origin for Achilles' preceptor (Ormenion), whereas Crates locates him in Phocis (at a village called Eleon, mentioned in *Iliad* 10.266). As presented by Strabo, the controversy involved two Homeric lines: *Iliad* 10.266 and *Iliad* 9.447.[199] For this last line, Demetrios suggests an alternative reading where the Thessalian place name Ormenion replaces that of Hellas. This is clearly a question of textual criticism, but for the time being, it is the fact that Demetrios answered to a position defended by Crates of Mallos that interests us. The evidence seems to suggest that Demetrios of Scepsis dealt with the same issues as those focused on by Crates of Mallos, and therefore probably also by the scholars working in the library of Pergamon. He must, therefore, have had access at least to the debates going on in Pergamon, if not to the works in which the different hypotheses were stated. This second statement has, however, to remain in the form of a hypothesis, as we have seen previously that the wording of the part of Strabo's text involved here is not clear enough to allow us to define more closely how Demetrios reacted to Crates. Strabo only juxtaposes the statements of the two scholars (φησὶ δ' ὁ Σκήψιος "Demetrios says"; Κράτης δὲ ποιεῖ [...]: "Crates considers" [...] and again ὁ δὲ Σκήψιός φησι "Demetrios says"). We therefore only have access to the interaction between the two scholars through the description by Strabo, and cannot rule out that he is responsible for the juxtaposition of the two statements, which would then diminish the directness of the connection. The passage has, however, been used to claim such a close interaction between Demetrios and Crates, particularly by Pfeiffer and by Broggiato, who both suggest that Crates

---

[196] Fr. 68 [Gaede/Biraschi] = Crates fr. 10 [Broggiato] = Strabo 9.5.18 [C438–439].

[197] See further the comment given by Broggiato 2001:153–154.

[198] For a short overview, see Hainsworth 1993:121–122, Brügger/Stoevesandt/Visser 2003:158–159 and 237, Danek 1988:121–122, Visser 1997:698–700, Mader 1991:532, and finally Watson 2011:612–613 and Finkelberg 2011b:45.

[199] See also *Iliad* 2.500, where an Eleon belongs to the Boeotian contingent and *Iliad* 2.734, another line of the Catalogue of the Ships, where Ormenion is mentioned.

was quoted by Demetrios.[200] Still, even if we do not go as far as Pfeiffer and Broggiato in this matter of the closeness between the two scholars and the issues it involves, and leave the question open, we may nonetheless gain some interesting insights about the nature of the interaction. First, we see that the discussion in which both scholars participated was on topographical issues, where the origin of one of the Homeric heroes, Phoenix, was involved. We may also note here that the issue is a question of homonymy, because the place name under discussion in the fragment, Eleon, was identified in several regions, for instance in Boeotia and in Thessalia.[201] Furthermore, there are also several contradicting Homeric lines involved, two from the Catalogue of the Ships (*Iliad* 2.500 and *Iliad* 2.734) and one from book 9 (*Iliad* 9.447), for which Demetrios preferred another variant,[202] and finally one from book 10 (*Iliad* 10.266). This illustrates that some textual criticism was involved and brings Demetrios' considerations closer to what we would expect from Crates of Mallos. It is, however, less clear in what kind of work Crates would have discussed these issues, and this is perhaps one of the reasons, which makes the definition of the interaction between the two scholars so difficult. Finally, it is also hard to see how, with regard to Demetrios, a topic linked to a line of the Catalogue of the Ships could have entered a work dedicated to the Trojan Catalogue. However, this question of how topics linked to lines from the Catalogue of the Ships could have been included in a work on the Trojan Catalogue and vice versa is also relevant for Apollodoros of Athens, the next scholar we shall discuss in connection with Demetrios.

We know from Strabo that Apollodoros of Athens wrote a response to Demetrios and used several elements from Demetrios' work for his own research.[203] The relation between the two scholars seems therefore to be rather well-established and gains in interest when we add that Apollodoros was a pupil of Aristarchos, and that we could obtain, through him, an indirect link to this famous Homeric scholar.[204] However, when trying to find out how Apollodoros' response was made, and on what points he disagreed with Demetrios, we have to acknowledge that we get very little from the remaining fragments. Unfortunately, this also applies to any investigation of the methodological basis on which Apollodoros may have constructed his work or the differences that may have existed between the two works.

---

[200] See Pfeiffer 1968:249 and Broggiato 2001:153–154.

[201] See also Σ T *Iliad* 10.266 [Erbse], and Mader 1991:532 and Visser 1997:261–264.

[202] Instead of the vulgate (οἶον ὅτε πρῶτον λίπον Ἑλλάδα καλλιγύναικα "as when I first left Hellas with its good-looking women"), Demetrios has οἶον ὅτε πρῶτον λίπον Ὁρμένιον πολύμηλον "as when I first left Ormenion with its many flocks," according to Strabo.

[203] Strabo 8.3.6 [C339] = T6 [Biraschi] and Strabo 1.2.38 [C45] = T9 [Biraschi].

[204] E.g. Montanari 1996b:857–860, Montanari 1993a:276–277, and Montana 2015:158–159.

Starting once again from the titles the two works were given, but without returning to the issue about the difference between *hypomnemata* and *sungrammata* we discussed in Section 1,[205] we may simply begin by noting that they are different (ὁ Τρωϊκὸς διάκοσμος versus Περὶ τοῦ τῶν νεῶν καταλόγου).[206] We have suggested in Section 1 that the difference between these terms, ὁ κατάλογος and ὁ διάκοσμος, may indeed not have been chosen arbitrarily, but the evidence cited is certainly not strong enough to consider this variation of the title as an indication of a different approach. For instance, even Strabo can call the work of Apollodoros ὁ Τρωϊκὸς διάκοσμος,[207] and this statement bears witness to the closeness of the two works rather than helping us to differentiate them. This is the same with the second element of the title we shall discuss here. The fact that the title of one of the works, ὁ Τρωϊκὸς διάκοσμος, would point to a work dealing with the part of the Homeric text enumerating the Trojan allies, whereas the other, Περὶ τοῦ τῶν νεῶν καταλόγου, would rather have been dealing with the Catalogue of the Ships is also misleading. Fragments from Apollodoros also touch upon topics linked to the territory that belongs to the Trojan Catalogue, and the fragments of both Demetrios and Apollodoros are quoted by Strabo in his books 8-10 (about Greece and topics linked to the Catalogue of the Ships) as well as in his books 12-14 (about Asia Minor where the topics linked to the Trojan Catalogue were discussed). Therefore, it seems that, even if the initial intention of the scholars, indicated by their choice of the wording of their titles, may have been to focus on one part of the Homeric text, either on the Catalogue of the Ships or on the Trojan Catalogue, the actual discussion must have been wider, including the issues raised by both Homeric passages and touching on both parts of the geographical area, mainland Greece as well as Asia Minor.[208] It seems, however, that very few fragments from the part on the Trojan Catalogue have been preserved from Apollodoros' work.[209]

With regard to the scholarly methods the two scholars may have used in their work, we encounter the same difficulty in defining the differences. Previous scholars have, for instance, tried to establish such a distinction by describing Apollodoros as someone who follows the principles of Eratosthenes and Aristarchos, whereas Demetrios' work is considered less closely linked

---

[205] See Section 1.1.3 (pp. 14-21).

[206] We follow here the suggestion made by Pfeiffer (1968:257). Jacoby 1930 (*Die Fragmente der griechischen Historiker* 244) reconstructs περὶ τοῦ Νεῶν καταλόγου. Other variants can be found in Schwartz 1894:2863-2864. See above Section 1.1.3 (p. 15).

[207] Strabo 12.3.24 [C552] = *Die Fragmente der griechischen Historiker* 244 F171.

[208] Niese 1877:267 and Jacoby 1930:778-779 (= commentary to *Die Fragmente der griechischen Historiker* 244 F154-207).

[209] Schwartz 1894:2870 and again Jacoby 1930:777 (= commentary to *Die Fragmente der griechischen Historiker* 244 F154-207).

to a specific school.[210] It is, however, interesting to note that the way Strabo describes Apollodoros' debt to Eratosthenes (τὰ πλεῖστα μετενέγκας παρὰ τοῦ Ἐρατοσθένους "having taken most if it from Eratosthenes")[211] is surprisingly close to the wording he chooses in the passage in which he speaks of Apollodoros' dependence on Demetrios' work (παρ' οὗ μεταφέρει τὰ πλεῖστα "from whom he took most of it").[212] Therefore, again the difference must not have been so clear-cut as suggested and may not help us to distinguish the two works. We shall, however, have to come back to Strabo's usage of both sources in Chapter 2 and see what we may learn about the two works when discussing the issue with regard to the authors who used them.

A similar closeness in methodology may also be adduced for the next scholar we should discuss: Hestiaia of Alexandria Troas. This time the link between the two scholars is clearly defined since Demetrios himself quotes the scholar.[213] However, unfortunately, we know very little about this woman and her work.[214] She dealt with Homer's *Iliad* (συγγράψασα περὶ τῆς Ὁμήρου Ἰλιάδος "she who has written about Homer's *Iliad*") as we learn from the passage quoted as a fragment from Demetrios, and seems to have focused at some point in her work, as far as the quotation lets us tell, on the topography of the Trojan land-scape described in the *Iliad* and more precisely on the fluctuations of the Trojan shore. The second fragment, in which some information about the content of her work is preserved, also points to the fact that she was dealing with Trojan topography and its link to the Homeric text.[215] This is all the information we can gather about her work. However, together with the context in which the passages have been transmitted, it allows us at least roughly to characterize her work. Because Demetrios uses her statement as evidence in favor of his own theory about the location of Troy, we may conclude, as did Cook, that she and Demetrios were among the scholars who spoke against the identification of the Hellenistic Ilion with Homeric Troy and that they based their argumentation on topographical elements.[216]

---

[210] Jacoby 1930:778-779 (= commentary to *Die Fragmente der griechischen Historiker* 244 F154-207) and Pfeiffer 1968:257-261.

[211] *Die Fragmente der griechischen Historiker* 244 T13 = Strabo 7.3.6 [C299].

[212] T6 [Biraschi] = Strabo 8.3.6 [C339].

[213] Fr. 26 [Gaede/Biraschi] = Strabo 13.1.36 [C599].

[214] See Funaioli 1913:1313-1314, Leaf 1923:184, and more recently Biraschi 2011, commentary ad fr. 26, and Ippolito 2006.

[215] In Σ D *Iliad* 3.64 [van Thiel] she is quoted because she uses the epitheton χρυσῆ given to Aphrodite in this Homeric line to explain the name of a plain (πεδίον ἐστὶν χρουσοῦν καλούμενον "a plain called golden"), of which the location is unfortunately not specified in the scholion. Allusions to the same topic are also found in Eustathius *Commentarii ad Iliadem* 3.64 (= 384, 20 or van der Valk I, 606-607). See also above Section 1.1.3 (p. 22).

[216] Cook 1973:186-188.

The situation is even more difficult with the two other lesser-known scholars we came across above: Parmeniscos and Menogenes. For Parmeniscos, who was probably also a pupil of Aristarchos, we have seen that he was dealing with the toponym of Ephyra as did Demetrios, but he could also deal with textual criticism unrelated to the Homeric topography. Furthermore, it seems that he focused not only on the Homeric text but may also have worked on some of Euripides' tragedies. However, this does not help us to define more closely the connection between Parmeniscos and Demetrios, or to define how the two ways of dealing with the issue of Ephyra were linked. It is the same with Menogenes who is mentioned in Eustathius along with Apollodoros.[217] He too seems to have written a work on the Catalogue of the Ships in twenty-three books, which suggested that he worked on a topic close to that of Demetrios, but nothing more is known about him.

Therefore, in order to find out more about the links between Demetrios' work and those of other scholars, we may turn to another category of works, the so-called Τρωϊκά. In Hegesianax of Alexandria Troas and Palaephatos we have two representatives of this category of works who are, moreover, linked to the fragments from Demetrios' work. We have seen that their names occur in some of the fragments of Demetrios' work and that they are praised by him.[218] Let us begin with Palaephatos, who is not strictly speaking a contemporary of Demetrios, but for whom the link to Demetrios is less complex. He is dated to the fourth century BCE and probably belonged to the entourage of Aristotle. He is best known for his work on *Unbelievable Tales* (Περὶ ἀπίστων),[219] but there are a few fragments from a Τρωϊκά that have been preserved and one of these as part of a fragment of Demetrios' work.[220] This passage belongs to a discussion in Strabo in which the Homeric lines of the contingent of the Halizones are discussed.[221] In this passage, Strabo first mentions Demetrios' opinion about three scholars, Hecataeus of Miletos,[222] Menecrates of Elaea,[223] and Palaephatos,

---

[217] Eustathius *Commentarii ad Iliadem* 2.494 (= 263, 36–37 or van der Valk I, 401). See above Section 1.2.1 (p. 37).

[218] See above Section 1.1.3 (pp. 23–24).

[219] Stern 1996:1–7, Santoni 2000:9–48, Brodersen 2005:44–57, and Hawes 2014a:37–91 and Hawes 2014b:125–147.

[220] *Die Fragmente der griechischen Historiker* 44 F4 = a part of fr. 45 [Gaede/Biraschi] = Strabo 12.3.22 [C551]. See further Trachsel 2007:165–177.

[221] See Trachsel 2017a:1–25 for this question.

[222] He is probably the one among the three about whom we have most evidence. See *Die Fragmente der griechischen Historiker* 1 for the fragments and Meister 1998:264–267. For his role in the history of historiography, see e.g. Meister 1990:20–24, and now also Bertelli 2001:67–94.

[223] Menecrates is a pupil of Xenocrates who was head of the Academy from 339 to 315 BCE. See also Göbel 1931:801, Radt 2008:375, and, for the few fragments, *Fragmenta historicorum graecorum* II, p. 342. For Xenocrates, see Stanzel 2002:620–623.

and gives a short summary of the statements of each of which the Hellenistic scholar approved. This piece of evidence not only suggests that Palaephatos is quoted by Demetrios as a valuable source, which establishes the link between the two scholars, but also that his name occurs together with those of two other scholars. Both elements are of interest to us here. First, with regard to the two other scholars, the passage not only establishes the link between Palaephatos and Demetrios but also between Demetrios and the two other scholars, Hecataeus and Menecrates. Demetrios used all three, and could combine in his argumentation aspects about the Homeric text found in Palaephatos' work with the topographical data from the two other texts, despite the difference in scope and methodology that modern authors postulate for these works. Furthermore, as far as Demetrios' working method is concerned, the passage reveals that the Hellenistic scholar not only used the content of his different sources, but also gave his opinion about the value of their contribution to the topic at hand. This seems to have been a general feature of Demetrios' working method and could also be applied to authors of whose works or opinions Demetrios did not approve. We find an example of this in the way Demetrios treated Ephoros, who is quoted a few lines above Palaephatos in the same passage. Demetrios seems to have discussed the opinions of this scholar and clearly stated that he disagreed with him. This is therefore an important feature of Demetrios' work that may, moreover, help us to define the link between Hegesianax, the second author of a Τρωϊκά, and Demetrios of Scepsis.

Indeed, the evidence preserved about Hegesianax in the fragments of Demetrios' work does not help us to define the link between the two scholars easily. We have four fragments of Demetrios' work that can be examined in connection with Hegesianax. Two of them concern episodes of Hegesianax's life;[224] a third, fr. 21 [Gaede/Biraschi],[225] constitutes the immediate context of a quotation of Hegesianax's name; and the fourth is fr. 20 [Gaede/Biraschi],[226] even if the connection is less explicit, as only Hegesianax's pseudonym Cephalon/Cephalion is mentioned. In none of them is the link between Demetrios and Hegesianax clearly stated.[227] Therefore, in order better to understand the potential link between the two works, we may start from the conclusion we reached above when discussing the link between Palaephatos and Demetrios, and hypothesize that Demetrios also stated his opinion about the sources he

---

[224] Fr. 7 [Gaede/Biraschi] = Athenaeus 4.155b and fr. 9 [Gaede/Biraschi] = Athenaeus 3.80b.

[225] Strabo 13.1.27 [C594].

[226] Stephanus Byzantius s.v. Ἀρίσβη (= Stephanus Byzantius 119, 3 [Meineke] = Stephanus Byzantius α 426 [Billerbeck].

[227] We may add the discussion about Oenone: fr. 22 [Gaede/Biraschi] = Strabo 13.1.33–34 [C596] and *Die Fragmente der griechischen Historiker* 45 F2 = Parthenius *Narrationum amatoriarum, libellus 4*, to further illustrate the closeness between the two scholars and the topics they discussed.

used. Such a hypothesis would conveniently explain the fact that Demetrios mentioned episodes of Hegesianax's life in his work on the Trojan Catalogue. For, when accepting that Demetrios may not only have taken pieces of information from the works of his sources, but may also have judged the value of these sources, it becomes likely that in order to be able to do so, Demetrios adduced elements other than those linked to the position under discussion. Among these could figure episodes of the scholars' lives that may have helped Demetrios either to justify his preference for a given author or to explain why he rejected the work. However, even if this may be an attractive idea, it must remain for the moment a hypothesis, as we have no other elements to enable us to go further. It would, however, have two interesting consequences for our discussion. First, as suggested, it would provide an attempt to explain why episodes of Hegesianax's life were discussed in Demetrios' work. Second, such an assumption could also provide a fitting explanation for at least one further fragment. Indeed, in fr. 72 [Gaede/Biraschi][228] an episode from the life of Diocles of Peparethos is mentioned. We know that this scholar wrote a history of the origin of Rome that was used by Fabius Pictor.[229] Such a topic would certainly have interested Demetrios, as much as the content of Hegesianax's Τρωϊκά may have done, and the Hellenistic scholar may have used it in his work and then have given, as we have supposed with Hegesianax, some indications to his readers about the value of the source by alluding to some of the episodes of the author's life. For Diocles such an explanation is even more necessary than for Hegesianax. As Hegesianax is a contemporary of Demetrios, who, moreover, actively took part in the political events of his time,[230] Demetrios may have mentioned him when discussing the more recent events of the history of the Troad. Such an assumption is not possible for Diocles, who is neither a contemporary of Demetrios (he is dated to the third century BCE) nor lived or originated in the Troad (Peparethos is an island near Euboea). Therefore, we have to assume that it was the work that interested Demetrios and that an episode of his life may have been mentioned in connection with his work, probably when discussing the value of its content.

We may not, however, completely dismiss the idea that Demetrios may have mentioned contemporaneous authors from the Troad in his work when dealing with more recent events taking place there in his time, as it may be fitting for two other authors who appear in the fragments of Demetrios' work. Indeed, for

---

[228] Athenaeus 2.44e.

[229] He has been identified as the author Fabius Pictor followed in his account of the foundation of Rome and is dated to the third century BCE. See e.g. Meister 1997:613, Biraschi 2011, commentary ad fr. 72 (= Athenaeus 2.44e), and Cornell 2013a:174 and Cornell 2013b:15–21.

[230] Evidence suggests that he was an envoy of Antiochos III about 193 BCE. We shall see that in more detail in Section 1.3.2 (pp. 62–64).

Ctesiphon, the Athenian citizen who became a judge at the court of the first Attalids,[231] and for Seleucos, son of Mnesiptolemos who was another historian at the court of Antiochos the Great,[232] such a hypothesis would even be more convenient than for Hegesianax. As we have seen, Hegesianax was the author of a Τρωϊκά, which may have interested Demetrios. For the two others we only know that they wrote drinking songs (κόλαβροι and ἱλαροὶ ᾄσματα), the topics of which seems to be less connected with Demetrios' domains of interest, even if it is not impossible to think that one of these songs may have been related to the story or the setting of the Trojan war.

Returning to Hegesianax, we must admit that the two remaining fragments quoted in connection with his name, but not yet discussed, do not help us to define the link between Demetrios and Hegesianax more closely either. In the passage from Strabo, the geographer only juxtaposes the statement from Hegesianax about the state of preservation of Ilion in the time of the invasion by the Galatians to Demetrios' narration of his experience when visiting Ilion in his youth. Strabo's formulation does not, however, enable us to find out whether Demetrios was quoting Hegesianax, a situation that would then imply that Strabo found this information in Demetrios' work, or if Strabo was himself compiling several sources, among them Demetrios and Hegesianax. The same occurs with the second example, from the entry about Arisbe in Stephanus of Byzantium. This text is actually a list of several statements about Arisbe attributed to different scholars. None among them is Demetrios, but Gaede has attributed the whole entry to Demetrios because it alludes to the tradition that makes Ascanios, the son of Aeneas, the foundation hero of several of the cities in the Troad.[233] In this case, the modern editor's choice would suggest that Demetrios quoted all the scholars mentioned in Stephanus' entry, Hegesianax included, but again the wording of the preserved text does not allow us to say whether the whole piece of information has been taken from the work of Demetrios or if Stephanus or his source compiled his information from several independent sources.

The only statement we can make about Hegesianax and the way his work or works were linked to Demetrios of Scepsis, therefore, is the fact that authors

---

[231] Fr. 6 [Gaede/Biraschi] = Athenaeus 15.697c. See Kroll 1922b:2079 for the very meager information we have about this Ctesiphon.

[232] Fr. 13 [Gaede/Biraschi] = Athenaeus 15.697d. See Laqueur 1932:2280, Meister 2000:308, Jacoby 1930:594–595 (= commentary to *Die Fragmente der griechischen Historiker* 164), and Primo 2009:88–90.

[233] See Gaede 1880:26. The passage is therefore in close connection with Strabo 13.1.52 [C607], which is not counted as a fragment by Gaede, but which occurs in Strabo's text between the passage that has been considered as fr. 33 [Gaede/Biraschi] = Strabo 13.1.51 [C606] and the one printed as fr. 35 [Gaede/Biraschi] = Strabo 13.1.53 [C607].

like Strabo found the works of the two scholars quite similar and could use them to illustrate the same point, in our case the bad state of preservation of Ilion. As far as Demetrios is concerned, we must content ourselves with the hypothesis that Demetrios may have used episodes of the lives of some scholars to justify his judgments about them. Hegesianax would then be among these sources and the two fragments about his life would belong to Demetrios' statements about the value of Hegesianax's scholarly contribution.

Another contemporary of Demetrios who should briefly be mentioned here is King Attalos I, who seems to have written a work in which he gave a very detailed description of the Pine Tree (περὶ τῆς Καλῆς Πεύκης [...] γράφει). The unique reference to this work comes from a passage that is considered as a fragment of Demetrios' work,[234] and it could therefore have been among the sources Demetrios used. Unfortunately, as this is the only reference to such a work by the Pergamene king, we cannot tell much more about it than what the few preserved lines reveal. Finally, as far as Neanthes of Cyzicos is concerned, we certainly know from fr. 50 [Gaede/Biraschi][235] that Demetrios contradicted his statements about some of the episodes concerning Cyzicos, but we must acknowledge a difficulty about the identity and the dating of the scholar. If in one of the hypotheses he may have been a contemporary of Demetrios, other evidence speaks for a date in the third century BCE instead,[236] and we may therefore postpone the discussion about the issues dealt with in this fragments to the next section, where we shall see the political implication of the fragments topic, at least in Demetrios' time.

There is, however, one last author we should discuss here as a contemporary of Demetrios, even if he is surprisingly absent from the collection of fragments. This is Polemon of Ilion whom we mentioned previously as a periegetical author and who is also dated to the beginning of the second century BCE.[237] The absence is even more surprising, because we know that Polemon wrote works against Timaeus and Neanthes of Cyzicos, two authors whose positions Demetrios must have been acquainted with as he criticized them. This mutual ignoring may be explained partly by the fact that Polemon and Demetrios may not have responded to the same works, as at least Neanthes seems to have written several works. It is also true that we have lost much of both authors (Polemon and

---

[234] Strabo 13.1.44 [C603] = part of fr. 31a [Biraschi]. Even if Gaede believes that this part belongs to Demetrios' work, he does not print it. He only states that his fr. 29 goes until the end of Strabo 13.1.45 [C603].

[235] Strabo 1.2.38–40 [C45–47].

[236] For a short summary of the question, see Shepens 1997:158–159, Schorn 2007:115–117, and, most recently, the biographical essays in *Brill's New Jacoby* 84 and *Brill's New Jacoby* 171.

[237] On Polemon, see, besides Donohue 2001:7, also Hutton 2005:251–261 and Angelucci 2003:165–184, and for the fragments still Preller 1838 and *Fragmenta historicorum graecorum* III, pp. 108–147.

Demetrios) and therefore have a distorted image of each of them. It is not, then, difficult to believe that the presumed passages in which they were quoting each other may no longer exist. However, despite all these hesitations, it still seems clear that they must have worked in rather different fields, as for instance the authors quoting them, Pausanias and Strabo, who may have had access to the works in their entirety, had a clear preference for one of them. Strabo quoted Demetrios extensively, whereas he quoted Polemon only twice by name.[238] In Pausanias, on the contrary, Gaede has included only one passage in his collection of the fragments of Demetrios.[239] This would certainly not be so if the works of the two scholars were as close as the works of Apollodoros of Athens and Demetrios, or those of Hegesianax and Demetrios. We have seen that Strabo used works of all of these scholars on the same issue, and sometimes stated the link between them. But, even so, with all the differences we may assume between the two scholars, it is still necessary to mention Polemon in a study on Demetrios. His works still belong to the literary background of Demetrios, and the discussion of his contribution may give some information about the context in which Demetrios carried out his research.[240] For instance, Polemon is still one of the authors working in the time of Demetrios on all kinds of evidence from the past, either preserved in the Troad, as the fragments from his Περιήγησις Ἰλίου prove,[241] or found in a larger geographical area.[242] The fact that he is not mentioned by Demetrios shows that the range of work could be very wide in those days and that authors who focused more on one aspect of literary activity could leave out authors who were focusing on other aspects, even if the topics they dealt with were very closely related, because they may have chosen their sources not only because of the subjects they dealt with, but also because of the methodological approach they used or the scholarly tradition they belonged to.

We may therefore conclude this second section by noting that our discussion showed a rather diversified picture. On the one hand, Demetrios could choose his sources among quite different categories of authors and combine the information he found in their works. He was closer to Crates of Mallos and the Pergamene scholars than for instance to Polemon of Ilion, even if the latter came from the same place as Demetrios. On the other hand, authors who took Demetrios as their source could associate him with other authors if they found

---

[238] Strabo 1.2.2 [C15] and Strabo 9.1.16 [C396]. See Radt 2011:233 and Preller 1838:35, and 85–87. At *Fragmenta historicorum graecorum* III, p. 116 only Strabo 9.1.16 [C396] is mentioned. However, Strabo 7, fr. 3 [Radt] gets attributed to Polemon by Müller (*Fragmenta historicorum graecorum* III, p. 124).

[239] Fr. 65 [Gaede/Biraschi] = Pausanias 10.12.2–7.

[240] See Montana 2015:147–148 and Schironi 2016:5.

[241] *Fragmenta historicorum graecorum* III, fr. 31–33.

[242] See *Fragmenta historicorum graecorum* III, pp. 110–111.

relevant information in both of the works. However, we have also seen how difficult it was to define the links between the scholars, that is mainly due to the way in which the fragments have been transmitted: largely through quotations made by other scholars. The discussion has therefore also shown how indirect our access to Demetrios is, and has prepared us for Chapter 2 in which we shall precisely discuss the ways in which Demetrios was used or appreciated by ancient authors. Before doing so, we shall give a brief description of the historical background in which Demetrios lived.

1.3 The Historical Background of the Troad

In the previous discussion on the testimonia, outlined in the first section of this chapter, we have not only defined the first part of the second century BCE as the chronological framework for the lifetime of Demetrios, but we were also able to highlight the link that Demetrios retained, throughout his life, to his hometown and more generally speaking to the Troad. Therefore, and also in order better to understand the scopes and aims of Demetrios' work, we should now join these two aspects and discuss the events that took place in the Troad during the first part of the second century BCE. This aspect has not yet been developed in our discussion: after the close reading of the testimonia, we focused in Section 2 on the literary background and tried to explain how Demetrios' work could be understood within the tradition of Homeric scholarship. During this investigation, we did not give much attention to chronological considerations, except maybe when we focused on the contemporaries of Demetrios. However, the scholarly activity we described in Section 2 was never entirely disconnected from historical events, and it is therefore important to give a short overview of the major events and changes of the second century BCE, and particularly its first part, which corresponds roughly to the lifetime of Demetrios. Our discussion does not, however, aim to be exhaustive, as a complete analysis of the events taking place in the Troad at this time is extremely complex and would exceed the scope of this section. Our intention here is to highlight the aspects that are most relevant to Demetrios' work.

In order better to understand the impact and significance of some of the events occurring in the Troad at that time, we should bear in mind that the Troad has the characteristic of being associated with the setting of the *Iliad*. This association started well before the second century BCE and varied considerably over time in shape and intensity.[243] It is not the point here to draw a history of

---

[243] The starting point is difficult to establish. See for instance Latacz/Starke 2006:57–70, Bieg 2006:361–372, or, more succinctly, Tenger 1999:121.

this association. This has been done by Sage, Rose, and more recently also by Nagy, and the phenomenon can be observed from before Xerxes' visit to Troy in 480 BCE to well beyond Demetrios' time.[244] Nonetheless, some stages of this association are crucial for our understanding of the background of Demetrios' work, and we shall highlight them in this section. We must, however, also be aware that the situation may not have been the same everywhere and that this episode of the past may have been dealt with differently from city to city. In the case of Ilion, for instance, we are very well-informed, and the case is very specific, as Ilion could draw on the fact that it was identified with the Homeric Troy and could gain some advantages from this association.[245] However, for other cities of the Troad the situation may have been different, especially if they may only have been able to demonstrate links to minor places or heroes from the Trojan legend. If they were not mentioned at all in the Homeric poems, they had to find a way to overcome this difficulty if they wanted to follow their neighbors and make political use of mythology.[246] The ways in which each of the Trojan cities could use the episodes of its mythological past also depended on its political situation. Cities did not always belong to the same rulers and had to adapt to the point of view of the representatives of the kingdom to which they belonged, or from which they wanted some favors. Therefore, we see once again how important it is to remain aware of the historical background and to understand its major characteristics. Thus, we shall first give as accurate a picture as possible of the political situation in the Troad at the beginning of the second century BCE, and then expand our analysis and explain how the cities and their rulers made use of mythology, and in particular of the Homeric association, and how this may have differed between Ilion and other cities such as Scepsis, the hometown of Demetrios.

1.3.1 The Troad in the Second Century BCE

We shall begin by drawing a general overview of the changes that the Troad, and in particular Scepsis, underwent during the lifetime of Demetrios of Scepsis.[247]

---

[244] Besides the quoted authors (Sage 2000:211–231, Rose 2003:27–88, Rose 2006a:81–104, Rose 2006b:189–198, Nagy 2010), see also Georges 1994:58–66, Burkert 1995:139–148, Tenger 1996:125–147, and Landucci Gattinoni 2005–2006:15–29.

[245] The bibliography on this topic is very large. See e.g. Perret 1942:501–519 (in particular), Webster 1972:213–255, Gruen 1993:6–51, and more recently Erskine 2001:234–253. We shall come back to this later in this section.

[246] Some cities or states took even advantage of this, such as the Acarneans, who emphasized their absence in the Homeric poems when asking for help from the Romans (Corsten 1992:195–210).

[247] For a short overview of what happened before, see Lund 1992:107–152, Franco 1993:123–130 (more precisely on Lysimachos), or Cook 1988:7–19 (for evidence from coins and inscriptions).

During this period, the first part of the second century BCE, two frequently discussed events reshaped the homeland of Demetrios. These were, first, the ongoing struggles between the Seleucids and the Attalids over the Troad as part of western Asia Minor, and second, the arrival of the Romans in this region. As far as the first event was concerned, the situation was not new, as the fluctuation of the borders between the two Hellenistic kingdoms started well before the beginning of the second century BCE. Indeed, since 281 when, after the death of Lysimachos, the Troad, as part of Lysimachos' kingdom, passed over to Antiochos I, the borders between his realm and the territories belonging to the newly created Pergamene dynasty were subject to variation.[248] It was, however, only in the second part of the third century BCE that Attalos I had enough power to expand his influence to the Troad.[249] Some of the Greek cities, such as Ilion, Alexandria Troas, and Lampsacos, joined him.[250] During the time of Antiochos Hierax[251] and Achaios,[252] the situation was still more changeable, but at the beginning of the second century BCE, Antiochos III started successively to reconquer the kingdom of his ancestors until 198 before the war against the Romans.[253] The territory of the Troad belonged to this reconquest,[254] and, as far as Scepsis is concerned, modern scholars assume that in this time it must probably have been among the so-called free cities as it was allowed to have its own coinage.[255] However, after the war against the Romans and Antiochos' defeat,[256] its status must have changed as Scepsis was given to Eumenes II in the aftermath of the Roman victory.[257] This change may certainly have had some impact on the inhabitants of Scepsis, among whom Demetrios lived, and may have influenced the way he responded to it. However, in order to understand how different this

[248] Schmitt 1964:40–44, Tenger 1999:146–152, Ma 1999:53–105, Eckstein 2008:307–341, and Chrubasik 2013:83–119. For a short overview of the elements we know about what happened before, see Radt 1999:23–25.

[249] Kosmetatou 2003:159–162: The first steps towards an independent state were undertaken by Philetairos after the battle of Coroupedion in 281 BCE, and, in a second step, Eumenes I formally declared the independence of the realm. But it is only after 237 BCE and the victory over the Galatians won by Attalos I that the Pergamene kingdom got its first king, and was, therefore, equal to the other Hellenistic kingdoms. See e.g. Pollitt 1986:79-83 and Radt 1999:27–33.

[250] Schmitt 1964:263 and Kosmetatou 2003:171. The ancient source is Polybios 5.78.6 (see Walbank 1957:606–607 for further bibliography).

[251] Antiochos Hierax: between 230 and 226 BCE. Ma 1999:46–63 and Schmitt 1964:40–42.

[252] Achaios: between 223–213 BCE. Ma 1999:54–63 and Schmitt 1964:262–267.

[253] Schmitt 1964:86–90 and Ma 1999:86–94.

[254] Ma 1999:89.

[255] Kagan 1984:11–24 and Ma 1999:163. See also Tenger 1999:153 for other signs that Scepsis was acting in favor of the Seleucids.

[256] For an overall view of the events of this war, see for instance Grainger 2002:329–349.

[257] Ma 1999:283, Allen 1983:111, and Schmitt 1964:283. The ancient source alluding to this fact is Strabo 13.1.54 [C608–609], the passage about the fate of Aristotle's library we discussed previously in Section 1.1.2 (pp. 9–11).

situation may have been from that of other places in the Troad, we must turn to the second event we mentioned above, the arrival of the Romans after their victory over Antiochos the Great. This event is moreover of particular relevance for Demetrios as he mentioned it himself as an important chronological reference in one of the preserved fragments.[258]

If we begin now considering why contemporaneous witnesses gave so much weight to this event, we may adduce as one of the reasons the fact that, after the victory over Antiochos III, the Romans rearranged the territory of the Troad and created a completely different political situation for many of the cities. As far as we can see from the evidence, the Troad was now divided into three main parts: that belonging to Ilion, one of the cities whose status could be raised;[259] that belonging to Alexandria Troas, another winner from the Roman division;[260] and finally that containing the cities that were given to the Pergamene kingdom.[261] Furthermore, according to the analyses of modern scholars, the status of the cities within each of these parts was not uniform and depended on the degree of liberty, or rather independence, that the Romans granted them. John Ma, for instance, suggests that there were at least three different statuses among the free cities after the settlements made by the Romans: the genuinely independent cities like Lampscos, Smyrna, and Chios; the cities declared independent by the Romans themselves, after they had rallied the Romans; and those declared independent by the Seleucids.[262] But for this distribution other criteria must have been taken into account.[263] It is, for instance, extremely difficult to establish the reasons why the above-mentioned Lampsacos and Abydos, which both seem to have been among the independent cities before the conflict, even if their destinies during the conflict were different, were not rewarded as greatly as, for instance, Parion and Dardanos, which gained their independence only after Apameia.[264] It is certainly not our aim here to settle these difficult questions or

---

[258] This is T3 [Biraschi] = fr. 21 [Gaede/Biraschi] (= Strabo 13.1.27 [C594]). See also above Section 1.1.1 (p. 3).

[259] We shall explore the reasons for this later in this chapter.

[260] Probably because the city stayed with the Attalids (Ma 1999:89–90 and Tenger 1999:153) or its inhabitants asked the Romans for help (Eckstein 2008:312).

[261] Tenger 1999:155–159.

[262] Ma 1999:282–283. See also Allen 1983:98–121 for an overview including all the cities under Attalids' rule, not only those from the Troad.

[263] For instance, their faithfulness to the Romans in the war against Antiochos III, or if they had once paid tribute to Attalos I. For this see, additionally, Ma 1999:282–283, and also McShane 1964:151–152. Baronowski 1991:450–463 suggested other solutions. On these see further the recent discussion in Koehn 2007:263–285.

[264] Tenger 1999:155–159 and Schmitt 1964:284. For Lampsacos, for instance, the evidence suggests that it must indeed have had some autonomy for some time, resisted Antiochos successfully, and become one of the reasons for the conflict between Rome and Antiochos III (Ma 1999:94–96 and Ferrary 2001:94–95). For Dardanos, on the contrary, the reason for which it was rewarded with

to add new evidence to the debate. The short description should simply have shown how enormous the Roman intervention must have been, and how much it changed the political situation for almost every city in the Troad. Moreover, as has been suggested recently, the changes, especially when they were instigated by an outsider like the Romans, may have kindled anew old rivalries or created new quarrels amongst the cities in the Troad.[265]

Another rather clear consequence of this reshaping of the political situation in the Troad was that it was no longer possible to ignore the presence of the Romans, even if they remained at the beginning of the second century BCE rather at a distance.[266] Indeed, during this period many embassies were sent to the Romans about matters in the eastern part of the Mediterranean Basin, and they often functioned as judges and negotiators in an effort of conciliation in several of the still ongoing conflicts in this part of Asia Minor.[267] This behavior shows that their influence had some positive effects for the population and that the time after the Roman victory over Antiochos the Great, despite the novelty of the situation and the necessity for each city to adapt to it, was a period of calm and peace after the many conflicts between the Seleucids and the Attalids, which often had disastrous consequences for the cities and regions involved.[268] It is only after 170 BCE, at the earliest, that the presence of Rome was felt in a more negative way and created a reaction that ultimately led to the conflict between Rome and Mithridates VI Eupator in the first century BCE, which involved Metrodoros of Scepsis, the younger fellow citizen of Demetrios whom we encountered in the discussion about the testimonia.[269] This negative evolution further intensified after the end of the Attalid kingdom in 133 BCE and overshadowed the creation of the Roman province of Asia. But these events belonged to this second phase of the Roman presence in Asia Minor and probably took place after Demetrios' lifetime. Therefore, we shall not develop this further here, as it would take us beyond the scope of our research. We should, however, remain aware of this development in our subsequent discussion, and understand it as a progressive change that may already have started, in at least some of its aspects, in the time of Demetrios.

---

the status of free city is probably to be found in the position Dardanos held when the Romans landed there. See also Ma 1999:89.

[265] For the North of the Troad, see Tenger 1999:157.

[266] Eckstein 2008:346–347 or McShane 1964:157–162.

[267] Mainly the wars of the Pergamene kings against the Galatians (189–187 BCE), against the king of Bithynia (185–183 BCE), and against Pharnaces I of Pontos (182–179 BCE). See Eckstein 2008:353, Pollitt 1986:81–82, Sartre 1995:108–113, and, for more details, see McShane 1964:159–164.

[268] Bresson 2001:13–14. See also Tenger 1999:159 and Eckstein 2008:353.

[269] For a more detailed description of this evolution, see Sartre 1995:107–133. For Metrodoros see above Section 1.1.1 (pp. 5–6).

For Demetrios, however, as probably for most of the inhabitants of the Troad in the first part of the second century BCE, it was the immediate presence of the Attalid kingdom that was more perceptible than the Romans, who were still far away. Even if the Romans had made their appearance and could no long be ignored, it was primarily the Attalids who influenced the Troad in the time of Demetrios. Their kingdom was the most powerful state after the peace of Apameia in the western part of Asia Minor[270] and its rulers were rather well-disposed towards the inhabitants.[271] This situation lasted until 133 BCE, as mentioned, when the kingdom was bequeathed to the Romans and became the Roman province of Asia—in other words, it corresponds probably to the period of Demetrios' life. Two elements associated with the Attalid kingdom will be of great importance for our study. First of all, of course, the creation of the Pergamene library, which was most probably undertaken under the reign of Eumenes II, should be mentioned.[272] This brings us back to the literary background discussed in the previous section. As Eumenes' accession to the throne is dated to 197, Demetrios must have witnessed the creation or expansion of this institution and its activities[273] as he witnessed the Roman victory over Antiochos III. However, we have already seen how difficult it was to establish the type of link that Demetrios had to this institution. It should nonetheless have become clear by now that he could not have carried out his scholarly activity without referring to or taking note of this institution. The second feature of the Attalids' dynasty that will interest us here is the way the Attalid kings used mythology, and in particular the elements from the Trojan cycle, in their propaganda and in their relations with the Romans. The fact that Hellenistic kings used mythology for their own purposes is not surprising and had of course been done before. The Attalids too had already developed a particular way of using it before they had to deal with the Romans. But their practice acquired another dimension in this context and the scholars working in their realm may have reacted to this.[274] Therefore, we should develop this aspect further and find out how this may have influenced or shaped the surroundings of Demetrios of Scepsis.

---

[270] For instance, McShane 1964:148, Sartre 1995:108, and Mitchell 2005:527.

[271] McShane 1964:170–171.

[272] Nagy 1998:214. Or at least the activities of this center of research enormously expanded during his reign (Kosmetatou 2003:164).

[273] We have already discussed the link to the Pergamene scholar Crates of Mallos. See above Section 1.1.1 (p. 4) and Section 1.2.2 (pp. 39–40).

[274] Kosmetatou 2003:159. The most famous and most impressive example is certainly the so-called Pergamon Altar. For a thorough mythological and political interpretation of the monument, see now Pollitt 1986:79–110 and Ridgway 2000:19–66.

1.3.2 Political Use of the Trojan Myth in the Second Century BCE

Even if the phenomenon as such was not new and many local historians defended their hometown's claims with mythological episodes,[275] the usage made of mythology gained a new dimension in the second century BCE, not only, but especially, in the context of the peace of Apameia, in the interaction with the Romans, who were a new but increasingly influential power in the East.[276] Not only the Attalids, but also Antiochos III, as well as some more independent Greek communities—and then in a second step even the Romans themselves[277]—could use mythological episodes to underpin their claims, particularly when the Roman authorities were involved. We shall return to Antiochos III later in more detail, but we can mention briefly here the well-known examples of Lampsacos and Ilion.[278] In both cities the inhabitants highlighted the link to the Trojan story in order to obtain substantial advantages from the Romans.[279] Here again the phenomenon is not new and can be traced back at least to the beginning of the third century BCE, and more precisely to Pyrrhos I, who tried to justify his intervention against the Romans by emphasizing that, as a descendant of Achilles, he was entitled to join a battle against the descendants of the Trojans.[280] Then it was used by the Acarneans in the middle of the third century BCE[281] and in a second step by the Lampsacians who developed this mythological connection in their dealings with the Romans. Their position is believed to have become one of the problems between Antiochos III and the Romans before their open conflict.[282] As for Ilion, it is only in 188 BCE in the context of the peace of Apameia that we have evidence of its more active exploitation of this link.[283]

---

[275] Kosmetatou 1995:133–138, Scheer 2003:220–226, and for a broader approach, see Jost 1998:227–240.

[276] Eckstein 2008:352. It took still at least two decades, according to Eckstein 2008:377, until the power of Rome was substantially shaping the political situation in Asia Minor.

[277] Gruen 1993:31 insists, however, that the initiative often came from the Greek cities and/or communities.

[278] Another well-documented example is Aphrodisias, even if the city does not belong to the Troad. The evidence about the political usage of mythology is later (Augustan times), but it still shows how the Trojan legend was explored in a political context and this over a very long period. See Jones 2001:179–186, de Chaisemartin 2001:187–206, Chaniotis 2003:69–84, and Chaniotis 2009:313–338.

[279] Erskine 2001:223.

[280] Weber 1972:214 and Gruen 1993:26–27.

[281] See, for instance, Weber 1972:213–225, Corsten 1992:195–210, Coppola 1994:177–186, or Desideri 2005–2006:48-49). The bibliography on this topic is enormous and can be found in the aforementioned studies.

[282] Eckstein 2008:313, Desideri 2005–2006:49, and for more details, Schmitt 1964:290, Ma 1999:94–102, and in particular Desideri 1970–1971:501–511.

[283] Weber 1972:221 considers this date as rather late compared to the evidence from other cities.

This aspect of the political use of mythology was, however, not the only factor for its increase in the second century BCE. In order to understand this development fully, we should focus more closely on the Attalids and the strategy they created for their dealings with Rome and other interlocutors.[284] It is therefore necessary to develop this further in order to understand the whole dimension of the phenomenon and the implications it may have had on any scholar working in those days, in whatever context he may have worked, either in favor of the Attalids or more independently.

In order to understand the complexity and many layers of the Attalids' use of mythology, we should focus first on their foundation myth. They based this myth on several links to the Homeric past, mainly though their two foundation heroes, Telephos and Pergamos, and this since the time of Philetairos.[285] The legend of Telephos had the advantage of taking elements of two mythological cycles, those of Heracles and the Trojan war.[286] Within the Trojan story, the legend of Telephos could be used in two ways. It provided, on the one hand, elements that help to highlight the links of friendship with the Achaeans, ancestors of the Greeks, which could then be highlighted when the Attalids dealt with their Greek political interlocutors. On the other hand, however, through Telephos' sons, some episodes of the legend could also be linked to the Trojans.[287] This was an interesting aspect that the Attalids used, not only for their interaction with the Romans, but actually also when dealing with those who were believed to be the descendants of the Trojans in the Troad. The second foundation hero, Pergamos, also provided several links to the Trojan legend that could be exploited in various ways. On the one hand, through the similarity of the names of the two cities involved, Pergamos/Pergamon, the Attalid kingdom was already linked to the Trojan setting and the Homeric poems.[288] Furthermore, as Pergamos was believed to be a son of Andromache and Neoptolemos,[289] the dealings with the hero Pergamos could again provide elements for both sides: through his father, Pergamos was descendant of the best of the Achaeans, and this part of the myth could be used to emphasize the connection to the Greek past. Through his mother, however, Pergamos was the son of Hector's wife,

---

[284] Gruen 2000:17–31.

[285] Scheer 2003:221. For an earlier use of the myth of Telephos, see Dignas 2012:119–143.

[286] Kosmetatou 1995:140, Kosmetatou 2003:167, and Gruen 2000:23.

[287] Kosmetatou 2001:126, Kosmetatou 2003:167, who names three sons of Telephos: Tarchon, Tyrsenos, and the better known Eurypylos. For their link to a Roman context, see e.g. Erskine 2001:222–223 or Schmidt 1916–1924:291. Both explanations go back to Lycophron's *Alexandra* v. 1245–1249.

[288] The passages where a part of the acropolis of Troy is named Pergamos are: *Iliad* 4.508; *Iliad* 5.446; *Iliad* 5.460; *Iliad* 6.512; *Iliad* 7.21; and *Iliad* 24.700.

[289] Kosmetatou, 2003:168 and Scheer 2003:222–223.

which provided a link to the Trojans and thus to the Romans, their descendants, if need be. There was, however, yet another aspect of this legend that was exploited by the Attalids. In one version of the legend, Andromache fled to Epirus, and this geographical element allowed the Attalids to draw a link to Alexander the Great.[290] This connection was much needed for a dynasty that did not have as its founder a direct diadoch of Alexander.[291] This aspect was used again either in their relations with the Romans or with their Greek interlocutors, who could come either from within their territory or from outside.

Many such examples of political usage of mythology may be given. For instance, besides the famous altar in Pergamon, the victory monuments established in Athens and Delphi by the Attalids after the victory of Attalos I over the Galatians in 237 BCE could be mentioned, as they have been interpreted in this way.[292] Attalos I was seen, as was his mythological forerunner Telephos, as someone not only defending his homeland, but also fighting for the Greek world and its culture against the barbarian Galatians.[293] As far as the Troad is concerned, such early examples as the following should be mentioned: the favors for the Aristotelean philosopher Lyco from Alexandria Troas by Eumenes I and Attalos I; the alliance with Ilion, Lampsacos, and Alexandria Troas made by Attalos I in 218 BCE; and the presence of the *Koinon* of Athena Ilias on the Pergamene and Roman side in the war against Philip V.[294] It is therefore no surprise to see that the Attalids continued to privilege selected places in the Troad, even after the arrival of the Romans and probably even in connection with their arrival, but probably still independently from Romans' interests. One telling example of their favoring of special places in the Troad after the arrival of the Romans is connected to the city of Cyzicos and has, moreover, a direct link to our study of Demetrios of Scepsis. This characteristic makes it then perhaps worth being described here in more detail. The first historical link between Cyzicos and the Attalid dynasty is established by the fact that the wife of Attalos I came from Cyzicos. Her sons, Eumenes II and Attalos II, exploited this link first by honoring their mother in visiting the city in her company probably around 183 BCE and later by building a temple to the dowager queen at the sanctuary

---

[290] Kosmetatou 2003:168.

[291] Gruen 2000:17 and Kosmetatou 2003:167.

[292] Gruen 2000:18–19 and 24–25, and Scheer 2003:224.

[293] For further examples on Aegina and Tegea, see Scheer 2003:220–226.

[294] Kosmetatou 2001:117–122. This is certainly already a sign of the threefold link between Ilion, Pergamon, and Rome that can be observed later on, but it shows also that the connection between Pergamon and the Troad antedates it and persisted even after the peace of Apameia, as suggested by Kosmetatou 2001:123–125. For the link between Eumenes I and the philosopher Lyco, see also Pollitt 1986:79.

of Cybele in Cyzicos.[295] It is this goddess and her sanctuary that are mentioned in two of the preserved fragments from Demetrios. In fr. 50 [Gaede/Biraschi],[296] Demetrios speaks against Neanthes of Cyzicos,[297] another local scholar, who placed the sanctuary of the goddess, whom he calls, however, at least in Strabo's version, the Idean Mother (ἡ Ἰδαίας μήτηρ), in Cyzicos.[298] We know, therefore, that there must have been a scholarly debate going on about the localization of the sanctuary of this goddess, as Demetrios, a native of Scepsis, seems not to agree with Neanthes, a local scholar from Cyzicos. If we add the second piece of evidence, fr. 61 [Gaede/Biraschi],[299] we learn about Demetrios' own position: he seems to have located the goddess under discussion (now called Rhea) and her sanctuary on Mount Ida near Scepsis. In our context here, when knowing that the Attalid dynasty took some interest in the sanctuary of Cybele in Cyzicos, the scholarly discussion outlined in the two fragments takes on another dimension, and we guess the importance it had for the scholars and their contemporaneous readers with regard to their everyday life and the status of their hometowns.

There is, however, more to be said about this example, its implication for the cult of Cybele, and its connection to a scholarly discussion about the localization of the sanctuary of this goddess. As we shall see, it provides, on the one hand, the context for other fragments of Demetrios, and, on the other hand, brings us back to the link between the Attalids and the Romans. However, in order to understand all the implications, we have to start by going back to an event that actually happened before the Roman victory over Antiochos the Great. This is the transfer of the so-called Great Mother, *Magna Mater*, from Asia Minor to Rome in the year 204 BCE, which also brings us back to the first friendly relations between the Attalids and the Romans believed to have started as early as the first Macedonian war against Philip V.[300]

The motivation for this transfer is generally explained by the fact that the Romans received an oracle in the last years of the Second Punic war telling them that they should transfer this goddess from Asia Minor to Rome in order to be successful in their undertaking.[301] They turned to Attalos I for assistance, as the sanctuary of this goddess was located in his realm. There are, however,

---

[295] Kuttner 1995:168, Kosmetatou 2003:169, and Thonemann 2013:41–42. The ancient evidence for this are the epigrams collected as *Anthologia Palatina* 3.1–19.

[296] Strabo 1.2.38–40 [C45–47].

[297] For Neanthes of Cyzicos, see for instance Schorn 2007:115–156 and Schepens 1997:158–159.

[298] In this we follow the translation of Radt 2002:110 for the adjective Ἰδαία.

[299] Strabo 10.3.19–20 [C472].

[300] Gruen 2000:26. For a closer description of the events about this transfer, see e.g. Graillot 1912:25–69, and more recently Gruen 1990:5–33 and Roller 1999:263–285.

[301] For the difficulty in evaluating the contradicting evidence from Antiquity, see Erskine 2001:205–218.

several variants in the different narrations of the episode. The differences mainly concern the location of the sanctuary or the name of the goddess, and both topics can be linked to our discussion. To begin, as far as the issue of the localization of the sanctuary is concerned, three options are transmitted. First, in some versions the sanctuary was to be found in Pessinous in central Phrygia, others located it in Pergamon, and still others on Mount Ida in the Troad.[302] This last location was favored by later sources like Ovid and Vergil, who used it to speak in favor of a Trojan origin for the Romans.[303] None of them, however, is in accordance with what Neanthes seems to have suggested for his Idean Mother. We know, however, because of the evidence about the variations of her name, that Neanthes may have had the same goddess in mind. Indeed, the goddess was worshipped under several different names, the most relevant for us being *Magna Mater*, *Mater Idaea*, *Cybeleia*, and *Rhea*.[304] This list helps us to link the issue about the *Magna Mater* to the above-mentioned issue about the Attalids' veneration of the sanctuary of Cybele in Cyzicos. Indeed, because of the epithet *Cybeleia*, the goddess involved here seems to have been linked to Cybele in Cyzicos, who was probably named Idean Mother by Neanthes.[305] As she could also be called Rhea, we may reasonably think that she was thought to be the same as the one Demetrios located on Mount Ida, especially as we just saw that one of the possible origins of the *Magna Mater* was that very same mountain. The situation may even be more complex and bear evidence of an assimilation or amalgamation of several previously distinct divinities. We shall not go further into this question here, as this would drive us too far into issues dealt with by historians of religion.[306] In the context of Demetrios of Scepsis, it is enough to see that these names were combined in Antiquity and to examine how scholars reacted to this phenomenon. The example should, however, also show that these scholarly considerations were often motivated by political implications. In our case, we see that it was not only the Romans who were interested in this goddess and her cult, but also the Attalids. For the former it may have been the attempt to match the oracle's requirements for the outcome of the Second Punic war and to intensify their relationship with the Attalid kingdom

---

[302] Nauta 2007:79–80. For epigraphical evidence from Pessinous, see Holm Rasmussen 2002:159–164, whereas Gruen 1990:5-33 (and in particular 15–20) privileges the Trojan origin.

[303] Ovid *Fasti* 4.249–276 and e.g. Vergil *Aeneid* 9.80-122 and 10.219-255. See Nauta 2007:82–83 for further references.

[304] For a fuller list, see Erskine 2001:213–216.

[305] See Strabo 10.3.12 [C469] and *Brill's New Jacoby* 171 F17 (Strabo 1.2.38 [C45]) for Neanthes in particular.

[306] For this see: Graillot 1912:1–24; Borgeaud 1996, in particular pp. 19–30 and 108–130, where Borgeaud speaks in favor of Pessinous as place from where the cult of *Magna Mater* was brought to Rome; and most recently Roller 1999:119–234.

that motivated their interest in the goddess. For the latter, this transfer of the goddess and the controversy about the location of her sanctuary could also have some advantages, especially if the sanctuary came to be located on Mount Ida, which belonged in those days to their realm. Indeed, with such a location they could not only tighten their relationship with the Romans, but also highlight their mythological link to some of their own prestigious ancestors, especially to the Trojans.[307] It is believed by modern scholars, especially Andrew Erskine, that it is only through this episode that the link between Rome and the Trojan story become known in the Troad and could later be used, as we have seen, by Lampsacos around 196 BCE and by Ilion around 188 BCE.[308]

Turning once again to the scholarly aspects of the issue, we may even add a further link between the several names of the divinities involved and Demetrios. For this we must take into account a further list of names for a goddess. It belongs to a passage from Apollonios Rhodios, in which we find, among other names, also those of Idean Mother and Rhea.[309] The passage belongs to the episode from the Argonauts' outward journey taking place in Cyzicos, and we are told that, during their stay there, the Argonauts established an altar for a goddess who is defined by several names: Dindymian Mother, Idean Mother, Rhea, and Mother of all the Blessed.[310] This is precisely the passage about which a scholion has preserved some elements from Demetrios' work.[311] The scholion does not, however, deal with the issues outlined above, but is about the meaning of a rare Homeric word used in a particular way by Apollonios.[312] This suggests that Demetrios may not only have discussed the Homeric lines in his work, but also extended his comments to evidence from later works, such as Apollonios' *Argonautica*. Moreover, we may infer from this that the passage from Apollonios' poem was interesting in itself and contained aspects, mainly those about the creation of the altar for the local goddess, the interpretation of which not only had consequences for the reading of the Homeric text, but could also be

---

[307] Erskine 2001:219–224. See also Nauta 2007:79–92.

[308] Erskine 2001:223. It is also interesting to notice, in connection with this transfer of *Magna Mater*, that the evidence from Lampsacos is dated before the inauguration of her temple in Rome in 191 BCE, whereas the Ilians seem to have used the episode after it.

[309] Apollonios Rhodios 1.1123–1139. For further analyses about the importance of the goddess in this passage, see e.g. Vian 1951:14–25 and, with regard to a later Roman use of the episode, see Williams 1997:5–28.

[310] The expression "Mother of all the Blessed" occurs a few lines above (Apollonios Rhodios 1.1094). See further Erskine 2001:215, who prefers, however, to translate the expression Ἰδαία Μήτηρ as "Mother Idaia" rather than "Idean Mother."

[311] Fr. 70 [Gaede] (= fr. 70a [Biraschi]) = Σ Apollonios Rhodios 1.1123 [Wendel]. Fr. 70b [Biraschi] is *Etymologicum Magnum* s.v. χεράδες.

[312] It is the Greek term χέραδος occurring only once in the *Iliad*, in *Iliad* 21.319, which is reused by Apollonios in line 1.1123 and again only there.

interpreted in a more political way by the time Demetrios wrote his commentary. Furthermore, if Demetrios discussed elements from the passage as shown in fr. 70 [Gaede] and contradicted Neanthes about the location of the goddess (fr. 50 [Gaede/Biraschi]), asserting that she had her sanctuary on Mount Ida rather than near Cyzicos (fr. 61 [Gaede/Biraschi]), we see also how his argumentation may have been formed and how these fragments are linked. It is a debate that involves toponyms located in the Troad (Cyzicos, Mount Ida). The inhabitants of these places tried to explore mythological stories about these places that could be linked to prestigious epic narrations, such as the Homeric poems or the saga of the Argonauts. These attempts created disagreements among local scholars from different towns, and not only because of the scholarly implications the different versions had. These interpretations were also relevant, in a political context, for the status of these places with regards to their neighbors when dealing with ruling powers.

Likewise, the political context could also be significant for another issue dealt with by Demetrios, even if this is not as closely linked to the particular events we alluded to. This is his special treatment of the part of the Trojan legend connected to Aeneas and his destiny after the fall of Troy. Demetrios' claim that Aeneas stayed in the Troad and became the foundation hero of Demetrios hometown Scepsis[313] can better be analyzed when we are aware of this political aspect of the issue. This version has been stated in a time when the Attalids, as well as the Romans, began to exploit the relationship between the mythological Trojans and their several alleged descendants, such as the inhabitants of the Hellenistic Troad or the Romans themselves. Therefore, we see that with regard to this fragment too, it is important to know that such a position not only had literary consequences for the understanding of the Homeric text and its reception, but was also connected to the scholar's immediate political background—and that this background involved not only local issues, but also those related to the great political powers. This does not, however, mean that Demetrios' position was exclusively directed against Rome and her interests, but rather that it was a general attitude in this time, that every local historian may have adopted in order to defend his hometown against opponents from far or near.[314]

---

[313] This is only suggested in the wording of fr. 35 [Gaede/Biraschi] = Strabo 13.1.53 [C607]. It is fully stated in Strabo 13.1.52 [C607] in a passage just preceding fr. 35, which has not been included in the previous collections of the fragments of Demetrios.

[314] Gruen 1993:40–42. For a larger point of view, see Heller 2006. She focuses on a later period (129 BCE to 235 CE), but her diachronical analysis of rivalries between Greek cities is also illuminating for the time of Demetrios. For Ilion, see Heller 2006:76–77, and for Cyzicos, see Heller 2006:71–76.

As a final aspect of this section on the historical background, we would like to open up the discussion, having spent much of it on the Attalids' dealing with mythology, and include also, as far as possible, the evidence from other Hellenistic kingdoms. For this we turn briefly to Antiochos III and to what we know about the use of mythology at his court.[315] Even if we are missing extensive evidence, we at least know of one embassy sent to Rome by Antiochos III, which involved a scholar who is known to have dealt with parts of the Trojan mythology in his own research. This could therefore be a small sign of how Antiochos III made use of the Trojan mythology in his diplomatic interactions with Rome. It was the embassy of 193 BCE, in which Hegesianax from Alexandria Troas, the author of a work entitled Τρωϊκά and whom we encountered previously in the discussion about the literary background, was sent by Antiochos III to Rome.[316] Two of the few fragments that are preserved of this work allude to Aeneas and his fate and give a special version of the link between the Trojans and the Romans. In Hegesianax's version, Aeneas does not reach Rome himself, but dies in Thrace. It is then the task of one of his sons to reach Italy and to establish a genealogical link between the Romans and the Trojans.[317] However, even if this fragment bears witness to the use of mythology at the court of Antiochos III and may be seen as an answer to the political situation, its brevity does not allow us to go any further here. First, we do not know how the stance of Hegesianax in the question about Aeneas' travel was linked to the political decisions of Antiochos III, or whether this aspect somehow influenced the embassy or the claims he was presenting to the Romans. Modern scholars disagree about this and some believe that Hegesianax's version shows a hostile position towards Rome, whereas others point to a more diversified use of the Trojan myth with many different versions that had no specific targets.[318] It must indeed be acknowledged that Hegesianax's version, even if it loosens the link between the Trojans and the Romans, does not render their claim impossible, and it remains puzzling that Hegesianax, a scholar from the entourage of Antiochos the Great, an opponent of the Romans, defended a version that was compatible with the

---

[315] Primo 2009 gives a thorough overview of the use of erudition at the court of the Seleucids.

[316] Hegesianax seems already to have been involved in diplomatic missions in 196 BCE. See Ferrari 1988:225–226, Primo 2009:90–92, and *Brill's New Jacoby* 45 T4–T6 with an up-to-date commentary on these events. For Hegesianax as a scholar, see Fornaro 1998:235–236. The collection of his fragments is found in *Die Fragmente der griechischen Historiker* 45, *Brill's New Jacoby* 45, and now also in *Supplementum Hellenisticum* frr. 464–470 and Pagani 2005. See also above Section 1.2.2 (pp. 43–47).

[317] *Die Fragmente der griechischen Historiker* 45 F7 = Dionysius Halicarnassensis *Antiquitates Romanae* 1.49.1; *Die Fragmente der griechischen Historiker* 45 F8 = Dionysius Halicarnassensis *Antiquitates Romanae* 1.72.1, and *Die Fragmente der griechischen Historiker* 45 F10 = Festus p. 266, 13 [Müller] (= p. 326 [Lindsay]).

[318] E.g. Gruen 1993:39, 42–43, and Primo 2009:93–95 with further bibliography.

Romans' claim, whereas Demetrios developed a version that contradicted such a connection between the Romans and the Trojans. Also with regard to the attribution of Hegesianax's work to a specific genre, there are several difficulties that diminish the value modern scholars give to his Τρωϊκά. For instance, because Hegesianax uses the pseudonym of Cephalon/Cephalion of Gergis in his work, it has been reduced to being only the predecessor of fictive retellings of the Trojan myth, such as those of Dictys of Crete and Dares.[319] However, it has, especially in Antiquity, also been seen as an ancestor of more valuable histories of the Troad, as, for instance, Strabo and Dionysios of Halicarnassos used Hegesianax as authority on the same level as other authors like Ephoros, Hellanicos, and even Aristotle.[320] Furthermore, we have seen that the formula of its title, Τρωϊκά, has also sometimes been given to the work of Demetrios of Scepsis and that this may not be enough to judge the content of a work.[321] However, knowing all this, it becomes even more interesting to reconsider the link between the two scholars and to think about the reasons why Demetrios may have mentioned episodes of Hegesianax's life in his work. In the light of the discussion outlined above, our hypothesis that Demetrios may have alluded to Hegesianax's opinions and criticized them, perhaps also by adding episodes of the scholar's life, receives some support. We know from the Straboian context of fr. 21 [Gaede/Biraschi][322] that both scholars described the state of preservation of Ilion: Demetrios in his own time and Hegesianax during the invasion of the Galatians. We suggested, however, that the Straboian passages did not allow us to define precisely how the two statements were related, or whether one of the scholars quoted the other. Here, even if we do not get an answer for this difficulty, we see that it becomes very likely that Demetrios, if he knew about Hegesianax's works, which the two fragments about Hegesianax's life suggest,[323] must have discussed at some point the version of Aeneas' story defended by

---

[319] Jacoby 1957b:525 (= commentary to *Die Fragmente der griechischen Historiker* 45 T1–11), Perret 1942:512–513, Merkle 1989:46–55, and Fry 1998:75. Likewise, Cameron 2004:124–125 defines Hegesianax's Τρωϊκά as a pseudo-archaic novelistic work. But other fragments from this author depict him as a well-versed scholar, as shown by the circumspect comments in *Brill's New Jacoby* 45.

[320] Strabo 12.3.20–23 [C552] = fr. 45 [Biraschi/Gaede]. Dionysius Halicarnassensis *Antiquitates Romanae* 1.46–49 and 1.72 gives a list of Greek authors who were dealing either with the tradition of Aeneas' going to Italy or the foundation story of Rome. He enumerates a whole range of authors among whom the above-mentioned are the best known. Surprisingly, however, he does not quote Demetrios of Scepsis, at least not by name. See further Trachsel 2007:186–188 and Primo 2009:92–93.

[321] See above Section 1.1.3 (pp. 18–19).

[322] Strabo 13.1.27 [C594].

[323] Fr. 7 [Gaede/Biraschi] = Athenaeus 4.155b (= *Die Fragmente der griechischen Historiker* 45 T3) and fr. 9 [Gaede/Biraschi] = Athenaeus 3.80d (= *Die Fragmente der griechischen Historiker* 45 T2).

Hegesianax. It was contradicting his own version, moreover, in a context in which this question had more than scholarly implications.

Unfortunately, we are not able to go any further here, because of the scarcity of the evidence. We hope nonetheless to have shown, at least to some extent, how the work of Demetrios must be seen with regard to its historical background. Together with our research on the literary background we may now have achieved a picture of the original setting in which this work was created. In the next two chapters, we shall see how it has been used and appreciated by subsequent readers, either from Antiquity or from modern times.

2
Appreciation of Demetrios' Contribution in Antiquity

In this chapter, as well as in Chapter 3, we shall focus on evidence of the way in which Demetrios' work was judged and appreciated by subsequent readers. However, for the sake of clarity, we shall divide the topic into two chapters. In the first, we shall focus on the use ancient authors made of Demetrios' work, and in the second, we shall study the modern points of view about the scholar. This division is explained by the fact that the two approaches will be quite different: in the first chapter, we shall analyze the authors from Antiquity who quoted and therefore used Demetrios' work, whereas in the second, we shall focus on the perception of Demetrios as a scholar and its implications for establishing the subsequent editions of the fragments. We shall, however, see during the discussion how the two perspectives are linked, and that it is often only the modern understanding of a given passage that makes it a source text for the fragments of Demetrios.

2.1 Reevaluation of the Ancient Source Texts

As far as the ancient point of view is concerned, we begin with one of the results that emerged during the discussion of the testimonia. Demetrios enjoyed a certain fame in Antiquity from the very beginning of his reception, as Apollodoros of Athens, a contemporaneous scholar, made an almost immediate answer and responded to the work of Demetrios with his own treatise on the Catalogue of the Ships. We have also seen that his reaction could be very polemic and directed against Demetrios' statements. But even so, it bears witness to the fact that Demetrios had some impact on his immediate environment. However, the influence an author may have had on his contemporary and future readers cannot be seen only through the testimonia and the way in which ancient authors spoke about Demetrios, as we have tried to show in the first chapter. It can also be seen when analyzing the list of authors who quoted parts of his work, and where, therefore, the fragments have been preserved. This will be the main task of this chapter. We shall not only try to understand in what kind of texts Demetrios' work is quoted, at what period it was still available, to what extent it could be read from firsthand, and whether there are signs indicating that it was only consulted indirectly through other compilations, but also try to find out how the elements quoted were viewed by the authors who used them.

However, before looking at the authors who quoted Demetrios' work individually, we should describe in more detail the chronological framework, and explain what it may reveal about the usage ancient authors made of Demetrios' work. Indeed, taking as our first item the testimonia about Apollodoros' reaction to Demetrios' statements, we may begin by assuming that Demetrios' work was used from the second century BCE until the twelfth century CE, when Tzetzes mentioned Demetrios by name.[1] The situation is, however, more complex, especially because many quotations of Demetrios are found in the scholia, not only in those to the *Iliad*, but also in those to Pindar, Euripides, Apollonios Rhodios, and Theocritos. The history of the transmission of each of these corpora is extremely complex, and it is almost impossible to fix a date for their creation. One should rather see this as an ongoing process of compilation in which a large number of scholars working at different periods added comments from a great variety of sources to the lines of the Homeric text that they wanted to explain. They could summarize or paraphrase already existing comments, as well as amplify them with their own thoughts, or combine information they found either in the manuscripts themselves or in other scholarly works that had come down from the Alexandrian period or been compiled in later times.[2] Therefore, the fragments from the scholia blur the chronological framework with regard to its upper limit.

Furthermore, there are some additional difficulties when considering the other end of our timescale. The work of Apollodoros has been preserved only indirectly, and we rely, as with Demetrios, on quotations from other, later authors, the earliest being Strabo. It is therefore only in Augustan times, through Strabo, that we have extensive evidence about the use Apollodoros made of Demetrios,[3]

---

[1]   Fr. 75 [Gaede/Biraschi] = Tzetzes *Σ ad Lycophronem* v. 530.

[2]   For the scholia to the *Iliad*, see e.g. Erbse 1960 and van der Valk 1963 and 1964, and more succinctly Kirk 1985:38-43 and Montana 2011:105-161. For Apollonios Rhodios, see now Lachenaud 2010:xi-xxxvi. For Theocritos, see Wendel 1920, and for Pindar, see Irigoin 1952, in particular 93-121. Finally, for a more general approach, see e.g. Maehler 1994:95-127, Maehler 2000:29-36, and McNamee 1995:399-414. Still fundamental are Wilson 1967:244-256 and Zuntz 1975, in particular 61-110.

[3]   Strabo is indeed for both scholars the earliest author in whose work either testimonia or fragments of their works are preserved, even if some of the elements from the scholia may give us some ideas about the debate that took place in the Hellenistic period. We have, however, decided to treat the scholia in a separate group, as they show much more the state in which the Hellenistic debate was still available for the later scholars than the debate itself.

and we shall have to begin our discussion with Strabo. If we look more closely at the dates of the source texts, it is possible to divide them into five chronologically distinct phases: the Augustan period with Strabo; the second century CE when Demetrios was used by Athenaeus, Pausanias, and Harpocration; late Antiquity (fifth-sixth century CE) with Hesychios and Stephanus of Byzantium; the twelfth century when we have the meager witnesses from Eustathius and Tzetzes; and finally we shall discuss the evidence from the scholia as a category of its own. We may complete this list with the two additional authors, Diogenes Laertios (third century CE) and Photius (ninth century CE), in whose works we have testimonia about Demetrios rather than fragments from his work. Still, their knowledge of Demetrios and his work can tell us something about the way he was used and appreciated in Antiquity.

Each of the aforementioned groups yields, however, a different amount of information, as the number of preserved fragments per author varies greatly, and we shall have to take this into account in our discussion. Indeed, when considering this question not from the chronological point of view, but with regard to the amount of preserved fragments, we have Strabo first with thirty-eight fragments in Biraschi's edition.[4] He is followed by the corpus of the scholia to the *Iliad* with seventeen fragments and by Athenaeus with sixteen.[5] Next comes Stephanus of Byzantium (nine fragments)[6] and the corpus of the scholia to Apollonios Rhodios (six fragments). Three fragments are preserved in Harpocration and two in Hesychios, and again we find two in Eustathius. Finally, there remains a list of five fragments each of which comes from a different author (Pausanias, Tzeztes, the scholia to Pindar, the scholia to Euripides' *Andromache*, and those to Theocritos). This gives a completely different image of the way in which Demetrios was used in Antiquity. The bulk of Demetrios' fragments were preserved in a group of authors who combined, each at a different level, two main topics: geography, defined here as the interpretation of the evidence about mythological elements a given landscape may still bear, on the one hand, and the Homeric poems, the mythological stories they tell, their interpretation, and/or links to other mythological narrations, on the other. These, then, are Strabo and Stephanus of Byzantium, the latter who himself used Strabo

---

[4]   As Biraschi often makes different decisions about the length of the passages included and changes the presentation of them, the number is not the same as in Gaede's edition.

[5]   For Athenaeus, fr. 1, 3, 5–11, 13–16 [Gaede/Biraschi] and fr. 72–74 [Gaede/Biraschi]. For the scholia we keep for the time being to Biraschi's edition and count each occurrence of a scholion even if it is not counted as fragment. However, the presentation of the scholia is problematic in each of the editions.

[6]   This is again the number from Biraschi's edition. We shall see later that in Gaede's edition there are only eight. Fr. 17b [Biraschi] = Stephanus Byzantius s.v. Κάλυμνα (Stephanus Byzantius 350, 12 [Meineke] = Stephanus Byzantius κ 39 [Billerbeck]) does not figure in Gaede's edition.

abundantly,[7] the scholia to the *Iliad* and those to Apollonios Rhodios, and finally Eustathius.[8] Another small group is formed by the lexicographers like Harpocration and Hesychios. A rather independent case is Athenaeus and the use he made of Demetrios in his learned *Deipnosophistai*. A final group contains the authors in whose work Demetrios appears only once by name, and for which we must suppose that the use of this special source may have been rather incidental in comparison to the many other sources these texts contain. These are the two authors Pausanias and Tzeztes and the three corpora of scholia: those to Euripides' *Andromache*, to Pindar, and to Theocritos.

However heterogeneous these groups may be, they still share one common feature, which can also be applied to the evidence from Diogenes Laertios and Photius. They all contain works in which the authors themselves use many sources and display their erudition by quoting many often very specialized works, and this observation can already give us some information about the nature of Demetrios' work and how it was perceived. The authors of these works seem to share the same scholarly working method as Demetrios himself. In the testimonia we have seen that Demetrios was viewed as a rather learned scholar who tended to justify his statements by citing several learned and specialized sources.[9] By doing so, he displayed his erudition and extensive researches, which is exactly what the authors who quote him wanted to achieve for themselves. Therefore, the way in which Demetrios' work was perceived seems to have guided subsequent authors, and we may assume that, since Demetrios' work was that of a scholar himself using many learned and often seldom found sources, it was consulted by other scholars who precisely perceived him in this way.

In order to achieve a more precise idea of this usage, we shall discuss, as suggested above, each source text on its own and see how Demetrios' work was used by its author. It is, however, important to notice that this common feature of being perceived and used as a very specialized and learned source is also one of the difficulties we shall face when discussing the individual authors. Indeed, in most of them we shall see that, even if many of the fragments from Demetrios' work may have been preserved there, the number of quotations from Demetrios is rather small when compared to other sources the authors used. We may often not have enough evidence in the texts to understand the way in which the quoting author used Demetrios' work, or the attribution to Demetrios modern scholars have made for some passages from a given source text may be too hypothetical to use them in our discussion. However, this is not the case

---

[7]   Diller 1975:10–15 and Billerbeck 2008:315.

[8]   He is, however, also a scholar who uses Strabo frequently, as did Stephanus of Byzantium. See again Diller 1975:86–87 and Billerbeck 2008:308.

[9]   See above Section 1.1.3 (pp. 21–23).

with Strabo, the first author we shall discuss. We have enough quotations from Demetrios in his text to reach some conclusions, even though Strabo's text still illustrates the fact that Demetrios of Scepsis is not among the most frequently quoted authors.

2.1.1 Strabo

Looking at the index now available in the last volume of Radt's edition of Strabo's *Geography*,[10] we soon see that Demetrios is not among the authors whose work is most frequently quoted. In this list the first is Homer, from whose poems Strabo quotes more than eight hundred passages. This shows how important Homer and the interpretation of his poems were, even for Strabo, who claims to write a description of the inhabited world and follows a strictly geographical order in the outline of his work.[11] Next comes a group composed by Eratosthenes and Poseidonios whose texts are believed to be quoted a little more than one hundred times.[12] Half as many times (between forty and sixty times) we find works written by Artemidoros, Hipparchos, Ephoros, and Polybios. It is then only in the third group where we find authors for whom we have preserved as many fragments in Strabo's text as for Demetrios (between ten and forty times). This group is composed of Apollodoros of Athens (twenty-seven), Onesicritos (twenty), and Callisthenes (thirteen), if we keep to the authors relevant to Demetrios of Scepsis.[13] Less often quoted than Demetrios' works are those of authors like Eudoxos, Hecataeus, Hellanicos, and Pytheas (between eight and

---

[10] Radt 2011:337–392.

[11] See now Kim 2010:47–84 and Lightfoot 2017:251–262 for a recent treatment of Strabo's attitude toward Homer.

[12] In Radt's list we find 169 entries for Eratosthenes and 102 for Posidonios. For both authors, in most of the cases the entries counted correspond to fragments of previous editions. Some of the fragments are, however, composed of more than one passage from Strabo. Therefore, such a counting allows us to draw only a very approximate picture. It gives, however, an idea of the proportion of quotations from these authors in Strabo's text, and the result, at least, confirms what we know about Strabo and how these two authors influenced Strabo's conception of the ideal geography. See for instance Aujac/Lasserre 1969:xxxvii–xxxix and more recently Dueck 2000:53–58, 62–66, and 180–186.

[13] Here again the numbers correspond to the entries in Radt's list. In some cases, as with Eratosthenes and Posidonios previously, the entry can be composed of more than one passage from Strabo. For Apollodoros, only twenty-two of the twenty-seven listed entries actually come from the *Catalogue of the Ships*. This is also the reason why there are only thirty entries in Radt for Demetrios, whereas the edition of Biraschi counts up to thirty-eight passages from Strabo as fragments from Demetrios (e.g. fr. 62 [Gaede/Biraschi] is composed of two items and T1 [Biraschi] = Strabo 13.1.55 [C609] is the only testimonium about Demetrios from Strabo that is not embedded in a fragment). The additional fragments are those in which the name of Demetrios does not appear, but which have nevertheless been attributed to Demetrios, either by Biraschi or already by Gaede.

ten times). As far as Crates of Mallos and Aristarchos are concerned, Crates' works appear only eight times in Radt's index of passages from other authors quoted by Strabo,[14] and Aristarchos is not listed in this part of Radt's index.[15] Finally, Polemon is quoted twice,[16] and Palaephatos, Hegesianax, and Neanthes of Cyzicos are among those authors for whom only one fragment is preserved in Strabo's text. Moreover, in this last group, all except Polemon are quoted in the immediate context of passages considered as fragments of Demetrios.[17]

This distribution is certainly mainly due to Radt's method of counting occurrences of more or less clear indications to the authors' names or works in Strabo's text, and it tells us a lot about the way modern editors understood Strabo's work, but it can nonetheless give us some initial indications about how Strabo used Demetrios and how this influenced our perception of the scholar. First of all, we can, for instance, see that the ranking Demetrios takes in this list is in accordance with what Strabo himself tells about the way he uses Demetrios. Even if Demetrios is not among the authors at the top of the list, the number of thirty quotations of his name does not contradict Strabo's statement that he used Demetrios frequently (οὗ μεμνήμεθα πολλάκις "whom we mention often")[18] and perhaps also τἄλλα δὲ ὑπολαμβάνομεν, ἢ τά γε πλεῖστα, δεῖν προσέχειν [...] "for the rest, however, or at least for most of it we assume that we have to follow [him/ Demetrios] [...]."[19] Second, we see that in the group of authors Strabo mentions as often as Demetrios we also find Apollodoros of Athens. This fact suggests that Strabo found as much useful information for his own topic in Apollodoros as in

[14] In the collection of fragments by Broggiato 2001, a whole range of passages from Strabo are linked to Crates of Mallos, but among those Broggiato selects as fragments, only Strabo 9.5.18 [C439] is missing. Radt 2011:378 is following here the older editions of Wachsmuth 1860 and Mette 1936.

[15] Aristarchos' name occurs nonethelss eight times througout Strabo's *Geography*. However, according to modern editors, none of these passages can be identified as a fragment of his works, so that Aristarchos does not appear in this part of Radt's index. For an more detailed analysis of these passages, see Trachsel 2017c:263–275.

[16] Strabo 1.2.2 [C15] and Strabo 9.1.16 [C396]. The second passage is only mentioned in Radt's index of proper names (Namensregister, Radt 2011:233), which is distinguished by Radt from the list of fragments from a given author preserved in Strabo (Von Strabo zitierte Stellen anderer Autoren, Radt 2011:337–392).

[17] For Neanthes, Strabo 1.2.38 [C45] (= Demetrios fr. 50 [Gaede/Biraschi]), for Palaephatos, Strabo 12.3.22 [C551] (= Demetrios fr. 45 [Gaede/Biraschi]), and for Hegesianax, Strabo 13.1.27 [C594] (= Demetrios fr. 21 [Gaede/Biraschi]).

[18] T1 [Biraschi] (= Strabo 13.1.55 [C609]).

[19] T4 [Biraschi] (= Strabo 13.1.45 [C603]). Here it is important to remember the fact that the number of thirty corresponds to the quotations of Demetrios' name as figuring in Radt's list. Strabo may indeed also include in his acknowledgment passages in which he follows Demetrios closely, but without giving the scholar's name. Therefore, we should say that there are at least thirty passages in which Strabo uses Demetrios as his source, and there are certainly more than that. But even so, this minimum number does not contradict Strabo's statement.

Demetrios, or that the content of their work was similarly relevant to his own research interests. However, a similar number of quotations from two authors in a source text does not necessarily prove that their works had the same content. However, in our case of Demetrios and Apollodoros, we actually have other elements that may suggest that these numbers are more than a coincidence. First, we may adduce that the testimonia show that Apollodoros made an immediate answer to Demetrios' work, and that, moreover, he often contradicted his fellow scholar in this response.[20] Then, we see that such a thematic closeness between the two authors, as presupposed here, is also suggested when the parts within Strabo's work in which the two authors are quoted are compared. When looking at the distribution of the quotations from the two scholars throughout the books of Strabo's *Geography*, we see that most of the time they appear in the same books. Demetrios' work is adduced, according to modern editors,[21] three times in book 1[22] and four times in book 7.[23] All the other fragments belong to the books on Greece (books 8 to 10)[24] and to those on Asia Minor (books 12 to 14).[25] We have a similar distribution for Apollodoros of Athens, at least for his

---

[20] See T6 [Biraschi] = Strabo 8.3.6 [C339] and T9 [Biraschi] = Strabo 1.2.38 [C45] and previously Section 1.1.3 (pp. 26–27) and Section 1.2.2 (pp. 40–42).

[21] We are well aware that such a distribution depends again on the choices modern scholars made when establishing the collections of the fragments of these authors. We shall follow here Biraschi's edition, which is based on Gaede's choices, for Demetrios of Scepsis. For Apollodoros of Athens, the reference edition is still the collection made by Jacoby in his *Fragmente der griechischen Historiker* (*Die Fragmente der griechischen Historiker* 244).

[22] This means the name appears twice in fr. 50 [Gaede/Biraschi] (= Strabo 1.2.38–40 [C45–47]) and once in fr. 48 [Gaede/Biraschi] (= Strabo 1.3.17 [C58]).

[23] Here the situation is even more complex. The name occurs for sure in two fragments (fr. 46 [Gaede/Biraschi] = Strabo 7, fr. 15a [Radt] and fr. 47 [Gaede/Biraschi] = Strabo 7, fr. 22a [Radt]). In fr. 55b [Biraschi] (= Strabo 7.7.10 [C328]), modern authors conjecture the name of Demetrios in a lacuna of the text. And finally in the two items of fr. 62 [Gaede/Biraschi](= Strabo 7, fr. 20b and fr. 20a [Radt]), the name of Demetrios does not occur. They were therefore dismissed by Radt in his index. However, he counts a piece of fr. 45 [Gaede/Biraschi] (= Strabo 12.3.22 [C550]) as an additional fragment from Demetrios (Strabo 7, fr. 27 [Radt]). According to Baladié 1989:26–27, even more of the passages from book 7 should be attributed to either Apollodoros or Demetrios, especially in those parts of the book where Strabo speaks about regions where either the Trojans or the Achaeans recruited their allies.

[24] We have three fragments with quotations of the name of Demetrios from book 8 (twice in Strabo 8.3.6 [C339] = fr. 55a [Biraschi] or part of fr. 55 [Gaede]; in Strabo 8.3.15 [C344] = fr. 59 [Gaede/Biraschi]; and in Strabo 8.6.15 [C374–375] = fr. 67a [Biraschi] or fr. 67 [Gaede]). The other passages from book 8 counted as fragments are again those without the name of Demetrios. From book 9, we have only one quotation of Demetrios' name (Strabo 9.5.18 [C438–439] = fr. 68 [Gaede/Biraschi]). In book 10, the name of Demetrios occurs five times (once in Strabo 10.2.16 [C456] = fr. 49 [Gaede/Biraschi], three times in Strabo 10.3.19–21 [C472–473] = fr. 61 [Gaede/Biraschi], and once again in Strabo 10.5.19 [C489] = fr. 17a [Biraschi] or part of fr. 17 [Gaede]).

[25] Here we have: one fragment with five quotations of Demetrios' name from book 12 (Strabo 12.3.20–23 [C549–552] = fr. 45 [Gaede/Biraschi]) and again one from book 14 (Strabo 14.5.28 [C680] = fr. 44 [Gaede/Biraschi]). In book 13, there are twelve occurrences of the name of Demetrios

Catalogue of the Ships. His work is considered to be quoted by Strabo in twelve passages in the books about Greece (8 to 10)[26] and in four passages in those about Asia Minor (12 to 14).[27] In the previous books, we have six fragments: three in book 1,[28] one in book 6,[29] and two in book 7.[30] It seems therefore that it is for the description of Greece and Asia Minor that Strabo found the works of our two scholars most useful. This distribution suggests then not only that the two treatises had similar contents, geographical elements about Greece and Asia Minor, which helps us to make sense of Strabo's use of the two authors, but it is also in accordance with other elements from the testimonia. Strabo presented Demetrios as a scholar who was particularly well acquainted with the landscape of the place in which he lived, in other words the Troad.[31] Therefore, it is indeed unsurprising that Strabo used Demetrios as source precisely for the parts of his work that dealt with the places Demetrios knew best. For Apollodoros of Athens we have seen that he was focusing on the Catalogue of the Ships, and it can

---

(including T1 [Biraschi]), but eighteen passages are mentioned as fragments in Biraschi's edition. We do not give here the entire list in the footnote, but the reader may find the exact reference to these passages in Pagani 2006 and in Biraschi 2011.

[26] Seven fragments come from book 10, one, however, without an explicit occurence of Apollodoros' name: Strabo 10.2.10–11 [C453] = *Die Fragmente der griechischen Historiker* 244 F201; Strabo 10.2.16 [C457] = *Die Fragmente der griechischen Historiker* 244 F202; Strabo 10.2.17 [C457] = *Die Fragmente der griechischen Historiker* 244 F178b; Strabo 10.2.21 [C460] = *Die Fragmente der griechischen Historiker* 244 F203; Strabo 10.2.22 [C460] = *Die Fragmente der griechischen Historiker* 244 F204; Strabo 10.3.4 [C464] = *Die Fragmente der griechischen Historiker* 244 F205; Strabo 10.4.3 [C474] = *Die Fragmente der griechischen Historiker* 244 F206. In book 8, there are three fragments: Strabo 8.3.6 [C338] = *Die Fragmente der griechischen Historiker* 244 F181; Strabo 8.6.1 [C368] = *Die Fragmente der griechischen Historiker* 244 F199 and Strabo 8.6.5–6 [C370] = *Die Fragmente der griechischen Historiker* 244 F200. According to Radt 2007:397–398, there could even be a fourth one (Strabo 8.3.12 [C342]). In book 9 there are two fragments: Strabo 9.2.14 [C405] = *Die Fragmente der griechischen Historiker* 244 F168 and Strabo 9.2.40–42 [C416] = *Die Fragmente der griechischen Historiker* 244 F169, where only the title of his treatise on the Catalogue of the Ships is mentioned.

[27] The two fragments from book 12 are: Strabo 12.3.24–25 [C552–553] = *Die Fragmente der griechischen Historiker* 244 F171 (where the name occurs twice), and Strabo 12.3.26 [C553] = *Die Fragmente der griechischen Historiker* 244 F157b (only pronom αὐτῷ, but no full name). His name occurs also in Strabo 12.3.27 [C555], but this has not been counted as a fragment. In book 14 the relevant passages are: Strabo 14.2.28 [C661] = *Die Fragmente der griechischen Historiker* 244 F207 and Strabo 14.5.22–29 [C677–680] = *Die Fragmente der griechischen Historiker* 244 F170 (where the name occurs five times).

[28] Strabo 1.2.24 [C31] = *Die Fragmente der griechischen Historiker* 244 F157e; Strabo 1.2.35 [C 43] = *Die Fragmente der griechischen Historiker* 244 F157f; and Strabo 1.2.37 [C44] = *Die Fragmente der griechischen Historiker* 244 F157d. Apollodoros' name also occurs in Strabo 1.2.38 [C45], but this passage has not been considered as a fragment of his work.

[29] Strabo 6.1.3 [C254] = *Die Fragmente der griechischen Historiker* 244 F167.

[30] Strabo 7.3.6 [C298] = *Die Fragmente der griechischen Historiker* 244 F157a and Strabo 7.7.10 [C328] = *Die Fragmente der griechischen Historiker* 244 F198. Here again, the scholar's name occurs in 7.3.10 [C 303], but the passage is not listed as a fragment.

[31] T4 [Biraschi] = Strabo 13.1.45 [C603]; T5 [Biraschi] = Strabo 13.1.43 [C602]; and T8 [Biraschi] = Strabo 12.3.23 [C552]. See above Section 1.1.2 (pp. 8–9).

therefore be anticipated that he was mentioned more often in the books about Greece, and was, for instance, completely absent from book 13. However, the fact that Strabo quoted elements from both authors about these regions should make us more cautious, and should remind us that the geographical boundaries were certainly not so clear-cut in the two works, and that Strabo could find information about the landscape of Greece in Demetrios and vice versa.[32] Furthermore, we should repeat here that, until now, we were guided in our analysis by Radt's index about passages for which modern scholars agreed about the attribution to a given author. We must, however, acknowledge that there are often important disagreements among modern editors about the number of passages from Strabo they consider as fragments from Demetrios' work. This is due to the fact that they often take into account passages in which the name of our scholar does not appear and for which, therefore, their choices depend on their understanding of the context of the Straboian passage. This is especially so for the part of book 8 about Elis (chapter 3) and the part on the Troad in book 13 (chapter 1).[33] For our discussion here, these elements are, however, only of limited use and cannot provide us with further evidence about the way in which Strabo used the works of the two scholars, as they depend on the choices made by modern editors, who were influenced in their readings by what they already knew about him from the more securely attributed fragments and from the testimonia.[34]

Therefore, in order to investigate further the question of Strabo's use of Demetrios' work, we may turn to the books in which the topic is less obviously linked to those of Demetrios' and Apollodoros' works, and find out what the distribution there may tell us about Strabo's usage of the two authors. Unfortunately, the passages of book 7, in which Demetrios is quoted, are all but one among those transmitted only through the *Chrestomathy and the Vatican Epitome*.[35] Therefore, we have only very indirect access to Strabo's text of this

---

[32] We have already alluded to this briefly in Section 1.2.2 (pp. 40–43). See also Jacoby 1930:778–779 (= commentary to *Die Fragmente der griechischen Historiker* 244 F154–207).

[33] See for instance Baladié 1978:24–27 for book 8. In book 8, it is the question of the localization of Homeric places, such as Ephyra, Pylos, and Bouprasion, which makes Strabo use abundantly the evidence from the two Hellenistic scholars. Further such considerations are found in Schwartz 1894:2868–2869, Bölte 1934:319–347, Atenstädt 1937:378–382, and Bölte 1938:142–160. We may come back to that in Chapter 3 (Sections 3.4.1 and 3.4.2). However, for a more recent survey on the question, but unfortunately without focusing on Strabo's text and its sources, see Kiechle 1960:1–67.

[34] See Jacoby 1957a:viii, Lenfant 2000:315–316, and more succinctly Lenfant 2002:418–419, for the criterion of the name as a selection principle for the creation of a collection of fragments.

[35] Fr. 55b [Gaede/Biraschi] (= Strabo 7.7.10 [C328]) comes from the part of Strabo's book 7 that is still preserved, but the name of Demetrios is not securely attested. All the others come from the fragmentary parts: fr. 46 [Gaede/Biraschi] = Strabo 7, fr. 15a [Radt]; fr. 47 [Gaede/Biraschi]

book, which makes it almost impossible to draw any conclusions about the way he used the two scholars there, so we shall have to rely on the two examples from book 1. It must, however, be mentioned that some recent papyrological findings have proved that Demetrios must have been present as an important source in the lost parts of book 7.[36] Moreover, as the new fragment, quoted in Biraschi's edition as fr. 67b, is also linked to a passage of book 8,[37] there must have been some links between the two books with regard to Demetrios and the use Strabo made of this author in both books. Such a connection is even more likely when we cite the evidence gained through the two passages gathered under fr. 55a and fr. 55b in Biraschi's edition. Both passages deal with the localization of the river Selleis, but the first part belongs to book 8,[38] whereas the second comes from book 7.[39] Furthermore, in fr. 55a [Biraschi], a statement of Apollodoros of Athens is followed immediately by the opposite view given by Demetrios, and this passage is one of those that show the disagreement between the two Hellenistic scholars. From all this, we may infer how important these two Straboian books may have been for our research. However, as mentioned above, the state of preservation of book 7 does not allow us to go further here. Thus, we shall focus on book 1 for the time being.

In book 1, as it is well known, Strabo defends Homer's geographical knowledge against the attacks made mainly by Eratosthenes, and both authors are quoted several times in this book. This is at first sight not surprising, as both authors were also dealing with the geographical content of the Homeric poems, but a closer analysis of the passages will reveal more relevant aspects, particularly when we focus on the places within the discussion where the scholars are quoted. We may begin by noting first that the quotations are not evenly distributed. They belong to two different parts of Strabo's discussion. In the first part, which deals precisely with Strabo's defense of Homer's geographical knowledge, the two scholars are quoted together, moreover in very close proximity. In the second passage, which concerns Strabo's critique of Eratosthenes' geological research, only Demetrios is quoted. They therefore give us two different images of Strabo's use of Demetrios, and we shall analyze them separately.

= Strabo 7, fr. 22a [Radt]; fr. 62 (items 1 and 2) [Gaede/Biraschi] (= Strabo 7, fr. 20b and Strabo 7, fr. 20a [Radt]), and now also Strabo 7, fr. 27 [Radt]. For a new edition of the *Chrestomathy* and the *Vatican Epitome*, see now Radt 2010.

[36] We refer here to P. Köln 1.8 (papyrus 5861). It is quoted as Strabo 7, fr. 11a and fr. 12a [Radt] in Biraschi's edition under her fr. 67b. However, Biraschi quotes the fragment by referring to Baladié's edition (Strabo 7, fr. 20c [Baladié]). For the different editions of the papyrus, see Krebber 1972:204–221, Kramer/Hübner 1976:27–32, and Luppe 1994:115–118.

[37] Strabo 8.6.15 [C374–375] (= fr. 67 [Gaede] or fr.67a [Biraschi]).

[38] Fr. 55a [Biraschi] = Strabo 8.3.6 [C339].

[39] Fr. 55b [Biraschi] = Strabo 7.7.10 [C328].

In the first passage it is not surprising that Strabo mentions the two scholars, as he uses sources who have also dealt with the geographical knowledge of Homer. It is, however, more surprising to see, when looking more closely at the places where Strabo quotes Apollodoros and Demetrios within this discussion, that Demetrios is only quoted at the very end of the discussion and that moreover both scholars are criticized in this section. For Apollodoros of Athens, Strabo's critique occurs in two places. The first is to be found in the discussion about Menelaos' journey.[40] Strabo severely criticizes Apollodoros, who, having compared Homer's geographical knowledge with that of Hesiod and other later poets, concludes that Homer was ignorant on geographical matters.[41] The second is stated, a few lines later, in an independent passage squeezed between the discussion on Charybde and the one about Jason's journey. Strabo reproaches Apollodoros for having criticized Callimachos about his localization of Odysseus' journey.[42] Demetrios is mentioned only after the two statements about Apollodoros in the last part of Strabo's defense of Homer. There, Strabo discusses Jason's journey and then attempts to locate it in the inhabited world.[43] As Strabo shares the conviction of those believing to be able to locate the itinerary of Jason in the inhabited world, he criticizes Demetrios for having claimed that Homer did not know about Jason's expedition. The passage has been quoted as fr. 50 by Gaede and Biraschi,[44] but the quotation actually falls into two parts. First, Strabo criticizes Demetrios on another point. For Strabo, Demetrios has gone too far in his refutation of Neanthes of Cyzicos' theory about the location of the sanctuary of the Mother-goddess of Mount Ida near Cyzicos. We have already spoken about this passage in Chapter 1 in the section on the historical background, and mentioned the political implications the location in Cyzicos of this goddess, who could also be identified with Cybele, could have.[45] Here we see that Strabo singles out Demetrios' reaction in the same way as he criticized just a few lines earlier the over-vigorous critique made by Apollodoros against Callimachos. But in opposition to his treatment of Apollodoros, Strabo develops his objections to Demetrios' position. According to Strabo, Demetrios

---

[40] This part of Strabo's discussion is presented in much detail. It starts with Strabo 1.2.31 [C37] and ends at Strabo 1.2.35 [C43].

[41] Strabo 1.2.35 [C42–43] = *Die Fragmente der griechischen Historiker* 244 F157f.

[42] Strabo 1.2.37 [C44] = *Die Fragmente der griechischen Historiker* 244 F157d. The third quotation of Apollodoros in book 1 occurs a little earlier (Strabo 1.2.24 [C31] = *Die Fragmente der griechischen Historiker* 244 F157e), but it still belongs to the same discussion. Furthermore, the passage has a similar content: Apollodoros reproves Homer for having given topographical indications that have no correspondance to a real landscape.

[43] The discussion starts with the quotation of Demetrios in Strabo 1.2.38 [C48] and extends until the end of chapter 2 (Strabo 1.2.40 [C46]).

[44] Strabo 1.2.38–40 [C45–47].

[45] See above Section 1.3.2 (pp. 57–61).

is not only contradicting Homer's wordings with his position, but also his own statements. In order to prove his stance, Strabo adduces that Demetrios explained, at some point in his work, which neither Strabo—or his source—indicates, that Achilles spared Lemnos in his raids against the Troad because of his kinship with Jason. This kinship can, however, only be explained through Jason's staying in Lemnos during his journey to Colchid. Therefore, concludes Strabo, either Demetrios' statement about Homer's ignoring Jason's journey is wrong or the scholar's explanation of Achilles sparing Lemnos is based on an incorrect assumption. After this first part of his critique, Strabo adds a list of other passages from Homer in which the poet's knowledge of Jason's journey is proved, and concludes his digression by reaffirming that Demetrios' statement is not in accordance with Homer's text. This is the second part of fr. 50 [Gaede/Biraschi], and it corresponds to the second part of Strabo's critique. The passage mainly reaffirms Strabo's conclusion of the first part, but contains an additional allusion to Demetrios' own sources. By expanding his critique, Strabo mentions the fact that Demetrios' position was based on Mimnermos' version of Jason's journey. This further information not only gives us a glimpse of Demetrios' working method, suggesting that Demetrios was using evidence from previous poets and scholars to justify his statements and therefore prove his erudition, but also shows how much Strabo valued evidence that came from Demetrios' work. It seems that even when criticizing Demetrios, Strabo still analyzes the scholar's statements carefully and thinks Demetrios' work worthy of being quoted more extensively. Such behavior is again in accordance with what Strabo has told us about Demetrios in the testimonia: Strabo considers Demetrios as a great expert in his field to whom he owes much.[46]

However, this treatment of Demetrios is not only in accordance with Strabo's own judgment of the Hellenistic scholar, but also with more general principles that the geographer uses for the selection of his sources. In the introductory section, for instance, Strabo first declares that he will only mention the geographers he considers as being of some value. Indeed, when justifying his attitude towards Eratosthenes, he claims that:

εἰ δ᾽ ἀναγκασθησόμεθά που τοῖς αὐτοῖς ἀντιλέγειν οἷς μάλιστα ἐπακολουθοῦμεν κατ᾽ ἄλλα, δεῖ συγγνώμην ἔχειν· οὐ γὰρ πρόκειται πρὸς ἅπαντας ἀντιλέγειν, ἀλλὰ τοὺς μὲν πολλοὺς ἐᾶν – οἷς μηδὲ ἀκολουθεῖν ἄξιον –, ἐκείνους δὲ διαιτᾶν οὓς ἐν τοῖς πλείστοις κατωρθωκότας ἴσμεν· ἐπεὶ οὐδὲ πρὸς ἅπαντας φιλοσοφεῖν ἄξιον, πρὸς Ἐρατοσθένη δὲ καὶ Ποσειδώνιον καὶ Ἵππαρχον καὶ Πολύβιον καὶ ἄλλους τοιούτους καλόν.

---

[46] See T4 [Biraschi] = Strabo 13.1.45 [C603]; T5 [Biraschi] = Strabo 13.1.43 [C602]; and T6 [Birasch] = Strabo 8.3.6 [C339].

But, when we shall be compelled to contradict at some point those very ones we follow most closely for all other things, we should be excused. Indeed we do not intend to contradict all, but to leave aside most of them—those who are not at all worthy to be followed—, and to discuss those we know are right most of the time. For it is not worth engaging in conversation with everyone, but it is honorable to do so with Eratosthenes, Poseidonios, Hipparchos, Polybios and others of such quality.

Strabo 1.2.1 [C14]

According to this principle, the fact that Strabo mentions both Demetrios and Apollodoros in his discussion suggests that he considers them as two scholars worthy of being mentioned; otherwise he would not have bothered to do so. Therefore, he takes them as his guides for some of his topics, as he does with Eratosthenes; but, again as with Eratosthenes, they are not beyond critique.

For the more detailed critique he addresses to Eratosthenes, Strabo announces that he will do so in a moderate way, not exaggerating as did Polemon of Ilion when he claimed that Eratosthenes never visited Athens.[47] This is exactly the attitude that Strabo takes in the passage mentioned above. We have seen that, despite the credit Strabo gives to Demetrios' statements, he was described as a scholar who was too excessive in his judgments against Neanthes, and was criticized for this particular behavior, as were others like Apollodoros just a few lines earlier, and, more prominently, Eratosthenes himself.

These factors help us better to understand how Strabo made use of Demetrios as one of his sources. We see that Strabo adduces Demetrios only for very specific parts of his discussion. It is only in the last part of his long defense of Homer, when he is discussing the link between Jason's journey and the journey of Odysseus, that Demetrios is quoted, even after Apollodoros. When he is mentioned, he is, however, treated as a worthy scholar even if he may be criticized for his attitude towards other scholars. This critique is not only directed against Demetrios himself,[48] but is to be seen as a more general attitude that Strabo takes when making his way through the sources at his disposal. He strongly disapproves of scholars who are too excessive in their critique. This may also apply to scholars whose achievements he appreciates, such as Eratosthenes and Apollodoros, besides Demetrios himself.

---

[47] Strabo 1.2.2 [C15] = *Fragmenta historicorum graecorum* III, p. 130 (see Preller 1838:86 who quotes the passage as evidence for Polemon's writing against Eratosthenes, but does not consider it as a fragment).

[48] For a modern discussion about the way Strabo uses Demetrios, see Leaf 1917–1918:23–47, Leaf 1923:xxxvii–xlvii, and more recently Biraschi 2000:55–59 and Nicolai 2005–2006:57–59.

However, we may obtain even further indications of the way Strabo used our scholar's work if we turn now to the second passage from book 1, particularly as this second passage belongs to a completely different context. It is no longer related to Apollodoros of Athens, as only Demetrios is quoted there, however still in connection with other scholars, as we shall see. Indeed, this second passage from book 1, fr. 48 [Gaede/Biraschi],[49] appears in Strabo's critique against Eratosthenes' research on geological phenomena. In this discussion, Demetrios' statement about the changes happening to the two springs of the Scamandros is quoted. However, if we look again in more detail at the structure of Strabo's discussion[50] and at the place within this discussion where Demetrios is mentioned, we see that he is quoted once again in a specific part. Having discussed and criticized in great detail Eratosthenes' theories on geological changes, for which the power of water is held responsible, Strabo comes to a part of the discussion where he mentions other natural phenomena able to change substantially the shape of a landscape, and he gives a list of examples of places where such changes happened. He even seems to leave Eratosthenes for a moment and comes back to him only in the last two paragraphs of chapter 3.[51] In this list of examples, he quotes, among others, Demetrios' example about the geological changes in the Troad and their consequences for the Scamandros and its springs. However, when looking at where Demetrios' example occurs within this list, we see that even though the whole passage appears at the end of Strabo's discussion against Eratosthenes, the quotation of Demetrios appears rather at the beginning of the list, just after the example from Poseidonios. Demetrios seems therefore to have a kind of priority within Strabo's exposition. This special treatment of the Hellenistic scholar is also underlined by the way Strabo formulates the evidence from Demetrios' work. The geographer not only mentions the name of the source for this example, which he does not always do with the subsequent examples on his list, but also gives a positive statement about his source and more precisely about the way Demetrios composed his report (οἰκείως παρατεθέντα).[52] Furthermore, the passage taken from Demetrios is among the longest and most elaborated examples on Strabo's list. Strabo not only quotes the Homeric lines under discussion,[53] but also gives substantial parts of Demetrios' line of argument. In particular, as in the first passage from book 1 we discussed above, Strabo again mentions Demetrios' source, as

[49]   Strabo 1.3.17 [C58].
[50]   Strabo's refutation of Eratosthenes extends over the whole of chapter 3 (Strabo 1.3.1–23 [C47–62]), but the part that interests us here concerns the discussion about the natural causes that changed the form of the landscape (Strabo 1.3.16–20 [C57–61]).
[51]   Strabo 1.3.22–23 [C61–62].
[52]   Strabo 1.3.17 [C58] (= part of fr. 48 [Gaede/Biraschi]).
[53]   *Iliad* 22.147–151.

we learn that Demetrios seems to have relied on the research that Democles[54] carried out in his discussion about the geological changes in Asia Minor.[55] This is in sharp contrast with the subsequent examples. None of them, except the one about Pharos and Egypt, for which Strabo can rely on his own experience, are as elaborated as the one from Demetrios. Most extend only over a few lines and, if sources are quoted, only their names are given and Strabo does not expand upon their statements. This manifest emphasis on Demetrios' example may then not only help us to define Strabo's use of his work, but also may reveal several aspects of Strabo's perception of the scholar and his achievements. On the one hand, we may, for instance, suggest that, because of his overall aim to defend Homer's geographical accuracy, Strabo may have thought that the example about Homeric geography (the two springs of the Scamandros) that he found in Demetrios' work was worthy of more expanded consideration than those of the others scholars. Furthermore, Strabo's esteem for Demetrios may have been such that he wanted to single him out next to Poseidonios. Finally, as a combination of the two statements just mentioned and perhaps more independently from Strabo's own point of view, we may assume that Strabo's emphasis on Demetrios could also bear witness to the fact that Demetrios was such an expert on these topics that Strabo simply found most of the information he needed there.

There is, however, more to be said about this list and about what it may reveal with regard to the place Strabo gave to Demetrios' work while elaborating his *Geography*. For this we must expand our considerations and focus for a moment on the way modern scholars understood the passage and used it in their own research on Demetrios of Scepsis. In particular we must focus on Gaede's choice to introduce a further passage from this list into his collection of fragments from Demetrios. This additional passage concerns a much later example dealing with Asteria (the Homeric Asteris), a place in the neighborhood of Ithaca, about which Strabo says that it was first, in the time of the Homeric poems, an island that later became a promontory. Gaede believes that this passage too belongs to Demetrios' work and counts it as part of his fr. 49.[56] He is entirely justified in this, because Asteria/Asteris is mentioned again in book 10 when Strabo describes the surroundings of Ithaca. There he quotes again

---

[54]   For details about Democles, see Fowler 2000:78 and Fowler 2013:369 and 648.

[55]   Indeed, fr. 48 [Gaede/Biraschi] is, again, as fr. 50 [Gaede/Biraschi] discussed above, one of the fragments in which Demetrios' sources have been preserved. See above 1.1.3 (pp. 21–23).

[56]   Strabo 1.3.18 [C59]. However, this passage is actually not numbered as a fragment by Gaede. It is the passage from book 10 (Strabo 10.2.16 [C456]) that is counted as fr. 49 [Gaede/Biraschi]. The passage from book 1 is only printed as a parallel passage. See Gaede 1880:46. In Biraschi's edition even less weight is given to the passage. She does not add it to her collection, but mentions it in her commentary (Biraschi 2011, commentary ad fr. 49).

the Homeric lines under discussion (*Odyssey* 4.844 and 846–847) and explicitly mentions Demetrios for having asserted that the place had changed since
Homeric times and no longer fitted the Homeric description.[57] The statement is
directly opposed to that of Apollodoros, who claims, on the contrary, that the
place is still preserved in the shape described by Homer. Knowing the passage
from book 10, it is then very easy to follow Gaede and attribute the passage from
book 1 about Asteria/Asteris to Demetrios too. It is therefore very likely that
Demetrios treated the case of Asteria, and its Homeric name of Asteris, some-
where in his work, and that his considerations about this topic then found their
way into Strabo's *Geography*.

However, precisely because the elements of Demetrios' work are present
in two different forms, the two passages under discussion may reveal several
features either about Strabo's way of using his sources or about the steps we
have to consider between the statement in Demetrios' work and its reuse in
Strabo. Or, at the very least, it allows us to see all the possibilities for explaining
how a passage from Demetrios' work may have been accessible to Strabo. The
fact that in one place Strabo quotes his source but at the other does not proves
that Strabo used more sources than he mentions, an assumption already made
by Karl Lehrs in 1865.[58] For Demetrios of Scepsis, as for any other source used by
Strabo, this means that there are more elements from Strabo's *Geography* that
may belong to his work than those for which Demetrios is quoted, and this is the
basis on which Gaede constructed his edition. However, this is also one of the
main difficulties one has to face with Strabo's text, and his peculiar way of incor-
porating his sources into his text creates much disagreement among modern
editors when it comes to attributing parts of it to a given ancient author. For our
discussion here this means that, even if Demetrios' work must have been present
in the background throughout Strabo's exposition of the list of examples about
physical changes, and despite the fact that Strabo may have followed closely
Demetrios' own wording about the issue, there was still a certain independence
from Strabo with regard to his source. Indeed, the fact that the Hellenistic
scholar is not named in the second passage could be a sign that Strabo may have
worked independently of any of his sources and introduced pieces of information from several of them in his own exposition, presenting a text in which his
own experiences and thoughts could be interwoven with those of his sources
without making this explicit to his readers. Furthermore, the context also shows
in how many different ways Strabo could treat various aspects from Demetrios'
work. The difference between the example about the springs of the Scamandros

---

[57] Strabo 10.2.16 [C 456] (= fr. 49 [Gaede/Biraschi]).
[58] Lehrs 1865:244. We shall return to this later in Section 3.2.1.

and the one about Asteria/Asteris seems to indicate that among the questions about Homeric geography that were, taken together, more important for Strabo than other matters, there was also a kind of hierarchy, especially with regard to Demetrios. The question about the localization of the two springs of the Scamandros, involving the landscape of the *Iliad*, seems to be described in more detail and linked to Demetrios more openly than the one about Asteria/Asteris, which belongs to the landscape of the *Odyssey*. The prioritization may then also help us to improve our understanding of how subjects from outside the Troad could have entered a work that seems to have taken as its starting point the Trojan Catalogue. It seems that Demetrios' considerations about the geological changes occurring in the Troad began with the question about the two springs of the Scamandros, which is closely linked to issues about the Homeric landscape of the *Iliad*, and then extended to other examples, one among them being Asteria/Asteris.

Moving to the second aspect of our discussion, the different ways in which Demetrios' work may have been accessible to Strabo, we must first acknowledge that the discussion of the passage from book 1 and its counterpart in book 10 reveals the complexity of the situation rather than provides any answers to our questions. It is clearly stated in the passage from book 10 that Apollodoros' opinion contradicted Demetrios' statement, but the formulation leaves two possibilities open: either Apollodoros contradicted Demetrios in his own work, or his statements, given in a more independent way in his work, were later placed in opposition to those of Demetrios by a subsequent scholar. This may have been Strabo himself, if he had both works at his disposal when composing this part of his work, or by his source, if we consider the hypothesis that there was an intermediary source between the two Hellenistic scholars and Strabo. Modern scholars have suggested this second hypothesis, at least for the passage from book 1 under discussion here. They believe that Strabo did not take the elements attributed to Demetrios directly from his work, but found them in an intermediary source that has been identified, for this passage, with Poseidonios.[59] Apollodoros of Athens has also been suggested as such an intermediary source between Demetrios and Strabo, for instance by Niese in the nineteenth century.[60] His claims have, however, been dismissed by Gaede,[61] and we shall discuss this controversy in more detail in Chapter 3. The question,

---

[59] See Aujac/Lasserre 1969:159 and 211. But this hypothesis is not admitted by Biraschi 2011, commentary ad fr. 48. For a more critical approach on the question about the presence of Poseidonios as source for Strabo, see also Floratos 1972:71–77. In this book the emphasis is, however, on the first two chapters of Strabo's introduction ([C1–47] = 1.1.1–1.2.40 [C1–47]), not on the third one.

[60] Niese 1877:303–304.

[61] Gaede 1880:3–4.

however, remains open for other authors who could have been the source of Strabo, but who have not been so closely analyzed by modern scholars as Apollodoros has been by Niese. For our passage here, it is indeed extremely difficult to decide whether Strabo used a secondary source, or if he had Demetrios' work at his disposal, and if so, whether he found there only the examples about the springs of the Scamandros and about Asteria/Asteris or a more complete list of examples that he then reproduced in his work. We simply do not have enough evidence for any of the three hypotheses. The fact that the passage just before the example about Asteria/Asteris has been attributed to Artemidoros, even though Strabo does not quote the name of the author,[62] may, however, suggest that Strabo used several sources for the composition of his list, some of them being even later than Demetrios. The situation therefore seems much more complex than previous scholars thought.

There is, however, one last aspect of these passages that should be noted here and that allows us to return to the first passage from book 1. As discussed above—and this applies precisely also to fr. 50 [Gaede/Biraschi], the passage about Neanthes of Cyzicos, which was our first example of book 1—Strabo reports Demetrios' statement about the two springs of the Scamandros in such detail that he also mentions Demetrios' sources. These two passages are certainly not the only ones in which Strabo does so,[63] but it is worth noting that in both passages from book 1 this is the case. This may perhaps suggest that, for the issues Strabo dealt with in book 1, he had a particularly close look at Demetrios' work, and that he may have showed this not so much by the number of quotations as in book 13, for instance, but by the longer quotations he gave.

We have seen in all the passages discussed, not only those from book 1, that Demetrios is perceived by Strabo as a specialized scholar whom he uses, most of the time, for the subjects on which he was considered an expert. Strabo did this either by quoting him many times, as in book 13 for instance, or perhaps, as has just been shown in book 1, by expanding the elements from Demetrios more than those from other scholars. This is, moreover, in accordance with what Strabo himself says about Demetrios. When Strabo speaks about the Hellenistic scholar, he considers him as an expert in his domain, worthy of being used as guide. However, Strabo could also depart from Demetrios' opinion, especially

---

[62] The passage has been associated with Artemidoros fr. 56 [Stiehe] = Stephanus Byzantius s.v. Ἀρτέμιτα (= Stephanus Byzantius 128, 8 [Meineke] or Stephanus Byzantius α 462 [Billerbeck]). For a recent discussion of the link between the two passages, see Billerbeck 2009:68 and for the edition of Artemidoros, see Stiehle 1856.

[63] See for instance fr. 26 [Gaede/Biraschi] = Strabo 13.1.36 [C599]; fr. 44 [Gaede/Biraschi] = Strabo 14.5.28 [C680]; and fr. 61 [Gaede/Biraschi] = Strabo 10.3.19–21 [C472–473]. Furthermore, in fr. 45 [Gaede/Biraschi] (= Strabo 12.3.20–23 [C550–552]), Strabo not only mentions Demetrios' sources, but also quotes elements from these works.

when the scholar's judgment about one of his fellow scholars is not compatible with Strabo's own principles about how to use his sources. We have also seen that Demetrios falls into the same category of authors as Apollodoros of Athens, and both were used, or at least mentioned, more or less the same number of times, moreover in the same parts of Strabo's *Geography*. This could indicate how close the two works must have been, even if some individualities may have existed for each of the works. Apollodoros is quoted more often in the books about Greece, whereas Demetrios is quoted more in those about Asia Minor. Finally, while discussing the second occurrence of Demetrios in book 1 we have also seen how many different ways Strabo could use his sources. He could quote them explicitly and give, for instance, parts of Demetrios' line of argument. He could, however, also use only the information taken from Demetrios without giving the source's name. Furthermore, it has been hypothezised by modern authors that Strabo may have found elements from Demetrios in other sources, such as Posidonios or Apollodoros of Athens, which would render our access to Demetrios even more indirect.

Still, even with all these difficulties, we have also seen that we are in rather a good position when analyzing Strabo's text with regard to his usage of Demetrios as one of his sources. Strabo is indeed, as we have highlighted in our discussion, a scholar who mentions some of his methodological principles, and we can therefore judge from this whether he kept to them during his research, and what this could mean for the sources he uses, particularly for Demetrios of Scepsis. Furthermore, as some testimonia about Demetrios are preserved in Strabo's text, we are also able to compare his own statement about Demetrios with the way he uses the pieces of information taken from Demetrios and with their actual content. This will unfortunately not be the case with most of the other authors we will be dealing with in this chapter. This applies already to Athenaeus, the next author we shall analyze, even though there are, proportionally speaking, many fragments from Demetrios in his work. We have, for instance, no testimonia from Athenaeus about Demetrios, and even though he occasionally states his judgment about the authors used,[64] this does not apply to Demetrios of Scepsis. We shall therefore rely only on our analysis in order to understand what the presence of Demetrios in Athenaeus' text may yield about the Hellenistic scholar, his work, and about the way the book was used and the scholar appreciated by Athenaeus.

---

[64] For some reflections about Athenaeus' judgments on historians, see Zecchini 2007:21–24. Indeed, Demetrios is often classified into the group of historians by modern scholars who are dealing with Athenaeus' sources, as Athenaeus himself qualified Demetrios as συγγραφεύς, a term he uses for other historians. See Athenaeus 15.697d (= fr. 13 [Gaede/Biraschi] and Zecchini 2007:20). For the difficulties linked to the words Atheneaus uses for historians, see e.g. Bouvier 2007:307.

2.1.2 Athenaeus

In Athenaeus, sixteen fragments of Demetrios' work are preserved.[65] This is again an important proportion in the collection of fragments of Demetrios,[66] but with regard to the number of authors quoted in Athenaeus it is a rather small amount.[67] In Athenaeus, the quotations of comic poets come first, with 260 occurrences for passages coming just from comic plays dated to the fifth-fourth century BCE.[68] Then we have the rather heterogeneous group of historians,[69] with, for instance, sixty-four quotations from Xenophon and eighty from Theopompos.[70] These are extremely telling numbers to compare with those for Demetrios, and they show how seldom his name actually appears in the *Deipnosophistai*. However, to get a more accurate picture, we should put these numbers in perspective by taking into account other authors mentioned in our discussion about Strabo. For instance, according to the list of Russo 2001,[71] we find twenty-eight fragments from Apollodoros of Athens and one testimonium about him in Athenaeus, and among these fragments only one belongs to the *Catalogue of the Ships*.[72] This is slightly greater when compared to the number of fragments we have from Demetrios in Athenaeus, but it is quite similar to the number of times we found the name of Apollodoros of Athens in Strabo, where we had twenty-seven occurrences of the scholar's name.[73] Another interesting case is that of Polemon of Ilion, for whom the situation is quite different with regard to the way he is used in Strabo and Athenaeus. He was quoted only twice in Strabo,[74] much less then Demetrios, whereas in Athenaeus he is

---

[65] Fr. 1, 3, 5–11, 13–16 [Gaede/Biraschi], and fr. 72–74 [Gaede/Biraschi].

[66] Ragone 2009:661 estimates it to be a little more than a fifth.

[67] Lenfant 2007:13 mentions the number of 2500 works from which the quotation in Athenaeus come. (This number is also given by Maisonneuve 2007a:74 and by Jacob 2004b:134: both refer to a statement Gulick made in the context of his Loeb edition from 1927. It is, however, difficult today to find this statement and to verify on what basis it was made.) In Russo 2001:1887–1987 there is a list of authors quoted in Athenaeus that can provide a similar tool to the list of Radt 2011:337–392 for Strabo.

[68] This is the number given by Sidwell 2000:137.

[69] See Sidwell 2000:136–152 and Quaglia 2001:611–633 for comic poets. For the historians, see Zecchini 1989:25–194, Zecchini 2007:19–28, and Wilkins 2007:36–38.

[70] These are the approximate numbers given by Maisonneuve 2007a:76 and 103–106. For Theopompos, see also Chávez Reino/Ottone 2007:142–146.

[71] Russo 2001:1898.

[72] Athenaeus 3.82b, which is a very short mention of a village called Sidous (Σιδοῦς) near Corinth. There are, however, two passages (Athenaeus 9.483a and Athenaeus 14.663c) in Russo's list that do not refer to Jacoby's edition (*Die Fragmente der griechischen Historiker* 244).

[73] Trachsel 2017c:264.

[74] See above Section 2.1.1 (p. 70). Strabo 1.2.2 [C15] and Strabo 9.1.16 [C396]. See further *Fragmenta historicorum graecorum* III, p. 116 and p. 130 and Preller 1838:35 and 86.

mentioned up to forty-eight times, according to Zecchini.[75] This is also the case for Neanthes of Cyzicos. He is quoted eight times in Athenaeus, but, as we have seen, only once in Strabo, moreover in the context of a fragment of Demetrios. For Onesicritos and Callisthenes, who were quoted, as was Apollodoros of Athens, approximately the same number of times as Demetrios by Strabo, the situation is different again. Onesicritos is not mentioned at all in Athenaeus, and Callisthenes only five times. Finally, for the authors who are mentioned less often than Demetrios, Palaephatos is mentioned, as in Strabo, only once by Athenaeus, whereas Hegesianax's name occurs three times. With such numbers, as with those from Strabo, it now becomes interesting to take a closer look at the distribution of the quotations of Demetrios within the work of Athenaeus and to find out if we could learn something from this about the way Athenaeus used or appreciated Demetrios' work.

An interesting starting point for such an analysis is fr. 8 [Gaede/Biraschi].[76] Here Athenaeus not only introduces the quotation in an unusual way compared to the other fragments, but also quotes it at a special place in the outline of his work. Indeed, just before the fragment, in Athenaeus 14.643e, there is an interruption of the narration that most likely brings us back to the level of the frame story, as Atheneaus himself seems to address Timocrates.[77] Before that, Pontianos had given a long speech about desserts, and afterwards, we find two catalogues of cakes.[78] In between these two large sections we have the passage in which Demetrios is quoted. The overall mood of this passage seems to be a kind of justification of the value given to the lists of cakes that follows. The narrator presents several attitudes that people can have toward cakes, and clearly puts himself among the scholars who are very serious about this subject. He starts, for instance, with an example about Callimachos, who is said to have even mentioned books about cakes in his *Pinakes*, and he clearly reproves Xanthippe, who smashed a cake Alcibiades had sent her, therefore showing little consideration, but with regard to the physical object of a cake rather than to any scholarly theme linked to it. Furthermore, by adding the lines from the comic poet Plato about someone, probably a divinity, complaining about having been deprived of cakes for one entire year, the narrator shows that cakes, just like

---

[75] Zecchini 1989:227–228. Unfortunately, he only gives the number without enumerating the passages. In Russo's list, there are three passages that have been added to Preller's edition where forty-five passages are enumerated (the missing passages are Athenaeus 4.140b–d, Athenaeus 10.416b–c, and Athenaeus 12. 541b). See also Zecchini 1989:224–235 for further considerations about the two authors, Demetrios and Polemon.

[76] Athenaeus 14.644a.

[77] This is the interpretation given by Ceccarelli 2000:285–286.

[78] Athenaeus 14.640d–643e for the part attributed to Pontianos and Athenaeus 14.644c–647c and 647c–648a for the two catalogues.

frankincense and entrails, can be longed for. Then comes the quotation from Demetrios of Scepsis:

ἀλλὰ μὴν οὐδὲ τῆς κώμης ἀμνήμων εἰμὶ ἣν Πλακοῦντά φησι καλεῖσθαι Δημήτριος ὁ Σκήψιος ἐν δωδεκάτῳ Τρωικοῦ Διακόσμου, τῶν Ὑποπλακίων Θηβῶν φάσκων αὐτὴν ἀπέχειν σταδίους ἕξ.

But for sure, nor do I forget the village that Demetrios says, in Book 12 of his Trojan Catalogue, was called *Plakous*, explaining that it was six stades away from the hypoplacian Thebes.

Athenaeus 14.644a

And finally after a few lines where someone, most probably the narrator, gives some indication about the spelling of the word *Plakous*, we have a final quotation from the poet Alexis about the cakes from Parion, which were of particular quality, before the first catalogue begins.

The whole passage, and in particular the reference to Callimachos, seems therefore to be a way of giving a special dimension to the topic the narrator is dealing with, or the performance that he or his protagonist are about to give by enumerating the two catalogues that follow. Such self-reflective statements are not uncommon before the relating of a catalogue,[79] and it has been suggested that, by referring here to Callimachos, Athenaeus wants to suggest that the catalogues of the cakes, and more so his *Deipnosophistai*, as a work on banquets where cakes may play an important role, could have a claim for literary status.[80] Christian Jacob underlines further the closeness between the banquets where dishes are presented (παρατίθεσθαι) on plates (*pinakes*) and the literary conversations held during the banquets where quotations are adduced (παρατίθεσθαι) according to quoting methods and utensils, such as, for instance, the *Pinakes* from Callimachos.[81]

In such a context, if our interpretation is correct, it becomes interesting to find out what the occurrence of a fragment from Demetrios' work could mean, and how it could help us to understand the status Demetrios had for Athenaeus. For such an approach, it is first important to see that Demetrios seems to have been quoted alongside Callimachos as someone who has shown, in the eyes of the narrator, an appropriate attitude towards the topic under discussion.

---

[79] Perceau 2002:23–28 and 153–164, and for Athenaeus see in particular also Athenaeus 13.555a–b.

[80] This is a reading suggested by Ceccarelli 2000:285–286. She quotes two other passages where Callimachos' *Pinakes* are quoted and where such a meaning could be underlying (Athenaeus 6.244a and 13.585b).

[81] Jacob 2001:l. For the verb παρατίθεσθαι used for introducing quotations, see also Svenbro 2004:274–275 and Jacob 2004a:167–168.

After all, he did not consider it unworthy to mention a place called *Plakous* and consider it in his work on the same level as other places such as the Homeric Thebes-under-Placos and probably many others. Second, when focusing on the verb Athenaeus uses to introduce the quotation, we may also cite the fact that he seems to single out his own act of quoting Demetrios, as he says that he will not forget the evidence from Demetrios (οὐδὲ ... ἀμνήμων).[82] Such a choice of vocabulary, even if the verbs μιμνῄσκεσθαι/μνημονεύειν are certainly not uncommon to introduce quotations,[83] could suggest that Athenaeus considers the quotation of Demetrios' work as a kind of performance.[84] He was not a very well-known author, and so to have thought of him in the discussion may have been regarded as a special sign of erudition. In order to strengthen this assumption, it is perhaps worth mentioning that it has been shown that memory had an important position in the work of Athenaeus,[85] and we could also adduce here the fact that memory and its importance for the performer is often alluded to in the context of the enumeration of a catalogue.[86] Finally, such an interpretation would also help us to highlight a feature that is common to several of the other fragments from Demetrios' work quoted in Athenaeus.

Indeed, when analyzing the context in which the other quotations of Demetrios occur, we see that they are almost always found at the end of a list. This could suggest that several of the quotations were meant to be perceived as a special performance or as a kind of comprehensiveness that was reached in the exposition or documentation of a topic, if the list of quotations about a theme had been extended to such remote and rare works as that of Demetrios of Scepsis.[87] This is the case with fr. 1 [Gaede/Biraschi],[88] in which the example taken from Demetrios about the Spartan feats of the Carneia is mentioned at the end of the list of feasts in Sparta before the topic moves to feasts in Crete; with fr. 3 [Gaede/Biraschi],[89] occurring at the end of an enumeration of cheeses;

---

[82] The most common formula of introduction of a quotation in Athenaeus is: [author's name] + [φησί/γράφει] + [quotation]. This schema comes from Jacob 2000:92. For Demetrios, eleven out of the sixteen quotations are introduced with this formula (ten with the verb φησί and one with the verb ἱστορεῖ).

[83] See Too 2000:121–122 who quotes as one of her examples our passage here and also Jacob 2000:108–110.

[84] See also Jacob 2004a:168–174 who defines the quotations as a game in which the goal would be to cover a maximum portion of literature and/or of a library by starting from a single element such as an author, a text, or a quotation.

[85] See Jacob 2001:lxxi–lxxxiii.

[86] Bouvier 2002:135–137 and in more detail Minchin 2001:73–99.

[87] For the idea of memory as a performance, see Jacob 2001:lxxv–lxxx and Jacob 2004a:162–163.

[88] Athenaeus 4.141e–f. For this passage, this final position in the development of the topic at hand has already been noticed by Bruit/Schmitt-Pantel 1986:209.

[89] Athenaeus 14.658b.

with fr. 5 [Gaede/Biraschi],[90] in which the last examples of gluttons come from Demetrios of Scepsis; and with fr. 6 and fr. 13 [Gaede/Biraschi],[91] following each other at the end of the discussion about the classification of poems and songs. This is also true for the two fragments about Hegesianax (fr. 7 and fr. 9 [Gaede/Biraschi]).[92] One appears among the final examples at the end of a discussion about different sorts of entertainments accompanying a banquet, even if it is not among the very last examples, whereas in the other the anecdote about Hegasianax eating figs is at the end of the section dealing with figs. Fragment 10 [Gaede/Biraschi] and fr. 14 [Gaede/Biraschi][93] are again, like fr. 6 and fr. 13, quoted together at the end of a list of cooking utensils. Fragment 11 [Gaede/Biraschi][94] occurs at the end of a list of eels, whereas fr. 15 [Gaede/Biraschi][95] occurs at the end of a list of shellfish. Finally, fr. 16 [Gaede/Biraschi][96] is at the end of a list of wine-pourers, and fr. 72 [Gaede/Biraschi][97] is quoted at the end of the list about people drinking only water. Only two fragments, besides fr. 8 [Gaede/Biraschi], which we mentioned at the beginning, do not fit this pattern. These are fr. 73 [Gaede/Biraschi][98] and fr. 74 [Gaede/Biraschi].[99] Fragment 73 [Gaede/Biraschi] comes from book 4, which also has a rather peculiar position with regard to Demetrios, as five out of the sixteen fragments come from book 4. We may assume that this may have affected, in one way or another, the distribution of the quotations from Demetrios' work in that book, even if we may not be able to explain this accumulation of quotations yet. When focusing, for instance, on fr. 73 [Gaede/Biraschi] in particular, we see that its context unfortunately does not help us to go any further here. Demetrios is quoted for a story about a Corinthian man called Aithiops who accompanied Archias on his trip, which led to the foundation of Syracuse.[100] The episode is mentioned in the middle of a section in which Ulpian speaks about spendthrifts and profligates.[101] Then

---

[90] Athenaeus 8.346c.

[91] Fr. 6 [Gaede/Biraschi] = Athenaeus 15.697c and fr. 13 [Gaede/Biraschi] = Athenaeus 15.697d.

[92] Fr. 7 [Gaede/Biraschi] = Athenaeus 4.155b and fr. 9 [Gaede/Biraschi] = Athenaeus 3.80d. Here again for fr. 7 [Gaede/Biraschi] coming from book 4, Bruit/Schmitt-Pantel 1986:216~217 describe the context in which it appears as a kind of final heterogenous passage where Athenaeus wants to add everything that is still to be said about the topic, for the sake of completeness, before moving on to the next section.

[93] Fr. 10 [Gaede/Biraschi] = Athenaeus 4.173f–174a and fr. 14 [Gaede/Biraschi] = Athenaeus 4.174a.

[94] Athenaeus 7.300d.

[95] Athenaeus 3.91c.

[96] Athenaeus 10.425c.

[97] Athenaeus 2.44e.

[98] Athenaeus 4.167d.

[99] Athenaeus 6.236c.

[100] The story is told in Strabo 6.2.4 [C269–270] and in Pausanias 5.7.3. However, none of them mentions our Aithiops.

[101] Athenaeus 4.165d–169a.

follows a rather long discussion that Aemilianus starts about the cook's utensils and about the different names and functions associated either with the preparation of food before a banquet or with the serving of it during the meal.[102] This long section is only interrupted after the next two quotations of Demetrios (fr. 10 and fr. 14 [Gaede/Biraschi]) in Athenaeus 4.174a, when some music coming from a hydraulic organ in the neighborhood is heard, and the conversation switches to this theme and several instruments are discussed. The situation is a little different with fr. 74 [Gaede/Biraschi], even if the quotation occurs again in the middle of a discussion that goes on well beyond the quotation of Demetrios.[103] Indeed, when analyzing the context of the fragment in more detail, we see that the fragment takes a rather particular position in the outline of the discussion. With two other quotations it stands apart from the rest of the discussion, as it is more focused on the question of the origin of the word under discussion than on its use, and the short section marks a kind of transition between the part dealing with the ancient, often different, use of the word παράσιτος and the list of authors using the word in their poems that follow our passage. Our section starts with an attack against Carystios of Pergamon,[104] who claims that Alexis invented the role of the parasite for drama. His statement is proved to be wrong, as evidence is shown that Epicharmos had already used such a character in his plays. Then follows the claim, stated by an unspecified authority, that it was Homer who first introduced the character of the parasite in his poems. The passage under discussion comes from book 17 of the *Iliad* and concerns the hero Podes who is, however, designated by the word εἰλαπιναστής instead of that of παράσιτος, which was under discussion:

> ἔσκε δ' ἐνὶ Τρώεσσι Ποδῆς, υἱὸς Ἠετίωνος,
> ἀφνειός τ' ἀγαθός τε· μάλιστα δέ μιν τίεν Ἕκτωρ
> δήμου, ἐπεί οἱ ἑταῖρος ἔην φίλος εἰλαπιναστής·

> Podes, son of Eetion, was among the Trojans a rich and valiant man. Hector honored him most among his people, as he was, as his companion, a dear guest at his feasts.

> *Iliad* 17.575–577

---

[102] We follow here the division suggested by Maisonneuve 2007b:392–393.

[103] Athenaeus 6.234c–248c. After that we have a change of speakers moving from Plutarch to Democritos and a change of topic moving from parasites to flatterers. See again Maisonneunve 2007b:396–397 for further details.

[104] See Montanari 1999:311–312 and Jacoby 1919:2254–2255. The fragments are to be found in *Fragmenta historicorum graecorum* IV, pp. 356–359 (the passage from Athenaeus under discussion (Athenaeus 6.235e) is listed as fragment 17 there).

Therefore, with regard to the line of argument developed in this passage from Athenaeus, the quotation may not be the best evidence in the discussion about the word παράσιτος and may seem slightly out of place. But also with regard to its content and its connection to the Homeric text the passage is peculiar, especially when we compare it to other fragments from Demetrios in the *Deipnosophistai*. Whereas it is difficult or almost impossible to link the content of a fragment preserved in Athenaeus to the Homeric text or to any issue it may have raised, our passages shows several possible links to the Homeric text.

A first hint is provided by Pandaros, the second hero alluded to in the fragment. The link between this figure and the Homeric text is rather obvious, as he is mentioned as leader of the third contingent,[105] and the scholia that have been preserved to the passage show that there were some ancient discussions about these lines. Some of the comments allude to controversies about Pandaros' origin (Zeleia or Lycia),[106] and others focus on his bow, which is said in book 2 to have been given to Pandaros by Apollo, whereas in book 4 we have a description of how Pandaros made the bow himself.[107] Furthermore, there is a comment in Eustathius suggesting that there was also a discussion about the fact that the bow is mentioned in book 2, as it has been interpreted as a kind of announcement about Pandaros' breaking of the oath by shooting an arrow from this same bow in book 4.[108] In book 5, when he is killed by Diomedes with a spear that is cutting off his tongue,[109] there is again a D-scholia that alludes, though very briefly, to an attempt to explain why it was this special part of his body that was wounded:

πρυμνήν: ἐσχάτην. ἐξέκοψεν δὲ αὐτοῦ τὴν γλῶσσαν, ὅτι ἐφιώρκησεν.

At the root: at the lowest part. He (Diomedes) cut his (Pandaros') tongue, because he broke his oath.

Σ D *Iliad* 5.292 [van Thiel]

This element of the ancient discussion has been singled out by Gaede, who reproduced this scholion, in a slightly different version,[110] in his collection as a parallel passage to fr. 74 [Gaede/Biraschi], and we may assume that it is

---

[105] *Iliad* 2.824–827.

[106] Σ b *Iliad* 2.826–827 [Erbse] and Σ D *Iliad* 2.826 [van Thiel].

[107] *Iliad* 4.105–111.

[108] Eustathius *Commentarii ad Iliadem* 2.827 (= 354, 27–29 or van der Valk I:556).

[109] *Iliad* 5.291–293.

[110] Our quotation comes from van Thiel's edition, whereas Gaede prints, under the heading Σ DL *Iliad* 5.292, ἔτεμε τὴν γλῶσσαν Πανδάρου ὅτι ἐπιώρκησεν "he cut Pandaros' tongue because he broke his oath."

plausible that a commentator like Demetrios, even if he may have started from the topographical issues about the contingent of Pandaros, may also have developed the issues about Pandaros' later appearances in the *Iliad*, about the contradictions linked to it, and about his death in book 5.[111] In this overall discussion, Demetrios may also have mentioned the similarity between Pandaros and Podes with regard to the way they were wounded and their action in the narration, as fr. 74 [Gaede/Biraschi] shows.

But actually, it is not only through Pandaros that Podes and the Homeric passage in which he is mentioned can be linked to issues discussed about the lines of the Trojan Catalogue. Two ζητήματα, moreover linked to the Homeric lines quoted in Athenaeus, can be found about Podes himself. First, according to the scholia to line 575–577 of book 17, there was a difficulty with the name of Podes' father.[112] He is called Eetion and this makes him a namesake of two others mentioned in the *Iliad*: the better-known father of Andromache;[113] but the Homeric poet also mentions an Eetion of Imbros, who ransomed Lycaon, a further son of Priam, from Lemnos and sent him back to Arisbe.[114] Such a coincidence certainly triggered the need for explanations and the scholia bear still witness to it. In the wording transmitted by the aforementioned scholia to the relevant passage of book 17, we see that this question of homonymy also influenced the understanding of the surrounding lines about Podes. Two expressions in particular appearing in this Homeric passage were problematic with regard to the identification of Podes' father. First, if Podes' father was, by error, identified with that of Andromache, there was a difficulty as this Eetion was king of the Cilicians and therefore Podes could not have belonged to the Trojans as the passage from the *Iliad* states (ἔσκε δ' ἐνὶ Τρώεσσι Ποδῆς "among the Trojans was Podes"). Likewise, it would have been difficult to understand why Podes was singled out as being specially honored by Hector among his people (μάλιστα δέ μιν τίεν Ἕκτωρ δήμου "and Hector honored him most among his people"), if his father was the Cilician king. For this second difficulty, we have preserved in the scholia at least one attempt to solve it by changing the line under discussion (μάλιστα τῶν βασιλέων ἐτίμα αὐτὸν ὁ Ἕκτωρ "Hector honored him most among the kings"). These are all fitting examples of what kind of difficulties the passage about Podes raised and that may therefore have been discussed by Demetrios. There is, however, also a second, more

---

[111] See Ebbott 2011:617 and Mueller 2011:942–943 for a short summary of the issues discussed in relation to Pandaros.

[112] Σ bT *Iliad* 17.575–577 [Erbse].

[113] *Iliad* 1.366; *Iliad* 6.395–398 and 416; *Iliad* 8.187; *Iliad* 9.188; *Iliad* 16.153; *Iliad* 22.472 and 480; and *Iliad* 23.827.

[114] *Iliad* 21.39–43. For all three heroes called Eetion, see Dué 2011:239 and Steiner 1991:899–900.

independent ζήτημα that can be linked to the hero Podes, and this bring us back to the passage of Athenaeus. This is the question about the origin and the explanation of the word εἰλαπιναστής (guest at one's feasts). Here again the scholia show that there was some discussion going on about this topic in Antiquity.[115] This is the reason why Gaede quoted, under the heading of his fr. 74, along with the passage from Athenaeus and the aforementioned D-scholion, some elements of the other branches of the scholia, especially when there is evidence that the word was discussed and explained.[116]

As for the reason why Demetrios may have mentioned such issues about Podes and book 17 in a commentary on the Trojan Catalogue, two links between Podes and the Trojan Catalogue should be considered. First, Podes, being explicitly defined as a Trojan, could have been mentioned while Demetrios was discussing the first lines of the Trojan Catalogue, in which the Trojans themselves were mentioned. There was indeed a huge debate about the term of the Trojans, the peoples who were defined by such a name, and the boundaries of their territories. Furthermore, there was also the difficulty of taking into account the fact that the delimitation between Trojans and Dardanians was not always very clear in the *Iliad*.[117] In particular, the alternation Trojan-Dardanian-Trojans at the beginning of the Trojan Catalogue was problematic and needed some explanation, especially with regard to the passages in which both peoples, or only one of them, were mentioned. Such a discussion could certainly also have developed from the lines mentioning Pandaros as leader of the third contingent, and then evolved to a discussion about the passage in book 17 and Podes. There is, however, a second link we may discuss in connection with Podes. For this we should go back to the homonymy concerning the name of Podes' father. In a discussion that may have aimed at distinguishing the several heroes named Eetion, the story of Lycaon may have been mentioned. However, as seen before, this story involved Arisbe, a place name also occurring in the Trojan Catalogue, even if the story itself is only given in book 21, when Lycaon is killed by Achilles.[118] It could therefore also be plausible that, when discussing the occurrence of Arisbe in the Trojan Catalogue, Demetrios may have developed all the issues, controversies, and difficulties linked to this place name in his commentary, which would have included the mention of Lycaon's

---

[115] See Σ A *Iliad* 17.577 [Erbse] and Σ D *Iliad* 17.577 [van Thiel], besides those quoted by Gaede and Biraschi (Σ B *Iliad* 15.577; Σ V *Iliad* 15.577 and Σ DL *Iliad* 5.292). It is, however, difficult to find these passages in modern editions of the scholia. Parts of Σ V *Iliad* 15.577 correspond to Σ bT *Iliad* 17.577b [Erbse], and, as told above, the end of Σ D *Iliad* 5.292 [van Thiel] is similar to Σ DL *Iliad* 5.292. Unfortunately, Σ B *Iliad* 15.577 no longer figures in Erbse's edition of the scholia.

[116] Part of Σ bT *Iliad* 17.577b [Erbse]. See further Gaede 1880:58 and Biraschi 2011, fr. 74.

[117] Kelly 2011:895–896, Dueck 2011:194, and Trachsel 2011:164.

[118] *Iliad* 21.34–114.

passage in Arisbe and the role that Eetion of Imbros played in this episode. In such a context, Demetrios could then at least have reminded his readers that this Eetion is not to be mistaken either for the father of Andromache or for that of Podes.

All these considerations may then show how different fr. 74 [Gaede/Biraschi] is in comparison with other fragments of Demetrios' work preserved in Athenaeus. We have observed that it does not figure at the end of a list, as do almost all the other fragments from Demetrios. Now we must admit that a closer analysis leads us, in opposition to the others, directly to several issues linked to the Trojan Catalogue, and, in addition to this, it must be noted that the fragment figures among the three from Demetrios for which there is no indication about the book in which they originally stood in Demetrios' work. All these peculiarities suggests then that we may be confronted in this case with a completely different situation with regard to the presence of the fragment in the work of Athenaeus, and we may therefore have to consider it as a kind of exception.

If we return now to the entire set of the fragments from Demetrios in Athenaeus, there is a further characteristic that could strengthen our assumption that Demetrios was perceived as a specialized scholar whose work was not widely available and was therefore quoted as a kind of special performance. This is the fact that, in the fragments from Demetrios, other authors, very often poets, are frequently mentioned, even if not all of them are quoted by Demetrios himself.[119] Besides Homer, who was quoted in the above discussed fr. 74 [Gaede/Biraschi], we find Simonides,[120] Mimnermos,[121] Sappho,[122] Archilochos,[123] Antimachos,[124] and also two more recent authors: Seleucos, a poet at the court of Antiochos the Great,[125] and Ctesiphon, who was appointed judge by Attalos I.[126] We may add that Demetrios also mentions, but without actually quoting them, the prose writers Hegesianax,[127] Diocles,[128] and Mnesiptolemos,[129] as well as the painter Cleanthes of Corinth.[130] This is a rather large list given that we have only sixteen rather small fragments of Demetrios in Athenaeus; and, because

---

[119] See above Section 1.1.3 (pp. 23–23).
[120] In fr. 3 [Gaede/Biraschi] (= Athenaeus 14.658b).
[121] In fr. 14 [Gaede/Biraschi] (= Athenaeus 4.174a).
[122] In fr. 70 [Gaede] or fr. 70a [Biraschi] (= Σ Apollonios Rhodios 1.1123 [Wendel]) and fr. 70b [Biraschi] (= *Etymologicum Magnum* s.v. χεράδες).
[123] In fr. 73 [Gaede/Biraschi] (= Athenaeus 4.167d).
[124] In fr. 11 [Gaede/Biraschi] (= Athenaeus 7.300d).
[125] In fr. 13 [Gaede/Biraschi] (= Athenaeus 15.697d).
[126] In fr. 6 [Gaede/Biraschi] (= Athenaeus 15.697c).
[127] In fr. 7 [Gaede/Biraschi] (= Athenaeus 4.155b) and fr. 9 [Gaede/Biraschi] (= Athenaeus 3.80d).
[128] In fr. 72 [Gaede/Biraschi] (= Athenaeus 2.44e).
[129] In fr. 13 [Gaede/Biraschi] (= Athenaeus 15.697d) together with Seleucos his son.
[130] In fr. 5 [Gaede/Biraschi] (= Athenaeus 8.346c).

this feature reappears so often despite the rather small amount of Demetrios' work involved here, it could perhaps be a sign that it was a distinctive feature of Demetrios' work[131] that may have come through even with the peculiar selective principle Athenaeus uses for the quotations in his work, or despite the intermediary sources Athenaeus may have used.

Indeed, such an intermediary step has to be considered here, as it is not clear, from what remains and from the way Athenaeus uses Demetrios, whether he may have had firsthand access to his work or accessed it through intermediary sources, despite the analysis Zecchini made a few years ago.[132] We are alluding here to the two criteria Zecchini suggests for the distinction among Athenaeus' sources between a firsthand usage and more indirect access. These are the length of the quoted fragment and the number of works from one author that are quoted.[133] Both of them seem to be less appropriate for Demetrios. Zecchini suggests that when Atheneaus quotes a lot of text from a few works this would be a sign of firsthand usage, whereas when many works are quoted, with just a few lines per work, this would rather suggest secondhand usage. We know, however, of only one work written by Demetrios, and we therefore cannot find out as, for instance, with Polemon of Ilion, how many works from this author Atheaneus quoted and how much content from each. For Demetrios, however, Zecchini suggests, even without extensive justification, that Athenaeus may have used him firsthand.[134] However, this assumption may not be entirely right and for this we may have to come back to the peculiarities we highlighted about fr. 74 [Gaede/Biraschi] and suggest that Athenaeus may have had access to Demetrios' work in several ways. This has already been suggested for instance by Jacob,[135] who also draws attention to the fact that Athenaeus may have gone through series of quotations from a given author, where the cumulation of evidence was required,[136] but used the information with much more circumspection at other places, for which our fr. 74 [Gaede/Biraschi] could be an example. We have demonstrated that the content of this fragment seems much closer to issues dealt with in Homeric ζητήματα than others. We may then tentatively suggest that such a passage may have come from another source, either Demetrios' work itself or an intermediary work, than, for instance, the

---

[131] Also in many of the fragments preserved in source texts other than Athenaeus, scholars are quoted. See Ragone 2009:667 who counts up to thirty-one authors.

[132] Zecchini 1989.

[133] Zecchini 1989:231.

[134] Zecchini 1989:232–233. He mainly notes that, because of Demetrios' encyclopaedic erudition, his work was a valuable source for Athenaeus, because it was more than a philological explanation of Homer.

[135] Jacob 2004a:157.

[136] Jacob 2004a:173.

series of rather unknown heroes with names that are formed on elements linked to meals (Matton, Keraon, and Daites), quoted in fr. 10 [Gaede/Biraschi] and fr. 14 [Gaede/Biraschi].[137] To underline our hypothesis we may return to the fact that fr. 74 [Gaede/Biraschi] is among the three passages in which Athenaeus does not give the precise indication of the title and the place within the original book where he has found the fragment. This is rather unusual for Athenaeus, who is most of the time, or at least with Demetrios, very precise for his quotations with regard to where he found them. This peculiarity suggests therefore that Athenaeus may have taken a piece such as fr. 74 [Gaede/Birascchi] from a different source than fr. 10 and fr. 14 [Gaede/Biraschi], where the precise indications were present. In this case, we would have to account for the fact that such indications are also absent in fr. 72 [Gaede/Biraschi] and in the aforementioned fr. 73 [Gaede/Biraschi]. This seems more difficult, as they do not share the other particularities of fr. 74 [Gaede/Biraschi]. However, despite these difficulties, such an assumption could still provide some insights for other fragments, such as, for instance, fr. 8 [Gaede/Biraschi], for which we may even be able to define more closely what kind of intermediary source could have been used. Indeed, even if the passage may show, by the way Atheneaus is introducing and using the quotation from Demetrios, how self-conscious he was about his own position as an author and scholar, the fact that the considerations about the village *Plakous* are followed immediately by details about the correct spelling and accentuation of the word πλακοῦς could suggest a lexicographical context for the place Athenaeus may have found this particular quotation from Demetrios, even if this may not be the only possibility. For instance, we may add here that the correct spelling of the word *Plakos* in the expression Thebes-under-Placos was also under discussion in a context in which topographical issues were discussed,[138] and this would lead us back to a context that may be closer to the original work, if not to Demetrios' commentary itself. However, fr. 16 [Gaede/Birachi],[139] a similar case in the sense that it deals with two special words from the Hellespontian dialect (ἐπεγχύτης and κρεωδαισία), brings us back to lexicographical considerations as a context for the fragment. Moreover, in this case, it is not only the wording of the passage that suggests a lexicographical context, but also the fact that it may be linked to the two fragments mentioned above, fr. 10 and fr. 14 [Gaede/Biraschi], in which the three heroes Matton, Keraon, and Daites are mentioned. First, the closeness between the name Daites and the word κρεωδαισία could suggest a lexicographical link as they are both formed from the Greek word ἡ δαίς or ἡ δαίτη (meal, banquet). There are, however,

---

[137] Athenaeus 4.173f–174a.
[138] See Strabo 13.1.65 [C613–614]. The two options are Πλάξ or Πλάκος.
[139] Athenaeus 10.425c.

some further aspects that allow us to go in this direction. An almost similar wording to that found in fr. 10 [Gaede/Biraschi] (about the two Spartan heroes) is attributed in book 2 to Polemon of Ilion:

Πολέμων φησὶν ἐν Μουνυχίᾳ ἥρωα Ἀκρατοπότην τιμᾶσθαι, παρὰ δὲ Σπαρτιάταις Μάττωνα καὶ Κεράωνα ἥρωας ὑπό τινων μαγείρων ἱδρῦσθαι ἐν τοῖς φειδιτίοις. τιμᾶται δὲ καὶ ἐν Ἀχαίᾳ Δειπνεὺς ἀπὸ τῶν δείπνων σχὼν τὴν προσηγορίαν.

Polemon says that in Mounychia a hero called Akratopotes (drinker of neat wine) is honored, and among the Spartans statues of the heroes Matton (Kneader) and Keraon (Mixer) were erected by some cooks in the common messes. Further, also in Achaia, a Deipneus who takes his name from the meals is honored.

Athenaeus 2.39c–d[140]

In this passage, the list is longer and includes two further heroes, one called Akratopotes and the other Deipneus. This makes it even more obvious, especially as we have in this new passage an explicit allusion to the fact that the name Deipneus derived from the word δεῖπνον, that this may have been originally a list of heroes whose names are all connected to words that mean feast or meal. The closeness among the four passages is further suggested by the fact that in two of them, fr. 16 [Gaede/Biraschi] and the passage from book 2 attributed to Polemon, the same fragment from Sappho is quoted.[141] Therefore, there must have been some connections between all of them, despite the fact that the statement about Matton and Keraon is attributed to different scholars, and this link was probably the lexicographical background from which they were taken. Therefore, we see how complex this question of accessibility may be in the case of Athenaeus, and it is indeed likely that he may have used a source, or elements from this source, in different ways at different places in his *Deipnosophistai*.

It is, however, difficult to go further on this question, as on any of the other questions raised by the distribution of Demetrios' fragments within Athenaeus' work. There is, for instance, no special pattern with regard to the speakers who may have mentioned Demetrios. The quotations are distributed among several of the participants of the banquet,[142] and, as we have seen, probably even Athenaeus as narrator in the frame story may quote him. It is the same with

---

[140] = Polemon fr. 40 [Preller]). See further Preller 1838:72.

[141] Athenaeus 10.425c–d = Athenaeus 2.39a = Sappho fr. 141.1–3 [Voigt].

[142] Besides Athenaeus himself (as narrator or participant), mainly Plutarch, Democritos, Aemilianus, and even the physician Daphnos.

the accumulation of five of the sixteen fragments in book 4. There is nothing special about this book, its structure or its topic, that could explain why so many fragments from Demetrios occur there. Bruit/Schmitt-Pantel have given a very detailed analysis of the first part of book 4.[143] They show, for instance, how Athenaeus composes this part of his book on alternations. When focusing on the topic, there are two alternations, one between descriptions of Greek and non-Greek banquets and one between luxurious meals and frugal ones. With regard to the sources used too, they show how Athenaeus plays with parts where longer pieces from better-known authors are followed by sections in which the sources are more heterogeneous, which creates an impression of cumulation of information. This last feature corroborates our previous statement that the fragments of Demetrios function as signaling a kind of exhaustivity or end point of a specially detailed performance. But the two authors of the article emphasize at the end of their outline that the part they analyzed did not have any special status within Athenaeus' work, and that such a close analysis of further parts of the *Deipnosophistai* would certainly reveal a similar structure displaying Athenaeus' witty playing with sources, themes, and the staging of the banquet, during which the learned discussion took place.[144] Such analyses have, however, not yet been carried out, even if the structure and the composition of the *Deipnosophistai* have been subject to several recent studies.[145] The fact, however, that there is an accumulation in book 4, even if we are not able to explain it, is a feature we find again, although to a lesser degree, for other quotations of Demetrios. Indeed, at least at three other places, the quotations of Demetrios appear in series following each other directly. This is the case for fr. 10 [Gaede/Biraschi] and fr. 14 [Gaede/Biraschi] from book 4 discussed previously,[146] and for fr. 6 [Gaede/Biraschi] and fr.13 [Gaede/Biraschi] in book 15.[147] Also in books 3 and 14, the two quotations from Demetrios that they contain are rather close, even though they do not follow each other directly.[148] Therefore, we may at least retain from this that the appearance in series is a further distinctive feature of a large group of the fragments of Demetrios from Athenaeus, as was the fact that they often appear at the end of lists.

---

[143] Bruit/Schmitt-Pantel 1986:203–221.

[144] Bruit/Schmitt-Pantel 1986:218.

[145] Lukinovish 1985:14–16, Lukinovish 1990:263–271, Friedrich/Nothers 1998:xiii–xxiii, Ceccarelli 2000:272–291, Jacob 2001:xxxviii–xlv, and Maisonneuve 2007b:387–412.

[146] Athenaeus 4.173f–174a (= fr. 10 [Gaede/Biraschi]) and Athenaeus 4.174a (= fr. 14 [Gaede/Biraschi].

[147] Athenaeus 15.697c (= fr. 6 [Gaede/Biraschi]) and Athenaeus 15.697d (= fr. 13 [Gaede/Biraschi]).

[148] For book 3: Athenaeus 3.80d (= fr. 9 [Gaede/Biraschi]) and Athenaeus 3.91c (= fr. 15 [Gaede/Biraschi]). For book 14: Athenaeus 14.644a (= fr. 8 [Gaede/Biraschi]) and Athenaeus 14.658b (= fr. 3 [Gaede/Biraschi]).

For our question about how this may help us to understand how Athenaeus perceived Demetrios, we may conclude that, despite the very few elements we have, Demetrios seems to be used as a learned scholar in special positions where the erudition of the person quoting, either a character of the *Deipnosiphistai* or the narrator himself, was at the same time highlighted. It was, however, more difficult to discover how Athenaeus had access to the work. There may have been several different ways of accessing Demetrios' work, either in a lexicographical context or from works more linked to the topic of the Trojan Catalogue, if we accept the hypothesis of an intermediary source between the work of Demetrios and Athenaeus.

Finally, as a more positive statement, we may add that, with regard to the inclusion of the passages from Athenaeus' text into a collection of the fragments of Demetrios' work, there seems to be no difficulty. All of them contain, at least, the name if not the title and the reference to the book from which the piece of information originated, and belong therefore to the work of Demetrios. This is unfortunately not the case with our next source. In Pausanias, a slightly older contemporary of Athenaeus, the identification of the passage involved as a fragment from Demetrios' work is highly hypothetical, and the discussion will show how important the selection process of modern editors is in this case, rather than giving us any information about the way Pausanias may have perceived Demetrios and his work. This aspect will unfortunately become even more important during the discussion of the subsequent authors. After Pausanias, our discussion of the source texts where Demetrios' fragments can be found will lead us, with Harpocration, Hesychios, and Stephanus of Byzantium, to works in which there is no narrative thread that could indicate the structuring principle followed by the author. The works are the results either of compilation or of accumulation of information that is then displayed in small comments, most of the time in the form of alphabetical entries. In this case, even if the name of our author occurs fairly often, the way the scholars use and appreciate their sources remains unexpressed. But first let us discuss the rather special case of Pausanias.

2.1.3 Pausanias

There is only one passage from Pausanias' *Description of Greece*[149] that is counted as a fragment from Demetrios' work in Gaede's collection. Moreover, the chosen passage does not contain the name of Demetrios. Therefore, it is unfortunately only of limited use here for our question of how Demetrios was perceived by

---

[149] Fr. 65 [Gaede/Biraschi](= Pausanias 10.12.2–7).

the authors who used his work. The discussion of the fragment can nonetheless reveal a lot about how Pausanias' passage was composed and what status Demetrios' work may have had in this process, if we follow Gaede in considering the passage as a fragment from Demetrios' work. There is indeed no reason, at first sight, to dismiss Gaede's decision. The German scholar bases his choice on the thorough analysis Ernst Maass made of the passage in his doctoral dissertation on the Sibylline oracles, which was published just a year before Gaede's edition.[150] However, we have to remain aware of the fact that there is no ancient evidence to support their assumptions. Therefore, in order to analyze this piece of evidence in the context of our investigation about the status Demetrios may have had among the sources of Pausanias, we must first understand Ernst Maass's interpretation of the passage involved.

Ernst Maass's dissertation was not about Demetrios of Scepsis, but focused on the Sibylline oracles. The German scholar analyzed the sources of the information about the several Sibyls recorded in Antiquity and therefore also discussed our passage from Pausanias, which is actually a rather extensive report about some of the recorded Sibyls. It starts, however, as a digression, when Pausanias reaches, in his description of Delphi, the place where the Delphian Sibyl was believed to have uttered her oracles.[151] The German scholar's analysis of this passage leads him to conclude that Demetrios' work was the source, although indirectly, of the report about one of the mentioned Sibyls.[152] It is the part that is dedicated to the second Sibyl, the one who was called Herophile and who was supposed to come from Marpessos in the Troad. She is also believed to have visited Delphi and given her oracles there.[153] The reason why Maass considers this passage as being inspired by Demetrios' work lies in the fact that in this section a large part is given to a controversy about the places to which this woman should be linked, and two Trojan settlements, Marpessos and Alexandria Troas, as well as the Ionian Erythraea, were involved in the debate. In favor of Marpessos, one of her poems in which she explicitly stated that this was her place of origin was invoked, whereas the inhabitants of Alexandria

---

[150] Maass 1879. It is actually another dissertation from Greifswald that Maass must have elaborated as fellow student of Gaede under the supervision of Wilamowitz.

[151] Pausanias' account has been discussed thoroughly in serveral of the studies focusing either on the origin of the Sibylline tradition or on the reliability of the ancient sources about this tradition, but it is not our aim here to summarize this issue. For this, see Parke 1988:23–70, Potter 1990:471–483, and more succinctly Lightfoot 2007:3–7.

[152] Maass 1879:22–27. Some further considerations about this issue can be found in Maass 1883:326–336.

[153] Pausanias 10.12.1–7. After that Pausanias mentioned a further Sibyl who was called Demo and he quotes his source for this section. He follows Hyperochos of Cumae whose fragments have been collected in *Die Fragmente der griechischen Historiker* 576. See now also *Brill's New Jacoby* 576.

Troas claimed that she died in the temple of Apollo Smintheus, which belonged to their territory. Finally, the Erythraeans dismissed both Trojan claims and asserted that the Sibyl was born in a cave in their territory, contesting the lines about Marpessos in her poem. In all of these accounts, but especially in the one about Marpessos, very detailed descriptions of the landscape are given, and this peculiarity of the report convinced Maass that these elements must have come from a periegetical work.[154] He hesitates then between two possible options for the scholar who may have been the author of such a work: either Polemon of Ilion or Demetrios of Scepsis. For us here it is, however, the reason for his choice rather than the actual choice that is interesting. He decides on Demetrios of Scepsis because he believes that Demetrios, influenced by his local patriotism, may have been capable of going as far as defending the Marpessos-tradition against the Erythraeans, whereas Polemon may have been too trustworthy a scholar (*homo verissimus et summae fidei*) to defend such a claim.[155] In doing so, he bases his decision primarily on the opinions modern scholars had in those days about Demetrios, and we shall see this in more detail in Chapter 3.

For our discussion here, however, the outline of Maass's argumentation should have shown how hypothetical the attribution of this passage to Demetrios is. This is even more so when we go back to Gaede and discuss in more detail what he did in his edition with Maass's conclusion. He includes, for instance, not only the passage from Pausanias as his fr. 65, but adds his fr. 66 as further evidence about this Marpessos-tradition. This is the entry from Stephanus of Byzantium about Mermessos,[156] which Maass already mentioned and discussed in connection with the passage from Pausanias and its alleged attribution to Demetrios of Scepsis.[157] Gaede dismissed, however, a third piece of evidence that comes from Dionysios of Halicarnassos' account about Aeneas' travels,[158] and his decision is due to the fact that Maass found no evidence in this passage that would point to Demetrios as its source. He therefore does not treat the passage the same way as the two others.[159] Maass's conclusions have, however, been challenged, and divergent opinions about the sources for this Marpassos-tradition have been defended since Maass's publication. On the one hand, we find the scholars who prefer to attribute all three pieces of evidence, Pausanias, Stephanus of Byzantium, and Dionysios of Halicarnassos, to one same source, which is most of

---

[154] Maass 1879:23.

[155] Maass 1879:24.

[156] Stephanus Byzantius s.v. Μερμησσός (Stephanus Byzantius 445, 15 [Meineke] = Stephanus Byzantius μ 148 [Billerbeck]), corrected to Marpessos by Maass 1879:24.

[157] Maass 1879:24–26.

[158] Dionysius Halicarnassensis *Antiquitates Romanae* 1.55. For the context of the passage, see e.g. Perret 1942:578–617.

[159] Gaede 1880:55. The passage is only alluded briefly to in a footnote.

the time identified with Demetrios of Scepsis, as for instance Diels did only a few years after Gaede's publication.[160] On the other hand, Vanotti suggested more recently that none of the three passages should be attributed to Demetrios. He bases his argument on the fact that it is very unlikely that an author like Demetrios, who dismissed Aeneas' travels, would have mentioned the prophecy that was related to Aenaes' settling in the new lands.[161] He prefers to suggest as the source Hegesianax of Alexandria Troas, who was not only defending, as we have seen in Chapter 1, a version in which Aeneas left the Troad, but was also quoted previously by Dionysios.[162] Finally, we find more skeptical scholars, like Frazer, who highlights, even if he accepts Maass's attribution of the passage to Demetrios, the fact that this is only the hypothesis of a modern scholar and that there is no evidence in Pausanias' text to strengthen it.[163] This then should also be our conclusion here. We may add, however, in favor of Gaede's hypothesis to count the passage from Pausanias among the fragments from Demetrios, and with regard to our question about Pausanias' usage of his sources, that when dealing with Polemon of Ilion, Maass's second option, Pausanias' text is again peculiar. The Hellenistic scholar seems not to have been quoted by name, even if many of the fragments preserved from his works share content with passages from Pausanias' text, and this coincidence triggered a huge debate about how closely Pausanias may have followed Polemon's work or whether he composed his work more independently.[164] For us here, it is interesting to note that such hesitations also occur with authors other than Demetrios of Scepsis, and this makes Pausanias' work even more difficult to analyze with regard to his sources. We may therefore pursue our discussion with the next category of sources in which we find fragments from Demetrios, and leave Pausanias' passage as a somewhat difficult exception in our list of authors using Demetrios' work.

2.1.4 Lexicographers

In Harpocration and Hesychios, we also have very little evidence about Demetrios' work. In Harpocration, we find three fragments,[165] whereas Gaede

---

[160] Diels 1890:94–95 (note 1).

[161] Vanotti 1993:155–157. His argumentation is not entirely convincing, as it is still possible to think that an author like Demetrios would have mentioned a tradition he is opposed to in detail before dismissing it.

[162] Dionysius Halicarnassensis *Antiquitates Romanae* 1.49.1 and 1.72.1.

[163] Frazer 1898 (vol. 5):288–289.

[164] See Frazer 1898 (vol. 1):lxxxii–xc and Hutton 2005:247–263.

[165] Harpocration s.v. Θυργωνίδαι (= fr. 4 [Gaede/Biraschi]); Harpocration s.v. Ἀδράστειαν (= fr. 18 [Gaede] or fr. 18a [Biraschi]); Harpocration s.v. Ἴων (= fr. 69 [Gaede/Biraschi]). As a Demetrios is also mentioned in the entry about Ἄκη it has been suggested that this author could be our Demetrios. At least this is what the SoudaOnline suggests for the very similar entry about Ἀκή

attributes two entries from Hesychios to Demetrios, in which, however, the name of the scholar again does not occur.[166] We are facing, therefore, the same difficulties with Hesychios' text as with the example of Pausanias discussed above. The explanation of Gaede's choice will absorb most of our attention when dealing with these passages, and we shall therefore begin our discussion with Harpocration, who is not only prior from a chronological point of view, but for whose passages we are in a slightly better position, even if we have only three entries in which Demetrios' name appears. This number, no matter how small it may be, tells us at least, as for Athenaeus, that Demetrios was not among the main sources of Harpocration. This is not surprising as Harpocration composed a lexicon for readers interested in the works of Greek orators and presumably focused mainly on the texts of such kind of writers. Therefore, the orators, and first of all Demosthenes, are also the most frequently quoted authors.[167] The historians such as Herodotus, Thucydides, Xenophon, and Theopompos come next, followed by Aristotle, who is mainly quoted for his *Constitution of the Athenians*.[168] Among the authors closer to Demetrios of Scepsis, we have first Apollodoros of Athens, even if none of the fragments, as far as we can tell from the preserved indications, come from the work on the Catalogue of the Ships. Next come Eratosthenes and Polemon of Ilion, but for these authors the preserved quotations have almost nothing in common with Demetrios' work. For Eratosthenes, most of the preserved fragments are from his work on comedy, and Polemon is quoted for elements touching on mainland Greece. Only the two fragments from Paleaphatos we find in Harpocration come closer in content to those from Demetrios. Both preserve elements from his Τρωϊκά and concern problems of localization. However, one is about the hero Dysaules linked to the Eleusian mysteries and the neighborhoods of Corinth,[169] and the other is about the Macrocephaloi, whom Palarphatos locate in Libya.[170] Unfortunately, both topics are too little known today to allow us to draw any further insights about Demetrios' work from them. Finally, to complete the picture we may add that Homer is quoted surprisingly few times and Strabo only twice.

---

in the Souda (α 858 [Adler]). See further SoudaOline http//www.stoa.org/sol/ and *Fragmenta historicorum graecorum* IV, pp. 381–382. The passage has, however, been dismissed since Stiehle 1850:529.

[166] Hesychios s.v. Θύμβρα (= fr. 24 [Gaede] or fr. 24b [Biraschi]); Hesychios s.v. Κάρησος (= fr. 30b [Gaede/Biraschi]). A further entry in Hesychios (s.v. Ῥοδίος) is quoted as parallel evidence for fr. 31, which is, in Gaede's edition, a whole cluster of texts that come mainly from the scholia to the *Iliad*, sharing their content with a passage from Strabo (Strabo 13.1.44–45 [C602–603]).

[167] For more details about the orators quoted and the exact number of quotations per author, see Keaney 1991:277–293.

[168] Zecchini 2000:156.

[169] Harpocration s.v. Δυσαύλης and for further information about the hero, see Pausanias 2.14.1–4.

[170] Harpocration s.v. Μακροκέφαλοι.

From this meager evidence Zecchini is still able to draw some interesting conclusions about the presence of Demetrios in Harpocration's work, especially when comparing Athenaeus and Harpocration as quoting authors. He notices first that as a general rule one can observe that works of scholarship are less frequently used in Harpocration than in Athenaeus,[171] but adds that the topic of Troy was an exception and received much interest from Harpocration despite his focus on Attica.[172] Moreover, the few fragments preserved in Harpocration still bear witness to the fact that Demetrios' work was still available in some way, even if it is as difficult as with Athenaeus to decide whether Harpocration was able to use Demetrios' work firsthand or via another source. The simple mention of the name does not allow us to draw any conclusions in this direction. The only rather indirect evidence about this problem we may adduce here comes from Diogenes Laertios. He mentions our scholar among the many others he lists,[173] and this may allow us to presume that even in the third century CE Demetrios' work was still known in one form or the other, otherwise Diogenes would perhaps not have considered Demetrios worthy of being quoted.

Turning now to Hesychios, the situation is extremely complex, as both fragments cannot be discussed individually, but each has to be understood in connection with other passages Gaede counts as fragments from Demetrios' work. This is due to the fact that in some cases Gaede assembles a cluster of several texts as evidence for one fragment of his collection. This feature of Gaede's edition means that we must first explain the special status the passages from Hesychios take in Gaede's collection, before we can consider whether they may be used in our discussion here.

In the first case, which is fr. 24 [Gaede],[174] Hesychios' entry about Thymbra is quoted by Gaede as a fragment from Demetrios because it shares the content of one sentence of paragraph 35 in Strabo's book 13.[175] In this Straboian passage the name of Demetrios does not, however, appear either, and we must take into account the whole sequence from fr. 23a to fr. 25 [Gaede][176] to understand Gaede's choice. The name of Demetrios occurs only in the two scholia that are counted under fr. 23a and fr. 23b. However, the topographical indications

---

[171] This means for Demetrios three fragments in Harpocration against sixteen in Athenaeus. See Zecchini 2000:159.

[172] Zecchini 2000:157.

[173] T2 [Biraschi] = Diogenes Laertios 5.83–85.

[174] Fr. 24b [Biraschi] = Hesychios s.v. Θύμβρα.

[175] Strabo 13.1.35 [C598].

[176] Fr. 23a [Gaede/Biraschi] = Σ bT *Iliad* 20.53c [Erbse]; fr. 23b [Gaede/Biraschi] = Σ A *Iliad* 20.3 [Erbse] (or Σ D *Iliad* 20.3 [van Thiel]); fr. 23c [Biraschi] = Strabo 13.1.35 [C597]; fr. 24 [Gaede] (or fr. 24b [Biraschi]) = Hesychios s.v. Θύμβρα; fr. 24a [Biraschi] = Strabo 13.1.35 [C 598]; fr. 25 [Gaede] (or fr. 25b [Biraschi]) = Σ A *Iliad* 11.166–168 [Erbse]; and fr. 25a [Biraschi] = Strabo 13.1.35 [C598].

in these two comments are identical with those mentioned by Strabo at the beginning of his paragraph 35, which leads Gaede to print this part of the Straboian text as parallel passage alongside the two scholia. Furthermore, as the whole paragraph 35 belongs, together with paragraphs 33 and 34 and paragraph 36, to a very detailed description of the Trojan plain, Gaede believes that the whole passage comes from Demetrios' work, and goes on quoting part of it as parallel passages for further fragments. One is our fr. 24 [Gaede], and the other is fr. 25 [Gaede]. The German scholar is certainly justified in doing so, as the whole passage is encompassed by two occurrences of Demetrios' name, one at the beginning of paragraph 33 and the other at the end of paragraph 36.[177] But for our discussion here, the analysis of Gaede's procedure reveals how indirect the evidence from Hesychios is. It is actually only in a second step, having decided that the Straboian passage about Thymbra is from Demetrios, that Gaede adduces the entry from Hesychios and includes it into his collection. Knowing this, it becomes obvious that the evidence cannot be used to find out how Demetrios' work was available to, or perceived by, Hesychios. The inclusion of this entry in the collection is a construction based mainly on Gaede's understanding of Strabo's passage, and, even if it is correct, it does not allow us to decide whether Hesychios knew from whose work he was quoting, or whether he found the information already embedded anonymously in other sources.

It is unfortunately the same with the second fragment from Hesychios. This time it is a remark about the river Caresos that Gaede associates, however only indirectly, to Strabo's excursus about the river system of the Troad.[178] Here again the Straboian passage is cut in two by Gaede and printed under three different fragments: paragraph 43 and the beginning of paragraph 44 count as fr. 29 [Gaede], whereas parts of the rest of paragraph 44 and paragraph 45 are printed as parallel passages to fr. 30 and fr. 31 [Gaede].[179] Under fr. 30a and fr. 30b [Gaede] we find a passage from Eustathius and our entry from Hesychios,[180] whereas the main entries of fr. 31 [Gaede] are three scholia to the same line of the *Iliad*.[181]

---

[177] Strabo 13.1.33 [C596] = fr. 22 [Gaede/Biraschi] and Strabo 13.1.36 [C599] = fr. 26 [Gaede/Biraschi].

[178] Strabo 13.1.43–45 [C602–603].

[179] Here Biraschi does not cut the Straboian text the same way as Gaede. Still, fr. 29 [Biraschi] corresponds at the beginning to fr. 29 [Gaede]. For fr. 30 and 31, Biraschi decides to consider the Straboian passage as fr. 31a (Strabo 13.1.44–45 [C602–603]).

[180] Eustathius *Commentarii ad Iliadem* 12.20–21 (= 890, 5 or van der Valk III:345) = fr. 30a [Biraschi] and Hesychios s.v. Κάρησσος = fr. 30b [Biraschi].

[181] Fr. 31a [Gaede] = Σ T *Iliad* 12.20a [Erbse] corresponding to fr. 31b [Biraschi], fr. 31b [Gaede] = Σ T *Iliad* 12.20c [Erbse] corresponding to fr. 30c [Biraschi], and finally fr. 31c [Gaede] = Σ T *Iliad* 12.20e [Erbse], which is also fr. 31c [Biraschi]. For a better understanding of the complex relationship between all these scholia and their positions on the page of the manuscript, see the digitization of the manuscript under http://www.bl.uk/manuscripts/Viewer.aspx?ref=burney_ms_86_f123r. It is also in this cluster where we find Hesychios' entry about the river Rhodios (Hesychios. s.v.

We see therefore that the evidence from Hesychios is only one among a whole series of passages that Gaede believes to belong to Demetrios' work. In none of them does the name of Demetrios occur. It is only in the passage from Strabo in which the Hellenistic scholar is mentioned twice, and we have to acknowledge that all the rest depends again on Gaede's understanding of the Straboian passages and on the links he sees between the Straboian passage and the contents of the others. It is therefore not possible to use the entry of Hesychios to say anything about the way Demetrios may have been used by the lexicographer. The only positive statement we may actually make is the fact that through Gaede's association we may guess how much material from Demetrios' work was circulating and may still have been accessible in late Antiquity, as some of it found its way into the lexicon of Hesychios. We may therefore conclude from our discussion about the lexicographers that Demetrios' work starts to fade away in late Antiquity, remaining only perceptible though rather vague allusions to its content. This statement may unfortunately also apply to Stephanus of Byzantium, the next author we shall discuss, despite the fact that there is a relatively large number of fragments from Stephanus in Gaede's collection.

2.1.5 Stephanus of Byzantium

According to Biraschi's edition there are nine fragments from Demetrios preserved in Stephanus of Byzantium.[182] All but one of these fragments deal with places in the Troad, as the fragments correspond to the entries about Silindion,[183] Kalymna (one of the Calydnian islands),[184] Percote,[185] Arisbe,[186]

Ῥόδιος), quoted, however, only as a parallel passage without a proper number either in Gaede's or in Biraschi's edition. It is therefore extremely difficult to understand what status this entry may have had for the two editors.

[182] This is again a rather small number if we compare it to other sources. The Hellenistic poets seem to be the group that comes first, followed by works of authors like Artemidoros and Pausanias. See Billerbeck 2005:411, Billerbeck 2008:314–317, and finally Billerbeck 2009:65–66.

[183] Fr. 12 [Gaede/Biraschi] = Stephanus Byzantius s.v. Σιλίνδιον (= Stephanus Byzantius 569, 6 [Meineke] = Stephanus Byzantius σ 159 [Billerbeck]).

[184] Fr 17b [Biraschi] = Stephanus Byzantius s.v. Κάλυμνα (= Stephanus Byzantius 350, 12 [Meineke] = Stephanus Byzantius k 39 [Billerbeck]). Gaede only quotes the passage from Strabo (Strabo 10.5.19 [C489]) as fr. 17.

[185] Fr. 19c [Biraschi] = Stephanus Byzantius s.v. Περκώτη (= Stephanus Byzantius 517, 21 [Meineke] = Stephanus Byzantius π 112 [Billerbeck]). Gaede prints it without giving a number as a parallel passage to the text of the scholion to the *Iliad* considered as fr. 19.

[186] Fr. 20 [Gaede/Biraschi] = Stephanus Byzantius s.v. Ἀρίσβη (= Stephanus Byzantius 119, 3 [Meineke] = Stephanus Byzantius α 426 [Billerbeck]).

Scepsis,[187] Alybe,[188] Polichna,[189] and Mermessos (for Marpessos).[190] The last one is about the toponym Esonia, which is, according to some traditions, either the ancient name given to the surroundings of Sardis or an alternative appellation of Asia.[191] However, and despite this geographical deviance, this entry is one of the fragments from Stephanus for which we actually have some evidence from Antiquity that it may have come from Demetrios' work, even without his name appearing. Indeed, as we shall see, the full name of Demetrios occurs only in the entry about Silindion. All the others are again included in the collection by Gaede or Biraschi only because of the closeness of their content with passages from Strabo, which the editors believe come from Demetrios' work. This is also true, as we shall see later, for fr. 17b [Biraschi] in which Demetrios is alluded to through the formula ὁ Σκήψιος. For fr. 42 [Gaede/Biraschi] on Esonia, on the contrary, there is a clear although indirect link to Demetrios of Scepsis. In fr. 41 [Gaede/Biraschi], a further passage from Strabo,[192] the assumption that Esonia is an alternative name for Asia, also stated in fr. 42 [Gaede/Biraschi], is explicitly attributed to Demetrios of Scepsis. Moreover, this parallel of the two names is mentioned in a discussion about the Homeric toponym Maeonia, which is the homeland of one of contingent of the Trojan allies.[193] This links the passage clearly to a discussion about the Homeric text, and we can even obtain some insights into the debate that developed about the place names involved: hesitations occurred about the identification and localization of Maeonia. Some scholars, like Demetrios, tried to associate the toponym with two other names, Esonia and Asia. In connection with this second toponym a further line of the Homeric text was involved. This is line *Iliad* 2.461, in which we find the expression Ἀσίῳ ἐν λειμῶνι. From this, we may see how the remark about Esonia can not only be linked to the name of Demetrios, but also how it fits the scope of his work, at least according to what we can gather from what we discovered so far in the remaining testimonia. This is unfortunately not always the case for the other fragments, as for most of them it is again Gaede's interpretations

---

[187] Fr. 34 [Gaede] or fr. 34b [Biraschi] = Stephanus Byzantius s.v. Σκῆψις (= Stephanus Byzantius 574, 8 [Meineke] = Stephanus Byzantius σ 202 [Billerbeck]).

[188] Fr. 60 [Gaede/Biraschi] = Stephanus Byzantius s.v. Ἀλύβη (= Stephanus Byzantius 79, 6 [Meineke] = Stephanus Byzantius α 233 [Billerbeck]).

[189] Fr. 63 [Gaede/Biraschi] = Stephanus Byzantius s.v. Πολίχνα (= Stephanus Byzantius 532, 4 [Meineke] = Stephanus Byzantius π 202 [Billerbeck]).

[190] Fr. 66 [Gaede/Biraschi] = Stephanus Byzantius s.v. Μερμησσός (= Stephanus Byzantius 445, 15 [Meineke] = Stephanus Byzantius μ 148 [Billerbeck]). As seen above, the lemma has been changed from Mermessos to Marpessos by Maass 1879:24.

[191] Fr. 42 [Gaede/Biraschi] = Stephanus Byzantius s.v. Ἠσιονία (= Stephanus Byzantius 304, 15 [Meineke] or Stephanus Byzantius η 25 [Billerbeck]).

[192] Strabo 13.4.8 [C627].

[193] *Iliad* 2.864–866.

that provide the strongest links to Demetrios. Nonetheless, we shall discuss the fragments individually here, starting with the one about Silindion, in which the name of Demetrios actually occurs.

The entry about Silindion is extremely succinct and only locates the place in the surroundings of Mount Ida.[194] There are, however, two interesting elements from these few lines for our investigation here. First, the passage contains a full reference to Demetrios' work, being one of the few pieces of evidence from outside Athenaeus' work in which it is specified from which book of Demetrios' work the passage comes. We know that the remark was located in book 16 of Demetrios' work, even if this piece of information does not help us much to find out more about Silindion and about how it could have been dealt with in Demetrios' work. But this absence of information is precisely the second interesting element about this fragment. The place name does not appear in Strabo, and therefore the remark must have entered Stephanus' work though a source other than Strabo's *Geography*. This independence from Strabo's text is even more striking, as for other fragments it is clear that it is through Strabo's text that the piece from Demetrios was incorporated into Stephanus' *Ethnica*. A telling example is fr. 17b [Biraschi],[195] which does not figure in Gaede's collection. In this entry, Stephanus quotes Strabo explicitly, and the sequence where allusion to Demetrios is made, is acutally a shorter rendering of a sentence in Strabo's paragraph 10.5.19 [C489]. The passage does not therefore give us any additional information for Demetrios' work, but illustrates how much Stephanus sometimes depended on Strabo's work.[196]

All the other passages have been chosen by Gaede, mainly because they fit discussions dealt with in other passages, most of them from Strabo, which can be linked to Demetrios. In some of them the name of Demetrios does not even appear in Strabo's text. Fragment 19 [Gaede],[197] about Percote, and fr. 20 [Gaede/Biraschi],[198] about Arisbe, are good examples to show how thin the evidence is adduced by Gaede is. Both places are mentioned in the Trojan Catalogue, in the Hellespontos contingent led by Asios, son of Hyrtacos. It is therefore likely that

---

[194] Stephanus Byzantius s.v. Σιλίνδιον (= Stephanus Byzantius 569, 6 [Meineke] = Stephanus Byzantius σ 159 [Billerbeck]).

[195] Stephanus Byzantius s.v. Κάλυμνα (= Stephanus Byzantius 350, 12 [Meineke] = Stephanus Byzantius k 39 [Billerbeck]).

[196] See for instance Diller 1975:10–15 and Billerbeck 2008:315.

[197] Again Biraschi chooses a different presentation for the texts assembled by Gaede under this number. Fr. 19a [Biraschi] = Strabo 13.1.20 [C590]; fr. 19b [Biraschi] = Σ T *Iliad* 11. 229 [Erbse] and fr. 19c [Biraschi] = Stephanus Byzantius s.v. Περκώτη (= Stephanus Byzantius 517, 21 [Meineke] = Stephanus Byzantius π 112 [Billerbeck]).

[198] Stephanus Byzantius s.v. Ἀρίσβη (= Stephanus Byzantius 119, 3 [Meineke] = Stephanus Byzantius α 426 [Billerbeck]).

Demetrios may have commented on the lines and discussed the issues linked to the two toponyms. Furthermore, the passage from Strabo, quoted under fr. 19a by Biraschi,[199] gives some additional details about the content such comments may have had. It comes from a part of Strabo's work in which the lines of the Trojan Catalogue under discussion are explicitly quoted and then followed by a mainly topographical comment about several of the toponyms mentioned. The name of Demetrios does not occur during the whole discussion, as the first occurrence of his name is found only seven paragraphs later, together with his statement about the shape of the historical Ilion in his own day.[200] There is therefore no evidence in Strabo's text to support Gaede's assumption, even if it is still highly probable that Strabo may have found the main elements of the discussion in Demetrios and followed the work of the Hellenistic scholar while composing his paragraph. It is again a construction based on Gaede's understanding of Strabo's text and his assumption about Demetrios' work, and therefore cannot help us to find out what Stephanus knew about Demetrios' work and how he may have used it. This conclusion does not, however, mean that Gaede was not justified in including the passage in a collection of Demetrios' work. His intuition may even turn out to have been correct, as his hypothesis can now be strengthened by a newly deciphered papyrus (P. Oxy. 76.5094).[201] The papyrus contains the quotation of Demetrios' name, together with, a few lines later, an allusion to a daughter of Dymas, who should most probably be identified with Hecuba.[202] This would then allude to the second passage from the *Iliad*, which is quoted in Strabo's text under discussion here. Indeed, at the end of the passage, Strabo quotes another passage from the *Iliad* in which Hecabe's brother Asios is mentioned (*Iliad* 16.718), and points to the homonymy between this Asios and the leader of the Hellespontos contingent, the Asios mentioned by Strabo at the beginning of the passage, who is son of Hyrtacos and dwells in Arisbe near the river Selleis. Therefore, all the four passages under discussion here, the two entries from Stephanus (Arisbe and Percote), the passage from Strabo, and the scraps from the papyrus, seem to deal with the same problem, the interpretation and localization of the toponyms and persons mentioned in the lines dedicated to the Hellespontos contingent. These may certainly be a fitting topic for Demetrios to have alluded to, and they prove the unity of the discussion of which all four pieces of evidence illustrate some parts, but they also show the distance that unfortunately exists between Demetrios' work and

[199] Strabo 13.1.20 [C590].
[200] Strabo 13.1.27 [C594] (= fr. 21 [Gaede/Biraschi] = T3 [Biraschi]).
[201] For the edition of the text, see Perale/Henry 2011:172–177, Colomo/Perale 2012:1–3, West 2012:11–13, Luppe 2012:8–10, Luppe 2013:105–106, and Perale/Vecchiato 2015:11–27.
[202] West 2012:11–13, Luppe 2013:105–106, and Trachsel 2014:5–11.

the evidence that remains. None of the preserved texts can be attributed to Demetrios' work for sure. First, the little pieces and bits from the papyrus are not actually from Demetrios' commentary, but from another scholarly work in which Demetrios is only quoted as an authority who attests the existence of a line from a poem, probably written in hexameters, in which Hecabe is explicitly defined as daughter of Dymas. However, the remaining text on the papyrus is not long enough to draw any conclusion about where in Demetrios' work such a line would have been used, and the author of the preserved passage seems not to have developed Demetrios' contribution beyond the simple quotation of the line under discussion. Second, the passage from Strabo's text, because the name of Demetrios does not appear and because of Strabo's peculiar way of using his sources, has to be taken with extreme caution. Furthermore, even if he quotes the passage about Hecabe's brother that must be the background for the discussion on the papyrus, he does not mention any difficulty about Hecabe's paternity and keeps to strictly topographical matters, except for the mention of the homonymy between Hecabe's brother and the son of Hyrtacos. There are therefore no overlapping elements between the two pieces of evidence, and we have to conclude that they illustrate several different aspects of the same problem. Finally, the two entries from Stephanus are only related to Demetrios through the passage of Strabo, and without further certainty about Strabo's passage nothing independent can be said about them, at least not with regard to the way in which they may be related to Demetrios' work. Therefore, it is obvious that even if the newly deciphered papyrus proves that Demetrios took part in this discussion, there is still no way to define his contribution clearly and to establish how close to the original work the remaining elements are.

The situation is similar with the other entries from Stephanus that Gaede includes in his collection (Scepsis, Alybe, and Polichna). All of them are linked to passages in Strabo, where it is likely that Demetrios may have been the source, but without explicit evidence. It is for instance highly probable that Demetrios could have spoken about the etymology of the name of Scepsis as it is given in fr. 34 [Gaede][203] (Scepsis linked to the verbal form σκήψασθαι), especially if we take into account the alternative etymology given in a passage from Strabo quoted by Gaede as a parallel passage for fr. 34[204] (Scepsis explained as coming from the adjective περίσκεπτος). However, the name of Demetrios is only quoted by Strabo in the subsequent paragraph about the assumption that Scepsis belonged to the realm of Aeneas, and the extent of Demetrios' influence on what precedes is therefore subject to interpretation. This does not change, even if we take

---

[203] Fr. 34b [Biraschi] = Stephanus Byzantius s.v. Σκῆψις (= Stephanus Byzantius 574, 8 [Meineke] = Stephanus Byzantius σ 202 [Billerbeck]).

[204] This is actually fr. 34a [Biraschi] = Strabo 13.1.52 [C607].

into account the link that exists between this entry of Stephanus about Scepsis and the one about Alybe counted as fr. 60 [Gaede/Biraschi].[205] Indeed, in both there is some allusion to the myth of Zeus' birth and the role Rhea played in this episode. Because of this thematic link, both entries and especially the one about Alybe can be linked to fr. 61 [Gaede/Biraschi],[206] in which we find several remarks about Demetrios' position concerning the birth of Zeus. The Hellenistic scholar claims that Zeus was born in the Troad and that the confusion between Crete and the Troad occurred because of the homonymies between place names from both regions. In Stephanus' entry about Alybe the place is designated as a retreat where Rhea went when she was pregnant with Zeus, and this statement is in accordance with Demetrios' position in fr. 61 [Gaede/Biraschi]. It therefore becomes highly probable that this statement belongs to the tradition about Zeus' birth that Demetrios also defended. But, still, we cannot grasp the distance between Demetrios' work and the wording preserved in Stephanus' entry to understand how Stephanus may have had access to Demetrios' work. It is the same with the second issue from the entry about Alybe, which can be linked to elements attributed to Demetrios' work. As the line from the Trojan Catalogue where the toponym Alybe occurs is quoted in the entry,[207] it can be linked to fr. 45 [Gaede/Biraschi],[208] again a passage from Strabo, in which we have a very detailed discussion about textual problems for the Homeric line involved, during which the name of Demetrios occurs several times. But, still, the contents of the two passages, the one from Stephanus and the one from Strabo, do not overlap, and we have two pieces of evidence for which, even if they illustrate different aspects of the same issues, and among which, one is certainly linked to Demetrios, it is not possible to prove that they come from the same source.

Finally, for the entry about Polichna[209] a similar conclusion has to be drawn. The toponym appears, on the one hand, in Strabo's discussion about the river system of the Troad, which is considered as inspired by Demetrios and is counted by Biraschi as fr. 31a.[210] On the other hand, the homonymy stated in Stephanus' entry between a Polichna in Crete and the one in the Troad may be seen as an extension of the issue developed in fr. 61 [Gaede/Biraschi], which we mentioned in the context of our discussion about Alybe. But in this case too,

---

[205] Fr. 60 [Gaede/Biraschi] = Stephanus Byzantius s.v. Ἀλύβη (= Stephanus Byzantius 79, 6 [Meineke] = Stephanus Byzantius α 233 [Billerbeck]).

[206] Strabo 10.3.19–21 [C472–473].

[207] *Iliad* 2.857.

[208] Strabo 12.3.20–23 [C550–552].

[209] Fr. 63 [Gaede/Biraschi] = Stephanus Byzantius s.v. Πολίχνα (= Stephanus Byzantius 532, 4 [Meineke] = Stephanus Byzantius π 202 [Billerbeck]).

[210] Strabo 13.1.44–45 [C602–603]. Polichna is mentioned twice in Strabo 13.1.45 [C603].

because of the extreme shortness of the entry and because its content does not overlap, either with elements of the passage considered as fr. 31a [Biraschi] or with those developed in fr. 61 [Gaede/Biraschi], it cannot be used as evidence that would be independent from Gaede's interpretation and help us to see how elements from Demetrios' work were used in Stephanus' *Ethnica*. Eventually, as far as Stephanus' entry about Mermessos is concerned, we have already developed the issues in the section about Pausanias and we have seen that it leads us to exactly the same conclusion. Even if its content may be inspired by elements from Demetrios' work, the absence of any explicit mention of Demetrios' work or name does not allow us to use it in our discussion here.

The discussion should have shown that, with the evidence preserved in Stephanus, it is hardly possible for us to say anything here about the way the scholar may have used Demetrios. This is even more so as some recent studies have shown how complex Stephanus' use of sources was.[211] But we may still keep in mind, as a kind of conclusion of our discussion about Stephanus of Byzantium, that, in opposition to Hesychios for instance, at least in one entry the name of Demetrios is mentioned moreover independently from Strabo. This could then indicate, on the one hand, that the work was available to Stephanus through a source other than Strabo's *Geography* where, if Demetrios is quoted, no indication is given about the place within Demetrios' work from which the information was taken. Furthermore, as such a precise reference is preserved in the entry about Silindion, we can associate it tentatively with the other fragments in which such a way of quoting Demetrios' work is preserved, which means most of the quotations in Athenaeus and one of the entries in Harpocration, and suggest that in this case the information entered Stephanus' work through similar kinds of sources as those used in Athenaeus and Harpocration.

2.1.6 Photius and Eustathius

Turning now to Eustathius, we move rather far in time and reach a contemporary of Johannes Tzetzes in the twelfth century. However, as we said at the beginning, as Stephanus' *Ethnica* and Strabo's *Geography* figure among Eustathius' main sources,[212] a strong tie exists between the three works and this allows us to treat Eustathius next. Moreover, we shall see that the testimonium from Photius will be involved in the discussion and illustrates the way Demetrios is perceptible in the timespan between Stephanus and Eustathius.

---

[211] In particular the research of Professor Billerbeck should be mentioned here. See for instance Billerback 2008:301–322.
[212] Diller 1983:184 and Billerbeck 2008:308 for Stephanus, and for Strabo, van der Valk 1971:lxxiv–lxxvi and Diller 1975:86–86.

Chapter 2

The fact that the only fragment from Demetrios preserved in Tzetzes comes from the scholia to Lycophron and not from his works on Homer may also create a distance between Tzetzes and Eustathius. The passage could indeed illustrate a completely different aspect of the transmission of Demetrios' work, whereas Eustathius is closely linked to Stephanus and Strabo not only because they are among his main sources, but also because Homer takes a central role, at least for Strabo and Eustathius. Finally, we shall see that the situation is actually quite similar to what we have found out about Stephanus with regard to the status of the fragments from Eustathius in Gaede's collection. The name of Demetrios does not occur, and the selected passages have been introduced into the collection because of the associations either Gaede or Biraschi made between aspects of their contents and statements found in other fragments more or less securely attributed to Demetrios. They can therefore again be of only limited use in our discussion here about the ways in which ancient authors used Demetrios' work. Still, as with Stephanus, because he also drew heavily on Strabo for some of his comments, we may have much material in Eustathius that could be linked, through Strabo, to Demetrios. We shall therefore examine the two passages from Eustathius' commentary to the *Iliad* that Gaede selected for his collection, as well as a third one, which does actually not belong to the collection of fragments but might still reveal interesting insights into the way elements from Demetrios' work entered Eustathius' commentary. Finally, we shall also extend the discussion to a passage from Eustathius' commentary to the *Odyssey*, which Biraschi adds as her dubious fr. 76.[213]

The two passages that Gaede includes in his collection are fr. 40 [Gaede/Biraschi][214] and fr. 30a [Gaede/Biraschi].[215] The first (fr. 40) is an extract from Eustathius' commentary about the Maeonian contingent in book 2 of the *Iliad*. The whole excursus on this topic repeats several of the elements found in two passages from Strabo: one has already been quoted above and contains the hypothesis that Asia was an alternative name of Maeonia,[216] whereas the other, occurring two paragraphs earlier in Strabo's text, discusses a plus-verse that was added in the Trojan Catalogue between the Maeonian contingent and the Carian one.[217] As we have seen, only in the second Straboian passage, the one about Esonia/Asia (actually fr. 41 [Gaede/Biraschi]), is the discussion attributed to

---

[213] Eustathius *Commentarii ad Odysseam* 11.538 (= 1696, 40–49 [Stallbaum]).
[214] Eustathius *Commentarii ad Iliadem* 2.865–866 (= 366, 14–15 or van der Valk I:577).
[215] Eustathius *Commentarii ad Iliadem* 12.20–21 (= 890, 5 or van der Valk III:345).
[216] Strabo 13.4.8 [C627] (= fr. 41 [Gaede/Biraschi]). See above Section 2.1.5 (pp. 106–107).
[217] Fr. 39 [Gaede/Biraschi] = Strabo 13.4.6 [C626]. The plus-verse is quoted as *Iliad* 2.866a. This makes a whole group of texts alluding to the same issue, including, besides the passages from Strabo and the one from Eustathius, also one of Stephanus' entries discussed above (fr. 42 [Gaede/Biraschi] = Stephanus Byzantius s.v. Ἠϊονία (= Stephanus Byzantius 304, 15 [Meineke]

Demetrios, although only through the rather vague formula οἱ περὶ τὸν Σκήψιον. All the rest is built on Gaede's interpretations. Moreover, the passage from Eustathius (fr. 40 [Gaede/Biraschi]) alludes to one of the editions that contained the plus-verse involved and is therefore more closely linked to the first passage from Strabo (fr. 39 [Gaede/Biraschi]) in which the discussion is precisely about the legitimacy and implications of this plus-verse, but no indication is given about the scholars involved in the controversy. Furthermore, at the beginning of fr. 41 [Gaede/Biraschi] Callisthenes is mentioned as having taken part in the discussion, which brings a further authority into the discussion, moreover one for whom we know, from another passage from Strabo, that he inserted two further plus-verses about the Cauconians into the Trojan Catalogue.[218] We see, therefore, that already, in the few pieces of evidence involved here, the names of three scholars who took part in the discussion appear. Besides Euripides, the scholar in whose edition the plus-verse was located, we have Callisthenes and then Demetrios, however in the particular formula (οἱ περὶ τὸν Σκήψιον), and this suggests that more than one scholar could have defended that position. This should make us cautious about making too strict an attribution of part of the debate to individual scholars, even if it is proper to see all the pieces of evidence involved as belonging to one thematic cluster about the Homeric text of the Trojan Catalogue to which Demetrios contributed.

As for fr. 30a [Gaede/Biraschi], we have to go back to the group of texts Gaede gathered under his fr. 29, fr. 30, and fr. 31. In Biraschi's edition, two of them, fr. 29 [Gaede/Biraschi] and fr. 31a [Biraschi], contain Strabo's description of the river system of the Troad.[219] The other pieces quoted under these numbers, among them the passage from Eustathius, contain elements that can loosely be linked to the content of the Straboian passage, as all of them give some details about the rivers of the Troad or reproduce some elements of Strabo's wording. However, the comment from Eustathius is not about Strabo's passage, even if the geographer is often quoted, but belongs to his discussion about the beginning of book 12 of the *Iliad*, in which the destruction of the Achaean wall by the Trojan rivers is announced.[220] This famous passage from the *Iliad* had indeed triggered many comments, as it is still possible to see through the scholia to this passage, some reproduced by Gaede as fragments from Demetrios,[221] and when reading

---

or Stephanus Byzantius η 25 [Billerbeck])) and a scholion to Apollonios Rhodios (Σ Apollonios Rhodios 2.777–779 [Wendel] = fr. 43 [Gaede/Biraschi]).

[218] Strabo 12.3.5 [C542] and *Iliad* 2.855ab for the two plus-verses.

[219] Strabo 13.1.43–44 [C602] and Strabo 13.1.44–45 [C602–603].

[220] Eustathius *Commentarii ad Iliadem* 12.20–21 (= 890, 5 or van der Valk III:345) and *Iliad* 12.1–35.

[221] Fr. 31a [Gaede] = Σ T. *Iliad* 12.20a [Erbse] corresponding to fr. 31b [Biraschi], fr. 31b [Gaede] = Σ T *Iliad* 12.20c [Erbse] corresponding to fr. 30c [Biraschi], and finally fr. 31c [Gaede] = Σ T *Iliad* 12.20e [Erbse], which is also fr. 31c [Biraschi].

the passage from Strabo involved. Also Eustathius' discussion about these lines is much longer than the few elements Gaede prints as fr. 30a in his edition, and should for instance also include the two passages alluded to under fr. 31a.[222] The scholion printed as fr. 31a and the passage in Eustathius Gaede equals to the scholion are about the river Rhesos and they locate it almost at the same place and almost with the same wording. This proximity is certainly more than just a coincidence and shows a certain closeness between the two witnesses, which has also been recognised by Erbse in his edition of the scholia to the *Iliad*.[223] But the situation may be too complex and the evidence about the scholars involved too scarce to say how much from Demetrios' work may have entered Eustathius' text, even if it may still be enough to include the passages in a collection of the fragments of Demetrios' work.

However, from our analysis we gain an interesting picture of the extension of the discussion involved here. First, we can see clearly that the discussion started from the Homeric lines in book 12 of the *Iliad*. There, eight rivers of the Troad are named, and the passage therefore provided much material to be commented upon by scholars who wanted to compare the information from the Homeric text with the landscape of the Troad that they could visit. Some parts of this discussion are developed in Strabo's description of the Trojan river system, but without a direct link to the text of the *Iliad*, whereas others are preserved in Eustathius' commentary on the passage from book 12. The content of his comments does not always overlap with the elements we find in Strabo, even if the geographer is often quoted, and reveals, therefore, further aspects of the discussion. Still other elements are preserved, albeit in an extremely abbreviated form, in the scholia to the *Iliad*. The outline of the debate is therefore fairly clearly established, even if not all gaps are filled. Demetrios must have taken part in the discussion, as his name is quoted in the Straboian passage, but we cannot find out from the elements that are preserved how much of his work ended up in Eustathius' commentary, or in what form. Demetrios' work could have been used directly by Eustathius, or elements that originally came from Demetrios could have been taken either from Strabo or from other sources who may have written their own commentaries or summarized Demetrios' work in a different way from Strabo.

What such a different way of entering Eustathius' work may have looked like can be seen when we discuss a further passage from his commentary that was not, however, included either in Gaede's or Biraschi's collection, but may

---

[222] Fr. 31a [Gaede] = Σ T. *Iliad* 12.20a [Erbse] corresponding to fr. 31b [Biraschi]. Both editors also quote Eustathius *Commentarii ad Iliadem* 12.20–22 (= 889, 5 or van der Valk III:344) where we find a very close paraphrase of the content of the scholion.

[223] Erbse 1973:299.

contain elements from Demetrios' work. The passage belongs to the very end of Eustathius' commentary and concerns line 802 of book 24, where we find a brief allusion to the feast in honor of the dead Hector taking place in Priam's palace. In his remark, Eustathius tries to account for the fact that no indications about the number of guests gathered at this feast are given in the Homeric text, and he quotes parts of the passage from Athenaeus that is counted as Demetrios' fr. 1 [Gaede/Biraschi].[224] Eustathius does not mention the name of his source, but paraphrases it by the expression κατὰ τὸν ἱστορήσαντα ὡς + content, whereas in Athenaeus the name of Demetrios is quoted together with the indication that the quotation comes from the first book of his work. There is, therefore, no doubt that the two passages ultimately came from the same source, which is probably Demetrios of Scepsis. But it is less obvious to find out whether Eustathius used Demetrios' work in its original form or took the information for instance from Athenaeus, which the closeness of the wording suggests,[225] or from a third source unknown to us. Indeed, such a third hypothesis seems necessary as there are two additional remarks in Eustathius' passages that do not overlap with Athenaeus' text. One is about Homer's fondness for the number nine, and the second suggests a link to a line in the *Odyssey* in which again the number nine is associated with feasts.[226] Therefore, even if the way these two remarks are introduced into the wording of Eustathius' passage does not allow us to make a hypothesis about their source, we can at least be sure that the work was not Athenaeus' *Deipnosophistai*. This is also confirmed if we take into account the places within the two works where the passage was located. As mentioned above, Eustathius alluded to Demetrios' considerations about the Carneia festival in Sparta at the very end of his commentary on the *Iliad*, while commenting on one of the last lines of the Homeric poem. However, we know from Athenaeus that Demetrios mentioned this issue in book 1 of his work, at its very beginning. Therefore, Eustathius cannot have found Demetrios' remark, for instance, in a comment on the same lines of the Homeric poem, as it is hardly possible that Demetrios would have started his work with comments on lines of book 24. It is much more likely that there could have been an element at the beginning of Demetrios' work that called for his comment on the Carneian festival, where he then expanded his considerations and included elements taken from book 24. In this case, the presence of these secondary elements could then have been interesting for Eustathius, or for an intermediary source, for his comment on the last lines of the *Iliad*, and this would then explain why a comment given in an original work at its beginning could figure at the end of

---

[224] Athenaeus 4.141e–f.

[225] It is well known that Eustathius used Athenaeus' work abundantly; Wilson 1983:200–201.

[226] The line as it is quoted in Eustathius is actually a mixture of lines forming *Odyssey* 3.7–8.

the second work. The presumed adaptation of the outline of the original work that such a reuse implies could then have been made either by Eustathius, if we considered a direct use, or by an intermediate source that Eustathius used for his comment. These changes may have been quite substantial, as the example from Athenaeus may show. Nothing in his quotation from Demetrios' work allows us to trace a path back to the original context of the remark about the Carneian festival, and we must conclude that Athenaeus, or his source, used this element in a way that is completely unrelated to the original context. This conclusion makes it even more difficult to consider Athenaeus' passage as a direct source of Eustathius in this particular case, despite the closeness of the wording. Indeed, it seems improbable that Eustathius used a quotation from Athenaeus' book 4, moreover in a context completely unrelated to the Homeric text, for his comment on the last few lines of the *Iliad*. But even so, and no matter what we may decide about such questions, it becomes obvious from the discussion that the structure of Demetrios' work has been lost in the course of the history of transmission, probably already at the time of Athenaeus, as it is no longer possible to determine from the evidence in Athenaeus or in Eustathius about which element in the *Iliad*, or in the Trojan Catalogue, the remark about the Carneian festival was given by Demetrios. The situation is then certainly more complex than suggested by previous scholars such as Stiehle, who claimed that because Sparta and its Carneian festival was mentioned in book 1 of Demetrios' work, this would have contained some preliminary considerations about the causes of the Trojan war.[227] We may also add here that, from what we know so far from Demetrios' work, we may have to look at the first lines of the Trojan Catalogue and examine how issues related to these lines may have triggered such a comment on the Carneian feast.[228]

As the last element in our discussion about the evidence in Eustathius' text we should analyze Biraschi's dubious fr. 76, a passage from Eustathius' commentary to the *Odyssey*.[229] The link between the passage, in which a Demetrios of Ilion is mentioned, and our Demetrios of Scepsis, has already been made by Carl Müller in his *Fragmenta historicorum graecorum*.[230] Under his entry of Demetrios of Erythraea, three different scholars who are all named Demetrios are associated, namely, Demetrios of Erythraea, the Demetrios of Ilion from Eustathius' passage under discussion here, and our Demetrios of Scepsis. Müller quotes the passage from Eustathius where Demetrios of Ilion is mentioned *in extenso* as belonging to Demetrios of Erythraea, but he is more cautious about Demetrios

---

[227] Stiehle 1850:544–545.
[228] See Trachsel 2018:203–221, for such a hypothesis.
[229] Eustathius *Commentarii ad Odysseam* 11.538 (= 1696, 40–49 [Stallbaum]).
[230] Müller 1851:382.

of Scepsis. He only suggests a possible identification of this scholar with the two others by relegating a list of fragments in which Demetrios of Scepsis is quoted to a footnote.[231] Gaede did not follow Müller's choice and we find nothing about this possible association in his work. This is mainly due to the fact that Müller's suggestion to consider all three names as referring to one scholar is controversial. It involves six passages from very different works and relies almost entirely on the way some of them have been transmitted by Photius. Indeed, besides the passage from Eustathius quoted as fr. 76 [Biraschi], which is the first piece of evidence, scholars adduce, as second item of their demonstration, a passage from Photius' summary of Ptolemaios Chennos' *New History*.[232] The remark, occurring in Photius' summary of Ptolemaios' book 3, is shorter than the passage from Eustathius and does not repeat the name of the authority, but shares its content. It has therefore been attributed by Jacoby to Demetrios of Ilion, but without going back to Demetrios of Erythraea as suggested by Müller.[233] The third passage involved comes from the *Eudociae Augustae Violarium*, a highly controversial work.[234] In one of the entries of this compilation (n° 281), Demetrios of Ilion is said to have written a Τρωϊκά in twenty books, and this piece of information has been taken as T11 by Biraschi, who associates Demetrios of Scepsis again with this Demetrios of Ilion.[235] The fourth passage comes, once again, from the same summary of Ptolemaios Chennos' work. When Photius summarizes book 5 of Ptolemaios' work, we find the passage quoted as T10 [Biraschi] where we learn that Demetrios of Scepsis had the book of a Tellis nearby when he died. This Tellis—or at least a Tellis—seems also to have been quoted by Eustathius, just next to the first passage involved here,[236] as the authority for the episode of Achilles' killing of Penthesileia, and this is the fifth passage that must be taken into account to understand the line of argument. Finally, this episode about the death of Penthesileia is again alluded to in the same summary of Ptolemaios'

---

[231] *Fragmenta historicorum graecorum* IV, pp. 381–382. See now also *Digital Fragmenta Historicorum Graecorum* at http://www.dfhg-project.org/DFHG/index.php?volume=Volumen%20quartum#.

[232] Photius *Bibliotheca* 190, 148b 21–24.

[233] *Die Fragmente der griechischen Historiker* 59 F1a (= Eustathius *Commentarii ad Odysseam* 11.538 (= 1696, 40–49 [Stallbaum]) and *Die Fragmente der griechischen Historiker* 59 F1b (= Photius *Bibliotheca* 190, 148b 21–24). See now also *Brill's New Jacoby* 59 with further comments on Demetrios of Ilion, and Cameron 2004:141–142 for a more skeptical point of view on this Demetrios. Kim 2010:18–21 joins Cameron in his skepticism about most of Ptolemy's sources.

[234] For an edition of its text, see Flach 1880. It has, however, been proved at the end of the nineteenth century that this work was a Renaissance creation; see Cohn 1907:912–913 and Pulch 1882:177–192.

[235] T11 [Biraschi] = Eudocia 128 (= Flach 1880:221). See further Stiehle 1854:509 and Jacoby 1957b:562 (= commentary to *Die Fragmente der griechischen Historiker* 61).

[236] Eustathius *Commentarii ad Odysseam* 11.538 (= 1696, 51 [Stallbaum]) = *Die Fragmente der griechischen Historiker* 61 F1a.

work, in the part dealing with book 6.[237] This makes the sixth passage in our argumentation, and it has been attributed by Jacoby, because of the closeness of content, to the Tellis mentioned in the passage quoted under T10 [Biraschi].[238] We therefore have the following situation: in Photius' summary of Ptolemaios Chennos' *New History* as it is preserved now, we have Demetrios of Scepsis mentioned in a context where, just beforehand, elements that can be attributed to Demetrios of Ilion are quoted, and just after it, elements that came from Tellis' work. This closeness has been taken as evidence to prove the assimilation of the two scholars named Demetrios: Demetrios of Ilion and Demetrios of Scepsis. However, according to Photius' summary, the pieces attributed to Demetrios of Ilion come from book 3, the quotation of Demetrios of Scepsis from book 5, and the episode narrated by Tellis from book 6. This suggests that there may not have been such a tight connection in the original work as the wording of the preserved summary suggests. It is the same for the passages from Eustathius. Demetrios of Ilion is quoted there next to Tellis, and apparently about the same line of the Homeric text (*Odyssey* 11.538). This could indeed suggest that the pieces came from the same comment about this line. But we have no evidence about Demetrios of Scepsis in this context, and nothing tells us that, if we accept the hypothesis of one single comment as the origin for the two remarks, this comment may not already have been a mixture of elements from several sources so that it is not possible to attribute it to Demetrios of Scepsis. Certainly T10 [Biraschi] proves that Demetrios must have known the work of Tellis, as he had it by his side when he died. But this statement provides a chronological framework that helps us to date this Tellis, rather than gives us any further information about Demetrios. Furthermore, there is no incontestable evidence that would allow us to identify the Demetrios of Ilion quoted just before Tellis with the Demetrios of Scepsis who may have used the work of Tellis, and Jacoby even suggests that the existence of one name (Demetrios of Scepsis) may have influenced the creation of the other (Demetrios of Ilion).[239]

In this situation, it becomes obvious that we cannot use the passage from Eustathius' commentary to the *Odyssey* for our present discussion. Its attribution to Demetrios' work is simply too hypothetical. But the discussion did involve the witness from Photius who summarized the work of Ptolemaios Chennos in which Demetrios of Scepsis was certainly used at least for an episode about his life. We therefore see again through how many steps elements from Demetrios' book may have gone in the course of time. Ptolemaios, living probably at the end

---

[237] *Die Fragmente der griechischen Historiker* 61 F1b (= Photius *Bibliotheca* 190, 151b 29–32).

[238] Photius *Bibliotheca* 190, 151a 6–8 (=*Die Fragmente der griechischen Historiker* 61 T1).

[239] Jacoby 1957b:533 (= commentary to *Die Fragmente der griechischen Historiker* 59). See also *Brill's New Jacoby* 59 with its commentary.

of the first century CE or at the beginning of the second century CE, probably knew Demetrios of Scepsis and may have used elements from his work. We only have an allusion to it in the summary Photius made in the ninth century. Some of the elements that have been mentioned in this summary, in the surrounding of the quotation of Demetrios' name, also appear in Eustathius' commentary on the *Odyssey*. Some are attributed to Demetrios of Ilion and some to Tellis, but it is impossible to find out from what is left through what kinds of sources Eustathius had access to the information he quoted. He may have taken it from summaries like that of Photius, or from work like that of Ptolemaios Chennos, or even, although less likely, from the original works of Demetrios of Ilion or Tellis. But we have to acknowledge that we lose at least the name of Demetrios of Scepsis in this process. We have therefore reached a similar conclusion as the one we obtained in the discussion about the two passages quoted in Gaede's edition. Elements from Demetrios' work may have come down to Eustathius, who incorporated them into his comments given in his two commentaries on the Homeric text, but it is impossible for us to find out from what is left whether Eustathius was aware of the fact that he was using elements from Demetrios' work, but did not quote his name, or if he took them from intermediate sources in which the name of Demetrios had already been lost. That both options existed even in the twelfth century is proved by the fact that the name of Demetrios of Scepsis is preserved in the fragment from Tzetzes, to which we shall now turn. It is, however, obvious that Demetrios ceased to be a main source for scholars in those days. Authors like Strabo, who certainly built their own statements on elements from Demetrios, are much more present at that point and had probably substituted the work of Demetrios.

2.1.7 Tzetzes

Even if we have to assume that Tzetzes had a good library at his disposal when he wrote his several commentaries and must have had access to books now lost, it is still difficult to measure today how much he read firsthand and what he found in other sources.[240] We are therefore back to the same hesitation we encountered with many of the authors mentioned above, with regard to the way Demetrios' work may have been accessible, even though his name is quoted in the passage involved and the attribution is therefore beyond doubt. On the one hand, this situation is certainly due to the fact that there is only one passage from Demetrios in Tzetzes' work. On the other, however, the fact that the remark occurs in Tzetzes' commentary on Lycophron also seems to

---

[240] Wilson 1983:96.

detach it from the source where Tzetzes may have found it. Demetrios' Τρωϊκὸς διάκοσμος does not seem to be the first work one would consult when trying to understand Lycophron's poems, even if it is certainly not impossible that one would do so. However, as far as the content is concerned, the passage from Tzetzes seems to be surprisingly close to what Demetrios' original comment may have been, and this may suggest that there were not too many interme-diate sources between Tzetzes and Demetrios. Indeed, it is quite easy to link the preserved remark to a line of the Trojan Catalogue, even if the comment is actu-ally about a line from the Catalogue of the Ships that alludes to Protesilaos.[241] Tzetzes tells his reader that Demetrios, as well as Sophocles, defended a rather unusual version of this episode, as both name Hector as the hero who killed Protesilaos. In the *Iliad* no name is given, and Protesilaos is said to have been killed by a Dardanian man (Δάρδανος ἀνήρ). This formulation triggered a huge debate among ancient scholars, and several options were discussed to iden-tify this Dardanian with a better-known hero such as Hector or Aeneas, and the debate can still be observed in some of the scholia and in a summary in Eustathius.[242] As one of the scholion that alludes to the debate is about a line from the enumeration of the Dardanian contingent in the Trojan Catalogue, we may guess where such a remark about the hero who killed Protesilaos may have occurred in Demetrios' work, namely, when he himself was commenting on the Dardanian contingent, its leaders, and probably the stories and controversies about them. Furthermore, the fact that the fragment is concerned with textual criticism and speaks about a variant reading of a Homeric line is in accordance with the topics of other fragments from Demetrios, and could suggest that the distance between the version we have preserved and the original comment from Demetrios is not too great. For instance, in fr. 17 [Gaede],[243] fr. 39 [Gaede/Biraschi],[244] and fr. 40 [Gaede/Biraschi],[245] Demetrios argues in favor of variants of given lines or mentions plus-verses. Fragment 75 [Gaede/Biraschi] there-fore fits this context and, together with the other examples, illustrates that Demetrios must also have worked on this level of textual criticism, even if it was certainly to a large extent in combination with his topographical approach, as we have seen in Chapter 1.[246] But it is difficult to go any further here. We simply do not know enough about Tzetzes to find out how the comment from

---

[241] *Iliad* 2.701.

[242] Σ D *Iliad* 2.701 [van Thiel] (or Σ A *Iliad* 2.701 [Erbse]); Σ A *Iliad* 2.819 [Erbse]. Eustathius *Commentarii ad Iliadem* 2.701 (= 326, 5–6 or van der Valk I:508). See also Trachsel 2011:153–167 for a close discussion of this topic in relation with fr. 75 [Gaede/Biraschi].

[243] Strabo 10.5.19 [C489] (= fr. 17a [Biraschi]).

[244] Strabo 13.4.6 [C626].

[245] Eustathius *Commentarii ad Iliadem* 2.856–866 (= 366, 14–15 or van der Valk I:577).

[246] See above Section 1.2.1 (pp. 33–34).

Demetrios found its way into Tzetzes' work about Lycophron's poem. We have to assume that there was a wide range of material available for the study of one text, and Tzetzes may have combined the information he mentioned from different sources he read, or taken information from already existing comments and scholia he found in the margins of the texts.[247]

However, even if the discussion did not help us, despite the presence of Demetrios' name, to answer the question about how Demetrios' work was preserved by the author who quoted him, it is important for our study in two ways. It has not only revealed how the content can be linked to the Trojan Catalogue, but has also showed that the place the fragment takes in Gaede's collection is misleading. This is certainly to some extent due to the chronological approach taken, for instance, by Müller for his arrangement of the fragments, which led Gaede to quote the fragment as the last item. But, as we have suggested, Demetrios' comment about the hero who may have killed Protesilaos is more suitable for the Dardanian contingent, which is the second in the Homeric text. The remark may therefore have occurred at the beginning of Demetrios' work.

2.1.8 Scholia

As mentioned before, but also as a conclusion from the discussion outlined in the previous sections, we must change our approach when focusing on the scholia and the way the fragments of Demetrios have been preserved in these corpora. It is no longer possible to find out how the work has been appreciated by the many authors and scholiasts who contributed to the accumulation of comments in the margins of the medieval manuscripts. We have seen that it became more and more difficult to answer such questions with authors from late Antiquity and beyond, for whom we still can assume that the works were written by one person. It is therefore even more difficult for the scholia, with their many layers of composition for which works that were already compilations were often used.[248] Therefore, if Demetrios appears in the scholia, this means that his work may not only have been used directly by the contributors to the scholia if they had Demetrios' work still at their disposal, but may also have entered the corpus indirectly when he was used by the authors whose works were then summarized

---

[247] For the scholia to Lycophron, Tzetzes' comments correspond most of the time with the so-called ancient scholia, which were the scholia made to Lycophron's text before Tzetzes. See Dickey 2007:65, and more generally for the difference between scholia noted alongside the text and more independent commentaries, see Budelmann 2002:143–148. For the work on Homer in Byzantine times, see in addition Browning 1992:134–148.

[248] Dickey 2007:31–34, 38–40, 62–65.

into the scholia. It is therefore no longer possible to break down all these steps of the creation process of the scholia, and we have to acknowledge that there are too many lacunae in our knowledge about this process to infer from that how Demetrios' contribution was appreciated during this process. This is especially so, because we lose in the scholia the concept of single author, and have to assume that there was more than one contributor, each of whom may have appreciated Demetrios differently. Nevertheless, the fact that some of the elements from Demetrios' work appear in the scholia, moreover in different corpora of scholia,[249] may still say something about the way Demetrios' work has been preserved and used.

We shall separate our discussion into two sections, one on the scholia to Homer and one on the other scholia, and begin with this second group, as it will be more heterogeneous, composed of corpora for which each, taken separately, contains only very few elements from Demetrios' work. In the scholia to Homer we have exactly the opposite situation. There is only one corpus, more precisely the scholia to the *Iliad*, which contains all the seventeen preserved fragments.

In this second more heterogeneous group we shall begin with the scholia to Apollonios Rhodios in which six fragments have been preserved, which is the largest amount after those in the scholia to the *Iliad*. These may therefore give us the most complete picture about how the fragments occur in such kinds of corpora. Moreover, in five of them, the name of Demetrios is quoted in full,[250] which leaves us with only one fragment that Gaede attributes to Demetrios, indirectly through an association with two other fragments.[251] The first striking point about this corpus is the fact that they are not evenly distributed: four out of the six are found in the first book, moreover assembled in two groups in which two fragments follow each other quite closely. This is certainly due to the episode to which the lemma for the scholia belongs. The first two (fr. 51 [Gaede/Biraschi] and fr. 52 [Gaede/Biraschi]) are about two words, one in line 230 and the other in line 238 of book 1.[252] They both belong to a passage, following the catalogue of the heroes taking part in the expedition, that describes the place

---

[249] These are the scholia to Homer, Pindar, Euripides, Apollonios Rhodios, and Theocritos.

[250] Fr. 51 [Gaede/Biraschi] = Σ Apollonios Rhodios 1.230 [Wendel]; fr. 52 [Gaede/Biraschi] = Σ Apollonios Rhodios 1.238 [Wendel]; fr. 53 [Gaede/Biraschi] = Σ Apollonios Rhodios 3.134 [Wendel]; fr. 70 [Gaede] (or 70a [Biraschi]) = Σ Apollonios Rhodios 1.1123 [Wendel]; and fr. 71 [Gaede/Biraschi] = Σ Apollonios Rhodios 1.1165 [Wendel].

[251] Fr. 43 [Gaede/Biraschi] = Σ Apollonios Rhodios 2.777–779 [Wendel]. The fragment is only a small part of the entire scholion and deals with the toponym Asia. This is also the subject of fr. 41 [Gaede/Biraschi] = Strabo 13.4.8 [C627] and fr. 42 [Gaede/Biraschi] = Stephanus Byzantius s.v. Ἡσιονία (= Stephanus Byzantius 304, 15 [Meineke] or Stephanus Byzantius η 25 [Billerbeck]).

[252] Fr. 51 [Gaede/Biraschi] = Σ Apollonios Rhodios 1.230 [Wendel] and fr. 52 [Gaede/Biraschi] = Σ Apollonios Rhodios 1.238 [Wendel].

where they gathered to launch the Argo. There is therefore no link to Trojan landscape here, and this could suggest that, precisely because of the absence of any geographical closeness between the two topographical frameworks involved, it is rather the position this passage takes in the narration that proves the link to Demetrios' work. The Hellenistic scholar may indeed have compared the place where the Trojans stood when the narration is left for the enumeration of the Trojan Catalogue to the one where the Argonauts were during Apollonios' catalogue, and may then have discussed the topographical elements from the second setting. If our hypothesis is correct, the first fragment may illustrate how large the geographical area could be in Demetrios' work, whereas the second would add a further element in favor of our hypothesis. Indeed, in the first fragment the discussion is about the adjective Minyan, which is given to the Argonauts. The attribution of this adjective to the Argonauts causes some topographical concerns, as the Minyans are thought to be associated with Orchomene in Boeotia,[253] and, as just mentioned, the focus is therefore on an issue concerning mainland Greece and not on the Trojan landscape. Now, when accepting our hypothesis that the Hellenistic scholar discussed the catalogue of the Argonauts when he compared it to the one of the Trojans in the *Iliad*, and analyzed the place where the two troops stood at the moment of the narration of the catalogues, we should be able to guess from that how considerations about mainland Greece may have entered Demetrios' work and to what depth Demetrios discussed these issues. Such a hypothesis may indeed be supported by the second fragment. It is about the name of the place where the Argo was launched. It is called Pagasai, and Demetrios is quoted for giving an alternative etymology of the name. It is again rather difficult, at first sight, to work out how such a comment could have been triggered by the Homeric lines of the Trojan Catalogue, even if Demetrios' dealings with etymology can also be observed in other fragments. We may, however, think of several topographical elements in the context of the Trojan Catalogue, which may be compared to Pagasai where the Argo was launched. Bateia, the hill where the Trojans gathered before the enumeration of their contingents, is one of the possibilities, but there is, for the time being, certainly not enough evidence to make this more than a guess. It may, however, get some support later during the discussion on the second cluster of passages to which we shall turn now.

It is a little easier to attribute such a link to the Homeric text when we proceed to the second cluster in book 1, fr. 70a [Biraschi] and fr. 71 [Gaede/ Biraschi], both occurring in the episode that takes place in and around

---

[253] For a short summary of this issue, see Vian/Delage 1974:10–12.

Cyzicos.[254] As this peninsula is located on the shore of the Propontis, it would actually belong to a region covered by the enumeration of the Trojan Catalogue, even if the toponym does not appear in the enumeration itself. In the Homeric text only Zeleia from the Trojan contingent under Pandaros and Adrasteia in the contingent from the Propontis are mentioned among the places that come closest to Cyzicos. Moreover, in the Mysian contingent, in which Cyzicos could be located from a geographical point of view, no place is mentioned, only the two leaders.[255] It seems, therefore, that Cyzicos belonged to the places that are absent from the Homeric text and for which its inhabitants had to create another past, if possible as prestigious as the one referring back to the *Iliad*. A version of such a past, which was based on the passage of the Argonauts and alluded to by Apollonios, may certainly have been attractive for the inhabitants of Cyzicos. Demetrios, on the other hand, may have had access during his research to the same mythological traditions about Cyzicos as Apollonios had previously, but he may have used them in another way. For instance, he may have tried to distinguish, when discussing the region common to both mythological stories, mainly the Propontis, the topographical elements belonging to the Trojan myth from those linked to the legend of the Argonauts. At least in fr. 50 [Gaede/Biraschi][256] such a line of argument is preserved. Strabo quotes Demetrios for having spoken against the version of Neanthes of Cyzicos, another of the local historians of the Troad, who claimed that the Argonauts founded the cult of the great Mother in Cyzicos on their way to Aietes. We have spoken about the political implications of this in the time of Demetrios in the chapter on the historical background. Here we may add that the fact that Demetrios is not only quoted by Strabo as speaking against Neanthes, but is also alluded to in the scholia to the passage of the *Argonautica* involved in the debate about Cyzicos, could indeed suggest that Demetrios must also have discussed evidence from the legend of the Argonauts when giving his topographical comments about the Trojan Catalogue. Furthermore, the words actually used as lemmata for the comments of the scholia would also allow such a conclusion.

The word discussed in the first scholion, χέραδος, is a hapax in the *Iliad*, which Apollonios used in a rather particular way in his episode about Cyzicos. In the *Iliad* the word is used in book 21 by the river Scamandros. He complains to his brother, the Simois, about the outrageous way Achilles is killing the Trojans in his riverbed, and threatens to bury the hero under a huge amount of stone (χέραδος). In Apollonios, however, the word is used for a hill of stones situated

---

[254] Fr. 70 [Gaede] or fr. 70a [Biraschi] = Σ Apollonios Rhodios 1.1123 [Wendel] and fr. 71 [Gaede/Biraschi] = Σ Apollonios Rhodios 1.1165 [Wendel].

[255] *Iliad* 2.858–861.

[256] Strabo 1.2.38–40 [C45–47].

on a mountain where no river is nearby. Furthermore, it is not created to become the tomb of a hero, as in the *Iliad*, but forms the altar for a goddess. Demetrios may have noted this reference to the *Iliad* made by Apollonios and discussed the difference in the usage of the word, which must have been striking.[257] It is, however, less clear where in his commentary Demetrios may have done this. Several possibilities may be mentioned here. First, there are some genealogical elements that could bring us back to the lines of the Trojan Catalogue. The mythological king Cyzicos is believed to be the son of Aenete who is the daughter of Eussoros. This Eussoros is also mentioned as the father of Acamas, one of the leaders of the Thracian contingent.[258] The wife of Cyzicos, Cleite, can also be linked to some of the heroes mentioned in the Trojan Catalogue. She is said to have been the daughter of Merops, who is mentioned as the father of the two leaders of the contingent from the Propontis region. With such connections, we could assume that a comment on the mythological ruler of Cyzicos could have been made when Demetrios was discussing the genealogy of either of the heroes mentioned. A further hypothesis would go back to the passage from Strabo quoted as fr. 50 [Gaede/Biraschi], already mentioned in our discussion. In this passage the central argumentation is about Jason's stay in Lemnos. Strabo criticizes Demetrios, who refused to acknowledge that Homer knew about the journey of the Argonauts, and bases his objections against the Hellenistic scholar on the fact that such a claim is in contradiction of Demetrios' own statements and also with what Homer says. Indeed, in three passages in the *Iliad* the link between Jason and Lemnos is alluded to.[259] One of the passages also occurs in book 21 and concerns the episode about Lycaon, who has been captured by Achilles and was sold to Euneos in Lemnos. From there he is ransomed by Eetion and sent to Arisbe. We see, therefore, that the discussion about Lemnos and its status as a connecting element between the Trojan story and the legend of the Argonauts implies toponyms that occur in the Trojan Catalogue and may have functioned as lemma for the development of a rather extensive comment: it may have started with Arsibe and the allusion to Lycaon's stay there. In order to understand this aspect, the episode of his being sold to Euneos of Lemnos had to be mentioned. This in turn may imply that the history of Lemnos and the genealogy of its ruler is explained, which can only be done with an episode from the legend of the Argonauts. We have therefore found another possible link between the preserved fragments and the Homeric lines

---

[257] For instance, in Pindar too, the word χέραδος is associated with the power of rivers in the sense that a river is able to carry such a great amount of stones. See Pindar *Pythian* 6.10–14.

[258] *Iliad* 6.8.

[259] *Iliad* 7.468–469; *Iliad* 21.41; *Iliad* 23.747: actually through the mention of Euneos, the son of Jason and Hypsipyle.

of the Trojan Catalogue. From this, and no matter which hypothesis we may favor, it becomes evident that the two fragments, fr. 50 (from Strabo) and fr. 70a (from the scholia to Apollonios Rhodios), can both be linked to the topographical framework, which is the background of three Trojan contingents located on the Hellespontian shore. Moreover, we may guess that one of the important elements in this discussion was Cyzicos, its status in the mythological past, and the disagreement between Neanthes of Cyzicos, defending his hometown, and Demetrios, who tries to dismiss this claim by stating that Homer did not know about the Argonauts' journey.

The lemma for the second scholion is the river Rhyndacos, even if the comment itself is about the Giant Briareos, also known as Aigaion, who was buried near this river, which empties into the Propontis a little further west of Cyzicos. The river is not mentioned in the *Iliad*, but Achilles alludes to Briareos and his human name of Aigaion in book 1.[260] There was a huge debate about this hero and his tomb in Antiquity,[261] and a scholar commenting on the landscape of the Troad must have mentioned these issues when speaking about the shore of the Propontis. Moreover, the readings of the Homeric lines from book 1 where the hero was mentioned varied in Antiquity, as for instance Zenodotos defended another version for this passage, and this may also have created many comments.[262] But again it is difficult to bring the debate we may presume from this evidence back to the lines of the Trojan Catalogue. We may suggest here one solution, which is built on Briareos who has an alternative human name. In several other places in the *Iliad* such a double name is alluded to.[263] Two of these examples are relevant for us here: the hill called Bateia, which takes its divine name from the Amazone Myrina, and the river Scamandros, whose alternative divine name was Xanthos. Neither of the two names occurs in the lines of the Trojan Catalogue, but for both it is reasonable to think that a commentator focusing on the Trojan Catalogue may have mentioned them. If we turn to the hill Bateia we may remember that this was already a possible lemma for a comment of Demetrios in the discussion about the fragment dealing with Pagasai. Now, with our discussion here we may not only strengthen, with the analysis of the present fragment, our guess about the two first scholia from book 1, but also adduce further evidence by mentioning that the discussion of topographical elements that do not figure in the lines of the Trojan Catalogue, but belong to the setting where the gathering of the troops took place, can also be

---

[260] *Iliad* 1.403–404.
[261] Some allusions to this ancient debate can be found in Delage 1930:114–115 and Vian/Delage 1974:30–31.
[262] Σ A *Iliad* 1.404a [Erbse] and the discussion in Kirk 1985:94–95.
[263] Kirk 1985:93.

found in other fragments of Demetrios' work. We have seen, when discussing the entries from Stephanus of Byzantium, that *Iliad* 2.461 could be linked to the discussion about Asia and therefore to fr. 40 [Gaede/Biraschi], fr. 41 [Gaede/Biraschi], fr. 42 [Gaede/Biraschi], and fr. 43 [Gaede/Biraschi].[264] This line belongs to the description of the setting before the two catalogues when the two armies gather on the battlefield. Also *Iliad* 2.783 about the Arimoi is connected to fr. 39 [Gaede/Biraschi] in which the contingent of the Maeonians is discussed.[265] This seems to hint at the fact, suggested above as a hypothesis, that Demetrios may also have commented on the setting where the two armies gathered before the two catalogues were given, not only on the toponyms mentioned within the enumeration of the Trojans.

However, the second hypothesis, the river Scamadros, could also figure as lemma for our discussion on fr. 71 [Gaede/Biraschi], especially as in the D-scholia to the passage about Briareos in book 1, the Scamandros is mentioned as one of the other examples where two names exist.[266] However, as Batieia, he is not mentioned in the lines of the Trojan Catalogue. It still is a river, as is the Rhyndacos, and we know, for instance from fr. 29 [Gaede/Biraschi] that Demetrios discussed abundantly the river system of the Troad, probably in connection with the adjective πολυπίδακος of Mount Ida.[267] It is explicitly said in the scholia to Apollonios Rhodios that Demetrios not only spoke about the hero Briareos (scholion c), but also about the river Rhyndacos (scholion a). It is therefore possible that the topic was mentioned in connection with the other rivers of the Troad in a long discussion for which the entry was either the Aisepos mentioned in the third contingent led by Pandaros or Mount Ida, which is named twice in the Trojan Catalogue, once in the Dardanian contingent, and once also in the one led by Pandaros. But this suggestion also remains hypothetical, and constitutes an alternative to the hypothesis about Batieia as a lemma. Both are probable, but the evidence is not sufficient to prove either of them.

The situation is better with fr. 43 [Gaede/Biraschi][268] from the scholia to book 2, even if the name of the Hellenistic scholar does not appear in the preserved wording and the attribution depends on Gaede's interpretation. Here the passage is explicitly linked to a particular line of the Homeric text (*Iliad* 2.461), and has therefore been associated by Gaede with a whole group of

---

[264] Fr. 40 [Gaede/Biraschi] = Eustathius *Commentarii ad Iliadem* 2.856–866 (= 366, 14–15 or van der Valk I:577), fr. 41 [Gaede/Biraschi] = Strabo 13.4.8 [C627]; fr. 42 [Gaede/Biraschi] = Stephanus Byzantius s.v. Ἠιονία (= Stephanus Byzantius 304, 15 [Meineke] or Stephanus Byzantius η 25 [Billerbeck]) and fr. 43 [Gaede/Biraschi] = Σ Apollonios Rhodios 2.777–779 [Wendel].

[265] Strabo 13.4.6 [C626].

[266] Σ D *Iliad* 1.403 [van Thiel] (or Σ A *Iliad* 1.403 [Erbse]).

[267] Fr. 29 [Gaede/Biraschi] = Strabo 13.1.43–44 [C602].

[268] Σ Apollonios Rhodios 2.777–779 [Wendel].

fragments (fr. 41 [Gaede/Biraschi] and fr. 42 [Gaede/Biraschi])[269] speaking about Asia. Together with fr. 39 [Gaede/Biraschi] and fr. 40 [Gaede/Biraschi],[270] this issue can be linked to the Maeonian contingent.[271]

We are, therefore, closer to the Homeric text with this scholion than with the four previous ones, even if the context in Apollonios' text, from which the lemma comes, does not give us any further indications about the issue. At this point of the story, Jason has reached the land of the Mariandynoi and gives a summary of their journey to Lycos, who rules this country. It is in Lycos' reaction to Jason's speech where the expression δι' Ἀσίδος ἠπείροιο, which is the lemma for the scholion, is mentioned. The particularity of the formula that generated the scholar's comments is to be found in its syntactic structure rather than in the explicit identification of Asia with Lydia. The element Ἀσίδος referring to Asia is used as an adjective here, which happens only twice in Apollonios' poem, in our passage here and in Apollonios Rhodios 1.444.[272]

However, also in *Iliad* 2.461 the term Ἀσίῳ (in the expression Ἀσίῳ ἐν λειμῶνι) seems to be used as an adjective, even if there is some evidence in the Homeric scholia of a hesitation among ancient scholars and some of them read Ἀσίῳ as a genitive form of the proper name Asias or Asios.[273] In light of this debate, we could suggest that Apollonios, as sometimes happens, used the wording of his poem to participate in such scholarly discussions and provided his own answers. In our case this would mean that he deliberately chose the adjectival form to express his scholarly convictions about the Homeric passage from book 2. This was then noticed by some of Apollonios' readers and led to the scholion, which shows how closely some of the scholiasts read the text, examining very carefully the wording Apollonios used and explaining the scholarly ζητήματα this may refer to.

This is, however, still rather far away from Demetrios, and the comment could be attributed to any scholar, even if the quotation of *Iliad* 2.461 in the scholion links the passage to fr. 41 [Gaede/Biraschi], a passage from Strabo in which Demetrios is mentioned for a comment on the same Homeric line.[274] If

---

[269] Fr. 41 [Gaede/Biraschi] = Strabo 13.4.8 [C627] and fr. 42 [Gaede/Biraschi] = Stephanus Byzantius s.v. Ἡϊονία (= Stephnus Byzantius 304, 15 [Meineke] or Stephanus Byzantius η 25 [Billerbeck]).

[270] Fr. 39 [Gaede/Biraschi] = Strabo 13.4.6 [C626] and fr. 40 [Gaede/Biraschi] = Eustathius *Commentarii ad Iliadem* 2.856–866 (= 366, 14–15 or van der Valk I:577).

[271] *Iliad* 2.864–866.

[272] Matteo 2007:515.

[273] See Σ A *Iliad* 2.461b [Erbse] and Σ D *Iliad* 2.461 [van Thiel] (for Asias) and Σ A *Iliad* 2.461c and d [Erbse] and Σ T in bT *Iliad* 2.461 (for Asios). See Krik 1985:164 for further details about the ancient debate.

[274] Strabo 13.4.8 [C627]. We have already mentioned this passage several times, for instance, in the discussions about Eustathius and Stephanus of Byzantium. This is due to the fact that Gaede considers fr. 39–43 as a group discussing several aspects of the same issue.

we accept Gaede's suggestion, this fragment may then show us that, as with the word χέραδος in fr. 70a [Biraschi],[275] the work of Demetrios may also have contained information about the wording of the *Iliad*, the variants that circulated about the text, and the issues they raised. This is important, as it would show how often the topographical elements have been overemphasized by modern commentators, giving, in doing so, an incomplete picture of Demetrios' concerns.

However, it remains true that Demetrios was certainly also used as a source for comments on the many local myths and topographical elements Apollonios introduced into his poem, as shown in the last fragment from the scholia to Apollonios Rhodios. Indeed, in the passage from book 3 in which the scholion mentions Demetrios of Scepsis, we are back to the topography of the Troad, as the passage is about the cave of Mount Ida.[276] In Apollonios' poem it is the goddess Aphrodite who mentions Mount Ida as the birthplace of Zeus. The scholiasts then add that there are two possible locations for Mount Ida: one in Crete and one in the Troad, where, according to Demetrios, people claimed Zeus was born. This brings us back to other fragments of Demetrios, for instance fr. 61 [Gaede/Biraschi],[277] which is a passage where the homonymy between places in Crete and places in the Troad is explained. Furthermore, when we consider that in Aphrodite's speech, one of Zeus' nurses, Adrasteia, is mentioned, we see that the discussion becomes even broader and involves the content of fr. 18a [Biraschi] and fr. 18b [Biraschi],[278] which are about the toponym Adrasteia occurring in *Iliad* 2.828. Moreover, the toponym Adrasteia is also mentioned in Apollonios Rhodios 1.1116, a few lines before the lemma to fr. 70a [Biraschi]. In the scholion to this line we find some further aspects about the debate and several ancient scholars are mentioned, probably Apollodoros of Athens among them.[279] Therefore, we see again how large the debate was in Antiquity and how many scholars took part. The occurrence of the name of Apollodoros of Athens brings us back to the question about the link between the two scholars as we developed it in the first sections of this chapter while discussing Strabo's text.

This allows us to conclude our discussion on the scholia to Apollonios Rhodios by comparing briefly the way the two scholars are quoted in this corpus and finding out what this may tell us about the way their works are presented or used. According to Lachenaud, Apollodoros of Athens is mentioned nine times

---

[275] Σ Apollonios Rhodios 1.1123 [Wendel] (= fr. 70 [Gaede]).

[276] Σ Apollonios Rhodios 3.134 [Wendel] (= fr. 53 [Gaede/Biraschi]).

[277] Strabo 10.3.19–21 [C472–473].

[278] Fr. 18a [Biraschi] (or fr. 18 [Gaede]) = Harpocration s.v. Ἀδράστειαν and fr. 18b [Biraschi] = Souda s.v. Ἀδράστεια (α 524 [Adler]).

[279] The passage has indeed been included in the collection made by Jacoby. See *Die Fragmente der griechischen Historiker* 244 F175.

in the scholia to Apollonios Rhodios.[280] This number is quite similar to the six fragments from Demetrios' work and may suggest that the two authors were of similar relevance for the readers of the *Argonautica*, who needed explanations for some of Apollonios' wording and composed the scholia. The parallel between the two scholars can also be extended to the distribution of the fragments within the corpus of the scholia. Apollonios is mentioned five times in book 1, three times in book 3, and once in book 4. Demetrios, as we have seen, is mentioned four times in book 1, once in book 2 (if we follow Gaede), and once in book 3. We see that, even if more than one of Apollodoros' writings is involved, the distribution is similar. It is for the first book, involving the topography of the Troad, that the two scholars were most used. This is slightly different, for instance, for Neanthes of Cyzicos, whom we have encountered several times in the discussion. His name appears only three times in the corpus of the scholia to Apollonios,[281] moreover twice in the same context, about the episode in Cyzicos where we also find, as we have seen, some of the fragments from Demetrios. He was probably one of Apollonios' main sources for this episode,[282] but this seems not to have been the case for the composers of the scholia who prefer to use, besides our two scholars, the work by the rather unknown Deilochos[283] or those of Ephoros, Timaeus, and Theopompos.[284] From these numbers we may therefore suppose that in the scholia to Apollonios, Demetrios is among one of the sources in which interesting elements could be found to explain Apollonios' text or story, as are other local historians. A commentator of this poem could then have used, in any of the different stages of the composition of the scholia, the work of Demetrios or elements from it, to comment on and explain Apollonios' work. Most of the time the content of these remarks alludes, as expected, to the landscape of the Troad, but it could also deal with issues linked more closely to the text, its wording or its variants, or to compare Apollonios' choices with Homeric vocabulary.

We may now turn to the remaining evidence from the other corpora of scholia and see how it may help us to complete the picture. We shall start with

---

[280] Lachenaud 2010:xxiv. He does not quote the references, but he is most probably alluding to the nine fragments from the scholia to Apollonios found as *Die Fragmente der griechischen Historiker* 244 F92, F107b, F114, F164, F174, F175, F240 [see apparatus], F242, and F277.

[281] Σ Apollonios Rhodios 1.308b [Wendel] (= *Die Fragmente der griechischen Historiker* 84 F42); Σ Apollonios Rhodios 1.1063 [Wendel] (= *Die Fragmente der griechischen Historiker* 84 F11) and Σ Apollonios Rhodios 1.1065 [Wendel] (= *Die Fragmente der griechischen Historiker* 84 F12).

[282] Delage 1930:92–113.

[283] *Die Fragmente der griechischen Historiker* 471.

[284] See Lachenaud 2010:xxi–xxii: Deilochos (or Deiochos) (twelve times), Ephoros (twelve times), Timaeus (seven times), and Theopompos (five times).

the scholion to Pindar quoted under fr. 54 [Gaede/Biraschi][285] as it is directly connected to the issue mentioned in fr. 53 [Gaede/Biraschi], the last scholion to Apollonios Rhodios. It is also about Zeus' birthplace and gives further insight into the difficulty, as now two alternative locations of the cave of Mount Ida, besides the one in Crete and the one in the Troad, are mentioned. Furthermore, precisely because of these further developments, the passage will yield additional information about the way Demetrios' work may have entered the different corpora of scholia. The context of Pindar's poem unfortunately does not help us much, as it is only in a short praise of Zeus that the poet mentions the cave of Mount Ida as the god's birthplace. However, as the Pindaric expression Ἰδαῖόν τε σεμνὸν ἄντρον is located in the poem near the river Alpheus, it was discussed and we have two comments preserved in the scholia: fr. 54 [Gaede/ Biraschi], and a paraphrase of the more commonly accepted version of Zeus' birth in Crete. When we look at the scholars who are quoted in these two entries of the scholia as authorities for the different versions, we see that, besides our Demetrios, Theon and Callimachos are quoted. Both names are extremely interesting for us. Theon, on the one hand, is the grammarian who composed several commentaries to different works of Hellenistic poets that were then incorporated into the corpora of the scholia we are discussing here.[286] Callimachos, on the other hand, is interesting in our context for two reasons. First, he is quoted in the scholion just preceding the one counted as fr. 53 [Gaede/Biraschi],[287] which is actually about Adrasteia, Zeus' nurse. Second, when turning back to fr. 54 [Gaede/Biraschi], we see that both comments, the scholion to Apollonios about Adrasteia and the scholion to Pindar, refer to the same poem, Callimachos' first Hymn, which is dedicated to Zeus and gives a large part to the story of the god's birth (lines 28–54). The Hellenistic poet alludes to hesitations about the localization of Zeus' birth, but chooses himself Arcadia. However, as he places at least the education of Zeus in Crete, he seems to have been more in favor of this version. There are, however, according to fr. 54 [Gaede/Biraschi], two other possible locations for the Idean cave, the one in the Troad, which seems to have been defended by Demetrios according to fr. 53 [Gaede/Biraschi] and fr. 61 [Gaede/Biraschi], and a third one in Elis, which Pindar may have mentioned in his poem, as is pointed out by Demetrios in fr. 54 [Gaede/Biraschi]. The wording of this scholion is, however, problematic, if taken on its own, as the alternative

---

[285] Σ Pindar *Olympian* 5.42a [Drachmann].

[286] This is explicitly claimed for the scholia to Apollonios Rhodios in the subscription, but modern scholars believe that his commentaries are also among the sources for the scholia to Theocritos and for those to Pindar. Guhl 1969:3–15 and Dickey 2007:62–65, who does not, however, mention this for the scholia to Pindar.

[287] Σ Apollonios Rhodios 3.133 [Wendel].

between Crete and the Troad for the location of the Idean cave is not attributed to Demetrios, but introduced by a impersonal ἔνιοι:

Ἰδαῖον ἄντρον ἐν Ἤλιδι Δημήτριος ὁ Σκήψιος νέων διακόσμου[288] ἱερὸν Διός. ἔνιοι δὲ νομίζοντες μὴ τῶν ἐν Ἤλιδι χωρίων αὐτὸν μεμνῆσθαι ὑπέλαβον μνημονεύειν Ἴδης τῆς ἐν Κρήτῃ ἢ τῆς ἐν Τροίᾳ. οὕτως Θέων φησίν.

Demetrios of Scepsis [says in the] Catalogue of the Ships that the Idean cave in Elis is dedicated to Zeus. Some scholars, however, who think that he does not mention the places in Elis, understand that he mentions either Mount Ida in Crete or the one in the Troad. So says Theon.[289]

Σ Pindar *Olympia* 5.42a [Drachmann]

In order to take account of the formulation of the scholion and to explain Demetrios' statement, Biraschi suggests that Demetrios may have adduced the evidence from Pindar's poem, where the Idean cave seemed to him to have been located in Elis, as an alternative variant to the localization in Crete, so that he could devalue this version by defining it as one among many and, by doing so, support his own Trojan hypothesis for Zeus' birthplace.[290] For us here, it is rather the fact that the whole comment was attributed, in a final remark, to Theon, which is interesting, especially as the formula as it stands may indicate several stages of the transmission. First, we may imply from the wording of the scholion that Theon may have alluded to the whole issue in his commentary to Pindar, and developed there Demetrios' particular position to which he may or may not have had direct access. Then, in the process of the creation of the scholia, Theon's comment seems to have been summarized. However, this was probably not carried out very accurately, so that the different hypotheses about the localization of the Idean cave were no longer attributed to the scholars who defended them and an impersonal ἔνιοι was substituted for at least one element of Demetrios' position, actually the most important one, the localization of Zeus' birth in the Troad. It is therefore an extremely indirect means through

---

[288] This formulation is highly problematic, as Demetrios' work was not on the Catalogue of the Ships but on its Trojan counterpart. The editors have suggested several restorations: see Gaede 1880:47 and Biraschi 2011, commentary ad fr. 54.

[289] As it is preserved, the first sentence of the scholion can unfortunately be understood in three different ways. Besides the translation given above, one could read: "Demetrios says ... that it is the Idean cave in Elis dedicated to Zeus" (given by Biraschi) or "Demetrios says ... that the Idean cave, which is dedicated to Zeus, is in Elis." Each of these readings points to a slightly different way that Demetrios may have dealt with the Idean cave in Elis in his work. All of them could be possible, and without another piece of evidence it seems impossible to decide.

[290] Biraschi 2011, commentary ad fr. 54.

which we have access to Demetrios' work in these fragments, and it would be misleading if we only had this one piece preserved on Demetrios' position in the question about Zeus' birthplace.

Such indirect use of Demetrios' work may also be suggested by the way the fragment from the scholia to Theocritos has been preserved.[291] It is in a long list of variant versions explaining the name of the Carneia festival in Sparta[292] that we find the one given by Demetrios, which figures, in the different editions, as fr. 2 [Gaede/Biraschi]. The discussion must have been quite lively in Antiquity, as we find another summary in Pausanias[293] and have altogether up to six different versions explaining either the name of this festival or the epithet of Apollo, for whom it was celebrated. Pausanias first summarizes a version involving a seer Crios and his daughter, which we do not find in the report from the scholia. Then we have a version, which is common to both sources, about a seer Carneios who is killed by a Hippotes, one of the Heracleidai. In the scholia, however, there are two slightly different versions of the same story, one of them attributed to Theopompos. Next we have, again in both sources, the one attributed to the poetess Praxilla, who claims that Carneios was a son of Zeus and Europe. The scholia have then two further versions, one from Alcman and the one from Demetrios, whereas Pausanias jumps directly to the last group given in the scholia, which explains the adjective κάρνειος not through a personal name, but through its closeness to the word for the cornel tree (κράνεια), the wood of which was said to have been used to built the wooden horse.[294]

Now, as far as Demetrios of Scepsis is concerned, several points can be made from this short summary about the context in which his contribution to the debate is to be found and the way it has been transmitted. First, Demetrios' explanation is classified among those that make a link between the festival and the Trojan story, as it is listed with that of Alcman, who claims that Carneios is a Trojan hero. Furthermore, his version must also be singled out as one of those that do not explain the name of the festival through a personal name, but through etymological considerations. In Demetrios' version it is the verb κρᾶναι that is believed to be at the origin of the adjective, moreover in a context where Menelaos is involved. This brings the whole story back to a Spartan setting and opposes it to an alternative version based on etymology where the Trojan setting is involved. This is the one, mentioned in both sources, in Pausanias and the scholia to Theocritos, at the very end of the list, where the word is explained through the association with the cornel trees growing on Mount

---

[291] Σ Theocritos 5.83a [Wendel] (= fr. 2 [Gaede/Biraschi]).

[292] For a modern account of the Carneia, see Pettersson 1992:57–72.

[293] Pausanias 3.13.3–5.

[294] See Trachsel 2018:203–221for further details.

Ida.[295] Pausanias does not mention Demetrios' version, but if we focus in more detail on the way the second Trojan explanation is rendered in the two sources, we may still find some further information about the way Demetrios' version was transmitted. In order to do so, we must first focus on the structure of the two passages. In the one from the scholia to Theocritos, we have four groups of explanations, three of them introduced by ἄλλως, a formula that was often used in the scholia to indicate the different sources from which the elements are taken.[296] As mentioned, Demetrios' version is listed together with Praxilla's and Alcman's in one group. This could then suggest that these three versions were already found together in one source before they were summarized and took the form they have in the scholion. Moreover, Demetrios' comment seems to be extremely summarized. The explanation of the adjective κάρνειος through the verbal form κρᾶναι works only if we take into account the shift of the letter ρ, which Pausanias mentioned as a necessary element for the last version, the one about the wooden horse (κάρνειος/κράνεια). Therefore, Demetrios' version must have shared one step with this last version, even though he is not listed in the same group in the scholia. In light of this, we may then distinguish among the versions bringing the explanation into the Troad: those linked to a person, like the one from Alcman; and those based on etymology, which depend on the shift of the letter ρ. In this second group, two versions existed, that of Demetrios, which connected the adjective to the verbal form κρᾶναι, and the one explaining the adjective through the cornel tree (κράνεια). The way the different versions were preserved in the two sources does not render this clearly and we seem to have a similar situation to the one we encountered with the scholion to Pindar. The way the scholion presented the situations was not very accurate, because it is too summarized, with important elements dismissed. In fr. 54 [Gaede/Biraschi], the preserved wording even suggested that, because his name is associated with the setting in Elis, Demetrios spoke against the alternative of Crete or Troia, whereas we know from other fragments that he was actually defending the localization in the Troad. With the scholion to Theocritos too, the wording of the passage suggests that Demetrios was speaking against a Trojan origin for the festival, because he linked the verb κρᾶναι to Menelaos, whereas we must assume, from our discussion, that he was rather opposed to

---

[295] Biraschi 2011 (commentary ad fr. 54) believes that this topographical link to Mount Ida is precisely the element that helps to link the fragment to other topics of Demetrios' work. She mentions in particular fr. 29 [Gaede/Biraschi] = Strabo 13.1.43–44 [C602] where the river system of Mount Ida is discussed. But all others, especially those about Mount Ida as Zeus' birthplace, could also be fitting in this respect.

[296] Dickey 2007:108–109 and Nünlist 2009:12–13. This feature has, however, been omitted by Wendel in his edition from 1914 (Wendel 1914:170–172). It is found in Dübner's edition from 1849. Moreover, the order of the four groups is not identical in the two editions.

the fact that its name was explained as coming from a personal name or that he was reacting against the version that explained the adjective κάρνειος through the episode of the creation of the wooden horse and the placing of this episode on Mount Ida. This may again be a hint that, when the element from Demetrios' explanation entered the scholion, it was very far from the original version of Demetrios' account, even if we may not say for sure whether this was due to an extreme epitomization at the moment of the creation of the scholion, or to a shortcut already present in previous stages of the reuse. As for Demetrios' original account, we know from fr. 1 [Gaede/Biraschi][297] that it was located in book 1 and must have been quite extensive, as Demetrios explained the festival at length, giving many details about its proceedings. The position of Demetrios' version in the scholia and its link to the Trojan setting, either because his version is mentioned in the same group as that of Alcman or because it is opposed to the last one about the wooden horse, should, however, remind us that the second fragment may be the one with which we should start when trying to link this topic to a commentary on the Trojan Catalogue, despite the fact that fr. 1 [Gaede/Biraschi] is more expanded and would probably give more accurate information about the Carneia festival.

The last scholion, taken from Euripides' *Andromache*, is even more difficult to take into account in our discussion. Once again the name of Demetrios does not occur in the text and Geade has only attributed the passage to Demetrios as fr. 37 [Gaede][298] because of a passage from Strabo where Thebes and Andromache's father Eetion are mentioned.[299] In Strabo's passage there is no name either, and even if Biraschi follows Gaede in printing this passage as a fragment of Demetrios, it does not appear as such in Radt's edition of Strabo.[300] Therefore, both pieces of evidence, the one from Strabo and the one from the scholia to the Euripidian *Andormache*, must be taken with extreme caution.

It is, however, interesting to note that, if we follow Gaede and take the passage as a fragment from Demetrios' work, it shows again that Demetrios' opinion is to be found, as in the scholion to Pindar and in the one to Theocritos, in a list of several comments from other authorities discussing the topographical issue at hand. This time it is the setting of Thebes, the birthplace of Andromache, which is explained. In the reported discussion, Dicaearchos, Phileas, and Theopompos, among the scholars, and Aeschylos, among the poets, are mentioned together with a group of scholars defined anonymously as ἔνιοι, which introduces the part attributed to Demetrios. Furthermore, among the Thebes mentioned in the

---

[297] Athenaeus 4.141e–f.
[298] Σ Euripides *Andromache* 1 (= fr. 37b [Biraschi]).
[299] Strabo 13.1.61 [C612] (= fr. 37a [Biraschi]).
[300] Radt 2011:345.

debate, there is, besides the former home of Andromache, the famous one in mainland Greece, another, less well-known, in Thessalia, and finally one near Cape Mycale. But we cannot say anything else about the fragment, its location within Demetrios' work, or the status it would have had there. The only link to the collection of fragments we could see is the fact that another fragment from Demetrios, fr. 8 [Gaede/Biraschi],[301] mentions a village *Plakous* in the neighborhood of the Cilician Thebes and that, therefore, it is very likely that Demetrios may also have discussed the localization of Thebes and the stories linked to this place.[302]

When proceeding, finally, to the scholia to the *Iliad* and to the passages Gaede included from this corpus in his collection, we must first acknowledge that we actually face the same difficulty with Gaede's procedure that we have already encountered throughout this section. In only five of the seventeen passages from the scholia to the *Iliad* figuring in Gaede's collection does the name of Demetrios occur. These are, first, the two comments from the D-scholia where we have the typical ending: ἡ ἱστορία παρὰ Δημητρίῳ (τῷ Σκηψίῳ).[303] Then we have two from the large group of fragments from the bT-scholia[304] and one from the A-scholia, which is moreover attributed to Nicanor.[305] For all the others we depend again on Gaede's choice. Most of them come from the bT-tradition and more precisely from the scholia Townleiana, which are quoted in Gaede's time by referring to the manuscript V (Victorianus).[306] As Biraschi takes over the old reference system from Gaede, she also prints them as V-scholia, even if the text she gives is often the one from Erbse's edition, in which they are divided into bT-scholia and A-scholia. Furthermore, the two scholia from the Venetus A are attributed to Nicanor, and finally there is one that comes from those elements in the Venetus B, which have, in the meantime, been attributed to Porphyry's *Quaestiones ad Iliadem*.[307]

However, despite their rather large number, they do not help us much with regard to the question of how ancient scholars used or appreciated Demetrios' work. First, for instance, when looking at the distribution among the books of the *Iliad* of the lines to which the passages considered as fragments are linked, we are not able to see any special pattern that would allow us to find out how

---

[301] Athenaeus 14.644a.

[302] For the interpretation of fr. 8 [Gaede/Biraschi], see above Section 2.1.2 (pp. 85–87).

[303] Σ D *Iliad* 20.3 [van Thiel] (= fr. 23b [Biraschi]) and Σ D *Iliad* 6.35 [van Thiel] (= fr. 32 [Gaede/Biraschi]). Both are also found in the A-tradition (Σ A *Iliad* 20.3 [Erbse] and Σ A *Iliad* 6.35 [Erbse]).

[304] Σ bT *Iliad* 20.53c [Erbse] (= fr. 23a [Biraschi]) and Σ bT *Iliad* 14. 229 [Erbse] (part of it is fr. 46b [Biraschi]).

[305] Σ A *Iliad* 11.757 [Erbse] (= fr. 58 [Gaede/Biraschi]).

[306] See Erbse 1969:xxix.

[307] Fr. 28b [Biraschi] = Σ B *Iliad* 6. 92 [Bekker] = Porphyry *Quaestiones ad Iliadem* (*Iliad* 6.273).

Demetrios' work was seen or at what stage it may have been when elements of it were incorporated into the corpus of the scholia. It is, however, surprising to observe that none of the passages selected by Gaede come from book 2 of the *Iliad*, for which we would assume that Demetrios' work would have been most useful. There may certainly be many reasons to explain this fact, but we might perhaps also hypothesize that this could be a sign that it was no longer obvious during the creation process of the scholia that Demetrios' work was specially linked to a part of this Homeric book. Still, as far as the content of Demetrios' work is concerned, most of the scholia selected as fragments from Demetrios' work are about places located in the Troad. Those in which the name of Demetrios occurs are the two scholia about the Callicolone,[308] from the beginning of book 20, and the one about Pedasos[309] linked to the occurrence of the toponym in book 6. Among those without the name of Demetrios we find the four scholia about the Trojan rivers (Rhesos, Caresos, Rhodios, and Simois)[310] at the beginning of book 12 and the one about the tomb of Dardanos[311] in book 11. Finally, there are the remarks about Percote given about a line occurring in book 11[312] and the scholion about Laris(s)a attached to its mention in book 17.[313] However, this coherence does not help us much here for two reasons: on the one hand, we depend on Gaede's choice, especially for the fragments without the name of our scholar and the coherence in the contents we have just noted may show the coherence in Gaede's choices rather than any special aspect of Demetrios' work. On the other hand, we should not forget that there are also a few other passages from the scholia attributed to Demetrios by Gaede that touch on elements located beyond the topographical area of the Troad. Here we find first the comment about Mount Athos, which is only mentioned in book 14.[314] As the name of Demetrios is preserved in this scholion, there is no doubt that the fragment belonged to Demetrios' work. Furthermore, we have the several remarks without Demetrios' name linked to the homonymy about Ephyra preserved about a line in book 15, which Gaede adduces under his fr.

---

[308] Fr. 23a [Gaede/Biraschi] = Σ bT *Iliad* 20.53c [Erbse] and fr. 23b [Gaede/Biraschi] = Σ A *Iliad* 20.3 [Erbse] (or Σ D *Iliad* 20.3 [van Thiel]).

[309] Fr. 32 [Gaede/Biraschi] = Σ A *Iliad* 6.35 [Erbse] (or Σ D *Iliad* 6.35 [van Thiel]). The fragment is, however, completed by elements from Σ bT and b *Iliad* 6.35 [Erbse].

[310] Σ T *Iliad* 12.20a [Erbse] = fr. 31a [Gaede] (or fr. 31b [Biraschi]); Σ T *Iliad* 12.20c [Erbse] = fr. 31b [Gaede] (or fr. 30c [Biraschi]); Σ T *Iliad* 12.20e [Erbse] = fr. 31c [Gaede/Biraschi] and Σ T *Iliad* 12.22b [Erbse] = fr. 64 [Gaede/Biraschi]).

[311] Σ A *Iliad* 11.166–168 [Erbse] (= fr. 25 [Gaede] or fr. 25b [Biraschi]).

[312] Σ T *Iliad* 11.229 [Erbse] (= fr. 19 [Gaede] or fr. 19b [Biraschi]).

[313] Σ T *Iliad* 17.301 [Erbse] (= fr. 38 [Gaede] or fr. 38b [Biraschi]).

[314] Σ T *Iliad* 14.229 [Erbse] (part of which is fr. 46b [Biraschi]).

56,[315] and those about the tomb of Alesios near Bouprasion, which come once again from the scholia to a line of book 11.[316] Therefore, we have to acknowledge that the evidence for the scholia is actually quite disparate, and, if we follow Gaede's choice, there is no dominant topic to be found in the preserved fragments from the scholia to the *Iliad*. From this discussion it should have become clear that, for the scholia to the *Iliad*, the context in which the fragments have been transmitted does not contain any indication that could help us to understand how Demetrios' work was perceived during this creation process or in what form it was still available. Our access to the original is simply too indirect.

We may, however, add as a final remark about the evidence from the scholia to the *Iliad*, that elements from the two scholia from book 20, fr. 23a [Gaede/Biraschi] and fr. 23b [Gaede/Biraschi],[317] were also found in two papyri that were attributed to the so-called *Mythographus Homericus*.[318] This may at least give some insights into the way the elements from Demetrios' works circulated during the several compilation-phases that scholarly works went through before taking the form of the scholia, but that is the most we can get from these pieces of evidence. The work we define now as the *Mythographus Homericus* is certainly already a mixture of several sources, some from the Hellenistic period and some from later additions.[319] These findings should give us a glimpse of the intermediate stages that Demetrios' work may have gone through before being incorporated into the scholia, and this may finally confirm our statement from the beginning of our chapter that it is almost impossible to trace a source occurring in the scholia back to its original form, if the work is lost.

2.2. Summary

With this very short section on the presence of Demetrios' work in the scholia to the *Iliad*, we have reached the final elements of what can be said about the way Demetrios' work was used and appreciated in Antiquity. If we now take a few moments to look back at our discussion, we must acknowledge that at some point, probably around or shortly after the time when Athenaeus and Harpocration wrote their works, we started to lose trace of Demetrios' work, and it became more and more difficult to say anything about the passages Gaede included in his collection that would actually be independent from Gaede's own

---

[315] Σ T *Iliad* 15.531c and d [Erbse] (= fr. 56 [Gaede] or fr. 56b [Biraschi]) together with the short Σ D *Iliad* 15.531 [van Thiel].

[316] Σ A *Iliad* 11.757 [Erbse] (= fr. 58 [Gaede/Biraschi]).

[317] Σ bT *Iliad* 20.53c [Erbse] and Σ A *Iliad* 20.3 [Erbse] (or Σ D *Iliad* 20.3 [van Thiel]).

[318] See van Rossum-Steenbeek 1998:85–118 for the most recent elements about the *Mythographus Homericus*.

[319] van Rossum-Steenbeek 1998:113–115. For a slightly different view see Montanari 1995c:166.

choices. For instance, in the section on the lexicographers, we have seen that Harpocration was still quoting Demetrios by name, whereas the passages from Hesychios collected by Gaede contained no external evidence about the attribution of the elements to Demetrios. This was also the case for the two fragments about the Trojan Sibyl, one from Pausanias' *Description of Greece* and the other from Stephanus of Byzantium.[320] Here it was not only Gaede's interpretation of the two passages, but also that of his colleague Ernst Maass, that influenced his choice, and this fact should allow us to pass now to Chapter 3, in which we shall discuss the modern appreciation of Demetrios' work, starting with the time in which the two German scholars, Gaede and Maass, lived. As for Chapter 2, we may conclude that Demetrios' work was highly appreciated by those scholars for whom we could establish that they either used his work or at least knew about him as a scholar. He was often associated with other scholars whose works were relevant for the topic the authors who quoted him discussed. The close link to Apollodoros of Athens was a particularly important issue in our discussion, at least at the beginning in the section dedicated to Strabo. However, we also had to acknowledge that from Athenaeus' work onwards the original structure of Demetrios' work must have been lost. Often the preserved remarks that were attributed to our scholar were completely unrelated to any issues that the lines of the Trojan Catalogue may have raised. We have discussed this question in relation with fr. 1 [Gaede/Biraschi], preserved in book 4 of Athenaeus' *Deipnosophistai*, and the reuse Eustathius made of it in a comment at the very end of his commentary on the *Iliad* when he discussed *Iliad* 24.802. These several steps in the transmission of Demetrios' work are, however, precisely one of the principal difficulties for our understanding of Demetrios' work. This will be particularly visible in the way modern scholars appreciated Demetrios' contribution to ancient scholarship, which will be the topic of our next chapter.

---

[320] Fr. 65 [Gaede/Biraschi] = Pausanias 10.12.2–7 and fr. 66 [Gaede/Biraschi] = Stephanus Byzantius s.v. Μερμησσός (= Stephanus Byzantius 445, 15 [Meineke] = Stephanus Byzantius μ 148 [Billerbeck]).

3

Appreciation of Demetrios' Contribution in Modern Times

Turning now to the chapter on the modern appreciation of Demetrios' work, we must first state that there is a gap between Chapter 2 and Chapter 3. As we have seen in the previous section, we lose trace of Demetrios' work, despite the evidence from the different corpora of scholia, by the end of the twelfth century, after the scarce evidence in Eustathius' and Tzetzes' works. The modern interest in our scholar seems, however, to emerge only in the nineteenth century, as we shall see below.[1] Nonetheless, there will be a link between the two chapters, since we shall use, as in the previous section on the ancient appreciation of Demetrios, some external elements to structure the outline of the present discussion. For the presentation of the point of view from Antiquity, we followed a chronological outline, using some considerations on genre as a secondary criterion for the description of the works in which Demetrios was quoted. In this section on modern times, we shall use as a first structuring principle the successive publications, in 1850, 1880, and 2011, of the different editions and collections of Demetrios' fragments. This is an obvious approach as these works provided, and still provide, new tools for the appreciation of Demetrios' contribution. However, the situation is more complex as the modern appreciation of Demetrios of Scepsis was also shaped by Schliemann's discovery in 1874 of the remains beneath Hissarlik. The huge debate about the Homeric landscape that ensued from the interpretation of his excavations between 1874 and 1891 constituted the background of Gaede's edition in 1880, and explains, to some

---

[1] It is extremely difficult to go beyond the very beginning of the nineteenth century. There are some disparate remarks on Demetrios by Friedrich August Wolf in his *Vorlesung über die Geschichte der griechischen Literatur* (see Gürtler 1831:325) and previously by Friedrich August Ukert in his work on Greek and Roman geography from 1816 (see Ukert 1816:153). This situation, and the difficulty to find any trace of Demetrios previously, may perhaps be related to a new scholarly approach to fragments, which started at the end of the eighteenth and developed during the nineteenth century. See Dionisotti 1997:1–33, Most 2009:9–20, and Most 2010:370–377 on the history of the treatment of fragmentarily preserved authors in classical studies.

extent, the interest in Demetrios' work in those days. The scholar's statements about the Trojan landscape were discussed intensely by the participants in the debate and this created the need for a scholarly edition of Demetrios' work. The archaeological discoveries should, however, be considered independently from the publication of the editions, as they shaped or influenced the scholarly appreciation of Demetrios in a different way. Therefore, our main divisions in this chapter will be constructed around the dates of publication of the three editorial contributions about Demetrios, whereas the discussion about Schliemann's discoveries and the controversy that ensued[2] will constitute a secondary feature of our outline.

Further, as the works dealing with Demetrios are extremely heterogeneous, we shall also divide them into two large categories, even if within these categories the approaches and methods may again differ widely. The first category will comprise the works focusing on the remaining fragments attributed to Demetrios. As we shall see, this group will turn out to be larger than the three editions just mentioned. There are indeed other contributions also dealing with the fragments but without taking the form of independent editions. None of these studies is, however, openly carried out in connection with the issues raised by the appraisal of Schliemann's discoveries. This absence could actually be seen as a characteristic of this first group, although the overall interest in Demetrios, to which these studies bear witness, might be the result of this controversy about Schliemann's excavations, as they brought the question of the topography of the Troad to the fore. Yet the authors of the studies from our first group focus mainly on textual criticism or on *Quellenforschung*, at least with regard to Strabo's *Geography* as one among the source texts for the fragments. Therefore, they take all the topics Demetrios may have alluded to in his work into account, not only those about the topography of the Troad. The second group of works about Demetrios consists of research, which deals with Demetrios as a scholar and focuses on his achievements, his background, or his methodology. Thus, most of them are not primarily aiming to contribute to the evaluation of the remaining fragments or to establish their exact wording. Among these studies we may not only find the many works dealing with the

---

[2] For a general overview of the archaeological investigation in relation to the Homeric text, see Buchholz 1991:11–44. He defines two great chapters in Homeric archaeology, one from Winckelmann (1717-1768) to Schliemann (1874) and one from Schliemann onwards. This shows the importance of Schliemann's contribution and allows us to use it as one of the pivots for the outline of our chapter. As Demetrios' work is much larger than the question of the localization of Troy and also involves philological questions, Bucholz's division has to be divided further and in particular the period after Schliemann's excavation should be analyzed more closely. Therefore, we shall follow Easton 1991:111–129 for the phases of the period before Schliemann and Korfmann 1991:89–102 for those in the twentieth century for the outline of our chapter.

topography of the Troad, in which Demetrios' contribution to this special topic is discussed, but also studies that attempt to give an overview of the remaining Greek literature and/or to outline the history of ancient scholarship.[3] We also find in this group the research undertaken for its own sake, dedicated either to Demetrios himself, or more often carried out in relation to contemporaneous scholars or authors, such as Apollodoros of Athens, Polemon of Ilion, Metrodoros of Scepsis, or Hegesianax of Alexandria Troas.[4] Finally, we shall also see that Demetrios is occasionally alluded to in works dealing with one of the many topics mentioned in his fragments. Therefore, it is in the second group that we shall find the greatest number of indications about the modern appreciation of Demetrios' contribution, as it is in these studies especially that the appreciation of Demetrios' achievement is most intensely discussed—often in relation to questions of the localization of the Homeric Troy, but it is not restricted to this subject, as we shall see.

We shall, however, discuss each of the subcategories of the two groups we have just defined in three phases. The first phase, from 1850 to 1880, covers the timespan between the first two collections of fragments, which also precedes the debate about Schliemann's discovery. A second phase will start around 1880 with the publication of Gaede's edition and is characterized by the fact that the controversy about the excavations in the Troad is at its peak. Finally, there is the third period, between 1880 and 2011, corresponding to the interval between Gaede's edition and that of Biraschi. In this last period, the longest one, two excavation campaigns were carried out in the Troad, one by Blegen and the other, still ongoing, which was initiated by Korfmann.

3.1 Works on Demetrios Between Stiehle and Gaede (1850-1880)

3.1.1 Stiehle's Collection of Fragments

In 1850, Robert Stiehle was able to claim that he was the first modern scholar to dedicate a work to Demetrios of Scepsis, and he used this statement to justify

---

[3] Although we are fully aware of the difference between the two kinds of research, we shall consider them as one category here. Our approach seems justified by the fact that the history of scholarship appears as one chapter in many of the works encompassing the whole history of Greek literature. Therefore, if Demetrios is mentioned in these works, he appears in the chapter on Hellenistic scholarship, which is often also dealt with in the first chapters of any history of scholarship.

[4] For more details on these authors, see above Section 1.1.1 (pp. 4–7, Methodoros) and Section 1.2.2 (pp. 40–42, Apollodoros; pp. 43–47, Hegesianax; pp. 47–48, Polemon), and finally Section 2.1.1 (pp. 70–77, for Apollodoros and Demetrios in Strabo's text).

his collection of fragments.[5] In his study he refers, however, to Theodor Bergk, who was interested in the Hellenistic scholar and had announced that he would speak about Demetrios more extensively.[6] Bergk seems never to have fulfilled his project, as such research is not listed in the collection of his published works.[7] Therefore, Stiehle's contribution is a good starting point for the analysis of modern studies about Demetrios, even if, as it took the form of an article published in an academic journal, it is rather short and contains only very brief comments on each fragment. However, several of the elements highlighted in this study are still relevant today. For instance, in the closing section of his article, Stiehle makes some very interesting remarks about Demetrios' work. First, he characterizes Demetrios as a very learned scholar, basing his judgment on the large number of authors Demetrios himself quotes in his work. This characteristic of Demetrios' working method has recently been highlighted once again by Ragone,[8] and we have seen in Chapter 1 how important this feature may already have been in Antiquity. Furthermore, Stiehle also gives a rather accurate and objective account of the scope and nature of Demetrios' work. He characterizes the rather heterogeneous content of the remaining fragments as belonging to topics involving either topographical, ethnographical, or mythological issues, which are, moreover, all more or less closely linked to places and people named in the Trojan Catalogue occurring in book 2 of the *Iliad*.[9] He also suggests that the comments given by Demetrios must have been enlarged by substantial digressions in which the Hellenistic scholar came to speak about events dated in historical times[10] and mentioned anecdotes about almost contemporaneous authors,[11] so that the fragments that we actually have are no longer directly linked to the lines of the Trojan Catalogue.[12] This last statement has been taken

---

5   Stiehle 1850:528. There are some additional fragments in Stiehle 1851:344–347.
6   Siehle 1850:528 referring to Bergk's *Index lectionum Marburgensium* 1844–1845, which can be found in Peppmüller 1886:287–288.
7   Peppmüller 1884:xi–xxxii.
8   Ragone 2009:649–691.
9   Stiehle 1850:544.
10   Besides the fragment about Ilion in his own time (fr. 21 [Gaede/Biraschi] = Strabo 13.1.27 [C594]), for instance fr. 6 [Gaede/Biraschi] (= Athenaeus 15.697c) and fr. 13 [Gaede/Biraschi] (= Athenaeus 15.697d), and maybe also fr. 69 [Gaede/Biraschi] = Harpocration s.v. Ἴων.
11   Fr. 7 [Gaede/Biraschi] = Athenaeus 4.155b; fr. 9 [Gaede/Biraschi] = Athenaeus 3.80d, and maybe also fr. 72 [Gaede/Biraschi] = Athenaeus 2.44e.
12   He quotes as examples fr. 39 [Stiehle] (fr. 17a [Gaede/Biraschi]) = Strabo 10.5.19 [C489]; fr. 40 [Stiehle] (corresponding to the second part of fr. 50b [Gaede/Biraschi]) = Strabo 1.2.40 [C47]; fr. 41 [Stiehle] (fr. 52 [Gaede/Biraschi]) = Σ Apollonios Rhodios 1.238 [Wendel]; fr. 42 [Stiehle] (fr. 51 [Gaede/Biraschi]) = Σ Apollonios Rhodios 1.230 [Wendel]; and fr. 38 [Stiehle] (fr. 49 [Gaede/Biraschi]) = Strabo 10.2.16 [C456]. Stiehle mentions also fr. 27 [Stiehle] (fr. 35 [Gaede/Biraschi]) = Str. 13.1.53 [C607], but this last example does not fit very well, as it is closer linked to Demetrios' topic than the others.

up by subsequent scholars who claimed that it was no longer possible to recover the structure of Demetrios' work because of the scarcity of the remaining fragments, the way most of them have been transmitted in Strabo, and their diversity in content.[13] Today, however, some attempts have been made to retrace the remaining fragments and their content back to the Homeric lines,[14] and we shall focus more closely on each of the suggested solutions for such an arrangement. Likewise, Stiehle's assumption that Demetrios must have spoken about the causes of the Trojan war at the beginning of his work should be revised today. The German scholar justifies his assumption by the fact that the content of some of the fragments, coming mainly from Athenaeus, who attributed them to the first book of the Τρωϊκὸς διάκοσμος, would otherwise not be explained.[15] We may, however, see that, at least for fr. 1 [Gaede/Biraschi][16] and fr. 2 [Gaede/Biraschi],[17] there may be other reasons that could explain their appearance at the beginning of Demetrios' work.[18]

The two most important features of Stiehle's works with regard to Demetrios' appreciation are, however, Stiehle's statements concerning the two recurring questions discussed in connection with Demetrios' contribution: the link between Demetrios and Apollodoros of Athens and the localization of the Homeric landscape. With regard to both issues Stiehle gives original answers, mainly because he antedates the main debate. As far as the first question, the link between Apollodoros and Demetrios, is concerned, we shall see that, even if the connection between the two Hellenistic scholars has already been stated in Antiquity,[19] it is only after Benedikt Niese's influential contribution of 1877 that modern scholars were really engaged with this issue. Stiehle wrote his contribution a little more than fifteen years earlier, and it is therefore important to see how this topic was perceived and described before Niese. Stiehle presents this link between the two scholars in a very circumspect way: he mentions, on the one

---

[13] E.g. Gaede 1880:16–17 and Schwartz 1901:2808, and even more recently Biraschi 2011, commentary ad T1–11.

[14] See Ragone 2009:674–691 for a very convincing attempt for fr. 11 [Gaede/Biraschi] = Athenaeus 7.300d, fr. 23a [Gaede/Biraschi] = Σ bT *Iliad.* 20.53c [Erbse] and fr. 23b [Gaede/Biraschi] = Σ A *Iliad* 20.3 [Erbse] (or Σ D *Iliad* 20.3 [van Thiel].

[15] Fr. 1 [Stiehle] (fr. 1 [Gaede/Biraschi]) = Athenaeus 4.141e; fr. 2 [Stiehle] (fr. 2 [Gaede/Biraschi]) = Σ Theocritos 5.83a [Wendel]; fr. 3 [Stiehle] (fr. 3 [Gaede/Biraschi]) = Athenaeus 14.658b; fr. 4 [Stiehle] (fr. 4 [Gaede/Biraschi]) = Harpocration s.v. Θυργωνίδαι. See Stiehle 1850:544.

[16] Fr. 1 [Gaede/Biraschi] = Athenaeus 4.141e-f.

[17] Fr. 2 [Gaede/Biraschi] = Σ Theocritos 5.83a [Wendel].

[18] See Trachsel 2018:293-22 for a hypothesis that would link the two fragments to Paris, who may have been mentioned in a comment on the contingent of the Trojans occurring at the very beginning of the Trojan Catalogue, even though his name was not enumerated there.

[19] Strabo 8.3.6 [C339] (= T6 [Biraschi]) and Strabo 1.2.38 [C45] (= T9 [Biraschi]). See above Section 1.1.3 (pp. 25–27), Section 1.2.2 (pp. 40–42), and Section 2.1.1 (pp. 70–77).

hand, the debt Apollodoros pays to Demetrios, but highlights, on the other hand, his independence in several of the issues. Furthermore, he places Apollodoros' achievement in a larger context as he mentions evidence from Eustathius, who quotes an otherwise unknown Menogenes, who composed, besides Apollodoros, a work on the Catalogue of the Ships in twenty-three books.[20] After Niese, the discussion takes another turn and focuses mainly on the way both authors are transmitted in Strabo's *Geography*. Also, when considering the second topic, the localization of the Homeric landscape, Stiehle's contribution has to be distinguished with regard to later works. In 1850, he could indeed expose the elements in Demetrios' work related to this issue in a convincingly objective way, and he had a rather good opinion about Demetrios, despite the fact that the investigations in the Troad had started as early as the end of the eighteenth century, with, for instance, the field work not only of Choiseul-Gouffier and Lechevalier, but of many other travelers, archaeologists, and surveyors.[21] Stiehle's positive judgment is partly explained by the fact that he encompasses the whole corpus of preserved fragments, not only those dealing with the Trojan landscape, and more precisely those about the localization of the Homeric Troy. Later scholars, as we shall see, are focusing only on these fragments and tend, therefore, to base their opinion only on this part of Demetrios' work. In conclusion then, we may say that Stiehle's contribution, even if it will be replaced soon by the edition of Richard Gaede, contains a large number of extremely interesting elements on Demetrios as a scholar and gains its interest from the fact that it was written before the time when Schliemann's discovery shaped the debate.

3.1.2 Bohle

Also before the publication of Gaede's edition, and, as we shall see, independently from Stiehle's first attempt to collect the fragments of Demetrios' work, Anton Bohle took Demetrios as his subject for a contribution published in 1858.[22] Like Stiehle's contribution, this article is written independently from the question about the localization of the Homeric Troy and stands therefore, again like Stiehle's consideration, in sharp contrast to the works dealing with the Homeric landscape and mentioning Demetrios only as evidence in relation

---

[20] Eustathius *Commentarii ad Iliadem* 2.494 (= 263, 36–37 or van der Valk I:401). See above Section 1.2.1 (p. 37) and Section 1.2.2 (p. 43).

[21] Easton 1991:111–129 defines two phases before Schliemann's excavations. The first is defined between 1784 and 1853 when many travelers and surveyors were working on the drawing of maps. The second phase is dated between 1855 and 1865 and sees the first excavations, mainly those of Frank Calvert. For this first phase of the exploration of the Troad, see also Cook 1973:14–51, Buchholz 1991:15–30, or Cobet 2003:331–377.

[22] Bohle 1858:1–9.

to their hypothesis of localization.[23] Furthermore, Bohle's work will also take an important position in our outline here, as it is the first, and for a long time the only, contribution that was entirely dedicated to Demetrios of Scepsis.[24]

However, even if Bohle's publication was the only one entirely and objectively dedicated to Demetrios, it was mostly dismissed, for instance, by Gaede himself,[25] by Susemihl in his influential *Geschichte der griechischen Litteratur in der Alexanderzeit*,[26] and by Schwartz in the *Realencyclopädie*-entry on Demetrios written in 1901.[27] The study therefore had very little impact on further considerations about Demetrios, even if it contains, in our opinion, two interesting statements, which will be of some importance for our own approach. The first are his comments concerning the link between Demetrios of Scepsis and the library of Aristotle, which Neleus took to Scepsis, the hometown of our scholar. The story about the hiding of the library is well known and was reported in detail by Strabo,[28] even if his account is still very controversial today.[29] Bohle makes a rather unconvincing, but nevertheless interesting, statement about this issue. He claims that Demetrios never used the books of Aristotle, because they were hidden at the time he was living in Scepsis. Bohle bases his statement on the assumption that, if Demetrios had known of the books, he would not have permitted them to be hidden.[30] This rather naïve claim is still interesting for us, as it is opposed to the opinions of most other modern scholars. They often claim, like for instance Schwartz, that Demetrios must have had a large library at his disposal to compose his work.[31] Certainly having a huge library at his disposal does not necessarily mean having Aristotle's library at his disposal, and Schwartz does not claim this. But he takes Demetrios' activity as evidence for the fact that the Aeolis, as a whole, may have been a somewhat independent scholarly center with either a Platonic or an Aristotelean tradition.[32] In such a context, the focus of the discussion lies on the scholarly working methods used

---

[23] We shall have to take into consideration the statements about Demetrios in previous works, but as the Hellenistic scholar is often not analyzed there for his own sake, but used as evidence in an argumentation either for Hissarlik or for other places in the Troad, or even for no places at all, we can start our overview with Bohle.

[24] This is not only true for the time span between Stiehle's first collection of fragments in 1850 and Gaede's edition in 1880, but also for the one between Gaede's edition and that of Biraschi.

[25] Gaede 1880:1n2.

[26] Susemihl 1891:681–685 (he classifies Bohle's study as worthless "*werthlos*").

[27] Schwartz 1901:2807.

[28] Strabo 13.1.54 [C608–609].

[29] For instance, Primavesi 2007:51–77, Schubert 2002:225–237, Nagy 1998:200–206, Lindsay 1997:290–298, Irigoin 1993:50–53, Richardson 1994:8–12, Gottschalk 1972:335–342, or even now Berti/Costa 2010:49–55. See also Section 1.1.2 (pp. 9–11).

[30] Bohle 1858:6.

[31] Schwartz 1901:2808.

[32] Schwartz 1901:2812–2813.

by Demetrios of Scepsis, and this shows that the opinion of a modern scholar about Demetrios not only depends on the scholar's position about Schliemann's theories, as we shall see throughout this chapter, but could also be influenced by other questions, such as the one concerning the destiny of Aristotle's books. Such presumptions are, however, often not directly acknowledged when a scholar describes Demetrios' achievements. They must still be taken into consideration when trying to analyze the attitudes of modern scholars to Demetrios' work, and Bohle's contribution shows this by focusing on the link between Demetrios and the fate of Aristotle's library. Finally, as far as the second statement from Bohle's contribution is concerned, we should highlight here his remarks on the state of research about Demetrios and especially the regret he expresses at the end of his article not to have had an edition of Demetrios' fragments at his disposal for this research. From this statement we can assume that he did not know the article written by Stiehle a few years earlier and may have developed an independent interest in the Hellenistic scholar. Unfortunately, he does not tell his readers the reasons for his interest in Demetrios of Scepsis.

3.1.3 Niese

In this respect, the article Benedikt Niese published in 1877, actually on Apollodoros of Athens, is more explicit. The author clearly states at the beginning of his article that he writes his contribution in reaction to a statement made by Karl Lehrs about Strabo's quoting methods.[33] Indeed, Lehrs highlighted a few years earlier, in his studies on Aristarchos, that Strabo's text contains quotations from the works of other scholars, even when Strabo does not mention their names, or, on the contrary, that, even if he is following a source he is quoting nominally, Strabo can introduce pieces from his own thoughts or even contributions from still other scholars.[34] Niese's studies aimed precisely at verifying Lehrs's statement by taking as a case study the fragments of Apollodoros of Athens.[35] This fact is important not only because it allows us better to judge Niese's contribution, but also because it shows that in 1877 Niese could still write an article on Demetrios without referring to any archaeological topic in relation to the question about the Homeric landscape.[36] Finally, the fact that

---

[33] Niese 1877:267–307.

[34] Lehrs 1865:244 expanded in Lehrs 1878:71 (reprinted as Lehrs 1902:300).

[35] Lehrs 1865:244 quoted by Niese 1877:267.

[36] In 1877 he actually could have done this as Schliemann's first works on his discoveries were already published. The first results of his excavation were published in German in 1874 under the title *Trojanische Alterthümer*. The following year, 1875, an English version entitled *Troy and its Remains* appeared. However, as we shall see, the bulk of the responses and objections were published only around 1880.

the study highlights some of the particularities characterizing the way modern scholars dealt with Demetrios and his contribution will also be of some interest here.

Niese's contribution illustrates the fact that Demetrios is seldom studied for his own sake. As just mentioned, Niese claims to undertake his study to focus on an assumption made by Karl Lehrs about Strabo and the geographer's working methods. The research is therefore not on Demetrios himself, but was triggered by the relation between Apollodoros' and Demetrios' works as it is described in Strabo's *Geography*. This situation shows, therefore, on the one hand, how seldom Demetrios was the subject of research, but highlights, on the other, the close relationship not only between Apollodoros and Demetrios, but also between the two Hellenistic scholars and Strabo. It is important to note here that already Lehrs saw the difficulty of Strabo's quoting methods and that, therefore, even more than the question about Aristotle's library developed in Bohle's article, the issue about the link between Strabo and Demetrios—not only through the question of the reliability of Strabo's text as a source for lost authors, but also with regard to the content of the two works—is a question that will recur when dealing with Demetrios of Scepsis and explains several of the modern contributions about the Hellenistic scholar.

Finally, the responses to Niese's article are also revealing. Niese reached the conclusion that Strabo must have used Demetrios only indirectly through the work of Apollodoros.[37] This conclusion has, however, not been accepted, as not only Lehrs dismissed Niese's claim,[38] but also Gaede, who refers to this work in his edition and claims to undertake his research against Niese's assumptions.[39] However, these reactions, and in particular Lehrs's response, lead us finally to the question about the Homeric landscape. It is indeed in the last paragraph of his response to Niese that Lehrs mentions the fact that Demetrios has been proved, through recent studies, to be a liar and that Strabo, as well as Apollodoros, is mistaken in giving so much credit to Demetrios.[40]

3.1.4 Demetrios in Works About the Homeric Landscape

Lehrs does not, however, quote his source for his assumption, but, through the wording of his statement, we see that he alludes to the debate about the

---

[37] Niese 1877:285–286. He is mainly analyzing the wording of two of Demetrios' fragments (fr. 5 [Gaede/Biraschi] = Athenaeus 8.346c and fr. 61 [Gaede/Biraschi] = Strabo 10.3.19–21 [C472–473]).

[38] Lehrs 1878:70–75 (reprinted as Lehrs 1902:299–305).

[39] As we shall see later, such a statement can certainly also be seen as a sign of the independence we claimed for the works dealing with the fragments of Demetrios with regard to the controversy about the Homeric landscape.

[40] Lehrs 1878:75 (reprinted as Lehrs 1902:305).

Trojan landscape and to the way Demetrios' contribution was appreciated in this debate. One of the earliest scholars who calls Demetrios of Scepsis a liar is Rudolph Hercher, who tries to prove, in the context of the debate about the localization of the Homeric landscape, that Homer did not know the Troad at all and that scholars like Demetrios invented the Homeric topography for their own purposes.[41] Hercher's demonstration is based mainly on the information we have in Strabo about the river system of the Troad.[42] He claims that the famous passage of the beginning of book 12 of the *Iliad*[43] is an interpolation and that the names of the rivers were added in later times. He even goes as far as claiming that, as Demetrios seems to be the only one who knows the names, he was the first to make this identification, moreover on a rather arbitrary basis. Hercher has a very negative opinion about Demetrios and it is precisely in this context the he calls him a liar.[44] However, Hercher's criticism of Demetrios does not come from any of Demetrios' special statements about the Homeric landscape, as often happens in the debate about the Homeric landscape, but should be seen as a kind of overall reaction to this controversy. It is based on Hercher's underlying skepticism against any research, ancient or modern, that had as its aim to prove that the Homeric setting of the *Iliad* could be found in a real landscape. Here we start to touch on the discussion about Schliemann's investigations in the Troad and the appreciation of Demetrios' contribution in this context. Yet, in 1875, Hercher alludes to the works by Heyne[45] and criticizes therefore mainly the previous investigations in the Troad, which had already started with Choiseul-Gouffier and Lechevalier at the end of the eighteenth century and went on throughout the nineteenth century, up to and including the phase characterized by Schliemann's publications. Hercher, however, maintains his opinion from 1875 throughout the debate, even after the discoveries of Schliemann, as he republishes parts of his line of argument unchanged again in 1881.[46] With regard to Demetrios, he adopts a seldom defended stance, as he

---

[41] Hercher 1875:101–103 and 116–117 (= Hercher 1881:26–29 and 46–47), and Hercher 1877:780 (= Hercher 1881:90). The only difference between the two earlier publications and the one in 1881 seems to be the fact that in 1881 Hercher quotes the passages from Strabo under discussion with the numbers of Gaede's collection of fragments.

[42] Strabo 13.1.43–45 [C602–603] (= fr. 29 [Gaede/Biraschi] and fr. 31a [Biraschi]). However, Hercher mentions mainly a passage from Eustathius (Eustathius *Commentarii ad Iliadem* 12.20–22 (= 889, 59 or van der Valk III:344) which is only alluded to in Gaede's or Biraschi's edition (under fr. 31a [Gaede] = fr. 31b [Biraschi]). See further Hercher 1877:772–773 (= Hercher 1881:76–77).

[43] *Iliad* 12.16–22.

[44] Hercher 1877:777 = Hercher 1881:86.

[45] Hercher 1875:101. Actually he refers to Heyne's introduction to Lechevalier's description of the Troad. See Lechevalier 1792:xi–xxxiii.

[46] As just mentioned, he reprints most of the content of the two previous articles (1875 and 1877) in 1881. See Hercher 1881:70–92. There he quotes the passages he mentions with the numbers

rejects not only the scholar's conclusion about the localization of the Homeric Troy, but Demetrios' overall undertaking of finding the setting of the *Iliad* in a real landscape. His negative opinion about Demetrios' scholarly achievement is, however, shared by many other scholars from the end of the nineteenth century, especially in relation to the question of the localization of Troy, even if their negative opinions can be rooted in several different positions about the Trojan landscape.

Indeed, besides those rejecting, like Hercher, any investigation aiming at a localization of the Homeric setting in a real landscape, scholars could dismiss Demetrios' theory because they thought they were able to identify the Homeric Troy with places other than the one Demetrios defended.[47] They do so mainly by denying his scholarly achievement, as shown by a curious but telling example from before Schliemann's discoveries: the French scholar, Antoine François Mauduit,[48] claims that Demetrios had a rather poor knowledge of the Troad, which was based, according to the French scholar's opinion, only on his experience from childhood and that, because of the rather long interval between his visit to the Troad in childhood and the writing of the work, which, according to Mauduit, Demetrios undertook in Alexandria, his account was full of errors and imprecision. For us the claim that Demetrios undertook his research in Alexandria is of particular interest, as it is based on the assumption, defended by several other modern scholars, that the presence of a library was necessary in order to explain Demetrios' achievement, even if Mauduit's hypothesis that this was the library of Alexandria is certainly not correct. Furthermore, examples among the scholars taking part in the debate before Schliemann and mentioning Demetrios' contribution are the German scholars Friedrich Gottlieb Welcker, who was one of the defenders of Bunarbashi as location of the Homeric Troy, and Gustave von Eckenbrecher, as someone speaking in favor of Hissarlik.[49] Both, even if they have a rather balanced view of Demetrios' achievements, dismiss his position,[50] anticipating the huge debate between the defenders of

---

Gaede gave to the fragments in his edition published the year before.

[47] A good summary of the situation before the publication of Gaede's edition is given in Brentano 1877:1–3. For the appreciation of Demetrios in this context, see in particular Brentano 1877:26–27 or also Frick 1876:302–303.

[48] Mauduit 1840:204–208.

[49] We are mainly following the presentation of Frick 1876:289–290 and Steitz 1875:225–226 alluding both to Welcker 1845:i–lxxxvi and Eckenbrecher 1843:1–49.

[50] Welcker 1845:xxxiii–xl dedicates a whole chapter to the analysis of Demetrios' position. He only blames Demetrios for local pride and even goes as far as defining his objections against the inhabitants of Ilion as accurate. This is certainly due to his own position. He locates Troy at Bunarbashi, which is neither Hissarlik nor the village of Demetrios. Eckenbrecher 1843:34–43 only states against Demetrios that his theory was not taken upon later and suggests that the Hellenistic scholar may have seen the Troad only in his youth.

Bunarbashi and those of Hissarlik after Schliemann's discoveries, where almost everybody attacked Demetrios for his peculiar position, which fitted neither of the two modern hypotheses; but we shall return to this later.

There were, however, also a few scholars in those early days who had a better opinion about Demetrios.[51] They often tried to find the village of the Ilians, which was the name Demetrios gave to the place that was located thirty stades inland from the Hellenistic Ilion and that he identifies with the Homeric Troy. They frequently did this in reaction against the two mainstream theories, Hissarlik (or before Schliemann the claim of the inhabitants of Ilion) and Bunarbashi. James Rennell, for instance, gives a passionate defense of Demetrios,[52] and Heinrich Nikolaus Ulrichs defines Demetrios' objections against the claims of the Ilians as perspicacious and entirely right.[53] Furthermore, we should also mention here the two contributions by Brentano, even if both allude to Schliemann and his discovery,[54] because Brentano uses an interesting argumentation in his defense of Demetrios, by citing in favor of the Hellenistic scholar the fact that the inaccuracies in the passages attributed to him are due to Strabo.[55] This statement is indeed very interesting as it shows us a further aspect of the link, already highlighted in the debate involving Lehrs and Niese, between Strabo's text and Demetrios. This time it is not the question of the more or less accurate use that Strabo made of his sources and the way he quoted them, but the appreciation of his scholarly methods and values that is under discussion. This is also an element that will come back in later works on Demetrios, and it is again interesting to note that such considerations started even before Gaede's edition.

3.1.5 Demetrios in the Histories of Greek Literature and/or Histories of Scholarship

This distribution of opinions about Demetrios and the later crystallization of the debate with regard to his position in connection with Schliemann's discoveries can also be observed in the histories of scholarship and/or Greek literature produced in those days. A first example, in which the question about

---

[51] Schliemann himself (1884:328) mentions only two scholars by name who have defended a location of the Homeric Troy that was neither Hissarlik nor Bunarbashi: Brentano and Jebb. Brentano 1877:3 adds two more: Rennell 1814 and Ulrichs 1845:573–608.

[52] Rennell 1814:4–16.

[53] Ulrichs 1845:573–608.

[54] Brentano 1877 and 1881. In the second contribution (Brentano 1881:33), he seems mainly to give an answer to Virchow who was one of the defenders of Schliemann's theories. See Virchow 1880a:673–685 or Virchow 1881:748–760.

[55] Brentano 1877:36–37.

the Homeric landscape is completely absent, is provided by the *Grundriß der griechischen Litteratur* by Bernhardy, published in 1845. Demetrios of Scepsis is mentioned twice, in a positive way even if only briefly, and his work is entitled "the first encyclopedia of Homeric antiquities."[56] Both remarks belong, however, to the chapter about the Homeric epics, and the Hellenistic scholar is mentioned in relation to the influence and importance accorded to the Homeric poems in Antiquity. There is no allusion to any kind of excavations in the Troad or to any debate that the question about the localization of the Homeric landscape may have raised, either in the first or in the later editions of Bernhardy's work. The addition in the third edition of the bibliographical reference to Stiehle's collection from 1850 and to Bohle's article from 1858 is the only difference that can be seen between the several editions of his work.

It is the same with Theodor Bergk's *Griechische Literaturgeschichte*, published a few years later, between 1872 and 1887. Demetrios is mentioned twice, both times, however, very briefly: in the first volume he appears in a list of exegetical works on Homer, alongside with others written by representatives of the Pergamene school;[57] then he is mentioned again in a short list of grammarians in the fourth volume, where Bergk is treating the Hellenistic period.[58] There are, however, once again no references to the question about the Homeric landscape.

The study by Ludwig Friedänder on the mores of the Romans (*Darstellungen aus der Sittengeschichte Roms: in der Zeit von August bis zum Ausgang der Antonine*), published between 1862 and 1871,[59] may be considered as taking an intermediary position. It is in the part about tourism and travels that Friedländer mentions Ilion as a well-known place where Roman tourists went because it was thought to be the heir of the Homeric Troy. He alludes there, as one might expect, to the attacks made by Demetrios and Hestiaia against this claim, and he tries to explain their hostility by local jealousy because they both come from neighboring cities.[60] In 1864[61] he can do this with no allusion to any kind of excavation in the Troad, in the same way Bernhardy did in 1877. It is,

---

[56] Bernhardy 1845:70 = Bernhardy 1877:83. The second remark, occurring a little earlier, is Bernhardy 1845:46 = Bernhardy 1877:70.
[57] Bergk 1872:905
[58] Bergk 1887:518.
[59] Friedländer 1862–1871.
[60] Friedländer 1864:60 (= Friedländer 1922:419–420).
[61] 1864 is the date of the edition of the second part of the first volume. In later editions, as in the ninth from 1919–1921 or in the tenth from 1922–1923, the division in volumes has been modified so that the chronological separation between the two parts of volume 1 is no longer perceivable.

however, interesting to note that the accusation of jealousy, also found later in Schliemann's works,[62] was already present in Friedländer's contribution.

A further example is the *History of Greece* written by the English scholar George Grote in 1869. There we find still more allusions to the question about the localization of the Homeric Troy, and a surprisingly large part is dedicated to Demetrios. As Grote approaches the question from the point of view of a historian rather than that of a philologist, he evokes first the destiny of the historical Ilion, and mentions Demetrios in opposition to a long list of more or less famous people having accepted the claim of the Ilians and visited the place as if it were the Homeric Troy. Grote claims that no one until Demetrios questioned the identification of Ilion with Troy and that only Strabo followed him. His presentation is given as a matter-of-fact description in which the position of Demetrios is mentioned as one single opinion standing against a long list of people before and after him who identified Ilion with Troy. Grote too makes some guesses about the reasons why Demetrios took this peculiar stance, but he is more general than, for instance, Friedländer. He mentions the "tendency toward criticism of those days," alluding to the working methods of the Hellenistic scholars, as reason for this statement of Demetrios. But even if he describes the situation in a rather neutral way, he alludes in a footnote to the debate about the archaeological research undertaken in the Troad.[63] However, he adopts, the point of view of an English scholar and mentions as the three main protagonists Bryant, Morritt, and Wakefield, even if he alludes to Lechevalier's account of the plain of Troy as the starting point of the debate. This is in contrast to the way the research in the Troad is presented by the people involved in the debate as it developed after Schliemann's publications,[64] and we should now turn to this aspect and focus on the period in which the debate was most intensely conducted.

3.2 Works in the Context of Gaede's Edition (Around 1880)

3.2.1 Demetrios in Works About the Troad

The debate about Schliemann's discoveries started a few years before Gaede's publication, as Schliemann published his first contribution about his discoveries in the Troad in 1874. In his excavation report he criticizes Demetrios severely, saying repeatedly that his excavations have proved Demetrios' theory

---

[62] For instance Schliemann 1881:193 and 199–200 (German version of Schliemann 1880:168 and 174).

[63] Grote 1869:320n3.

[64] See above Brentano 1877:1–4.

to be wrong.[65] Demetrios is, however, attacked most sharply by John Pentland Mahaffy,[66] whose contribution was published, together with those of Archibald Henry Sayce and Rudolf Virchow,[67] in Schliemann's second publication, which appeared, almost simultaneously with Gaede's edition of the fragments of Demetrios, in 1880 in English and in 1881 in German.[68] It is also between 1880 and 1883 that Schliemann and his followers are most vigorously criticized, for instance, by Richard Claverhouse Jebb, who is himself severely attacked by Mahaffy and Sayce.[69] We have therefore reached a first phase of the debate, in which, interestingly for our study, it is precisely the appreciation of the statements of Demetrios that is under discussion and that creates the disagreement between the modern scholars. Jebb approaches the question through the evidence from Antiquity and lists against the claim of Schliemann—but also of others before him—the statements from ancient authors who spoke against a continuous occupation of the site of Ilion, so that Demetrios' opinion no longer appears as isolated as it has been presented by the defender of Hissarlik. He is followed in his approach by Brentano, we mentioned before, who gives in his second work, published in 1881, a very large part to the defense of Demetrios' position, bringing it into line with descriptions found in Pliny.[70]

A reply by the defenders of Schilemann's theory is given in 1884 when the German archaeologist published his third monograph, which was now also taking account of the contributions that Wilhelm Dörpfeld made since 1882 to the excavations. It is, however, again Mahaffy who outlines the topic about the value of Demetrios' achievement. He attacks previous statements made by Jebb and Brentano[71] and focuses on the evidence from Antiquity about the continuation or interruption of the settlement at the site of Hissarlik. He once again tries to isolate Demetrios' opinion among the ancient ones so that his assumption appears to be a strange attempt of one jealous neighbor. As Dörpfeld's opinion is concerned, his statement is clear, even if his publication would only appear in 1902: Schliemann's excavations have proved, once and for all, that Demetrios and

---

[65] Schliemann 1874:xl–xli, 32, 39, and 134.

[66] Mahaffy 1880b:686–690 (= Mahaffy 1881:761–765) and Mahaffy 1882:69–80 calling Demetrios a "malevolent pedant." In his *History of Greek Literature*, he dedicates only one sentence to Demetrios, in a list of scholars considered as sources of the scholia. See Mahaffy 1880a:39.

[67] Sayce 1880:691–705 (= Sayce 1881:766–781) and Virchow 1880a:673–685 (= Virchow 1881:748–760). Virchow 1880b:31 and 35 has a surprisingly neutral opinion about Demetrios for someone defending Schliemann's opinions about Hissarlik.

[68] Schliemann 1880 is the first version published in English, whereas Schliemann 1881 is the German translation.

[69] Jebb 1881:7–43, Jebb 1882:185–217, Jebb 1883:147–155. The opponents are Mahaffy 1882:69–80 and Sayce 1883:142–146.

[70] Brentano 1881:75.

[71] Mahaffy 1884:372–393.

his followers were wrong in locating Troy at a place other than Hissarlik.[72] This is the same with Alfred Brückner, who contributed to Dörpfeld's publication. He has a rather negative opinion of Demetrios and calls his arguments "*tendenziöse Nachrichten.*"[73] In between these two dates, 1884 and 1902, and in order to exemplify the vehemence of the debate, the contributions of Ernst Bötticher should briefly be mentioned, even if they do not give us many new elements about the appreciation of Demetrios' contribution. Bötticher focused on the archeological remains and their interpretation, and tried to prove that the ruins discovered by Schliemann were the vestiges of a necropolis, not those of a city.[74] The controversy between Bötticher and Schliemann not only led to new excavations in Hissarlik, but also brought about two conferences on the site of Hissarlik during which scholars could see the remains and judge for themselves which hypothesis to follow; and Dörpfeld dedicated a large summary to these events in the introductory part of his work while outlining the history of the excavations in Hissarlik.[75] It is therefore in such a context that Gaede undertook to collect the remaining pieces of evidence from Demetrios' work and presented his edition as a doctoral dissertation at the University of Greifswald.

3.2.2 Gaede and the Approach of His Supervisor Wilamowitz

However, Gaede's work is meant to be, like Stiehle's, an edition of all the remaining fragments that can still be attributed to Demetrios of Scepsis. Therefore, it is quite obvious that his contribution distinguishes itself from the studies just mentioned, which constituted the controversy about Troy by the fact that it dealt not only with the fragments containing Demetrios' opinion about the localization of Troy,[76] but actually with all the remaining fragments with their many different topics. It is therefore not surprising that Gaede expresses a much more balanced view about the Hellenistic scholar's achievements. He calls

---

[72] Dörpfeld 1902:603.

[73] Brüchner 1902:568.

[74] E.g. Bötticher 1889 and Bötticher 1890. His opinion will leave some traces in later works and the necropolis will be associated with the tomb of the Achaeans built on the advice of Nestor. See Seyk 1926:23 and Vellay 1930:100–110.

[75] Dörpfeld 1902:14–15 and now Zavadil 2009:33–109.

[76] These are for instance fr. 21 [Gaede/Biraschi] = Strabo 13.1.27 [C594]; fr. 22 [Gaede/Biraschi] = Strabo 13.1.33–34 [C596–597]; fr. 23a [Gaede/Biraschi] = Σ bT Iliad 20.53c [Erbse]; fr 23b [Gaede/Biraschi] = Σ A Iliad 20.3 [Erbse] (or Σ D Iliad 20.3 [van Thiel]) and fr. 23c [Biraschi] = Strabo 13.1.35 [C597]; fr. 24 [Gaede] (or fr. 24b [Biraschi]) = Hesychios s.v. Θύμβρα and fr. 24a [Biraschi] = Strabo 13.1.35[C598]; fr. 25 [Gaede] (or fr. 25b [Biraschi]) = Σ A Iliad 11.166–168 [Erbse] and fr. 25a [Biraschi] = Strabo 13.1.35 [C598]; fr. 26 [Gaede/Biraschi] = Strabo 13.1.36 [C599]; fr. 27 [Gaede/Biraschi] = Strabo 13.1.39 [C600]; and finally fr. 28a [Gaede/Biraschi] = Strabo 13.1.41 [C601] and fr. 28b [Gaede/Biraschi] = Σ B Iliad 6.92 [Bekker] (now Porphyry *Quaestiones ad Iliadem* [*Iliad* 6.273]), see MacPhail 2011).

him a *vir doctus*, but suggests that one should refrain from judging Demetrios' scholarship before having an accurate collection of his fragments.[77] This statement explains then why we do not find any other comment from Gaede about the Hellenistic scholar's achievements in his edition.[78]

Therefore, but also in order to get a clearer idea of the scope and purpose of Gaede's edition, we should mention a few elements about the historical context of Gaede's work. First, it must, for instance, be noted that Gaede's edition is one of the dissertations that Wilamowitz supervised during his professorship at the University of Greifswald.[79] Furthermore, Gaede's work was not the only one among the dissertations supervised by Wilamowitz that dealt with Demetrios of Scepsis. Ernst Maass, who actually wrote his dissertation on the Sibylline oracles, also dedicated some pages to Demetrios of Scepsis.[80] This study was published just one year before Gaede's edition,[81] and we have highlighted in the previous section on Pausanias how much it influenced Gaede's treatment of some of the fragments.[82] Maass indeed believes that the parts of Pausanias' passage about the Delphian oracle dedicated to the Sibyls[83] should be attributed to Demetrios, even though the name of the scholar is not mentioned in Pausanias' text. This assumption of Maass allowed Gaede to include this passage as fr. 65 in his edition,[84] and his choice therefore shaped the way Demetrios of Scepsis was perceived later on. However, Maass's interpretation of Pausanias' passage and the consequences this view had for Gaede's collection of fragments does not necessarily mean that Maass had a good opinion of the Hellenistic scholar. His line of argument actually shows rather the opposite. Maass's main proof for his choice to attribute Pausanias' passage to Demetrios is the scholar's presumed vanity and impudence, which made him transfer to the Troad, his homeland, several well-known mythological episodes, such as the birth of Zeus or the rites of the Cabeiroi.[85] Maass's appreciation of Demetrios' achievements, however, goes further than the statements in his doctoral dissertation. In 1883,

---

[77] Gaede 1880:1 and 17.

[78] This is, for instance, also in contrast with Stiehle's contribution from 1850, where we have seen that Stiehle formulated several statements about Demetrios' scholarly achievements.

[79] Dräger 2003:343–344.

[80] Maass 1879:22–27.

[81] Maass 1879.

[82] See above Section 2.1.3.

[83] Pausanias 10.12.2–7.

[84] Gaede 1880:55. As mentioned before, also fr. 66 [Gaede/Biraschi] = Stephanus Byzantius s.v. Μερμησσός (= Stephanus Byzantius 445, 15 [Meineke] = Stephanus Byzantius μ 148 [Billerbeck]) should be added here.

[85] Maass 1879:24. He refers to Strabo 10.3.20 [C472], which is actually part of fr. 61 [Gaede/Biraschi], the part of Strabo's text that is most of the time described as speaking about the cult of Rhea. See further again Section 2.1.3 above.

the German scholar returns to this topic and analyzes how Tibullus' *Elegy* 2.5 may have been influenced by Demetrios' research.[86] In particular, Maass aims to prove that the Latin poet may have been using Demetrios' version of the story about Aeneas' destiny after the fall of Troy, because the events described in his poem presuppose a version in which Aeneas consulted the Sibyl before leaving, or at the moment he leaves, the Trojan soil.[87] However, he does not assume that Tibullus read Demetrios' work firsthand, but believes that Demetrios' version may have been known by Tibullus through the work of another historian, whom Maass identifies with Alexander Polyhistor.[88] Without further investigation, this statement may appear today as not entirely convincing,[89] but still, as it stands, it reveals several additional features of Maass's appreciation of Demetrios. First, it seems completely acceptable to the German scholar that Demetrios' work was read and used in Antiquity at least by someone like Alexander Polyhistor. Furthermore, Maass's interpretation of Tibullus' poem also presumes that Demetrios was used in a context other than the discussion about the Homeric landscape as it is, for instance, described in Strabo, even if the story about Aenaes' destiny after the fall of Troy is certainly still linked to the interpretation of the Trojan story at large. In the context of the end of the nineteenth century, especially in 1883, at a moment when the discussion about the Homeric landscape seems overwhelmingly present in the scholarly world, this focus on a more literary use of Demetrios' work is somehow striking. To some extent this is certainly due to the fact that, like Gaede, Maass did not focus primarily on the question about the localization of the Homeric Troy in his research, but was more interested in the way Demetrios' work may have been used by later scholars. In Maass's approach, it was indeed the transmission of the tradition about the Trojan Sibyl that was focused on, whereas Gaede undertook his work as an answer to Niese's contribution from 1877, in which Niese tried to prove that Strabo used Demetrios only through the work of Apollodoros of Athens.[90] Both works illustrate an interesting alternative to the mainstream approach to Demetrios' work, which was in those days, as we just have seen, overshadowed by the controversy about the localization of the Trojan landscape—and one could wonder to what extent this attitude may be seen in connection with their

---

[86] Tibullus 2.5.19–22 and 67–71. See Maass 1883:322–339. A further relevant passage for this question is Dionysius Halicarnassensis *Antiquitates Romanae* 1.55.

[87] Strabo 13.1.53 [C607] part of which is fr. 35 [Gaede/Biraschi].

[88] Maass 1883:334. For Alexander Polyhistor, see Montanari 1996a:478–479 and for the fragments *Die Fragmente der griechischen Historiker* 273, now also *Brill's New Jacoby* 273, and Andria 1989:115–144 for some of the remaining fragments.

[89] For an attempt to give more detail about Alexander Polyhistor as the source for this account, see Perret 1942:578–617.

[90] Gaede 1880:2–12.

supervisor's open contempt of Schliemann and his discoveries.[91] Therefore, we should also extend our investigation to Wilamowitz himself, and see what we can discover about his opinion of our scholar.

Unfortunately, the famous German scholar did not take much interest in Demetrios, and we are therefore only informed indirectly about Wilamowitz's opinion of the Hellenistic scholar. He mentions Demetrios only briefly and by allusion, rather than by developing his opinion fully. These short comments will still reveal some interesting aspects about how he perceived Demetrios and his contribution. In the first comment, which takes the form of a rather extensive footnote, Wilamowitz speaks about a passage from Strabo's book 13 in which the geographer actually quotes Thucydides.[92] Wilamowitz believes that this passage still belongs to Demetrios, who is quoted in Strabo's text a few lines above about Timaeus.[93] He calls the Hellenistic scholar a liar and suggests that the changes between Strabo's quotation of Thucydides' passage and the version that has been transmitted through the direct transmission of Thucydides' text are due to Demetrios.[94] Franz Rühl contested this statement in a rather aggressive way,[95] but for us, it is not his disagreement but his justification that is interesting. Rühl discharges Demetrios of the error Wilamowitz attributes to him, by claiming that the passage from Strabo under discussion does not come from Demetrios, but either from Strabo himself or from Apollodoros. We are therefore back to the question about Strabo's quoting methods and the link between Demetrios and Apollodoros that we have already alluded to previously and that was the acknowledged reason for Gaede's study. However, as Rühl himself notes, Wilamowitz mentions the Hellenistic scholar a second time, moreover in a more positive way, in a subsequent publication, when he is speaking about the prehistory of Athens.[96] He alludes there, again in a footnote, to another passage from Strabo and attributes it to Demetrios.[97] The passage is actually about an etymology of the Piraeus, which seems convincing to Wilamowitz who attributes it to Demetrios. Gaede follows his supervisor and quotes the passage in his edition under his fr. 48, however in a rather ambiguous way.[98] Gaede prints only an extract from Strabo 1.3.17 [C58] as the actual fr. 48, but alludes to the

---

[91] For instance Wilamowitz 1905:10. For more details, see Calder III 1980:146–151.

[92] Strabo 13.1.39 [C600]. The reference in Strabo's text is to Thucydides 3.50.3.

[93] Fr. 27 [Gaede/Biraschi] = Strabo 13.1.39 [C600]. Neither in Gaede's nor in Biraschi's edition is the passage from Thucydides included in the fragment.

[94] See Wilamowitz 1877:333–334.

[95] Rühl 1882:74–75.

[96] Wilamowitz 1880:97–172.

[97] Wilamowitz 1880:137 about Strabo 1.3.18 [C59].

[98] Gaede 1880:45. As with the suggestion of Maass, here too Gaede refers directly to Wilamowitz's argumentation as reason for his attribution of this part to Demetrios' work.

rest of Strabo's text up to Strabo 1.3.21 [C21] beneath the fragment as a kind of parallel passage, without making it clear whether or not this should be seen as a quotation of Demetrios' work. Both passages (Strabo 1.3.17 [C58] and Strabo 1.3.18 [C59]) belong to Strabo's list of examples of places where natural phenomena changed the landscapes, and we have already discussed these passages and modern scholars' disagreement about Strabo's sources for this part of his text in the chapter on Strabo's use of Demetrios.[99] We are therefore again back to the question of Strabo's quoting methods and his reliability with regard to the fragments of Demetrios of Scepsis.

For Wilamowitz's third allusion to Demetrios the context is slightly different. In 1881, he mentions Demetrios in a list of authors whom he believes to have been influenced by the scholarship carried out at the library of Pergamon, but he does not give any judgment about the scholars' achievements,[100] and therefore we cannot take much from this allusion to Demetrios. It is finally only in 1905, in his chapter *Griechische Literatur des Altertums*, that Wilamowitz comes back to Demetrios and to Schliemann's discoveries in Hissarlik. He does not mention Demetrios by name, but seems to have a more positive opinion about the Hellenistic scholar as he suggests that Demetrios' statements about Ilion and its history were in accordance with the most recent modern results concerning the Troad, despite Schliemann's earlier claims.[101] Therefore, this statement shows clearly how much Wilamowitz's attitude has changed between his first mention in 1877 when he calls Demetrios a liar and 1905. This change may be explained either by the reduced vigor of the debate about the discoveries in the Troad at the beginning of the twentieth century or in connection with the more balanced view that the works of his two students gave of Demetrios.

3.2.3 Further Independent Works on Demetrios

Despite the weight given in the scholarly world both to the debate about Schliemann's discovery and to the question about Strabo's quoting methods, a few more independent works at the end of the nineteenth century dealt with Demetrios of Scepsis. One of them is Marcel Dubois's *Examen de la géographie de Strabo*, published in 1891, just one year after Schliemann's death. He describes the achievements of Demetrios briefly, together with those of Apollodoros of Athens, however in a rather neutral way.[102] This attitude is certainly explained to

---

[99] See above Section 2.1.1 (pp. 78–82).

[100] Wilamowitz 1881:176–177.

[101] For instance, Wilamowitz 1905:10 (= 1907:12 or 1912:15; there were no changes in the second and third edition of this particular passage).

[102] Dubois 1891:312–313.

some extent by the fact that, because Dubois's main focus is on the geographical content of Strabo's work, which means that he considers our two scholars only as "*sources secondaires*,"[103] he does not develop the content of their works beyond a short summary of each, and prefers to privilege other geographers among Strabo's sources, such as Ephoros, Polybios, Artemidoros, and Poseidonios.

We should perhaps add here the two contributions, one on Demetrios and the other on Apollodoros of Athens, written by Eduard Schwartz in the *Paulys Realencyclolädie der classischen Altertumswissenschaft*.[104] Both entries were written, as was the study by Dubois, when the debate about the Homeric landscape was still present but had started to lose its vehemence after Schliemann's death. Therefore, it is perhaps not surprising to see that Schwartz's contributions establish once again a close link between the two Hellenistic scholars. Indeed, not only in the parts where he discusses the fragments themselves, he often alludes to the fact that the pieces attributed to one of the scholars contain elements that are likely to come from the work of the other,[105] but he also insists, when presenting the achievements of the two scholars, on the fact that Apollodoros wrote an Alexandrian answer to Demetrios and that it is mainly because of this response that the work of Demetrios was more widely known.[106] Furthermore, when we focus on the entry about Demetrios, we find a surprisingly well-balanced presentation of Demetrios' achievements, which is in contrast with the extreme positions scholars had about Demetrios in the debate that Schliemann's excavations raised. Schwartz describes Demetrios as a true scholar who presents his arguments in a clear and reproducible way, even if the conclusion he draws from these statements may be wrong, as it is the case, according to Schwartz, with the question about the localization of Troy. We, however, still feel the influence that the debate about Schliemann's discoveries had on Schwartz's presentation when he mentions the presumed jealousy of Demetrios against Ilion as reason for his peculiar position. It is also interesting for us to see that, like Stiehle before him, Schwartz uses as justification for his positive appreciation of Demetrios the long list of rather unknown authors that Demetrios quotes in his work. This is, according to Schwartz, a sign of Demetrios' scholarly activity, even if he judges it inferior to the research carried out in Alexandria. Furthermore, he considers the scholarly activity of Demetrios as an example of an independent tradition, which he believes to be typical of the ancient Aeolis and which Demetrios would then share with scholars like Polemon of Ilion, Hegesianax of Alexandria Troas, or Neoptolemos of Parion, in opposition to the one carried out in the center of

---

[103] Dubois 1891:332.
[104] Schwartz 1894:2855–2886 and Schwartz 1901:2807–2813.
[105] Schwartz 1894:2867–2870 and Schwartz 1901:2808, 2810.
[106] Schwartz 1894:2865 and Schwartz 1901:2808.

scholarship created in Pergamon. We have already alluded to this question in the chapter about Demetrios' literary background, and it brings us to the last group of works we have not yet dealt with in this part of our chapter, those either dealing with the history of ancient scholarship or giving a general overview of Greek literature.

3.2.4 Demetrios in Works on Greek Literature or on the History of Scholarship

Among the works focusing on Greek literature, Wilhelm von Christ's *Geschichte der griechischen Literatur* is one of the first that should be mentioned.[107] In his presentation of Demetrios, the influence of the debate about Schliemann's discovery is clearly visible at least in the first four editions in which it is explicitly mentioned.[108] He repeats, for instance, Mahaffy's statement about the alleged jealousy as the reason for Demetrios' attacks against the claims made by the Ilians. However, since the fifth edition of his work, which was reworked by Wilhelm Schmid and Otto Stählin and published between 1908–1913, the wording is more neutral, leading to a more positive description of Demetrios' achievements. His error about the localization of Troy is mentioned as a matter of fact, but his erudition is highlighted and serves as an example to illustrate how learned people could be in Asia Minor and especially in the Troad in those days.[109]

However, it is not only the chronological distance from the debate, as suggested by the changes in the presentations of Demetrios in von Christ's text, that determines the more or less neutral description of Demetrios' achievements as a scholar. For instance, between 1887 and 1899, the two French scholars Alfred and Maurice Croiset were able to write a chapter on Demetrios, in their *Histoire de la littérature grecque*,[110] in a very neutral way, without even mentioning the controversy about Troy. They even express some regrets about the loss of the work, although it is not the work itself, which they do not consider as of great literary value, that they regret the lack of, but the assembled material that it contained.[111] It is the same with Alfred Gudeman's *Grundriss der Geschichte der klassischen Philologie*, an enlarged German version of his *Outlines*

---

[107] The first edition was printed in 1889 (the dates for the subsequent editions are 1890, 1898, 1905, 1908–1913, and then 1912–1924).

[108] von Christ 1889:421 (§ 361) (= von Christ 1890:474–475 [§361] or von Christ 1898:555–556 [§ 392] or von Christ 1905:576–577 [§ 392]).

[109] von Christ/Schmid/Stählin 1911:189 (§ 465) or von Christ/Schmid/Stählin 1920:245 (§ 470).

[110] Croiset 1887–1899.

[111] Croiset 1899:94–95 (it is the fifth volume; the whole is published between 1887–1899).

of the *History of Classical Philology*.[112] He mentions Demetrios, but emphasizes the link to Apollodoros, alluding, only cursorily and without taking a position, to Demetrios' controversial position about the identification of Troy.[113] Such attitudes are in contrast with the one Susemihl takes in his *Geschichte der griechischen Litteratur in der Alexanderzeit*.[114] With this German scholar, we turn back to Gaede's environment, as Susemihl is a professor in Greifswald at the time when Wilamowitz supervised Gaede's dissertation.[115] He acknowledges that he was much influenced by Wilamowitz's views while composing his work,[116] and it is therefore not surprising to find in his description of Demetrios Wilamowitz's rather ambiguous attitude toward the Hellenistic scholar. On the one hand, Susemihl mentions the large scholarly knowledge Demetrios must have had in order to be able to write his commentary, but on the other he accuses Demetrios of having distorted and falsified some of the facts to bring them in line with his local patriotism.[117]

We turn fully back to the controversy about Troy, however, only with the *History of Classical Scholarship* written by Sir John Edwin Sandys.[118] Even if he publishes the first edition of his work only in 1903, his presentation of Demetrios, which is now for the first time more openly linked to the Pergamene library, is much influenced by Jebb, whose works we have discussed in the section on the controversy about the discoveries in Hissarlik. Sandys quotes Jebb's judgment about Demetrios in full, and emphasizes Demetrios' scholarly achievements, by highlighting the fact that Strabo quotes Demetrios in more than twenty-five passages. He also alludes to the controversy about the discovery made by Schliemann, but acknowledges only that the Greek Ilion had been identified by Schliemann, leaving open the question of whether this was also the Homeric Troy.[119] Furthermore, he cites the fact that scholars like Hellanicos and Polemon too acted with patriotism when they identified Ilion with the Homeric Troy, but refrains from giving any reason why Demetrios defended his peculiar opinion. Sandys's work was very influential,[120] and there was no other history of ancient scholarship written before Pfeiffer's *History of Classical Scholarship* in 1968, which

---

[112] The first version was Gudeman 1892 under the title *Syllabus on the History of Classical Philology*. A second edition follows in 1894 under the title *Outlines of the History of Classical Philology*. In both of them only Apollodoros of Athens is mentioned. See Gudeman 1892:12–13 = Gudeman 1894:16–17.

[113] Gudeman 1907:44 = Gudeman 1909:49–50.

[114] Susemihl 1891, 1892.

[115] From 1856–1898. See Kirstin 2000:175–176 and Dräger 2003:338.

[116] Susemihl 1891:v–vi.

[117] Susemihl 1891:681–685.

[118] Sandys 1903.

[119] Sandys 1903:153–154.

[120] Pfeiffer 1968:viii.

will lead us to the next section about the studies on Demetrios carried out in the twentieth century.

3.3 Works After Gaede (1880-2011)

As no new edition of the fragments from Demetrios' work was published in the twentieth century, our next section will have to take account of rather a long period. We shall see that only at the beginning of the twenty-first century both Laura Pagani and Anna Maria Biraschi came back to the fragments and made substantial improvements on this aspect of the research on Demetrios of Scepsis. This chronological division means that, with regard to the second criterion we defined at the beginning of the chapter—the several phases into which the excavations carried out in the Troad can be divided—the timespan we shall consider here saw two further such excavation campaigns.[121] Until now we have focused on the first phase, which corresponds to the excavations led by Schliemann and Dörpfeld. These are followed by the excavations carried out by Blegen between 1932 and 1938 and, finally, those undertaken by Korfmann from 1981 onwards. For the study and judgment of Demetrios, both, Blegen and Korfmann, add some further elements about the scholar and shape the perception one had of this scholar in different ways. Moreover, it is interesting to see that they are separated from each other by World War II and therefore belong to two different historical contexts. As far as Blegen's campaign is concerned, we see that it covers a timespan that can be dated before the war (1932–1938). The preliminary reports were then written between 1933 and 1948, before the final reports could be publish between 1950 and 1958.[122]

However, we find very little about Demetrios in Blegen's works. Our scholar is only alluded to in a very synthetic exposition of the results from Blegen's excavations, moreover only in a footnote in which Blegen reminds his readers that Demetrios was among the first who contested the identification of Ilion with the Homeric Troy.[123] Furthermore, an additional brief mention of Demetrios is made by Burr Thompson, who gives, in the introduction to her analysis of the terracotta figurines from Troy, a short summary of the history on the site of Ilion and discusses Demetrios' testimonium about the state of preservation of Ilion in his time.[124] We must, therefore, conclude that it is not in the strictly

---

[121] Korfmann 1991:91 and 93–101. See now also Rose 2015:157–176 for the link between the two more recent campaigns.

[122] See also Blegen 1950:24–26, Caskey 1948:119, and for Blegen's activities in connection with and as consequence of World War II, see Vogeikoff-Brogan 2015:28–31.

[123] Blegen 1962:386.

[124] Fr. 21 [Gaede/Biraschi] (= T3 [Biraschi]) = Strabo 13.1.27 [C594]). Burr Thomson 1963:3–5.

archaeological studies where we find most of the discussions about Demetrios of Scepsis in those days. This is in contrast with what we have seen in the previous section, where Demetrios took a rather large part in Schliemann's publications about his discoveries in the Troad. We shall indeed see that, in this new period of our analysis, it is actually in another category of works, those focusing on the Troad in a very broad sense where archaeological and more literary data are combined, that we find most of the new elements about Demetrios of Scepsis. The situation is not fundamentally different during the last phase of excavation, which started in 1981, by focusing on the bay of Beriska and the localization of the presumed Achaean camp, but turns back to Hissarlik-Troy itself only since 1988. As we shall see, this different focus has its importance with regard to the appreciation of Demetrios' achievements, and tends to blur the caesura that Word War II represents. Indeed, the results this campaign brought—and still bring—are more indirectly linked to Demetrios of Scepsis, and we do not find in these excavation projects the same interest in our scholar as in the previous campaigns. Yet even this distance between the excavation and our scholar's contribution influences the perception modern scholars had of Demetrios, and this will also be discernible in the outline of our presentation. However, this shift in the way Demetrios is dealt with in the twentieth century is perhaps also due to the approach Walter Leaf took in the research that he carried out at the very beginning of the twentieth century. He conducted it with a rather surprising independence from the archaeological investigations, when we compare his approach to those from the studies discussed so far, and this allows us to begin our section with his contributions.

3.3.1 Studies Dealing With the Troad in the Twentieth Century

In order fully to understand Walter Leaf's contribution on Demetrios, we still have to start by describing it in connection with what happened in the Troad at the beginning of the twentieth century from an archaeological point of view. In this respect, it is important to note first that most of Leaf's dealings with Demetrios fall in the time when no excavations were carried out in the Troad. Actually, it is the timespan between the publication of Dörpfeld's results about Troy, dated to 1902, and his last excavation campaign in 1924.[125] There is, however, a connection between the two scholars, as Leaf accepts Dörpfeld's assumptions and identifies Hissarlik with the Homeric Troy.[126] However, this

---

[125] We have already mentioned his work (Dörpfeld 1902) and the opinion about Demetrios he defended there previously (Dörpfeld 1902:603). For some details about Dörpfeld's last campaign, see for instance Korfmann 1991:100.

[126] Leaf 1912:vii, 8, 57–58.

does not prevent Leaf from developing his own opinion about Demetrios, precisely because he does not approach Demetrios from the point of view of an archaeologist. His interests in the Hellenistic scholar come rather from his studies about the Homeric text. In 1891, for instance, he starts by publishing an English translation of the *Iliad*.[127] The following year he adds a commentary[128] and in 1895 an edition of the Greek text.[129] However, in none of these early works is Demetrios mentioned. It is only when Leaf's interest shifts away from the text and focuses on its content, and more precisely on the question of the setting where the events narrated in the *Iliad* could have taken place, that the English scholar starts to speak about Demetrios and his achievements, moreover in a surprisingly positive way for someone in the tradition of Schliemann and Dörpfeld. In a first contribution on the Scamandros Valley, written after his experience of traveling in the Troad around 1910, Leaf discusses the testimonia of Demetrios without contesting their value.[130] In this article, however, he uses Demetrios' fragments mainly in relation to topics that do not touch on the question of the localization of Troy, and there is therefore no need for Leaf to allude to this controversial topic in his contribution. However, his positive attitude towards Demetrios does not change, even when he is dealing with the question of the localization of Troy. This is particularly visible in his well-known *Troy, a Study in Homeric Geography*, published in 1912.[131] By then, however, the archaeological approach to the Troad had also changed, and Leaf could, for instance, claim to be the first scholar to have detached the topographical research from Hissarlik and from the search for Troy by expanding them to the analysis of the entire territory of the Troad.[132] He even suggests that his research could be seen as a kind of continuation of Demetrios' commentary,[133] and from such statements, it becomes obvious how positive Leaf's opinion about Demetrios was, despite his acceptance of Schliemann's claims and Leaf's acknowledged debt to Dörpfeld. He accepts, for instance, without hesitation Demetrios' witness about the state of preservation of the Hellenistic Ilion at the beginning of the second century BCE, and claims that it is actually in accordance with the remains found in the Troad.[134] In other cases, as with the problematic question about the localization of the two springs of the Scamandros, he discharges Demetrios for not having found them by comparing his ignorance with that

---

[127] Leaf/Lang/Myers 1891.
[128] Leaf 1892.
[129] Leaf 1895 with a second edition in 1900–1902.
[130] Leaf 1910–1911:266–283.
[131] Leaf 1912.
[132] Leaf 1912:viii and also 5.
[133] Leaf 1912:171.
[134] Leaf 1912:57 and 115.

of modern scholars.[135] Furthermore, even if in relation with other topics he clearly states Demetrios' local pride, which made him defend strange versions of mythological stories so that he could privilege his hometown, he does it in a rather apologetic tone.[136] Finally, when he is dealing with the Trojan plain, he even acknowledges his regret to have lost so many details of Demetrios' work, due, according to him, to the distortions introduced by Strabo when he quotes elements from Demetrios' work.[137] To this specific topic he then dedicates an entire study, which he published in the 1917–1918 volume of the *Annual of the British School at Athens* under the title "Strabo and Demetrios of Skepsis."[138] This study restates his views that the contradictions and difficulties encountered in Demetrios' fragments are actually due to Strabo, and he therefore diminishes the value of Strabo's scholarly activity rather than that of Demetrios. In doing so, he shows once again how far he can go in his defense of Demetrios' achievements, and it is therefore not surprising to see that Leaf believes that Demetrios has invented a new approach to scholarly research on Homer.[139] This enthusiasm for Demetrios' approach, together with his conclusions about the link between Strabo's and Demetrios' texts, leads him to his last work, published in 1923, and dedicated entirely to Strabo's book 13 with its description of the Troad.[140] This evolution of Leaf's research interests reveals two interesting elements for our study. First, it shows how the analyses of the ancient testimonies about the Troad lead away from the Homeric text to the discussion of the quotations given in Strabo's *Geography*.[141] Second, it brings us back to one of the difficulties about Demetrios' work we have encountered several times previously: as a large number of the remaining fragments are transmitted in Strabo's text, scholars who wants to deal with Demetrios must first, before making any statement about Demetrios himself, ponder the question of how accurate Strabo's text is, either with regard to the transmitted information or with regard to his quoting methods, on which the accuracy of the preserved quotations depends. This situation has not changed, and we have encountered this question already in Niese's contribution from 1877 and also in Gaede's introduction.[142]

---

[135] Leaf 1912:49.

[136] Leaf 1912:135–138 (for the question of the Locrian maiden in relation with the claims of Ilion), 179 (for Dardania and the claims of Dardanos), and 195–197 (for Arisbe).

[137] Leaf 1912:171.

[138] Leaf 1917–1918:23–47.

[139] Leaf 1917–1918:23–24 (reaffirmed in Leaf 1923:xxviii).

[140] Leaf 1923.

[141] He acknowledges himself that his three journeys to the Troad prepared him to make a book about Strabo's Troad (Leaf 1912:7)

[142] Niese 1877 and Gaede 1880:17. See also above Section 3.1.3 and, for Gaede, Section 3.2.2.

In the same period (1890–1930), and therefore also without further new material from the archaeologists, there are a few other scholars who mention Demetrios in relation to the Troad and its exploration. One example worth mentioning here is the work by Felix Sartriaux, as his work shares several similarities with Leaf's contributions. The French scholar is, for instance, also defending Schliemann's position and especially Dörpfeld's work. Furthermore, like Leaf, he himself was able to travel in the Troad, and uses his experience as basis for his own contribution. However, in opposition to Leaf, Demetrios is not the main focus of Sartriaux's study and is therefore mentioned only three times, rather briefly. First, Sartriaux alludes to Demetrios in his summary of the several historical phases the Greek settlement of Ilion went through and uses the Hellenistic scholar's statement about the state of Ilion[143] as proof for the decline that Ilion underwent in the second century BCE.[144] In a second passage, he takes up the old position of the defenders of Hissarlik and presents Demetrios' position and that of his fellow scholar Hestiaia of Alexandria Troas as a unique attack against the claims made by the Ilians to see in their town the Homeric Troy.[145] But, in contrast with the scholars from the nineteenth century, Sartriaux can now also reflect on the debate that has taken place at the end of the nineteenth century, and he uses these new insights to isolate Demetrios' position even more by adding that also in modern times his position was only seldom defended, as it was only attractive at the end of the eighteenth century to the defenders of the Bunarbashi-theory. Finally, he briefly mentions Demetrios' work in a footnote, when he is giving a rather meticulous description of the Troad, aiming to prove Homer's accurate knowledge of the Troad.[146] It is therefore not surprising to see that, because Sartriaux gives so little weight to our scholar, he does not discuss or judge Demetrios' contribution in a way that would help us to learn more about Demetrios from Sartriaux's work than was already said at the end of the nineteenth century by the participants of the controversy over Schliemann's discoveries.

Unfortunately, we reach a similar conclusion when discussing the works by scholars from the beginning of the twentieth century who were speaking against Schliemann's theory. We may mention here two examples. First, there is Vaclav Wenzel Seyk, who in 1926 published a work entitled *Das wahre und richtige Troja-Ilion*.[147] He gives a long list of all the objections that could be adduced against Schliemann's identification and among these points we also find the question

---

[143] This is once again fr. 21 [Gaede/Biraschi] (= T3 [Biraschi]) = Strabo 13.1.27 [C594]).
[144] Sartiaux 1915:34.
[145] Sartiaux 1915:73.
[146] Sartiaux 1915:126.
[147] Seyk 1926.

about the distance between Hissarlik and the seashore, which was already discussed in Strabo's text, moreover in a passage attributed to Demetrios.[148] In this context he briefly mentions Demetrios and blames Schliemann for not having given more weight to the evidence from Antiquity. It is, however, difficult to understand from this Seyk's opinion about Demetrios. On the one hand, he acknowledges that Demetrios' indications about the distance between the seashore and Hissarlik were right,[149] but, on the other, he also criticizes Demetrios' identification of Troy with the so-called village of the Ilians.[150] Therefore, the analysis of his study suggests that Seyk did not have a very positive opinion about the Hellenistic scholar, despite his criticism of Schliemann.

Our second example is the work written by Charles Vellay in 1930 and entitled *Les nouveaux aspects de la question de Troie*. The French scholar refers to Dörpfeld's last excavation campaign carried out in 1924 and attacks him severely, in particular about the localization of the Achaean camp, which was actually the subject of Dörpfeld's last excavations.[151] The outline of his attacks reveals, however, how much Vellay is actually inspired by the previously mentioned work by Seyk. Like Seyk, Vellay focuses mainly on the Trojan shore and discusses the localization theories for the Achaean camp. In this context he mentions Demetrios occasionally, most of the time as a valuable source for the topography of the Troad.[152] However, once again the few comments on Demetrios we get from Vellay's work do not bring many new elements to the discussion, and we have to acknowledge that, by mentioning these studies, we are actually only highlighting the importance Leaf's contributions had for our question about the modern appreciation of Demetrios' work.

This conclusion is also true for the next work we mention here, John M. Cook's monograph from 1973, *The Troad, an Archaeological and Topographical Study*, which soon became the standard work on the Troad.[153] This is certainly to some extent due to the fact that its publication in 1973 falls once again in the interval between two excavation phases, now between that of Blegen and that of Korfmann;[154] it is therefore interesting to note that Cook comes to Demetrios in a similar way as Leaf at the beginning of the twentieth century, and this despite

---

[148] This is Strabo 13.1.36–37 [C598–599], part of which is fr. 26 [Gaede/Biraschi].

[149] Seyk 1926:20.

[150] Seyk 1926:48.

[151] Vellay 1930:1–8.

[152] Vellay 1930:12, 51, 85, and 97–98.

[153] Cook 1973.

[154] As just mentioned, the one led by Blegen was carried out between 1932 and 1938, and the one by Korfmann started only in 1981.

the break that World War II may have brought.[155] Indeed, before writing this very detailed study on the Troad, Cook started by publishing some considerations about textual issues in Strabo's text.[156] This more philological research, which is dated from 1959, is linked to the reevaluation, undertaken in the first half of the twentieth century, of the Vatican Palimpsest, which contains part of Strabo's text.[157] Among others, Cook discussed in this study a passage from book 13 in which the textual problems touch on a part of Strabo's text that was considered as a fragment of Demetrios' work.[158] This article and the context in which it was written, even if we do not learn from it anything about the way Cook appreciated Demetrios' work, remind us once again of the close link between Strabo and Demetrios, which has already been highlighted several times and which will actually be present throughout this part of our discussion until Biraschi's edition from 2011. We shall indeed see that she is also a scholar who started with works on Strabo[159] before editing the fragments of Demetrios. For the question of Cook's appreciation of Demetrios we should, however, return now to his archaeological study on the Troad, in which Cook's clearest statement about Demetrios is given in the discussion about the localization of the Achaean camp. There the English scholar takes not only the defense of Demetrios' investigations, but describes the ancient approach to the question of the localization of the Homeric landscape as a whole in an extremely positive way.[160] He parallels, for instance, the hypotheses they gave and the evidence they adduced with the lines of argument of modern scholars, by emphasizing that both groups face the same difficulties because the landscape they were focusing on remained the same. In other places, he is also rather positive towards the evidence from either Strabo or Demetrios.[161] Nonetheless, we have to acknowledge that Demetrios does not take much space in Cook's work, and we see that, even with this more positive touch in Cook's works, the situation does not change much with regard

---

[155] It is also interesting to mention here that Cook also published his work after Pfeiffer's *History of Classical Scholarship* from 1968. We shall come back to this later (see below Section 3.3.3).

[156] Cook 1959:19–26.

[157] Aly 1928:1–45, Aly 1931:1–32, Aly 1950:228–263, and for a transcription of the text, see Aly 1956. For the importance of this edition, see Aujac/Lasserre 1969:liii–lvii, Diller 1975:19–14, and Radt 2002:ix–x.

[158] Strabo 13.1.45 [C603] (= Fr. 31a [Biraschi]). The passage appears only as parallel evidence in connection with Gaede's fr. 31.

[159] See for instance Dueck 2005:260–261 for some of Biraschi's most relevant publications about Strabo.

[160] Cook 1973:186–188.

[161] See for instance his discussion about the localization of the Callicolone (Cook 1973:112–113), the identification of the springs of the Scamandros (Cook 1973:292), and the identification of Palaescepsis and Cebrene (Cook 1973:302–304 and 341–342). See also Cook 1973:245, 260 for shorter statements.

to the status Demetrios had in the works written in the twentieth century. With the exception of Leaf's works, the interest in Demetrios seems to have diminished gradually between the time of Schliemann's excavation and the third excavation campaign, despite the work Blegen carried out between 1932 and 1938. If Demetrios is mentioned, most of the time the scholars repeat elements we have already encountered in previous studies or they emphasize the connection between Strabo and Demetrios by focusing on the geographer's work. And this tendency is even intensified after Cook's contributions, as a rather quiet period follows with regard to Demetrios. We shall see that there were some important remarks in works with a wider scope than the Trojan landscape, such as Pfeiffer's *History of Classical Scholarship*, but for studies in connection to the Troad, we have to wait for the next excavation phase, which started, as mentioned above, in 1981, before we receive any new elements about Demetrios.

A first reaction to the new information from the Troad involving Demetrios can be seen in two works written by John Victor Luce. The first, taking the form of an article published in 1984, focused on the localization of the Achaean camp, which was also the target of the first campaign of the new phase of excavation. Luce discusses there the new hypotheses about the localization of the Achaean camp, which were now based on the latest evidence from the archaeological investigations in the Troad, and defends Demetrios of Scespis.[162] This extremely positive opinion is displayed even more clearly in Luce's second book, dedicated to the whole Troad and published in 1998. There he takes the stance that the descriptions found in the Homeric texts are accurate, and he outlines once again his proof for such a position. In this discussion, he also mentions the evidence from Strabo's text about Demetrios.[163] This involves mainly Demetrios' statements about the question of the localization of two springs of the Scamandros and his description of the problem about the distance between the seashore and the Trojan city. Luce's judgment of Demetrios, even if it involves well-known elements, is, however, an interesting mixture of these. He cites, for instance, Demetrios' presumed local pride, which led him to dismiss the claim of the Ilians that their city was the Homeric Troy. Nevertheless, Luce recognizes a certain value to Demetrios' objections against this localization because of the missing space for the battlefield between the seashore and Troy. It is the same with the difficulty Demetrios had in finding the two springs of the Scamandros. Luce dismisses Demetrios' position although he recognizes that it has a certain value.

---

[162] Luce 1984:31–43.
[163] Especially Luce 1998:132–133 and 160.

Also closely linked to the new phase of excavation are two contributions published in the *Studia Troica*,[164] even if neither of them gives much weight to the new archaeological results. The first, dated from 1993, illustrates once again how closely considerations about Demetrios are linked to the analysis of Strabo's text, as this contribution is Stefan Radt's preliminary presentation, which he gave together with Jan Willem Drijvers, of his new edition of Strabo's *Geography*.[165] For this preliminary publication of part of his work, he chooses the passage from Strabo's book 13 in which the geographer speaks about Troy, its localization, and Demetrios' statements. Therefore, he mentions Demetrios briefly in the introduction to his commentary and alludes to two characteristics about Demetrios' position that we have already encountered. He underlines, on the one hand, that the excavations in the Troad speak against Demetrios' hypothesis of localization, and suggests, on the other, that Demetrios denied the Ilians' claim because of his contempt towards his neighbors.[166] It is the same with the second article in the *Studia Troica* in which Demetrios is mentioned. A few years later, Demetrios is indeed again alluded to in Michael Sage's contribution about the visitors to the Troad.[167] He is named there briefly together with Strabo as one of the authors criticizing both the identification of Ilion with the Homeric Troy, and the several Roman visitors who went there because of this association.[168] Sage does, however, not comment on Demetrios' position, as he embraces a much wider point of view in his article and gives a thorough analysis of the phenomenon of the visits to the Troad without stopping too long on one single example.

His approach, despite its very few elements about Demetrios, leads us, however, to a further category of works that allude to the Hellenistic scholar, those dealing with the historical background of the Troad either in Strabo's or in Demetrios' time. They are not, strictly speaking, related to the excavations carried out in the Troad, but discuss Demetrios' achievements with regard either to the period in which the Hellenistic scholar wrote his work or to the cultural and literary background of Strabo's *Geography*. A first example of this more historical approach to Demetrios' achievement is provided by the works of Emilio Gabba who classifies Demetrios' position about the localization of Troy as an anti-Roman attitude, which would then reflect the political situation of the

---

[164] This is the academic journal that has been created for the publication of the annual reports of the new excavation campaigns. For more information, see the website of *Project Troia* at http://www.uni-tuebungen.de/troia/eng/sttroica.html.

[165] Radt/Drijvers 1993:201–231.

[166] Radt/Drijvers 1993:218.

[167] Sage 2000:211–231.

[168] Sage 2000:214.

second century BCE.[169] He is followed in his opinion by Jean-Louis Ferrary, even if the French scholar is not as affirmative as Gabba;[170] whereas Erich S. Gruen, who joined the debate a little later, sees Demetrios' attitude as the one of a scholar who speaks in favor of his hometown rather than against the Roman claims.[171] Erskine's study from 2001, *Troy between Greece and Rome*, is also dedicated to this aspect, and Demetrios' position is discussed as a witness of his time. Erskine does not, however, present the Greek reaction to the arrival of the Romans as being as polarized as it has been previously and focuses more on the context in which the statements were made (the local competition between neighboring cities) rather than on their content (e.g. his localization of the Homeric Troy).[172] Therefore, he does not, for instance, judge Demetrios' statements, but simply qualifies his position about the Homeric Troy as reflecting the prejudice against Ilion stated by one of its neighbors.[173] An even more balanced view is embraced by Desideri and Nicolai, who both publish their contributions in the 2005–2006 volume of the review *Geographia Antiqua*.[174] Desideri focuses on the way the inhabitants of the Troad reacted to the political use of the myth of the Trojan origin of Rome and discusses Demetrios' contribution along with those of Hegesianax of Alexandria Troas, Agathocles of Cyzicos,[175] and Polemon of Ilion. He emphasizes, however, the role Strabo played in the transmission of Demetrios' position, and then switches to the discussion on Strabo's intentions when he borrows from Demetrios' work, bringing us back once again to the question of Strabo's use of his sources. Nonetheless, Desideri's approach brings us some new elements as he discusses the issue in a very broad sense and focuses more on the reasons why Strabo chooses the sources he actually quotes rather than on the recurring question of how he uses them.[176] Nicolai explores this aspect even further and analyzes the status of philological considerations about the Homeric text in Strabo's *Geography*. He therefore mentions Demetrios several times in his study, but does not give any judgment about the Hellenistic scholar's achievements. He only focuses on Strabo's point of view and tries to explain what the geographer's intentions or aims may have been when he quotes

---

[169] Gabba 1974:630–632 and Gabba 1976:85–93. He has, however, a rather positive opinion about Demetrios and describes his work as a writing of great erudition and carried out with much commitment.

[170] Ferrary 1988:223–225.

[171] Gruen 1993:40–42.

[172] Erskine 2001:106–107.

[173] Erskine 2001:233.

[174] Desideri 2005–2006:45–53 and Nicolai 2005–2006:55–75.

[175] For the collection of the fragments, see *Die Fragmente der griechischen Historiker* 472 (and *Brill's New Jacoby* 472); otherwise, Gabba 1974:632 and Perret 1942:380–386.

[176] Desideri 2005–2006:51–52.

elements of Demetrios' work alongside witnesses from other sources.[177] This is the same with works like Franco's *La Troade di Straboe*[178] or Biraschi's contribution on the Homeric tradition within Strabo's text, published in the same collection of articles.[179] Both Italian scholars mention Demetrios several times as a source of Strabo, but they do not judge his contribution. Biraschi underlines the distance Strabo sometimes takes from his source and restates the anti-Roman aspects of Demetrios' work, whereas Franco imputes some of the inadequacies in Strabo's text about the Troad to Demetrios of Scepsis, therefore taking a position exactly opposite to that defended by Leaf at the beginning of the century, who discharged Demetrios by making Strabo responsible for the inadequacies.[180] Finally, also, in Biraschi's 2005 article on Homer and Strabo, very little case is made of Demetrios, who is mentioned only together with Apollodoros of Athens as sources of Strabo.[181]

The common feature of all these works seems therefore to be the fact that the modern scholars focus on Strabo and his time, mentioning Demetrios as only one among the many sources Strabo used. This has as its consequence that we drift away, with these more recent contributions, from the archaeological remains and the implications they had on Demetrios' position in the second century BCE to a more historical or literary approach that focuses on Strabo and the early imperial period. This is even more so with works like Nagy's *Homer the Preclassic* or Antonelli's *I Pisistratidi al Sigeo*.[182] Nagy, for instance, analyzes different aspects of Homeric reception in Antiquity and juxtaposes several traditions about the localization of the Homeric Troy. He defines an Athenian tradition that claims that Troy was destroyed, an Ionian tradition, represented by Demetrios of Scepsis, in which the Trojan survivors moved to Scepsis, and finally an Aeolian one, which is actually the position of the inhabitants of Ilion.[183] Nagy does not give any judgments about the different claims, but analyzes the perception and usage of Homer's poems to which they bear witness. A good example of Nagy's approach is, for instance, the way he analyzes the passage from Strabo about Timaeus, which is actually fr. 27 [Gaede/Biraschi].[184] The

---

[177] Nicolai 2005–2006:57–59.
[178] Franco 2000:263–282.
[179] Biraschi 2000:47–72.
[180] Biraschi 2000:56–65 and Franco 2000:267, 270–271. Interestingly, as one of his examples Franco uses the passage from Strabo 13.1.39 [C600], which has already been discussed by Wilamowitz and in the context of which the German scholar calls Demetrios a liar. See above Wilamowitz 1877:333–334.
[181] Biraschi 2005:80.
[182] Nagy 2010 and Antonelli 2000:9–58.
[183] Nagy 2010:197–198.
[184] Strabo 13.1.39 [C600].

American scholar states that Demetrios is Strabo's source, but does not clearly decide which of them should be taken as responsible for the inconsistency he sees in Strabo's interpretation of Timaeus' statement.[185] This is the same with Antonelli. He actually discusses the same passage from Strabo and analyzes Demetrios' critique towards Timaeus.[186] Moreover, he clearly states that Stabo is inspired by Demetrios' work in this passage and even suggests that Demetrios may have used Herodotus as his source, but he does not judge any of the ancient contributions.

We are, finally, back once again to the Troad with the short article about the settlement of Caresos by Gille Courtieux.[187] The French scholar again does not allude to any progress from the archaeological point of view, as the place he is interested in, Caresos, has not received much attention in recent excavation projects. Nevertheless, Courtieux believes he has found the site of Caresos in the Troad, by analyzing two passages about the city, one from Polybios and one from Strabo.[188] As the Straboian passage corresponds to Demetrios' fr. 31a [Biraschi], Courtieux recognizes Demetrios as Strabo's source and briefly alludes to his contribution. He reproaches Strabo for using his source sometimes without careful reexamination and suggests that Demetrios may have been too partial towards the Attalids in his exposition of the fate of Caresos. But, despite these rather new elements that would point to a close connection between Demetrios and the Attalids, Courtieux's analysis does not help us much in our research here. It is far too short and does not focus on Demetrios, but actually on a passage from Strabo that happened to be considered as a fragment of Demetrios. This approach is also the one scholars take when dealing with other fragments from Demetrios' work in which the topic is no longer the Troad. Often modern scholars are interested in the content of a fragment and allude to the fact that it is actually a statement attributed to Demetrios, but without making judgments about his scholarly contribution. One exception is Boshnakov's analysis of Strabo's account of the Thacians,[189] and therefore it is the first example we shall discuss in our next section.

For the present discussion, we may conclude that we saw a shift from archaeological studies on Troy to a broader approach that encompasses the Troad as a region, and analyzes, besides the physical remains, also the historical, social, and cultural background of its inhabitants. This development had already started at the beginning of the twentieth century, with Leaf's works,

---

[185] Nagy 2010:178–182.
[186] Antonelli 2000:24–29.
[187] Courtieux 2004:57–60.
[188] Polybios 5.77–78 and Strabo 13.1.44–45 [C602–603].
[189] Boshnakov 2003.

but intensified during the second part of the century and is still very influential today. For Demetrios, this means that studies tend now more to understand the context in which a work was created (may this be Strabo's *Geography*, in which Demetrios' work is transmitted, or his own work) and to investigate how these parameters influenced the literary productions rather then to formulate clear-cut judgments about a scholar's achievements.

3.3.2 Studies Dealing With Other Fragments From Demetrios' Work

Boshnakov focuses on the areas inhabited by the Thracians, and this leads us away from the Troad and opens up a new perspective on Demetrios' achievements, as it is no longer linked to the question of the localization of the Homeric Troy and the interpretation of Schliemann's discoveries. Moreover, Boshnakov's study is different from those just mentioned and this for two reasons: on the one hand, Boshnakov dedicates an extremely large part to the analysis of Demetrios' contribution;[190] and, on the other hand, he has a very good opinion of Demetrios, as he describes him as a careful and accurate scholar who is singled out by his autopsy.[191] Boshnakov seems sometimes, however, to overemphasize his point, not only because of his extremely good opinion of Demetrios, but also because, without hesitation, he attributes passages to Demetrios that are more controversial with regard to the sources Strabo may have used. He actually discusses only five fragments from Demetrios,[192] but adds a list of twelve other texts or groups of texts he believes to belong to Demetrios' work. In the case of most of them, the attribution to Demetrios is highly hypothetical, as, for instance, in his first example, in which he discusses a passage from Strabo's book 1, which belongs to the list of examples of places where geological changes reshaped the landscape involved. We have already mentioned this list several times as the example of Asteria/Asteris, also mentioned in this list, has been attributed to Demetrios.[193] However, as this island is not in Thracia, Boshnakov chooses another example from the list, that of cities having been inundated by the water of Lake Bistonis and Lake Aphnitis, which is given in Strabo's text just before the one about Asteria/Asteris. By doing so, he presupposes that the whole list

---

[190] Boshnakov 2003:205–297.

[191] E.g. Boshnakov 2003:209, 216, 226, and 275.

[192] Fr. 46 [Gaede] (or fr. 46a [Biraschi]) = Strabo 7, fr. 15a [Radt]; fr. 47 [Gaede/Biraschi] = Strabo 7, fr. 22a [Radt]; fr. 16 [Gaede/Biraschi] = Athenaeus 10.425c; fr. 45 [Gaede/Biraschi] = Strabo 12.3.20–23 [C550–552] and fr. 67 [Gaede] (or fr. 67a [Biraschi]) = Strabo 8.6.15 [C374–375] and fr. 67b [Birasch] = Strabo 7, fr. 11a [Radt].

[193] Fr. 49 [Gaede] second item. Biraschi does not print this passage even if in Strabo 10.2.16 [C456] (her fr. 49) the description of Asteria/Asteris is attributed to Demetrios.

from Strabo 1.3.17 [C58] to Strabo 1.3.21 [C61] belongs to Demetrios, which is not agreed upon by all scholars, as we have seen in the section on Strabo. Some think that the whole list comes from Poseidonios who is quoted at the very beginning, and some emphasize the contribution Strabo himself may have made to the list.[194] Boshnakov, however, does not allude to this controversy, and this makes his statements less convincing. His discussion should, however, be taken as one of the examples in which the authors are interested in the content of a given passage, here Thracia, rather than in the scholar who made the statements preserved there.

This is also the case with our next example, the article written by Matthew Leigh about Sophocles' version of the destiny of the Antenoridae after the fall of Troy.[195] As Strabo 13.1.53 [C607–608] is one of the largest witnesses about Sophocles' treatment of this part of the legend, Leigh discusses this passage abundantly and also alludes to the fact that the beginning of this passage is a fragment from Demetrios' work. He believes that Strabo quotes Sophocles only indirectly through Demetrios, and suggests an interesting hypothesis about the place where Demetrios could have discussed such a topic. As the link between the Antenoridae and Aeneas is already stated in the Trojan Catalogue,[196] Leigh suggests that Demetrios could have discussed the destiny of these heroes when commenting on the relevant Homeric lines. Furthermore, he also adduces fr. 75 [Gaede/Biraschi][197] to prove that Demetrios must have discussed Sophocles' Trojan pieces in his commentary.[198] Both of these ideas are highly interesting, in particular if we add that Leigh too has a rather positive opinion about Demetrios and qualifies the length of his work as "scholarly diligence," but without developing his opinion.

The same attitude towards Demetrios can be observed in the second article connected to this topic, Gabba's short contribution on Pseudo-Scymnos.[199] The Italian scholar analyzes the passage of the poem that speaks about the foundation of Rome, and, because the poem ignores Aeneas' travel, Gabba concludes that it should be classified among the works of scholars who contested the Trojan origin of Rome, as did Demetrios of Scepsis and Polybios.[200] He restates therefore his conclusion from the 1970s about the political use of this part of the Trojan myth, but does not develop it.

---

[194] Aujac/Lasserre 1969:159 and 211 and Biraschi 2011, commentary ad fr. 48. For more details, see above Section 2.1.1 (pp. 81–82).
[195] Leigh 1998:82–100.
[196] *Iliad* 2.819–823.
[197] Tzetzes *Σ ad Lycophronem* v. 530.
[198] Leigh 1998:86–87.
[199] Gabba 2003:143–147.
[200] Gabba 2003:146.

We can also be very brief about two further, rather recent contributions in which Demetrios is mentioned in connection with Strabo's text. Both are about the Homeric problem of the Halizones, which involves fr. 45 [Gaede/Biraschi], a part of Strabo's book 12.[201] However, neither of them is actually focusing on Demetrios' contribution to this debate. In the first, Ragone is dealing with the different variants of the myth of the Amazones and mentions Demetrios only in a footnote, even if he is the author who would publish only a few years later an important contribution about Demetrios himself.[202] In the second, Holford-Strevens is focusing on the form ἀλαζονία attested for the first time in the Straboian passage and not on the Hellenistic scholar.[203] He comments on a short fragment from Aristoxenos of Selinus in which the same form is attested,[204] and the topic of the contribution is this comic poet. It is therefore not surprising that we do not have any comments about Demetrios there.

A third example of such an attitude toward Demetrios is provided by the way fr. 1 [Gaede/Biraschi] from Athenaeus is dealt with. It concerns the Carneia festival and is therefore quoted and discussed in Pettersson's monograph on the cults of Apollo in Sparta. Here again a wide range of sources are quoted along with the piece of evidence from Demetrios, and therefore no comments are made about the achievements of the scholar, who is actually only mentioned twice by name in the whole monograph.[205]

Likewise, there are two short mentions of Demetrios made by Francesca Schironi in her monograph on the *Oxyrhynchos Glossary* (P. Oxy. 15.1802 and P. Oxy. 71.4812).[206] First, he is mentioned very briefly when Schironi discusses the hypothesis of Pergamon as the place where the *Glossary* may have been written. He is quoted there as one of the scholars working in the tradition of the Pergemene school, together with Polemon of Ilion and Apollodoros of Athens, even if Schironi acknowledges a direct link to Pergamon only for Apollodoros, which brings us back to the question about where Demetrios may have written his work. The second time Demetrios is mentioned is in the commentary about fr. 15 of the *Glossary*, where Schironi discussed the hypothesis that the title of Demetrios' work may have been quoted. The sequence ἐν τῷ Τρωικῷ has been identified in line 3, and it is indeed tempting to complete it with διακόσμῳ, but as Schironi rightly adds, this is not the only possibility. Either the formula

---

[201] Strabo 12.3.20–23 [C550–552].

[202] Ragone 2005:338n100. I am referring here to Ragone 2009:649–691, which we have already used and quoted several times and to which we shall return shortly.

[203] Holford-Strevens 2009:624–626. He actually alludes to the variant Ἀλαζονίαν, which figures in Kramer's and Baladié's editions of Strabo, but not in Radt's text. He reads Ἀλαζόνιον.

[204] Fr. 1 [Kassel-Austin]. For more details see Kaibel 1896:1056.

[205] Pettersson 1992:57 and 63.

[206] Schironi 2009:14–15.

ἐν τῷ Τρωικῷ [πολέμῳ] or the one ἐν τῷ Τρωικῷ [πεδίῳ] would be satisfactory alternatives too.[207] However, such considerations unfortunately do not give us further information about Demetrios and how he was perceived.

Finally, and in contrast to the previous examples, we should mention here the second, more substantial contribution made by Ragone to the studies on Demetrios of Scepsis. This is the article, published in 2009, in which he provides a close analysis of two fragments from Demetrios' work: fr. 11 [Gaede/Biraschi], which comes from Athenaeus,[208] and fr. 23 [Gaede/Biraschi], the cluster of two scholia to the *Iliad*[209] and a passage from Strabo.[210] As the Italian scholar focuses only on two fragments, the contribution certainly belongs in this section. However, because of the scholar's approach and of the study's scope, it can also be seen as one of the few works that is entirely dedicated to Demetrios of Scepsis. We have indeed seen, throughout our discussion, that Demetrios is seldom studied for his own sake. He is most often treated in relation to Strabo and to Apollodoros of Athens. It is therefore regrettable that Ragone's study does not go beyond the analysis of the two fragments mentioned. However, for the analysis of both of them, the Italian scholar has the whole work of Demetrios in mind and shows how the content of the two fragments can be linked to issues dealt with in the Trojan Catalogue and how they illustrate Demetrios' working methods.

Let us begin with fr. 11 [Gaede/Biraschi]. It is interesting to see that, precisely because the content of the fragment does not allow us to go any further, Ragone changes his approach and bases his argumentation on Athenaeus' selective principle, which made him include the quotation from Demetrios at this moment of the discussion narrated in his *Deipnosophistai*. The fragment occurs at the end of a long list about eels and this was, according to Ragone, the distinctive feature allowing Athenaeus to add the witness from Demetrios in his text. However, as Ragone notes, the eels are not mentioned in the Trojan Catalogue. There are only two occurrences of eels in the entire *Iliad* and both are found in book 21.[211] They both belong to the episode about Achilles' revenge of Patrocles' death, when the Achaean hero kills the Trojans whom he pursues to the Scamandros and spoils the river's water with the corpses of his victims. According to Ragone, there is, however, a link to be drawn between this episode and the Trojan Catalogue. He points out that one of the warriors killed by Achilles is Asteropaios, one of the

---

[207] Schironi 2009:114–115.
[208] Athenaeus 7.300d.
[209] Fr. 23a [Gaede/Biraschi] = Σ bT *Iliad* 20.53c [Erbse] and fr. 23b [Gaede/Biraschi] = Σ A *Iliad* 20.3 [Erbse] (or Σ D *Iliad* 20.3 [van Thiel]).
[210] Strabo 13.1.35 [C597].
[211] *Iliad* 21.154–156 and *Iliad* 21.203–204.

Paeonians, who claims to have come to Troy only eleven days prior to the events. There was a debate in Antiquity about this Asteropaios, as scholars wondered why he was not mentioned among the Paeonian leaders in the Trojan Catalogue. Moreover, Ragone notes that in some ancient editions there was even a plus-verse in the Homeric text about the Paeonian contingent in which Asteropaios was mentioned just after Pyraichmes. For Ragone, this is the link to Demetrios' work: it is in his discussion concerning the Paeonian contingent that Demetrios may have mentioned the plus-verse, which he either had in his version of the text or to which he alluded in his comments because he knew that the version existed. Certainly in such a discussion, starting with the lines of the Trojan Catalogue, Demetrios may have alluded to the death of Asteropaios, which was narrated in book 21 and mentioned during this digression the involvement of the eels. This is even more likely as there was also a discussion among Homeric scholars about the way the eels were mentioned in the Homeric text. There was a debate about why Homer distinguished, in this part of the poem, between fishes and eels.[212] Furthermore, Ragone suggests that, when the discussion had reached the Scamandros and the fishes and eels living in it, Demetrios may have alluded to other rivers, which were possibly tributaries of the Scamandros, and commented on the eels in them. One of these rivers may have been a Euleus, which would explain the name of this river in the preserved wording of fr. 11 [Gaede/Biraschi].[213] Ragone's attempt is very convincing, as he shows how the few elements (in our case the eels) that were retained in the preserved fragment can be linked to several well-attested Homeric ζητήματα. Moreover, as just seen, he is able to link this cluster of questions to a line of the Trojan Catalogue through the hero Asteropaios. He appears in the episode where the eels are mentioned, and there was a ζήτημα about him as scholars tried to find out why he was not mentioned in the Trojan Catalogue, despite the fact that he claims himself to be one of the Paeonian leaders in book 21.[214]

The power of Ragone's method can also be seen when he applies the same reasoning to fr. 23a and fr. 23b [Gaede/Biraschi], the two scholia to the *Iliad* that mention the Callicolone.[215] As we have said, the difficulty seems smaller, as the Callicolone is a topographical element mentioned in the Homeric text.[216] Furthermore, the detailed description of the Trojan plain given by Strabo in his paragraph 13.1.35 [C597] also mentions the issues about the Callicolone and

---

[212] Σ A and bT *Iliad* 21.203 [Erbse] and Ragone 2009:682–683.

[213] Matthews 1996:311–312 suggests that the name Euleus may have been a corruption for a river Cillaeus found in the Troad and mentioned by Strabo (Strabo 13.1.62 [C612]).

[214] *Iliad* 21.153–160.

[215] Σ bT *Iliad* 20.53c [Erbse] (= fr. 23a [Gaede/Biraschi]) and Σ A *Iliad* 20.3 [Erbse] (or Σ D *Iliad* 20.3 [van Thiel]) (= fr. 23b [Gaede/Biraschi]).

[216] As mentioned, the two occurrences are *Iliad* 20.53 and *Iliad* 20.151.

strengthens the link to an discussion about the Trojan landscape. However, as Ragone notes, the Callicolone is only mentioned in book 20, in the episode narrating the battle between the gods, and not in the Trojan Catalogue. Therefore, there is again no obvious link to this part of the Homeric text and this has to be reconstructed. Ragone does this by emphasizing one of the ζητήματα that was linked to the first occurrence of the Callicolone. There were two variants of the text: either θέων ἐπὶ Καλλικολώνῃ (running towards the Callicolone) or θεῶν ἐπὶ Καλλικολώνῃ (on the Callicolone of the gods/goddesses). Among the many elements about this discussion, there is one preserved in Eustathius that allows Ragone to make a link to the Trojan Catalogue. He notes that in Eustathius' comment on Batieia, which is a topographical feature of the Trojan plain mentioned, in the Homeric text, just before the enumeration of the Trojan Catalogue as the place where the Trojans and their allies gathered, Eustathius also mentions the Callicolone and makes a link between the two toponyms, through the word κολώνη, which applies to both of them.[217] Therefore, Ragone concludes that it is possible that, while discussing Batieia, Demetrios may also have discussed the difficulties linked to another hill (κολώνη), namely the Callicolone. His argument is based on the assumption that not only the topographical elements alluded to in the Trojan Catalogue could have been discussed in a commentary on these Homeric lines, but also those where, from a narratological point of view, the heroes stood during the enumeration. This is a very convincing assumption, and we may end our discussion on Ragone's contribution by recalling that we also formulated the hypothesis that elements that are preserved in the fragments from Demetrios' work could be linked to issues about Batieia, making it very likely that Demetrios may have mentioned this place in his work, even if no fragment about it has been preserved.[218]

3.3.3 Studies on Demetrios in Relation To Works on Classical Scholarship and/or Greek Literature

We may be justified in having postponed the discussion of this category of works until now, as there is rather a large gap between Sandys's study published at the beginning of the century, the last work we discussed in Section 3.2.4, and Pfeiffer's *History of Classical Scholarship*, first published in 1968. It is indeed only after Blegen's excavation, and in a very different scholarly context, that Pfeiffer's famous study is published and provides some new elements about the

---

[217] See Ragone 2009:689–691 and Eustathius *Commentarii ad Iliad* 2.811–815 (= 350, 40–351, 13 or van der Valk I:549–550).

[218] See our analysis of some of the fragments preserved in the scholia of Apollodius Rhodius (above Section 2.1.8, pp. 122–123 and 126–127).

way Demetrios' work is appreciated. We have already mentioned, in Chapter 1, the influence this study had on the later dealings with Demetrios, and we have discussed in particular the distinction Pfeiffer made between *hypomnemata* and *sungrammata* to differentiate Demetrios' work from that of Apollodoros of Athens. Here we shall focus only on his appreciation of Demetrios' work and mention first that he judges the contribution of Demetrios in a very balanced way. He alludes to the difficulties his position creates in the context of Schliemann's excavations and points unambiguously to the fact that the discoveries in the Troad speak against Demetrios' claim. However, he dismisses the old accusation of jealousy as motivation for Demetrios' position, and acknowledges that his statements were always held in good faith and argued with great pain. Finally, he ends his presentation by praising the merit of Demetrios' work as a "realistic exegesis" that furthered the understanding of a special part of the *Iliad*, even if he does not ignore the slight exaggeration of Demetrios' undertaking.[219] His statement may therefore have contributed to the development of more positive attitudes towards Demetrios at the end of the twentieth century, as we have seen in the previous sections.

We may leave out Frazer's *Ptolemaic Alexandria*[220] and Canfora's *Storia della letteratura greca*[221] here, as almost nothing is said about Demetrios of Scepsis in these works, and jump to 1993 where we find in Montanari's chapter on Pergamon belonging to the Italian collaborative work *Lo Spazio letterario della Grecia antica* a somewhat longer account of Demetrios.[222] In this study there is, however, no allusion to Demetrios' controversial position in the question of the Trojan topography, as Montanari instead emphasizes, in his presentation of Demetrios, the link to Crates of Mallos and to the library of Pergamon. He also underlines that Demetrios was used by Apollodoros of Athens, but adds a new element to the discussion by mentioning that Demetrios' work was probably also used during the creation process of the Homeric scholia. In doing so, Montanari emphasizes in his description of Demetrios' work the contribution he made to ancient scholarship rather than judges his position with regard to the Trojan landscape. This approach is certainly explained by Montanari's previous research on the transmission and creation of the corpus of the Homeric scholia. Indeed, in the years before writing the contribution to the Italian history of Greek literature, Montanari worked intensively on the analysis of the creation process of the scholia.[223] He was focusing on the so-called

---

[219] Pfeiffer 1968:249-250.
[220] Fraser 1972:465.
[221] Canfora 1989:740.
[222] Montanari 1993b:639–655.
[223] Montanari 1979:3–19 and Montanari 1995b:69–85.

Mythographus Homericus and its status in the scholia.[224] Moreover, among the papyrological findings attributed to this *Mythographus Homericus*, at least two fragments can be considered as referring to the content of Demetrios' works[225] and are linked to fr. 23a [Gaede/Biraschi] and fr. 23b [Gaede/Biraschi].[226] It is therefore Montanari's work on the *Mythographus Homericus* that explains why he emphasizes this peculiarity of Demetrios' work and uses him in his description of the scholarly activity in Antiquity as an example of the works characterizing the working method of the library of Pergamon.[227] It is the same with Montanari's contribution on Demetrios in the *Neue Pauly*.[228] The Italian scholar again does not allude to the controversy about Troy, but mentions only that Demetrios had a rather strange opinion about the story of Aeneas, alluding to Demetrios' belief that Aeneas never left the Troad and that his son and the son of Hector founded a dynasty in the Troad. The treatment is similar in the rather positive entry about Demetrios that we find in the *Kleine Pauly*,[229] as the achievement of Demetrios is characterized there as the one of an amazingly learned man who based his work on scientific criteria. We see, therefore, once again that the more the question of the localization of the Homeric landscape is neglected the more positive opinion one gets about Demetrios.

Finally, it is also in this section that we may add Laura Pagani's collection of fragments.[230] As it is part of a larger, still ongoing project on ancient Greek grammarians under the direction of Franco Montanari, it is certainly Demetrios' contribution to ancient scholarship that is highlighted, even if the form the collection takes leaves little room for statements about any judgment on the scholar's achievement.

The very last words of this section should, however, be dedicated to the two-volume *Companion to Ancient Greek Scholarship* published in 2015.[231] Expectedly, Demetrios is alluded to in the contribution on Hellenistic scholarship, although only briefly.[232] Nonetheless, as the scope of the collection of studies is much larger and encompasses a vast array of scholarly activities, it will certainly

---

[224] Montanari 1995c:135–172, Montanari 2002:129–144, and now also Rossum-Steebeek 1998:85–118 and 278–309, for an overview on the different publications about each papyrus attributed to the *Mythographus Homericus*.

[225] Montanari 1984:229–242 and Montanari 1995d:113–125.

[226] Fr. 23a [Gaede/Biraschi] = Σ bT *Iliad* 20.53c [Erbse]; fr 23b [Gaede/Biraschi] = Σ A *Iliad* 20.3 [Erbse] (or Σ D *Iliad* 20.3 [van Thiel]. See Trachsel/Schubert 1999:222–237 and Luppe 2000:237–239 for further papyrological findings related to the same issue.

[227] Montanari 1993b:651–652.

[228] Montanari 1997b:438.

[229] Gärtner 1964:1468.

[230] Pagani 2006.

[231] Montanari/Matthaios/Rengakos 2015.

[232] See Montana 2015:145–148 and 158–159.

influence any further research on Demetrios, or on any other ancient scholar. Therefore, the mention of this work may form an appropriate end to this section, which started with Pfeiffer's *History and Classical Scholarship*, in the footsteps of which the *Companion* was elaborated.[233]

3.4 Summary

By now, our overview should have demonstrated, even if it is not exhaustive, especially for the more recent times, how the modern appreciation of Demetrios' work evolved since Stiehle's first publication, and what kind of factors influenced the scholars who dealt with his work. In the nineteenth century, even if more moderate opinions circulated before, during, and after the controversy about Schliemann's discoveries in the Troad, it was mainly in this context that Demetrios' contribution was discussed, moreover in an extremely polarized way. This had its consequences in that, on the one hand, interest in the scholar and his work certainly increased. However, on the other hand, this increased interest was not always that beneficial, as the negative opinions about Demetrios were often exaggerated and based on only one part of the preserved fragments. Then it was mainly Walter Leaf's treatment of the Hellenistic scholar that shaped the modern perception of Demetrios of Scepsis, and in particular it was in connection with Strabo's text that his work was mentioned. We have also seen that the two subsequent excavation campaigns, by Blegen and by Korfmann, did not stir the same interest in Demetrios' work as the first excavations by Schliemann. The new data from the Troad was certainly incorporated into the more recent studies and modified or highlighted some of the aspects of the modern reception of Demetrios' work, but the Hellenistic scholar never regained the same status in the debate as he had at the end of the nineteenth century. Moreover, if modern scholars mention Demetrios, they often refrain from judging his contribution. He often becomes simply one of the many sources for a topic, or his statements are discussed in connection with Strabo's text where the focus is on the geographer and his working method rather than on Demetrios as one of his many sources. Therefore, we see that, especially in more recent years, the number of times Demetrios is alluded to increases, but, as the treatment of his contribution is often shorter and rather secondary with regard to the main topic of the given study, we actually receive less information about him. Also, the many different categories of works in which Demetrios is alluded to, mostly because he happens to be the source for the ancient witness that is adduced, makes it extremely difficult to follow all the traces and to bring them together

---

[233] Montanari/Matthaios/Rengakos 2015:ix.

in an overall picture of how Demetrios has been perceived in recent years. With these considerations we may then have reached the context, in which the most recent edition of the fragments of Demetrios' work appeared. This is the one by Anna Maria Biraschi, which is included, as mentioned at the beginning of our study, in the continuation project of Jacoby's *Fragmente der Griechischen Historiker*.[234]

---

[234] Biraschi 2011.

Conclusion

By analyzing three different forms of witnesses about Demetrios' work, we highlighted the indirectness of our access to his contribution. In doing so, we delineated two steps in the reception of Demetrios' work, the ancient readings of his work (Chapter 2) and the modern investigations aiming to individualize the remaining evidence that can be traced back to the lost work (Chapter 3). This was preceded by a close reading of ancient statements about the scholar, his purpose, and the literary and historical context to which he belonged (Chapter 1).

The aim of Chapter 1 was therefore to define a precise picture of the circumstances and the motivations that may have brought Demetrios to compose his monumental work. We saw that he was a scholar living in the second century BCE, which is not only a key moment for the Troad, but also a significant phase for ancient scholarship. On the political level, the second century BCE saw the Romans extending their influence in Asia Minor, shaping the development of the Hellenistic kingdoms in the East. For the Troad this meant a form of prominence, as its Homeric past was once again exploited in this context. Demetrios as a citizen of Scepsis, a neighbor city of Novum Ilion, may have experienced the consequences of this phenomenon and reacted to it by trying to defend the interests of his hometown. He may then indeed been defined as a local scholar who was aware of the larger implications of his scholarly activity (whether in connection with the Romans or with regard to the Attalids). Nonetheless, this feature of Demetrios' activity should not be judged as negatively as it has been in the past. Our investigations also demonstrated that, although he was probably not directly linked to any of the great centers of scholarship, he took part in the scholarly activities of these days, which had by then developed into several domains. He used, for instance, the same methodological tools as the great Homeric scholars to analyze the Homeric text, and must have had access to a large number of sources, as may be seen in the range of seldom-quoted authors we find in the remaining fragments of his work. His contribution should therefore be seen an integral part of Homeric scholarship, despite its personal and local colors. In this respect, it is also important to remember that he was a contemporary of Aristarchos and Crates of Malos and probably saw the creation of the library of Pergamon in his neighborhood. He must have reacted in one way or the other to this event, even if it is not possible today to find clear evidence about this. Moreover, his work was almost immediately discussed by Apollodoros of Athens, a pupil of Aristarchos, and, even if the response was developing into a rather severe critique, it proves that Demetrios' work was considered worth by fellow scholars of an answer. This led us to Chapter 2, which was dedicated to the ancient authors from whom we know that they quoted from Demetrios' work in one form or another.

Indeed, in Chapter 2 we focused on the perception that ancient readers of Demetrios' work had about the scholar and his contribution. We were particularly interested in defining how each of these authors used Demetrios' work, or at least parts of it, for their own purposes. In doing so, we were able to complete the picture of Demetrios that we discovered in Chapter 1. However, during our analysis, we also had to acknowledge that we only have indirect access to Demetrios' work, which faded away over time, leaving us with only a few hints diversely interpreted by modern scholars. At the beginning of the chapter, while dealing with Strabo's *Geography* and Athenaeus' *Deipnosophistai*, we were in rather a good position, as we had a reasonably large number of fragments preserved in their texts. Moreover, we were dealing with authors who gave their works a structure that allows us to consider the distribution of the fragments from Demetrios' work within these texts. Furthermore, with Strabo we could also rely on his own views about quotations, as he explained some of the principles that guided him in his choices among his sources. Unfortunately, such information was absent for later works, especially when we dealt with the lexicographers, Harpocration and Hesychios, and with Stephanus of Byzantium. We therefore had to acknowledge that our perception of Demetrios' work within these source texts depended on Gaede's way of understanding them, even if to some extent this was already true for Strabo's text, in which Gaede often identified passages without Demetrios' name as fragments from our scholar's work. Therefore, while progressing in our analysis of the ancient authors in whose texts the fragments were preserved, the interpretations that modern scholars made of the source texts involved became more and more important, and led us to Chapter 3, in which we examined their many and disparate opinions about Demetrios of Scepsis.

During the discussion carried out in Chapter 3, we realized that two factors influenced the way Demetrios was perceived in modern times. On the one hand, we highlighted Schliemann's discoveries in Hissarlik and the huge debate that ensued about the localization of the Homeric landscape in the Troad. On the other, we also took into account the date of publication of the different editions of Demetrios' fragments, which helped us to divide the chapter into several sections. The date of 1880, when Gaede's edition was published, and that of 2011, for Biraschi's contribution, were particularly important, and helped us to structure our analysis of the opinions modern scholars had about Demetrios.

We also saw that in a first phase of the modern reception, Demetrios' contribution was severely judged and considered poor scholarship. This was to a large extent the result of the archaeological investigations carried out at Troy in the nineteenth century and of the way scholars in those days weighted their discoveries against the opinions defended by ancient scholars, in particular by Demetrios. However, their judgments became more balanced when investigations were undertaken with a broader perspective moving away from the focus on Troy to an analysis of the ancient Troad. Likewise, scholars opened their approach so that they extended their research beyond Homer's poem to later texts such as Strabo's *Geography* and analyzed their historical and cultural background. In this context, Demetrios' contribution was also reevaluated and placed in a broader tradition, using it more as a witness of its time rather than as a guide to Homer's world. It is then within this newer appreciation of Demetrios' work that Biraschi's edition falls, fostering new interests in the scholar. Our own study should therefore be seen as a prolongation of this new outlook, as it not only focuses on presenting an accurate picture of the time in which Demetrios composed his work, but also investigates the process of transmission through which the work went. Therefore, our research has given much attention to the ancient readings of the work, as it could not benefit from direct und uninterrupted recopying. Indeed, the hazards of time led to the loss of the original work. Nevertheless, ancient readers carried on part of it in their quotations, and these pieces of evidence can be gathered, as it has been done for Demetrios by Gaede and by Biraschi. However, this process of gathering fragments should also be analyzed and understood in its broader historical, social, and scholarly contexts. This was the aim of Chapter 3, as a response to the most recent developments in this field of research.

The book should, therefore, be seen as a preliminary study, the aim of which is threefold: presenting the scholar and his contribution in a new light, which may hopefully trigger new interests and new research; analyzing the many different ways in which Demetrios' Τρωϊκὸς διάκοσμος has been read and apprehended throughout the ages, from its composition up to the present day; and, finally, providing a starting point for a new edition of the textual witnesses about a fascinating piece of ancient scholarship. In such an undertaking, as our research should also have demonstrated, the link to the Homeric text should be emphasized to a much larger extent than in previous editions, so that this central aspect of Demetrios' work receives the attention it deserves.

Bibliography

Online Resources

The Project Troia (University of Tübingen, and University of Cincinnati). http://www.uni-tuebungen.de/troia/eng/sttroica.html

Mertens-Pack 3 online Database (University of Liege). http://promethee.philo.ulg.ac.be/cedopalMP3/indexMP3.aspx

Digitised Manuscripts (British Library London). http://www.bl.uk/manuscripts/

Cited Bibliography

Allen, R. E. 1983. *The Attalid Kingdom. A Constitutional History.* Oxford.

Alonso Núñez, J. M. 1984. "Un historien antiromain: Métrodore de Scepsis." *Dialogues d'histoire ancienne* 10:253–258.

Aly, W. 1928. *Der Strabo-Palimpsest Vat. Gr. 2061A.* Sitzungsbericht der Heidelberger Akademie der Wissenschaften: Philosophisch-Historische Klasse 1928/29/1). Heidelberg.

———. 1931. *Neue Beiträge zur Strabo-Überlieferung.* Heidelberg.

———. 1950. "Testi e documenti. Zum neuen Strabo-Text." *Parola del Passato* 5:228–263.

———. 1956. *De Strabois codice rescripto: cuius reliquiae in codicibus Vaticanis Vat. Gr. 2306 et 2061A servatae sunt.* Vatican City.

Ambaglio, D. 2001. "Ἐπιχώριος: un termine tecnico storiografico?" In *Atti del Congresso Storiografia locale e storiografia universale*, ed. C. Bearzot, R. Vattuone, and D. Ambroglio, 7–21. Como.

Andria, R. G. 1989. *I frammenti delle "Successioni dei filosofi."* Naples.

Angelucci, M. 2003. "Polemone di Ilio: fra ricostruzione biografica e interessi antiquari." *Studi classici e orientali* 49:165–184.

Antonelli, L. 2000. "I Pisistratidi al Sigeo. Instanze pan-ioniche nell'Atene tirannica." *Anemos* 1:9–58.

Atenstädt, F. 1937. "Kaukonen und triphylisches Pylos." *Philologus* 92:378–382.

Aujac, G., and F. Lasserre. 1969. *Strabo: Géographie; Introduction Générale.* Vol. 1, Book 1. Paris.

Ax, W. 2000. "Parmeniskos." In *Der Neue Pauly: Enzyklopädie der Antike* 9, 343. Stuttgart.

———. 1991. "Sprache als Gegenstand der alexandrinischen und pergamenischen Philologie." In *Sprachtheorien der abendländischen Antike*, ed. P. Schmitt, 275–301. Tübingen.

Baladié, R. 1978. *Strabo. Géographie.* Vol. 5, *Book 8*. Paris.

———. 1989. *Strabo. Géographie.* Vol. 4, *Book 7*. Paris.

———. 1996. *Strabo. Géographie.* Vol. 6, *Book 9*. Paris.

Baltussen, H. 2004. "Plato Protagoras 340–48: Commentary in the making?" In *Philosophy, Science and Exegesis in Greek, Arabic and Latin Commentaries.* Vol. 1, ed. P. Adamson, H. Baltussen, and M. W. F. Stone, 21–35. London.

Baronowski, D. W. 1991. "The Status of the Greek Cities of Asia Minor after 190 BC." *Hermes* 119:450–463.

Baumbach, M. 2000. "Mnesimachos [2]." In *Der Neue Pauly: Enzyklopädie der Antike* 8, 307. Stuttgart.

———. 2002. "Tauriskos [1]." In *Der Neue Pauly: Enzyklopädie der Antike* 12.1, 54. Stuttgart.

Bergk, T. 1872. *Griechische Literaturgeschichte.* Vol. 1. Berlin.

———. 1887. *Griechische Literaturgeschichte.* Vol. 4. Berlin.

Bernhardy, G. 1845. *Grundriß der Griechischen Litteratur.* Teil 2.1. Halle.

———. 1877. *Grundriß der Griechischen Litteratur.* Teil 2.1. 3rd ed. Halle.

Bertelli, L. 2001. "Hecataeus: From Genealogy to Historiography." In *The Historian's Craft in the Age of Herodotus*, ed. N. Luraghi, 7–94. Oxford.

Berti, M., and V. Costa. 2010. *La Bibliotheca di Alessandria: Storia di un paradiso perduto.* Tivoli (Rome).

———. 2013. "Collecting Quotations by Topics: Degrees of Preservation and Transtextual Relations among Genres." *Ancient Society* 43:269–288.

Bieg, G. 2006. "Archäologie und Geschichte einer Landschaft—Die Troas von der griechischen Kolonisation bis in byzantinische Zeit." In Korfmann 2006:361–372. Mainz.

Billerbeck, M. 2005. "Lykophrons Alexandra in den Ethnika des Stephanos von Byzanz." In *Koryphaioi andri: Mélange en l'honneur d'André Hurst*, ed. A. Kolde, A. Lukinovich, and A.-L. Rey, 411–415. Geneva.

———. 2008. "Sources et technique de citation chez Etienne de Byzance." *Eikasmos* 19:301–322.

———. 2009. "Artemidorus' Geographoumena in the Ethnika of Stephanus of Byzantium: Source and Transmission." In *Images and Texts on the "Artemidorus Papyrus,"* ed. K. Brodersen, and J. Elsner, 65–87. Stuttgart.

Biraschi, A. M. 2000. "Omero e aspetti della tradizione omerica nei libri Straboiani sull'Asia Minore." In Biraschi and Salmeri 2000:45–72.

———. 2005. "Strabo and Homer: A Chapter in Cultural History." In *Strabo's Cultural Geography: The Making of a Kolossourgia*, ed. D. Dueck, H. Lindsay, and S. Pothecary, 73–85. Cambridge.

———. 2011. "Demetrio di Skepsis (2013)." In *Jacoby Online. Die Fragmente der Griechischen Historiker Part V*, ed. H.-J. Gehrke, and F. Maier. https://referenceworks.brillonline.com/cluster/Jacoby%20Online?s.num=0.

Biraschi, A. M., and G. Salmeri, eds. 2000. *Straboe e l'Asia Minore*. Perugia.

Blank, D. L. 1998. *Sextus Empiricus: Against the Grammarians*. Oxford.

Blegen, C. W. 1950. *Troy: General Introduction, the First and Second Settlements*. Princeton.

———. 1950-1958. *Troy*. Vols. 1–4. Princeton.

———. 1962. "The Principal Homeric Sites: Troy." In *A Companion to Homer*, ed. A. J. B. Wace, and F. H. Stubbings, 362–386. London.

Bodnár, I. 1997. "Demokritos [1]." In *Der Neue Pauly: Enzyklopädie der Antike 3*, 455–485. Stuttgart.

Bohle, S. A. 1858. "De Demetrio Scepsio grammatico." In *Jahresbericht über das Gymnasium zu Kempen (Schuljahr 1857-1858)*, 1–9. Kempen.

Bölte, F. 1934. "Ein Pylisches Epos." *Rheinisches Museum* 83:319–347.

———. 1938. "Triphylien bei Strabo eine Quellenuntersuchung." *Rheinisches Museum* 87:142–160.

Borgeaud, P. 1996. *La mère des dieux. De Cybèle à la Vierge Marie*. Paris.

Boshnakov, K. 2003. *Die Thraker südlich vom Balkan in den Geographika Strabos*. Wiesbaden.

Bötticher, E. 1889. *La Troie de Schliemann: une nécropole à incinération à la manière assyro-babylonnienne*. Louvain.

———. 1890. *Hissarlik wie es ist*. Berlin.

Bouvier, D. 2002. *Le septre et la lyre. L'Iliade ou les héros de la mémoire*. Grenoble.

———. 2007. "Usage et autorité de l'épopée homérique chez Athénée." In Lenfant 2007a:306–319.

Braund, D., and J. Wilkins, eds. 2000. *Athenaeus and his World*. Exeter.

Bravo, B. 1971. "Remarques sur l'érudition dans l'Antiquité." In *Acta conventus XI "Eirene,"* ed. K. Kumaniecki, 326–335. Warsaw.

———. 2002. "Felix Jacoby, Arnaldo Momigliano e l'erudizione antica." In *Aspetti dell'opera di Felix Jacoby*, ed. C. Ampolo, 227–257. Pisa.

———. 2007. "Antiquarianism and History." In *A Companion to Greek and Roman Historiography*, Vol. 2, ed. J. Marincola, 515–527. Oxford.

Breithaupt, M. 1915. *De Parmenisco grammatico*. Leipzig.

Brentano, E. 1877. *Alt-Ilion im Dumbrekthal: ein Versuch, die Lage des homerischen Troia nach den Angaben des Plinius und Demetrios von Skepsis zu bestimmen*. Heilbronn.

———. 1881. *Zur Lösung der troianischen Frage: nebst einem Nachtrag: einige Bemerkungen über Schliemann's Ilios; mit 1 Kt. der troischen Ebene und 2 Plänen.* Heilbronn.

Bresson, A. 2001. "La conjoncture du IIe siècle a.C." In *Les cités d'Asie mineure occidentale au IIe siècle a.C.*, ed. A. Bresson and R. Descat, 11–16. Bordeaux.

Briquel, D. 1997. *Le regard des autres. Les origines de Rome vues par ses ennemis.* Besançon.

Brodersen, K. 2005. "'Das aber ist eine Lüge!' Zur rationalistischen Mythenkritik des Palaiphatos." In *Griechische Mythologie und frühes Christentum*, ed. R. von Haehling, 44–57. Darmstadt.

Broggiato, M. 1999. "Krates [5]." In *Der Neue Pauly: Enzyklopädie der Antike* 6, 812–814. Stuttgart.

———. 2001. *Cratete di Mallo. I frammenti.* La Spezia.

———. 2014. *Filologia e interpretazione a Pergamo. La scuola di Cratete.* Rome.

Browning, R. 1992. "The Byzantines and Homer." In *Homer's Ancient Readers: The Hermeneutics of Greek Epic's Earliest Exegetes*, ed. R. Lamberton and J. J. Keaney, 134–148. Princeton.

Brückner, A. 1902. "Geschichte von Troja und Ilion." In *Troja und Ilion*, ed. W. Dörpfeld, 549–593. Athens.

Brügger, C., M. Stoevesandt, and E. Visser. 2003. *Homers Ilias: Gesamtkommentar. Band 2, Zweiter Gesang (B), Fasz. 2: Kommentar.* Munich.

Bruit L., and P. Schmitt-Pantel. 1986. "Citer, classer, penser: A propos des repas des Grecs et des repas des 'autres' dans le livre IV des Deipnosophistes d'Athénée." In *Annali Istituto Orientale di Napoli: Sezione di Archeologia Antica* 8:203–221.

Buchholz, H.-G. 1991. "Die archäologische Forschung im Zusammenhang mit Homer." In *Zweihundert Jahre Homer-Forschung, Colloquium Rauricum. Band 2*, ed. H.-J. Latacz, 11–44. Stuttgart.

Budelmann, F. 2002. "Classical Commentary in Byzantium: John Tzetzes on Ancient Greek Literature." In *The Classical Commentary. Histories, Practices, Theory*, ed. R. K. Gibson and C. Shuttleworth Kraus, 141–169. Leiden.

Burkert, W. 1995. "Lydia between East and West, or, How to date the Trojan War: A Study in Herodotus." In *The Ages of Homer: A Tribute to Emily Townsend Vermeule*, ed. J. B. Carter and S. P. Morris, 139–148. Austin, TX.

Burr Thompson, D. 1963. *Troy, the Terracotta Figurines of the Hellenistic Period.* Princeton.

Bury, R. G. 1949. *Sextus Empiricus. Against the Professors.* Vol. 4. Cambridge, MA.

Bux, E. 1932. "Mnesimachos [3]." In *Paulys Realencyclopädie der classischen Altertumswissenschaften* 15.2, 2279. Stuttgart.

Calder III, W. M. 1980. "Wilamowitz on Schliemann." *Philologus* 124:146–151.

Cambiano G., L. Canfora, and D. Lanza, eds. 1993. *Lo Spazio letterario della Grecia antica 1.* Vol. 2, *L'Ellenismo.* Salerno.

Cameron, A. 2004. *Greek Mythography in the Roman World.* Oxford.

Canfora, L. 1989. *Storia della letteratura greca.* Rome.

———. ed. 2001. *Ateneo, i Deipnosofisti.* Rome.

Caskey, J. L. 1948. "Notes on Trojan Chronology." *American Journal of Archaeology* 52:119–122.

Ceccarelli, P. 2000. "Dance and Desserts: An Analysis of Book Fourteen." In Braund and Wilkins 2000:272–291.

Chaniotis, A. 2003. "Vom Erlebnis zum Mythos: Identitätskonstruktionen im Kaiserzeitlichen Aphrodisias." In *Stadt und Stadtentwicklung in Kleinasien,* ed. E. Schwertheim and E. Winter, 69–84. Bonn.

———. 2009. "Myths and Contexts in Aphrodisias." In *Antike Mythen: Medien, Transformationen und Konstruktionen,* ed. U. Dill and C. Walde, 313–338. Berlin.

Chantraine, P. 1968. "μεῖραξ." In *Dictionnaire étymologique de la langue grecque, histoire des mots,* 678. Paris.

Chávez Reino, A. L., and G. Ottone. 2007. "Les fragments de Théopompe chez Athénée: un aperçu général." In Lenfant 2007a:139–174.

Chrubaski, B. 2013. "The Attalids and the Seleukid Kings, 281–175 BC." In *Attalid Asia Minor. Money, International Relations, and the State,* ed. P. Thonemann, 83–119. Oxford.

Cobet, J. 2003. "Die Troas als historische Landschaft." In *Geschichtsdeutung auf alten Karten: Archäologie und Geschichte,* ed. D. Unverhau, 331–377. Wiesbaden.

Cohn, L. 1896. "Aristarchos [22]." In *Paulys Realencyclopädie der classischen Altertumswissenschaften* 2.1, 862–873. Stuttgart.

———. 1907: "Eudokia Makrembolitissa." In *Paulys Realencyclopädie der classischen Altertumswissenschaften* 6.1, 912–913. Stuttgart.

Colomo, D., and M. Perale. 2012. "On P. Oxy. LXXVI 5094 Fr. 1." *Zeitschrift für Papyrologie und Epigraphik* 181:1–3.

Cook, J. M. 1959. "On Stephanus Byzantius' Text of Strabo." *Journal of Hellenic Studies* 79:19–26.

———. 1973. *The Troad. An Archaeological and Topographical Study.* Oxford.

———. 1988. "Cities in and around the Troad." *Annual of the British School at Athens* 83:7–19.

Coppola, A. 1994. "Memorie troiane e ambascerie romane." *Hesperia: Studi sulla grecità di occidente* 4:177–186.

Cornell, T., ed. 2013a. *The Fragments of the Roman Historians.* Vol. 1. Oxford.

Cornell, T., ed. 2013b. *The Fragments of the Roman Historians.* Vol. 3. Oxford.

Corsten, T. 1992. "Der Hilferuf des akarnanischen Bundes an Rom: Zum Beginn des römischen Eingreifens in Griechenland." *Zeitschrift für Papyrologie und Epigraphik* 94:195–210.

Courtieux, G. 2004. "Karésos, la cité 'totalement renversée' de Troade." *Anatolia Antiqua* 12:57–60.

Croiset A., and M. Croiset. 1887–1899. *Histoire de la littérature grecque*. Paris.

Danek, G. 1988. *Studien zur Dolonie*. Vienna.

Darbo-Peschanski, C., ed. 2004. *La citation dans l'antiquité*. Grenoble.

de Chaisemartin, N. 2001. "Le retour des Troyens: l'exemple d'Aphrodisias." In V. Fromentin and S. Gotteland 2001:187–206.

Delage, E. 1930. *La géographie dans les Argonautiques d'Apollonios de Rhodes*. Bordeaux.

Derda, T., J. Hilder, and J. Kwapisz, eds. 2017. *Fragments, Holes, and Wholes: Reconstructing the Ancient World in Theory and Practice*. Warsaw.

Desideri, P. 1970–1971. "Studi di storiografia eracleota." *Studi Classici e Orientali* 19–20:487–537.

———. 2005–2006. "Cultura della Troade." *Geographia antiqua* 14–15:45–53.

Dettori, E. 2000. "La 'filologia' di Filita di Cos (con qualche osservazione sulla filologia del III sec. a.C.)." In *La letteratura ellenistica. Problemi e prospettive di ricerca*, ed. R. Pretagostini, 183–198. Rome.

Dickey, E. 2007. *Ancient Greek Scholarship*. Oxford.

Diels, H. 1890. *Sibyllinische Blätter*. Berlin.

Dignas, B. 2012. "Rituals and the Construction of Identity in Attalid Pergamon." In *Historical and Religious Memory in the Ancient World*, ed. B. Dignas and R. R. R. Smith, 119–143. Oxford.

Dihle, A. 1998. "Eratosthenes und andere Philologen." In *Mousopolos Stephanos, Festschrift für Herwig Görgemanns*, ed. M. Baumbach, H. Köhler, and A. M. Ritter, 86–93. Heidelberg.

Diller, A. 1975. *The Textual Tradition of Strabo's Geography*. Amsterdam.

———. 1983. "The Tradition of Stephanus Byzantius." In *Studies in Greek Manuscript Tradition*, 183–198. Amsterdam. Orig. pub. 1938 in *Transactions of the American Philological Association* 69:333–348.

Dindorf, W. 1827. *Athenaeus*. Leipzig.

Dionisotti, A. C. 1997. "On Fragments in Classical Scholarship." In Most 1997:1–33.

Donohue, A. A. 2001. "Polemon aus Ilion [2]." *Der Neue Pauly: Enzyklopädie der Antike* 10, 7. Stuttgart.

Dorandi, T. 2000. "Le commentaire dans la tradition papyrologique: quelques cas controversés." In Goulet-Cazé 2000:15–27.

Dörpfeld, W. 1902. *Troja und Ilion*. Athens.

Drachmann, A. B. 1903. *Scholia vetera in Pindari carmina*. Vol. 1. Leipzig.

Dräger, P. 2003. "Otto Kern: Wilamowitz in Greifswald." *Eikasmos* 14:331–392.

Dreyer, B. 2009. "City Elite and the Administration of the Attalid Kingdom after the Peace of Apameia. Evidence, Research and Methodological Thoughts." In *Greek History and Epigraphy: Essays in Honour of P.J. Rhodes*, ed. L. Mitchell and L. Rubinstein, 33–46. Swansea.

Dubois, M. 1891. *Examen de la géographie de Strabo: étude critique de la méthode et des sources*. Paris.

Dubischar, M. 2015. "Typology of Philological Writings." In Montanari, Matthaios, and Rengakos 2015:545–599.

Dübner, F. 1849. *Scholia in Theocritum*. Paris.

Dué, C. 2011. "Eëtion." In Finkelberg 2011a:239.

Dueck, D. 2000. *Strabo of Amasia. A Greek Man of Letters in Augustan Rome*. London.

———. ed. 2005. *Strabo's Cultural Geography. The Making of a Kolossourgia*. Cambridge.

———. 2011. "Dardanians." In Finkelberg 2011a:194.

———. 2017. *The Routledge Companion to Strabo*. London.

Easton, D. F. 1991. "Troy before Schliemann." *Studia Troica* 1:111–129.

Ebbott, M. 2011. "Pandaros." In Finkelberg 2011a:617.

Eckstein, A. M. 2008. *Rome Enters the Greek East. From Anarchy to Hierarchy in the Hellenistic Mediterranean, 230–170 BC*. Oxford.

Erbse, H. 1960. *Beiträge zur Überlieferung der Iliasscholien*. Munich.

———. 1969. *Scholia graeca in Homeri Iliadem*. Vol. 1. Berlin.

———. 1973. *Scholia graeca in Homeri Iliadem*. Vol. 3. Berlin.

———. 1977. *Scholia graeca in Homeri Iliadem*. Vol. 5. Berlin.

Erskine, A. 2001. *Troy between Greece and Rome: Local Tradition and Imperial Power*. Oxford.

Ferrary, J.-L. 1988. *Philhellénisme et impérialisme. Aspects idéologiques de la conquête romaine du monde hellénistique*. Rome.

———. 2001. "Rome et les cités grecques d'Asie Mineure au IIe siècle." In *Les cités d'Asie Mineure occidentale au IIe siècle a.C.*, ed. A. Bresson and R. Descat, 93–106. Bordeaux.

Finkelberg, M., ed. 2011a. *The Homer Encyclopedia*. Wiley-Blackwell.

———. 2011b. "Amyntor." In Finkelberg 2011a:45.

Flach, I. 1880. *Eudociae Augustae Violarium*. Leipzig.

Floratos, C. S. 1972. *Strabo über Literatur und Poseidonios*. Athens.

Ford, A. 2002. *The Origins of Criticism*. Princeton.

Fornaro, S. 1998. "Hegesianax." *Der Neue Pauly: Enzyklopädie der Antike* 5:235–236. Stuttgart.

Fowler, R. L. 2000. *Early Greek Mythography*. Vol. 1. Oxford.

———. 2013. *Early Greek Mythography*. Vol. 2. Oxford.

Franco, C. 1993. *Il regno di Lisimaco. Strutture amministrative e rapporti con le città*. Pisa.

———. 2000. "La Troade di Straboe." In Biraschi and Salmeri 2000a:263–282.

Fraser, P. M. 1972. *Ptolemaic Alexandria*. Oxford.

Frazer, J. G. 1898. *Pausanias's Description of Greece*. Vols. 1 and 5. London.

Friedländer, L. 1862–1871. *Darstellungen aus der Sittengeschichte Roms: in der Zeit von August bis zum Ausgang der Antonine*. Leipzig.

———. 1920–1923. *Darstellungen aus der Sittengeschichte Roms: in der Zeit von August bis zum Ausgang der Antonine*. Leipzig. 10th ed. Leipzig.

Friedrich, C., and T. Nothers. 1998. *Athenaios. Das Gelehrtenmahl*. Book 1–6. Stuttgart.

Fromentin, V., and Gotteland S., eds. 2001. *Origines Gentium*. Bordeaux.

Fry, G. 1998. *Récits inédits de la guerre de Troie*. Paris.

Funaioli, G. 1913. "Hestiaia [4]." In *Paulys Realencyclopädie der classischen Altertumswissenschaften* 8.2, 1313–1314. Stuttgart.

Fournet, J.-L. 1999. *Hellénisme dans l'Egypte du VIe siècle. La bibliothèque et l'oeuvre de Dioscore d'Aphrodité*. Cairo.

Gabba, E. 1974. "Storiografia greca e imperialisme romano." *Rivista Storica Italiana* 86:625–642.

———. 1976. "Sulla valorizzazione politica della leggenda delle origini troiane di Roma fra III e II secolo a.C." In *I canali della propaganda nel mondo antico*, ed. M. Sordi, 84–101. Milan.

———. 2003. "Riflessione sui Giambi a Nicomede." In *Laurea internationalis, Festschrift für Jochen Bleicken zum 75. Geburtstag*, ed. T. Hantos, 143–145. Stuttgart.

Gaede, R. 1880. *Demetrii Scepsii quae supersunt*. Greifswald.

Gärtner, H. 1964. "Demetrios [23]." In *Der kleine Pauly* 1, ed. K. Ziegler and W. Sontheimer, 1468. Stuttgart.

Georges, P. 1994. *Barbarian Asia and the Greek Experience, From the Archaic Period to the Age of Xenophon*. Baltimore.

Göbel, P.E. 1931. "Menekrates [25]." In *Paulys Realencyclopädie der classischen Altertumswissenschaften* 15.1:801. Stuttgart.

Gottschalk, H. B. 1972. "Notes on the Wills of Peripatetic Scholarchs." In *Hermes* 100:314–342.

Goulet-Cazé, M.-O., ed. 2000. *Le commentaire, entre tradition et innovation*. Paris.

Graillot, H. 1912. *Le culte de Cybèle mère des dieux à Rome et dans l'empire romain*. Paris.

Grainger, J. D. 2002. *The Roman War of Antiochos the Great*. Leiden.

Grote, G. 1869. *History of Greece*. London.

Gruen, E. S. 1990. *Studies in Greek Culture and Roman Policy*. Leiden.

———. 1993. *Culture and National Identity in Republican Rome*. London.

———. 2000. "Culture as Policy. The Attalids of Pergamon." In *From Pergamon to Sperlonga: Sculpture and Context*, ed. N. T. de Grummond and B. S. Ridgway, 17–31. Berkeley.

Gudeman, A. 1907. *Grundriss der Geschichte der klassischen Philologie*. Leipzig.

———. 1909. *Grundriss der Geschichte der klassischen Philologie*. Leipzig. 2nd ed.

———. 1892. *Syllabus on the History of Classical Philology*. Boston.

———. 1894. *Outlines of the History of Classical Philology*. Boston. 2nd ed. of Gudeman 1892.

Guhl, C. 1969. *Die Fragmente des Alexandrinischen Grammatikers Theon*. Hamburg.

Gulick, C.-B. 1927. *Athenaeus, The Deipnosophists*. Vol. 1. Cambridge, MA.

Gürtler J. D., ed. 1831. *Friedrich August Wolf's Vorlesung über die Geschichte der griechischen Literatur*. Leipzig.

Gutzwiller, K. J. 2010. "Literary Criticism." In *A Companion to Hellenistic Literature*, ed. J. J. Clauss and M. Cuypers, 337–365. London.

Hainsworth, B. 1993. *The Iliad: a Commentary*. Vol. 3, *Books 9–12*. Cambridge.

Hammerstaedt, J. 1998. "Die Homerallegorese des älteren Metrodor von Lampsakos." *Zeitschrift für Papyrologie und Epigraphik* 121:28–32.

Harding, P. 2006. *Didymos. On Demosthenes*. Oxford.

Hawes, G. 2014a. *Rationalizing Myth in Antiquity*. Oxford.

———. 2014b. "Story Time at the Library: Palaephatus and the Emergence of Highly Literate Mythology." In *Between Orality and Literacy: Communication and Adaptation in Antiquity*, ed. R. Scodel, 125–147. Leiden.

Heller, A. 2006. *"Les bêtises des Grecs": conflits et rivalités entre cités d'Asie et de Bithynie à l'époque romaine; (129 a.C. - 235 p.C.)*. Bordeaux.

Hercher, R. 1875. "Über die Homerische Ebene vor Troja." In *Abhandlungen der Königlichen preußischen Akademie der Wissenschaften zu Berlin*, 101–134. Berlin.

———. 1877. "Vier Homerische Flüße." In *Commentationes philologae in honorem Theodori Mommseni*, 769–781. Berlin.

———. 1881. *Homerische Aufsätze*. Berlin.

Holford-Strevens, L. 2009. "Selinus or Athens?" *Classical Quarterly* 59:624–670.

Holm Rasmussen, A. 2002. "The Attalid Kingdom and the Cult of Cybele at Pessinous." In *Ancient History Matters: Studies Presented to Jens Erik Skydsgaard on His Seventieth Birthday*, ed. K. Ascani, 159–164. Rome.

Hunter, R. 2011. "Plato's Ion and the Origins of Scholarship." In Matthaios, Montanari, and Rengakos 2011:27–40. Berlin.

Hutton, W. 2005. *Describing Greece*. Cambridge.

Ippolito, A. 2005. "Parmeniscus." In Montanari, Montana, and Pagani 2015, https://referenceworks.brillonline.com/browse/lexicon-of-greek-gram marians-of-antiquity.

———. 2006. "Hestiaea." In Montanari, Montana, and Pagani 2015, https:// referenceworks.brillonline.com/browse/lexicon-of-greek-grammarians -of-antiquity.

Irigoin, J. 1952. *Histoire du texte de Pindare*. Paris.

———. 1994. "Les éditions de textes." In Montanari 1994:39–93. Vandoevres.

Jacob, C. 2000. "Athenaeus the Librarian." In Braund and Wilkins 2000:85–110.

———. 2001. "Ateneo, o il dedalo delle parole." In Canfora 2001:xi–cxvi.

———. 2004a. "La citation comme performance dans les Deipnosophistes d'Athénée." In Darbo-Peschanski 2004:147–174.

———. 2004b. "La construction de l'auteur dans le savoir bibliographique antique: à propos des Deiponosophistes d'Athénée." In *Identités d'auteur dans l'Antiquité et la tradition européenne*, ed. C. Calame and R. Chartier, 127–158. Grenoble.

Jacoby, F. 1919. "Karystios." In *Paulys Realencyclopädie der classischen Altertumswissenschaften* 10.2, 2254–2255. Stuttgart.

———. 1930. *Die Fragmente der griechischen Historiker, Kommentar zu Nr. 106–261*. Berlin.

———. 1957a. *Die Fragmente der griechischen Historiker, Nr. 1–63: Vorrede-Text-Addenda-Konkordanz (Neudruck)*. Leiden. Orig. pub. 1923. Berlin.

———. 1957b. *Die Fragmente der griechischen Historiker, Nr. 1–63: Kommentar-Nachträge (Neudruck)*. Leiden. Orig. pub. Berlin 1923.

Janko, R. 1997. "The Physicist as Hierophant: Aristophanes, Socrates and the Authorship of the Derveni Papyrus." *Zeitschrift für Papyrologie und Epigraphik* 118:61–94.

Jebb, R. C. 1881. "Homeric and Hellenic Ilium." *Journal of Hellenic Studies* 2:7–43.

———. 1882. "The Ruins at Hissarlik and their Relation to the *Iliad*." *Journal of Hellenic Studies* 3:185–217.

———. 1883. "The Ruins of Hissarlik." *Journal of Hellenic Studies* 4:142–155.

Jones, C. P. 2001. "Diplomatie et liens de parenté: Ilion, Aphrodisias et Rome." In V. Fromentin, and S. Gotteland 2001:197–186.

Jones, H. L. 1928. *Strabo. Geography*. Vol. 5, *Books 10-12*. Cambridge, MA.

Jost, M. 1998. "Versions locales et versions 'panhelléniques' des mythes arcadiens chez Pausanias." In *Les Panthéons des cités des origines à la Périégèse de Pausanias*, ed. V. Pirenne-Delforge, 227–240. Liège.

Kagan, J. H. 1984. "Hellenistic Coinage at Scepsis after its Refoundation in the Third Century BC." *American Numismatic Society Museum Notes* 29:11–24.

Kaibel, G. 1887–1890. *Athenaei Naucratitae Dipnosophistarum libri*. Leipzig.

———. 1896. "Aristoxenos [5]." In *Paulys Realencyclopädie der classischen Alter-tumswissenschaften* 2.1, 1056. Stuttgart.

Keaney, J. J. 1991. *Harpocration, Lexeis of the Ten Orators*. Amsterdam.

Kelly, A. D. 2011. "Trojans." In Finkelberg 2011a:895–896.

Kiechle, F. 1960. "Pylos und der pylische Raum in der antiken Tradition." *Historia* 9:1–67.

Kim, L. 2010. *Homer between History and Fiction in Imperial Greek Literature*. Cambridge.

Kirk, G. S. 1985. *The Iliad: a Commentary*. Vol. I, *Books 1–4*. Cambridge.

Kirstein, R. 2000. "Achill und Nestor in Greifswald: Ulrich v. Wilamowitz-Moellendorff und Franz Susemihl." In *Wilamowitz in Greifswald: Akten der Tagung zum 150. Geburtstag Ulrich Wilamowitz-Moellendorffs in Greifswald, 19.-22. Dezember 1998*, ed. W. M. Calder, et al. 168–196. Hildesheim.

Koehn, C. 2007. "Die Eumenesrede (Polybios XXI, 19–21) und die Neuordnung Kleinasiens 189/188 vor Chr." *Hermes* 135:263–285.

Korfmann, M. 1991. "Der gegenwärtige Stand der neuen archäologischen Arbeiten in Hisarlik (Troia)." In *Zweihundert Jahre Homer-Forschung: Rückblick und Ausblick; Colloquium Rauricum 2*, ed. H.-J. Latacz, 89–102. Stuttgart.

———, ed. 2006. *Troia Archäologie eines Siedlungshügels und seiner Landschaft*. Mainz.

Kosmetatou, E. 1995. "The Legend of the Hero Pergamus." *Ancient Society* 26:133–144.

———. 2001. "Ilion, the Troad and the Attalids." *Ancient Society* 31:107–132.

———. 2003. "The Attalids of Pergamon." In *A Companion to the Hellenistic World*, ed. A. Erskine, 159–174. Oxford.

Kramer, B., and B. Hübner. 1976. *Kölner Papyri. Band 1*. Opladen.

Krebber, B. 1972. "Naustologoi bei Strabo: ein neues Papyrusfragment." *Zeitschrift für Papyrologie und Epigraphik* 9:204–221.

Kroll, W. 1922a. "Krates [16]." In *Paulys Realencyclopädie der classischen Alter-tumswissenschaften* 11.2, 1634–1641. Stuttgart.

———. 1922b. "Ktesiphon [1]." In *Paulys Realencyclopädie der classischen Alter-tumswissenschaften* 11.2, 2079. Stuttgart.

Kuch, H. 1965. *ΦΙΛΟΛΟΓΟΣ Untersuchung eines Wortes von seinem ersten Auftreten in der Tradition bis zur ersten überlieferten lexikalischen Festlegung*. Berlin.

Kuttner, A. 1995. "Republican Rome Looks at Pergamon." *Harvard Studies in Classical Philology* 97:157–178.

Lachenaud, G. 2010. *Scholies à Apollonios de Rhodes*. Paris.

Lallot, J. 1998. *La grammaire de Denys le Thrace*. Paris.

———. 2012. *Etudes sur la grammaire alexandrine*. Paris.

Landucci Gattinoni, F. 2005-2006. "Diadochi ed Epigoni nell'Asia Minore di Straboe: Ilio e la Troade." *Geographia antiqua* 14–15:15–29.

Laqueur, R. 1932. "Mnesiptolemos." In *Paulys Realencyclopädie der classischen Altertumswissenschaften* 15.2, 2280. Stuttgart.

Latacz, J., and F. Starke F. 2006. "Wilusa und die Grossen Vier—Troia in der politischen Landschaft der Späten Bronzezeit." In Korfmann 2006:57–70. Mainz.

Leaf, W., A. Lang, and E. Myers. 1891. *The Iliad of Homer Done into English Prose.* London.

———. 1892. *A Companion to the Iliad, for English Readers.* London.

———. 1895. *The Iliad.* 1895. 2nd ed. 1900–1902. London.

———. 1910-1911. "The Topography of the Scamandre Valley." *Annual of the British School at Athens* 17:266–283.

———. 1912. *Troy: A Study in Homeric Geography.* London.

———. 1917-1918. "Strabo and Demetrios of Skepsis." *Annual of the British School at Athens* 22:23–47.

———. 1923. *Strabo on the Troad.* Book XIII, Cap. I. Cambridge.

Lechevalier, J.-B. 1792. *Beschreibung der Ebene vor Troja.* Leipzig.

Lehrs, K. 1878. "Drei Schriften über Apollodor II." In *Wissenschaftliche Monatsblätter* 6:70–75. Reprinted in *Kleine Schriften von Karl Lehrs*, ed. A Ludwich, 299–305. Königsberg i. Pr., 1902.

———. 1865. *De Aristarchi Studiis Homerici.* Leipzig.

Leigh, M. 1998. "Sophocles at Patavium (fr. 137 Radt)." *Journal of Hellenic Studies* 118:82–100.

Lenfant, D. 2000. "Nicolas de Damas et le corpus des fragments de Ctésias. Du fragment comme adaptation." *Ancient Society* 30:293–318.

———. 2002. "Les citations de Thucydide dans les scholies d'Aristophane: contribution à l'analyse de fragments d'historiens." In *Fragments d'historiens grecs, autour de Denys d'Halicarnasse*, ed. S. Pittia, 415–447. Rome.

———. ed. 2007a. *Athénée et les fragments d'historiens.* Paris.

———. 2007b. "Introduction. " In Lenfant 2007a:13–15.

———. 2013. "The Study of Intermediate Authors and its Role in the Interpretation of Historical Fragments." *Ancient Society* 43:289–305.

Lightfoot, J. L. 2007. *The Sibylline Oracles.* Oxford.

———. 2017. "Man of Many Voices and of Much Knowledge: Or, in Seach of Strabo's Homer." In Dueck 2017: 251–262.

Lindsay, H. 1997. "Strabo on Apellicon's Library." *Rheinisches Museum* 140:290–298.

Lohan, E. 1890. *De librorum titulis apud classicos scriptores graecos nobis occurrentibus.* Görlitz.

Luce, J. V. 1984. "The Homeric Topography of the Trojan Plain Reconsidered." *Oxford Journal of Archaeology* 3:31–43.

———. 1998. *Celebrating Homer's Landscapes.* New Haven, CT.

Lukinovich, A. 1985. "La Poikilia chez Athénée." *Revue des Études Latines* 63:14–16.

———. 1990. "The Play of Reflections between Literary Form and the Sympothic Theme in the Deipnosophistae of Athenaeus." In *Sympotica: A Symposium on the Symposion,* ed. O. Murray, 263–271. Oxford.

Lund, H. S. 1992. *Lysimachus. A Study in Early Hellenistic Kingship.* London.

Lundon, J. 2011. "Homeric Commentaries on Papyrus: A Survey." In Matthaios, Montanari, and Rengakos 2011:159–179.

Luppe, W. 1994. "Die Verfluchung der Methonaier, zum Strabo-Papyrus P. Köln I 8." *Archiv für Papyrusforschung und verwandte Gebiete* 40:115–118.

———. 2000. "Ein Nachtrag zum Genfer Topographie-Papyrus Pack² 1204." *Museum Hellveticum* 57:237–239.

———. 2012. "Zum Mythographie-Papyrus P. Oxy. LXXVI 5094." *Archiv für Papyrusforschung und verwandte Gebiete* 58:8–10.

———. 2013. "Ein neuer Textvorschlag für den Mythographie-Papyrus P. Oxy. LXXVI 5094 (fr. 1)." *Zeitschrift für Papyrologie und Epigraphik* 185:105–106.

Ma, J. 1999. *Antiochos III and the Cities of Western Asia Minor.* Oxford.

Maass, E. 1879. *De Sibyllarum Indicibus.* Berlin.

———. 1883. "Tibullische Sagen." *Hermes* 18:321–342.

MacPhail, J. A. 2011. *Porphyry's "Homeric questions" on the "Iliad": Text, Translation Commentary.* Berlin.

Mader, B. 1991. "Ἐλεών." In *Lexikon des frühgriechischen Epos* 2, 532. Göttingen.

Maehler, H. 1994. "Die Scholien der Papyri in ihrem Verhältnis zu den Scholiencorpora der Handschriften." In Montanari 1994:95–141.

———. 2000. "L'Evolution matérielle de l'Hypomnema jusqu'à la basse époque." In Goulet-Cazé 2000:29–36.

Mahaffy, J. P. 1880a. *A History of Greek Literature.* New York.

———. 1880b. "Appendix II: On the Relation of Novum Ilium to the Ilios of Homer." In *Ilios: the City and Country of the Trojans,* H. Schliemann, 686–690. London.

———. 1881. "Anhang II: Das Verhältniss von Novum Ilium zu dem Ilion des Homer." In *Ilios: Stadt und Land der Trojaner: Forschungen und Entdeckungen in der Troas und besonders auf der Baustelle von Troja,* H. Schliemann, 761–765. Leipzig. Trans. of Mahaffy 1880b.

———. 1882. "The Site and Antiquity of the Hellenic Ilion." *Journal of Hellenic Studies* 3:69–80.

———. 1884. "Anhang IV: Die Baustelle und das Alter des hellenistischen Ilion." In *Troja: Ergebnisse meiner neuesten Ausgrabungen auf der Baustelle von Troja, in den Heldengräbern, Bunarbaschi und anderen Orten der Troas im Jahre 1882*, H. Schliemann, 372–395. Leipzig.

Maisonneuve, C. 2007a. "Les 'fragments' de Xénophon dans les Deipnosophistes." In Lenfant 2007a:73–106.

———. 2007b. "Les Deipnosophistes: repères dans une structure complexe." In Lenfant 2007a:387–412.

Marastoni, S. 2007. *Metrodoro di Scepsi*. Alessandria.

Matteo, R. 2007. *Apollonio Rodio, Argonautiche, libro II: introduzione e commento*. Lecce.

Matthaios, St., F. Montanari, and A. Rengakos, eds. 2011. *Ancient Scholarship and Grammar*. Berlin.

Matthews, V. J. 1996. *Antimachus of Colophon, Text and Commentary*. Leiden.

Mau, J. 1954. *Sexti Empirici opera, Adversus mathematicos*. Vol. 3, *Books 1-6 continens*. Leipzig.

Mauduit, A. F. 1840. *Découvertes dans la Troade*. Vol. 1. Paris.

Mayor, A. 2010. *The Poison King. The Life and Legend of Mithridates, Rome's deadliest Enemy*. Princeton.

McNamee, K. 1995. "Missing Links in the Development of Scholia." *Greek, Roman and Byzantine Studies* 36:399–414.

McShane, R. B. 1964. *The Foreign Policy of the Attalids of Pergamum*. Urbana.

Meineke, A. 1858–1867. *Athenaei Deipnosophistae*. Leipzig.

Meister, K. 1990. *Die griechische Geschichtsschreibung: von den Anfängen bis zum Ende des Hellenismus*. Stuttgart.

———. 1997. "Diokles von Peparethos [7]." In *Der Neue Pauly: Enzyklopädie der Antike* 3, 613. Stuttgart.

———. 1998. "Hekataios aus Milet [3]." In *Der Neue Pauly: Enzyklopädie der Antike* 5, 264–267. Stuttgart.

———. 2000. "Mnesiptolemos." In *Der Neue Pauly: Enzyklopädie der Antike* 8, 308. Stuttgart.

Merkle, S. 1989. *Die Ephemeris belli Troiani des Diktys von Kreta*. Frankfurt am Main.

Mette, H.-J. 1936. *Sphairopoiia: Untersuchungen zur Kosmologie des Krates von Pergamon: mit einem Anhang: Texte*. Munich.

Minchin, E. 2001. *Homer and the Resources of Memory*. Oxford.

Mitchell, S. 2005. "Anatolia between East and West. The Parallel Lives of the Attalid and Mithridatid Kingdoms in the Hellenistic Age." In *Studi ellenistici XVI*, ed. B. Virgilio, 521–530. Pisa.

Montanari, F. 1979. "Introduzione." In *Studi di filologia omerica antica I*, 3–25. Pisa.

———. 1984. "Revisione di P. Berol. 13282. Le historiae fabulares omeriche su papiro." In *Atti del XVII Congresso internationale di papirologia*. Vol. 2, 229–242. Naples.

————. 1993a. "L'erudizione, la filologia e la grammatica." In Cambiano, Canfora, and Lanza 1993:235–282.

————. 1993b. "Pergamo." In Cambiano, Canfora, and Lanza 1993:639–655.

————. ed. 1994. *La philologie grecque à l'époque hellénistique et Romaine*. Vandoevres.

————. 1995a. *Studi di filologia omerica antica II*. Pisa.

————. 1995b. "Gli Homerica su papiro per una distinzione di generi." In Montanari 1995a:69–85. Pisa.

————. 1995c. "Revisione di P. Berol. 13282 I Papyri del Mythographus Homericus." In Montanari 1995a:113–125

————. 1995d. "The Mythographus Homericus." In *Greek Literary Theory After Aristotle*, ed. J. G. J. Abbenes, S. R. Slings, and I. Sluiter, 135–172. Amsterdam.

————. 1996a. "Alexandros Polyhistor [23]." In *Der Neue Pauly: Enzyklopädie der Antike 1*, 478–479. Stuttgart.

————. 1996b. "Apollodoros aus Athen [7]." In *Der Neue Pauly: Enzyklopädie der Antike 1*, 857–860. Stuttgart.

————. 1996c. "Aristarchos von Samothrake[4]." In *Der Neue Pauly: Enzyklopädie der Antike 1*, 1090–1094. Stuttgart.

————. 1997a. "Asklepiades aus Myrleia [8]." In *Der Neue Pauly: Enzyklopädie der Antike 2*, 92. Stuttgart.

————. 1997b. "Demetrios von Skepsis [34]." In *Der Neue Pauly: Enzyklopädie der Antike 3*, 438. Stuttgart.

————. 1997c. "Dionysios Thrax [17]." In *Der Neue Pauly: Enzyklopädie der Antike 3*, 632–635. Stuttgart.

————. 1998. "Zenodotus, Aristarchus and the Ekdosis of Homer." In *Editing Texts, Texte edieren*, ed. G.W. Most, 1–21. Göttingen.

————. 1999. "Karystios." In *Der Neue Pauly: Enzyklopädie der Antike 6*, 311–312. Stuttgart.

————. 2002. "Ancora sul Mythographus Homericus (e l'Odyssea)." In *La Mythologie et l'Odyssée. Hommage à Gabriel Germain*, ed. A. Hurst and F. Létoublon, 129–144. Geneva.

Montanari, F., St. Matthaios, and A. Rengakos, eds. 2015. *Brill's Companion to Ancient Greek Scholarship*. Leiden.

Montanari F., F. Montana, and L. Pagani, eds. 2015. *Lexicon of Greek Grammarians of Antiquity*. https://referenceworks.brillonline.com/browse/lexicon-of-greek-grammarians-of-antiquity.

Montana, F. 2011. "The Making of Greek Scholiastic Corpora." In *From Scholars to Scholia*, ed. F. Montanari and L. Pagani, 105–161. Berlin.

————. 2015. "Hellenistic Scholarship." In Montanari, Matthaios, and Rengakos 2015:60–183.

Most, G. W., ed. 1997. *Collecting Fragments/Fragmente sammeln*. Göttingen.

———. 2009. "On Fragments." In *The Fragment: An Incomplete History*, ed. W. Tronzo, 9–20. Los Angeles.

———. 2010. "Fragment." In *The Classical Tradition*, ed. A. Grafton, G. W. Most and S. Settis, 370–377. Cambridge, MA.

Mueller, M. 2011. "Wounds." In Finkelberg 2011a:942–943.

Müller, K. 1851. *Fragmenta historicorum graecorum*. Vol. 4. Paris.

Nagy, G. 1998. "The Library of Pergamon as a Classical Model." In *Pergamon. Citadel of the Gods*, ed. H. Koester, 185–232. Harrisburg.

———. 2010. *Homer the Preclassic*. Berkeley. New ed. pub. http://chs.harvard.edu/CHS/article/display/437.

Nauta, R. R. 2007. "Phrygian Eunuchs and Roman Virtus: The Cult of the Mater Magna and the Trojan Origins of Rome in Virgil's Aeneid." In *Tra Oriente e Occidente: Indigeni, Greci e Romani in Asia Minore*, ed. G. Urso, 79–92. Pisa.

Nesselrath, H.-G. 1997. *Einleitung in die griechische Philologie*. Stuttgart.

Nestle, W. 1932. "Metrodoros [14]." In *Paulys Realencyclopädie der classischen Altertumswissenschaften* 15.2, 1476–1477. Stuttgart.

Nicolai, R. 2005–2006. "Geografia e filologia nell'Asia di Straboe." *Geographia antiqua*:14–15, 55–75.

Niese, B. 1877. "Apollodors Commentar zum Schiffskataloge als Quelle Strabo's." *Rheinisches Museum* 32:267–307.

Novokhatko, A. 2015. "Greek Scholarship from its Beginnings to Alexandria." In Montanari, Matthaios, and Rengakos 2015:3–59.

Nuchelmans, G. R. F. M. 1950. *Studien über φολόλογος, φολολογία und φιλολογεῖν.* Zwolle.

Nünlist, R. 2009. *The Ancient Critic at Work*. Cambridge.

———. 2011. "Aristarchus and Allegorical Interpretation." In Matthaios, Montanari, and Rengakos 2011:105–117.

Pagani, L. 2005. "Hegesianax." In Montanari, Montana, and Pagani 2015, https://referenceworks.brillonline.com/browse/lexicon-of-greek-grammarians-of-antiquity.

———. 2006. "Demetrius [2]." In Montanari, Montana, and Pagani 2015, https://referenceworks.brillonline.com/browse/lexicon-of-greek-grammarians-of-antiquity.

———. 2007. *Asclepiade di Mirlea, I frammenti degli scritti omerici*. Rome.

Parke, H. W. 1988. *Sibyls and Sibylline Prophecy in Classical Antiquity*. London.

Pédech, P. 1991. "Deux grecs face à Rome au 1er siècle av. J.-C.: Métrodore de Scepsis et Théophanes de Mitylène." *Revue des Études Anciennes* 93:65–78.

Peppmüller, R. 1884. *Kleine Schriften von Theodor Bergk*. Vol. 1. Halle.

———. 1886. *Kleine Schriften von Theodor Bergk*. Vol. 2. Halle.

Perale, M., and W. B. Henry. 2011. "P. Oxy. 5094. Mythology." In *The Oxyrhynchus Papyri LXXVI*, ed. D. Colomo and J. Chapa, 172–177. London.

Perale, M., and S. Vecchiato. 2015. "More on P. Oxy. 5094: Hecuba's Father, Stesichorus, and a New Fragment of Ar(i)aethus of Tegea." *Zeitschrift für Papyrologie und Epigraphik* 194:11–27.

Perceau, S. 2002. *La parole vive. Communiquer en catalogue dans l'épopée homérique.* Louvain.

Perret, J. 1942. *Les origines de la légende Troyenne de Rome (281-31).* Paris.

Pettersson, M. 1992. *Cults of Apollo at Sparta: the Hyakinthia, the Gymnopaidiai and the Karneia.* Stockholm.

Pfeiffer, R. 1968. *History of Classical Scholarship.* Oxford.

Pollitt, J. J. 1986. "The Sculpture of Pergamon." In *Art in the Hellenistic Age*, 79–110. Cambridge.

Pontani, F. 2005. *Sguardi su Ulisse. La tradizione esegetica greca all'Odissea.* Rome.

Porter J. I. 1992. "Hermeneutic Lines and Circles: Aristarchus and Crates on the Exegesis of Homer." In *Homer's Ancient Readers. The Hermeneutics of Greek Epic's Earliest Exegetes*, ed. R. Lamberton and J. J. Keaney, 67–114. Princeton.

Potter, D. 1990. "Sibyls in the Greek and Roman World." *Journal of Roman Archaeology* 3:471–483.

Preller, L. 1838. *Polemonis Periegetae Fragmenta.* Leipzig.

Primavesi, O. 2007. "Ein Blick in den Stollen von Skepsis: vier Kapitel zur frühen Überlieferung des Corpus Aristotelicum." *Philologus* 151:51–77.

Primo, A. 2009. *La storiografia sui Seleucidi.* Pisa.

Pulch, P. 1882. "Zu Eudocia. Constantinus Palaecappa, der Verfasser des Violariums." *Hermes* 17:177–192.

Quaglia, R. 2001. "Citazioni da Aristophane e dalla comedia antica in Ateneo." *Maia* 53:611–633.

Radt, S., and J. W. Drijvers. 1993. "Die Groninger Neuedition von Strabos Geographika, vorgestellt anhand des Abschnittes über Troia." *Studia Troica* 3:201–232.

———. 2002. *Strabos Geographika.* Vol. 1, Prolegomena, *Book 1-4: Text und Übersetzung.* Göttingen.

———. 2003. *Strabos Geographika.* Vol. 2, *Book 5-8: Text und Übersetzung.* Göttingen.

———. 2004. *Strabos Geographika.* Vol. 3, *Book 9-13: Text und Übersetzung.* Göttingen.

———. 2007. *Strabos Geographika.* Vol. 6, *Book 5-8: Kommentar.* Göttingen.

———. 2008. *Strabos Geographika.* Vol. 7, *Book 9-13: Kommentar.* Göttingen.

———. 2010. *Strabos Geographika.* Vol. 9, *Epitome and Chrestomathie.* Göttingen.

———. 2011. *Strabos Geographika.* Vol. 10, *Register.* Göttingen.

Radt, W. 1999. *Pergamon. Geschichte und Bauten einer antiken Metropole.* Darmstadt.

Ragone, G. 2005. "Le Amazzoni in Eolide." In *Eoli ed Eolide. Tra madrepatria e colonie*, ed. A. Melle, M. L. Napolitano, and A. Visconti, 315–357. Naples.

———. 2009. "Polemica localistica e ZHTHMATA omerici in Demetrio di Scepsi." In *Tradizione e trasmissione degli storici greci frammentari*, ed. E. Lanzillotta, V. Costa, and G. Ottone, 649–691. Tivoli, Rome.

Razzetti, F. 2010. "Aristarchus." In *Lessico dei Grammatici Greci Antichi*, ed. F. Montanari, F. Montana, and L. Pagani, http://www.aristarchus.unige.net/LGGA/it-IT/Home. Accessed March 2010.

Rengakos, A. 1993. *Der Homertext und die hellenistischen Dichter*. Stuttgart.

Rennell, J. 1814. *Observations on the Topography of the Plain of Troy*. London.

Richardson, N. J. 1975. "Homeric Professors in the Age of the Sophists." *Proceedings of the Cambridge Philological Society* 21:65–81.

———. 1994. "Aristotle and Hellenistic Scholarship." In Montanari 1994:7–38.

Ridgway, B. S. 2000. "The Shadow of the Pergamon Altar." In *Hellenistic Sculpture 2, the Styles of ca. 200–100 B.C.*, 19–66. Madison, WI.

Roller, L. E., 1999. *In Search of God the Mother. The Cult of Anatolian Cybele*. Berkeley.

Rose, C. B. 2003. "The Temple of Athena at Ilion." In *Studia Troica* 13:27–88.

———. 2006a. "Am Schnittpunkt von Ost und West—Das westliche Kleinasien in griechischer und römischer Zeit." In Korfmann 2006:81–104.

———. 2006b. "Auf mythengetränktem Boden—Ilion in griechischer, römischer und byzantinischer Zeit." In Korfmann 2006:189–198.

———. 2015. "Carl Blegen and Troy." In Vogeikoff-Brogan, Davis, and Florou 2015:157–176.

Rühl, F. 1882. "Herodotisches." *Philologus* 41:55–77.

Russo, G. 2001. "Repertorio degli autori citati." In Canfora 2001:1887–1981.

Sage, M. 2000. "Roman Visitors to Ilium in the Roman Imperial and Late Antique Period: The Symbolic Functions of a Landscape." *Studia Troica* 10:211–231.

Sandys, J. E. 1903. *A History of Classical Scholarship*. 3rd ed. Cambridge. 1921. Repr. New York 1958.

Santoni, A. 2000. *Palefato, storie incredibile*. Pisa.

Sartiaux, F. 1915. *Troie, la guerre de Troie et les origines préhistoriques de la question d'Orient*. Paris.

Sartre, M. 1995. *L'Asie Mineure et l'Anatolie*. Paris.

Sayce, A. H. 1880. "Appendix III: The Inscriptions Found at Hissarlik." In *Ilios: the City and Country of the Trojans*, H. Schliemann, 691–705. London.

———. 1881. "Anhang III: Die Inschriften von Hissarlik." In *Ilios: Stadt und Land der Trojaner: Forschungen und Entdeckungen in der Troas und besonders auf der Baustelle von Troja*. H. Schliemann, 766–781. Leipzig. Trans. of Sayce 1880.

———. 1883. "The Ruins of Hissarlik." *Journal of Hellenic Studies* 4:142–155.

Scheer, T. S. 2003. "The Past in a Hellenistic Present: Myth and Local Tradition." In *A Companion to the Hellenistic World*, ed. A. Erskine, 216–231. Oxford.

Schenkeveld, D.M. 1994. "Scholarship and Grammar." In Montanari 1994:263–306.

———. 2006. "What Do we Do with Homer? Literary Criticism in the Hellenistic Age." In *Land of Dreams: Greek and Latin Studies in Honour of A. H. M. Kessels*, ed. A. P. M. H. Lardinois, M. G. M. van der Poel, and V. J. C. Hunink, 189–202. Leiden.

Schepens, G. 1997. "Jacoby's FGriHist: Problems, Methods, Prospects." In *Collecting Fragments, Fragmente sammeln*, ed. G. W. Most, 144–172. Göttingen.

———. 2000. "Probleme der Fragmentedition (Fragmente der griechischen Historiker)." In *Vom Text zum Buch*, ed. C. Reitz. 1–29. St. Katharinen.

Schironi, F. 2009. *From Alexandria to Babylon*. Berlin.

———. 2016. "Scholarship, Hellenistic." In *The Encyclopedia of Ancient History*, ed. R. S. Bagnall et al., 1–6. Wiley Online Library.

Schliemann, H. 1874. *Trojanische Alterthümer: Bericht über die Ausgrabungen in Troja*. Leipzig.

———. 1875. *Troy and Its Remains: a Narrative of Researches and Discoveries Made on the Site of Ilium, and the Trojan Plain*. London.

———. 1880. *Ilios: the City and Country of the Trojans; the Results of Researches and Discoveries on the Site of Troy and throughout the Troad in the Years 1871, 72, 73, 78, 79; Including an Autobiography of the Author*. London.

———. 1881. *Ilios: Stadt und Land der Trojaner: Forschungen und Entdeckungen in der Troas und besonders auf der Baustelle von Troja*. Leipzig. Orig. pub. as Schliemann 1880.

———. 1884. *Troja, Ergebnisse meiner neuesten Ausgrabungen auf der Baustelle von Troja, in den Heldengräbern, Bunarbaschi und andern Orten der Troas im Jahre 1882*. Leipzig.

Schmidt, J. 1916–1924. "Telephos." In *Ausführliches Lexikon der griechischen und römischen Mythologie*. Vol. 5, ed. W. H. Roscher, 274–308. Leipzig.

Schmitt, H. H. 1964. *Untersuchungen zur Geschichte Antiochos' des Grossen und seiner Zeit*. Wiesbaden.

Schorn, S. 2007. "'Periegetische Biographie' – 'Historische Biographie': Neanthes von Kyzikos (FGrHist 84) als Biograph." In *Die griechische Biographie in hellenistischer Zeit*, ed. M. Erler and S. Schorn, 115–156. Berlin.

Schrader, H. 1880. *Porphyrii Queastiones Homericarum ad Iliadem pertinentium reliquias*. Vol. 1. Leipzig.

Schröder, B.-J. 1999. *Titel und Text*. Berlin.

Schubert, P. 2002. "Strabo et le sort de la bibliothèque d'Aristote." *Les Études classiques* 70:225–237.

Schwartz, E. 1894. "Apollodoros [61]." In *Paulys Realencyclopädie der classischen Altertumswissenschaften* 1, 2855–2886. Munich.

———. 1901. "Demetrios [78]." In *Paulys Realencyclopädie der classischen Altertumswissenschaften* 4, 2807–2813. Stuttgart.

———. 1903. "Demokles [12]." In *Paulys Realencyclopädie der classischen Altertumswissenschaften* 5.1, 133. Stuttgart.

Seyk, V. 1926. *Das wahre und richtige Troja-Ilion.* Prague.

Sidwell, K. 2000. "Athenaeus, Lucian and Fifth-Century Comedy." In Braund and Wilkins 2000:136–152.

Stanzel, K.-H. 2002. "Xenokrates [2]." In *Der Neue Pauly: Enzyklopädie der Antike* 12.2, 620–623. Stuttgart.

Steiner, G. 1991. "Ἠετίων." In *Lexikon des frühgriechischen Epos* 2, 899–900. Göttingen.

Steitz, A. 1875. "Die Lage des Homerischen Troja." *Jahrbücher für classische Philologie* 21:225–264.

Stern, J. 1996. *On Unbelievable Tales.* Wauconda.

Stiehle, R. 1850. "Der Τρωϊκὸς διάκοσμος des Demetrios von Skepsis." *Philologus* 5:528–546.

———. 1851. "Nachtrag zu der Abhandlung 'Der Τρωϊκὸς Διάκοσμος des Demetrios von Skepsis.'" *Philologus* 6:344–347.

———. 1854. "Zu den Fragmenten der griechischen Historiker." *Philologus* 9:462–514.

Susemihl, F. 1891. *Geschichte der griechischen Litteratur in der Alexanderzeit.* Vol. 1. Leipzig.

———. 1892. *Geschichte der griechischen Litteratur in der Alexanderzeit.* Vol. 2. Leipzig.

Svenbro, J. 2004. "Façons grecques de dire 'citer.'" In Darbo-Peschanski 2004:265–279.

Tenger, B. 1996. "Die Troas zwischen Königsfrieden und Ankunft Alexanders." In *Asia Minor Studien, Band 22: die Troas, Neue Forschungen zu Neandria und Alexandria Troas II*, ed. E. Schwertheim and H. Wiegartz, 125–147. Bonn.

———. 1999. "Zur Geographie und Geschichte der Troas." In *Die Troas: Neue Forschungen III*, ed. E. Schwertheim, 103–180. Berlin.

Thonemann, P. 2013. "The Attalid State, 188–133 BC." In *Attalid Asia Minor. Money, International Relations, and the State*, 1–47. Oxford.

Too, Y. L. 2000. "The Walking Library: The Performance of Cultural Memories." In Braund and Wilkins 2000:111–123.

Trachsel, A., and P. Schubert. 1999. "Une description de Troie dans un papyrus de Genève (Pack² 1204): réédition." *Museum Hellveticum* 56:222–237.

Trachsel, A. 2007. *La Troade: un paysage et son héritage littéraire. Les commentaires antiques sur la Troade, leur genèse et leur influence.* Basel.

———. 2008. "Asklepiades of Myrlea (697)." In *Jacoby Online. Brill's New Jacoby*, ed. I. Worthington. https://referenceworks.brillonline.com/cluster/Jacoby%20Online?s.num=0.

———. 2011. "Textvarianten zum Tod des Protesilaos: Demetrios von Skepsis als Homerphilologe." In *Parva Mythographica*, ed. J. Pamias, 153–167. Oberhaid.

———. 2012. "Collecting Fragments Today: What Status Will a Fragment Have in the Era of Digital Philology?" In *Lire demain—Reading tomorrow*, ed. C. Clivaz et al., 415–429. Expanded ebook ed. Lausanne.

———. 2014. "P. Oxy. 5094: Asios, son of Dymas or Asios, son of Hyrtakos? Demetrios of Scepsis on Homonymies in the Iliad." *Zeitschrift für Papyrologie und Epigraphik* 188:5–11.

———. 2017a. "Démétrios de Scepsis et son Τρωϊκὸς διάκοσμος, ou comment ordonner le passé mythologique de la Troade au IIe siècle av. J.-C." *Polymnia* 3:1–25.

———. 2017b. "Presenting Fragments as Quotations or Quotations as Fragments." *Digital Classics Online* 3,2:17–27.

———. 2017c. "Strabo and the Homeric Commentators." In Dueck 2017:263–275.

———. 2018. "Kontexte und Kontextualisierungen im Bereich der Fragment-forschung: Beispiele aus der Fragmentsammlung des Demetrios von Skepsis." In *Text, Kontext, Kontextualisierung. Moderne Kontextkonzepte und antike Literatur*, ed. U. Tischer, A. Forst, and U. Gärtner, 203–221. Zürich.

Turner, E. G. 1968. *Greek Papyri. An Introduction.* Oxford.

Ukert F. A. 1816. *Geographie der Griechen und Römer von den frühesten Zeiten bis auf Ptolemäus.* Weimar.

Ulrichs, H. N. 1845. "Über die Lage Trojas." *Rheinisches Museum für Philologie* 3:573–608.

van der Valk, M. 1963. *Researches on the Text and Scholia of the Iliad.* Vol. 1. Leiden.

———. 1964. *Researches on the Text and Scholia of the Iliad.* Vol. 2. Leiden.

———. 1971. *Eustathii archiepiscopi thessalonicensis Commentarii ad Homeri Iliadem pertinentes.* Vol. 1. Leiden.

van Rossum-Steenbeek. M. 1998. *Greek Readers' Digests?: Studies on a Selection of Subliterary Papyri.* Leiden.

Vanotti, G. 1993. "Dionigi di Alicarnasso e la Sibilla 'troiana.'" In *La profezia nel mondo antico*, ed. M. Sordi, 151–157. Milan.

Virchow, R. 1880a. "Appendix I: Troy and Hissarlik." In *Ilios: the City and Country of the Trojans*, H. Schliemann, 673–685. London.

———. 1880b. *Troja und der Burgberg von Hissarlik.* Berlin.

—. 1881. "Anhang I: Troja und Hissarlik." In *Ilios: Stadt und Land der Trojaner: Forschungen und Entdeckungen in der Troas und besonders auf der Baustelle von Troja*. H. Schliemann, 748–760. Leipzig. Trans. of Virchow 1880a.

Vellay, C. 1930. *Les nouveaux aspects de la question de Troie*. Paris.

Vian, F. 1951. "Les Γηγενεῖς de Cyzique et la Grande Mère des dieux." *Revue Archéologique* 37:14–25.

Vian, F., and E. Delage. 1974. *Apollonios de Rhodes. Argonautique*. Vol. 1, *Chant I-II*. Paris.

Visser, E. 1997. *Homers Katalog der Schiffe*. Stuttgart.

Vogeikoff-Brogan, N., J. L. Davis, and V. Florou, eds. 2015. *Carl W. Blegen: Personal and Archaeological Narratives*. Atlanta, GA.

—. 2015. "The Life of Carl W. Blegen from a Grass Roots Perspective." In Vogeikoff-Brogan, Davis, and Florou 2015:17–38.

von Christ, W. 1889. *Geschichte der griechischen Literatur bis auf die Zeit Justinians*, Munich.

—. 1890. *Geschichte der griechischen Literatur bis auf die Zeit Justinians*, 2nd ed. Munich.

—. 1898. *Geschichte der griechischen Literatur bis auf die Zeit Justinians*, 3rd ed. Munich.

—. 1905. *Geschichte der griechischen Literatur bis auf die Zeit Justinians*, 4th ed. Munich.

von Christ, W., W. Schmid, and O. Stählin. 1911. "Geschichte der griechischen Literatur." In *Handbuch der Altertumswissenschaft*, ed. I. von Müller. Vol. 7, *Part 2.1*. 5th ed. Munich.

von Christ, W., W. Schmid, and O. Stählin. 1920. "Geschichte der griechischen Literatur." In *Handbuch der Altertumswissenschaft*, ed. I. von Müller, W. Otto, and H. Bengston. Vol. 7, *Part 2.1*, 6th ed. Munich.

von Eckenbrecher, G. 1843. "Über die Lage des homerischen Ilion." *Rheinisches Museum* 2:1–49.

Wachsmuth, C. 1860. *De Cratete Mallota*. Leipzig.

Walbank, F. W. 1957. *A Historical Commentary on Polybius*. Vol. 1. Oxford.

Watson, K. Janet. 2011. "Ormenion." In Finkelberg 2011a:613.

Weber, E. 1972. "Die trojanische Abstammung der Römer als politisches Argument." *Wiener Studien, Neue Folge* 6:213–255.

Welcker, F. G. 1845. "Über die Lage des homerischen Ilion." In *Kleine Schriften zur griechischen Literaturgeschichte*, i–lxxxvi. Bonn.

Wendel, C. 1914. *Scholia in Theocritum vetera*. Stuttgart.

—. 1920. *Überlieferung und Entstehung der Theokrit-Scholien*. Berlin.

—. 1934. "Tauriskos [2]." In *Paulys Realencyclopädie der classischen Altertumswissenschaften* 5a.1, 15. Stuttgart.

―――. 1935. *Scholia in Apollonium Rhodium vetera.* Berlin.

―――. 1949. "Parmeniskos [3]." In *Paulys Realencyclopädie der classischen Altertumswissenschaften* 18.4, 1570–1572. Stuttgart.

West, M. L. 2001. *Studies in the Text and Transmission of the Iliad.* Munich.

―――. 2012. "The Daughter of Dymas." *Zeitschrift für Papyrologie und Epigraphik* 183:11–13.

Wilamowitz-Moellendorff, U. 1877. "Die Thukydideslegende." *Hermes* 12:326–367.

―――. 1880. *Aus Kydathen.* Berlin.

―――. 1881. *Antigonos von Karytos.* Berlin.

―――. 1905. "Die Griechische Literatur des Altertums." In *Die Kultur der Gegenwart.* Teil 1, Abt 8, *Die Griechische und lateinische Literatur und Sprache.* Berlin.

―――. 1907. "Die Griechische Literatur des Altertums." In *Die Kultur der Gegenwart.* Teil 1, Abt 8, *Die Griechische und lateinische Literatur und Sprache.* 2nd ed. Berlin.

―――. 1912. "Die Griechische Literatur des Altertums." In *Die Kultur der Gegenwart.* Teil 1, Abt 8, *Die Griechische und lateinische Literatur und Sprache.* 3rd ed. Leipzig.

Wilkins, J. 2007. "Vers une histoire sympotique." In Lenfant 2007a:29–39.

Williams, M. F. 1997. "The Cyzicus Episode (Ap. Rh., Arg. I, 936–1158 and Aeneid V: Cybele and Ritual." In *Studies in Latin Literature and Roman History VIII,* ed. C. Deroux, 5–28. Brussels.

Wilson, N. 1967. "A Chapter in the History of Scholia." *Classical Quarterly* 17:244–256.

―――. 1983. *Scholars of Byzantium.* London.

Wouters, A., and P. Swiggers. 2015. "Definitions of Grammar." In Montanari, Matthaios, and Rengakos 2015:515–544.

Zavadil, M. 2009. *Ein trojanischer Federkrieg: die Auseinandersetzung zwischen Ernst Bötticher und Heinrich Schliemann.* Vienna.

Zecchini, G. 1989. *La cultura storica di Ateneo.* Milan.

―――. 2000. "Harpocration and Athenaeus: Historiographical Relationships." In Braund and Wilkins 2000:153–169.

―――. 2007. "Athénée et les historiens: un rapport indirect." In Lenfant 2007a:19–28.

Zuntz, G. 1975. *Die Aristophanes-Scholien der Papyri.* Berlin.

Index Locorum

Demetrios of Skepsis

Other Ancient Authors

Subject Index